BECOMING SUPERMAN

BECOMING SUPERMAN

My Journey from Poverty to Hollywood

WITH STOPS ALONG THE WAY AT
MURDER, MADNESS, MAYHEM, MOVIE STARS,
CULTS, SLUMS, SOCIOPATHS, AND WAR CRIMES

J. MICHAEL STRACZYNSKI

INTRODUCTION BY NEIL GAIMAN

HARPER Voyager
An Imprint of HarperCollinsPublishers

BECOMING SUPERMAN. Copyright © 2019 by Synthetic Worlds, Ltd. Introduction copyright © 2019 by Neil Gaiman. All rights reserved. Printed in the United States of America. No part of this book may be used or reproduced in any manner whatsoever without written permission except in the case of brief quotations embodied in critical articles and reviews. For information, address HarperCollins Publishers, 195 Broadway, New York, NY 10007.

HarperCollins books may be purchased for educational, business, or sales promotional use. For information, please e-mail the Special Markets Department at SPsales@harpercollins.com.

Harper Voyager and design are trademarks of HarperCollins Publishers LLC.

FIRST EDITION

Designed by Paula Russell Szafranski

Library of Congress Cataloging-in-Publication Data has been applied for.

ISBN 978-0-06-285784-2

19 20 21 22 23 LSC 10 9 8 7 6 5 4 3 2 1

CONTENTS

Dedicated with thanks and reverence to the Four Horsemen (or Horsepeople) in my life without whom very little good would have happened.

KATHRYN DRENNAN, who believed in the man she thought I could be;

HARLAN ELLISON, who through his work taught me what it was to be a writer;

NORMAN CORWIN, who through his life showed me what it was to be a human;

and MARTIN SPENCER, Paradigm agent provocateur, whose belief in my work led me to this place.

ACKNOWLEDGMENTS

To ensure the accuracy of the events described in this volume, as many still-living witnesses as could be found were interviewed or asked to read the manuscript to confirm, amend, or dispute these events from their own perspective. My thanks therefore to the following fact-checkers and interview subjects: Kathryn Drennan, Mark Orwoll, Cathi Skoor (née Williams), Tim Pagaard, Jeri Taylor, David Moessinger, Walton Dornisch, Frank Skibicki, and my sister Theresa.

My appreciation also goes to my assistant, Stephanie Walters; first-reader Jaclyn Easton; litigation attorney Karlene Goller, and my personal attorney of over twenty years, Kevin Kelly, of the Gendler-Kelly law firm, who reviewed the manuscript and steered me clear of danger; Buddy the Miracle Cat (BuddyTMC to his hip-hop friends); and the Astonishingly Insightful Axis of agent Emma Parry and editors Eve Claxton and Domenica Alioto for their assistance in wrestling this beast of a book to the ground.

INTRODUCTION

I properly met Joe Straczynski in, I believe, January of 1991. He was hosting the *Hour 25* radio show on KPFK-FM Los Angeles, and Terry Pratchett and I were on the show that night, to talk about our book *Good Omens*. Before Joe arrived, the station boss came and warned Terry and me that she knew how we British people liked to swear on the radio, and that no swearing on our parts would be tolerated. (We asked if it was all right to mention a fictional book in *Good Omens* called the *Buggre Alle This Bible*, and she went away and checked with the Authorities and said it was.) We'd neither of us ever sworn during any radio interview before, but were now terrified that we would, and we did our interview convinced that at any moment a fit of something resembling Tourette's syndrome might overtake us. I remember that it was late at night in a dim-dark studio, and when Joe went over from talking to us to taking questions from callers, at least one of the voices at the other end of the line made no sense at all, the words were random and confused, and Joe cut him off, but kindly, and we carried on talking.

I say *properly met*, because I think I had already met Joe before that, at dinner with Harlan Ellison, but maybe all those dinners with Harlan were afterward. And that's the hell of memoirs and autobiographies:

you are dealing with what you remember, and what you remember is fallible and it's unreliable and sometimes it's simply wrong, and yet it's still all you have to go on.

We've worked together once: Joe asked if I would write a script for *Babylon 5* for him before the show began, and each season I would apologize because my plate was filled with *Sandman* and with the original *Neverwhere* TV series, and then Joe got to his final season, and I said yes, because *Sandman* and *Neverwhere* were done and I had the time, and in 1998 I wrote an episode called "The Day of the Dead" for him. Joe was, for the record, the easiest and sanest television executive I've ever written for: he was writing the entire show himself (except for my episode), and overseeing it, and doing all this without giving any indication of breaking a sweat.

So I've known Joe for almost thirty years. His hair has changed in that time (long ago it was darker and there was significantly more of it), but from the hairline down he's still very much the same man I met in that voice-haunted radio studio late one night. He's decent, and he's good-hearted; he works harder than anyone I've met in film and TV; he's sane and he's sensible, accessible and wise. Which, you would think, would mean that the autobiographical volume you are reading would be as dull as insurance policy small print: people are as interesting as they are flawed, their stories as fascinating as the obstacles they encounter on the way.

In Joe's case, as you read his story you also start to realize the pressure and the force that created the ferociously hardworking and ethical entity that he is: you understand not only what he was reacting against, but the pressure that he was under. Superman, one of Joe's inspirations, could squeeze coal into diamonds. I was never convinced that it would work in real life, the whole coal-to-diamonds thing, suspecting that if you weren't Superman and you squeezed a lump of coal really hard, you'd get coal dust; but the pressures of Joe's life and childhood, the people who surrounded him, gave him something and someone not to be, gave him something to transcend, something to survive. Most people would have become coal dust. He didn't.

The childhood we read about here is like an iron key winding up the clockwork that might so easily have destroyed Joe or turned him into a monster: instead it gave him power and a place to stand, and, most of all, a willingness to learn.

We follow him through several careers, and in each career he learns how to do it, how to set out and make something happen that ought, by any stretch of the imagination, to have been impossible. It's his willingness to learn, his quiet persistence, and his willingness to do the work that are his superpowers. He has become a diamond.

And now he is finally willing to share.

Neil Gaiman
London
June 2017

BECOMING
SUPERMAN

CHAPTER 1

We Were Told

Iceland. March 14, 2014.

An hour earlier and a thousand feet nearer the ground we had been on a narrow strip of road bordered on both sides by a seemingly endless expanse of black volcanic rock and green moss, the air crisp but not cold. Then we started the long climb up a steep mountain, and within minutes the sky was swallowed by snow. The road turned from black to the brittle white of hard packed ice, then disappeared altogether. The world had no edges, the sky no shape, the sun no particular direction. We were inside a snow globe, with nothing before, behind, or beside us.

We climbed out to better experience the whiteout: location managers, production coordinators, directors, producers, and writers, myself among the latter two categories. We were warned to stay close: anyone walking more than twenty feet from the caravan would be lost to sight.

Iceland was the first stop in our round-the-world tour to scout locations for *Sense8*, a Netflix series I had written, created, and was producing with the Wachowskis. From here the show would travel to Mexico City, San Francisco, Seoul, Chicago, Berlin, Nairobi, and London.

The story that brought us here concerned a young woman who gives birth in the middle of the frozen tundra miles from civilization. Stranded after a car wreck, alone and on foot, the odds of her or her infant surviving the intense cold are nearly zero, but she keeps walking anyway, refusing to go down without a fight. Desperation and tears in the cruel bitter wind. Blood on snow.

We'd come to determine if this particular mountain would suffice, but someone had apparently backed up a U-Haul and taken it away before we arrived, leaving only a curtain of white void that stretched to infinity.

"We should get off the mountain before it gets dark," the location manager said, "while we can still see the road."

"Road, hell," someone said in reply. "We should go while we can still see the *mountain*."

As I climbed back into the van I paused to look out at the white void, two thousand seven hundred miles from where I began my journey in Paterson, New Jersey. And it occurred to me that the only thing more improbable than being on *this* road was the longer and considerably darker road that *brought* me there: the mistakes and wrong turns, the tragedies and lies, the wise and poor decisions . . . and the secrets I'd kept about myself, my family, and my past, afraid of what the world would think.

The whisper of things left long unsaid echoed out at me from the void. *We know who you are. Who you* really *are. You may be able to fool everybody else, but you can't fool us. And as long as we're out here, where you can't reach us, you will never be truly free.*

Writers tell stories. It's what we do. It's what I've done my whole life. But there's one story I've never told, trained into silence by people who wanted to make sure that my family's secrets *remained* secret.

And there's only one appropriate response when you discover you're afraid of something.

You get up and you *do* it.

That was the moment I decided to write this book and reveal my secret origin story to the world. The writing process took four years because there were still mysteries about my family to be unraveled and little to work with. Just as no one told Clark Kent he was an alien until he was ready to handle it, I was told as little as possible about our past because nobody was entirely sure when the statute of limitations ran out on some of this stuff. Records were systematically destroyed to expedite hasty departures and eliminate three generations' worth of incriminating evidence. It was only with great effort that the Clark Kent reporter-for-a-great-metropolitan-newspaper inside me was able to push past decades of convenient fiction to discover the fiercely guarded truth.

We were told that of four Straczynski brothers born in 1880s Vilnius (then a province of Russia, now the capital of Lithuania), Kazimier traveled throughout Europe representing the family's business interests before moving to America to make his fortune.

The truth, acquired much later, is that Kazimier was a drunk and a womanizer who spent his early twenties on an alcohol-fueled binge across four countries, at each stop luring young women into bed with stories of wealth and promises of marriage. It was only when the relationships turned serious and his lies were in danger of running into one another that he took off across the Atlantic, citing pressing family business.

America was the land of wealthy widows and trust-fund debutantes, and Kazimier was determined to land as many of those as possible. Armed with money the family wanted him to invest on their behalf, two good suits, Old World charm, and elaborate fictions about vast tracts of land owned by his family in Russia, he set out like a sexual Vasco da Gama sailing the seas of high society in search of a woman with sufficient means to give him the lifestyle he believed he deserved.

Then, just as he was in sight of his goal—a woman from a wealthy family who liked the idea of merging fortunes—he burned through the last of the family funds he had appropriated for his own purposes. With arrangements still to be made and proofs given to confirm his status as one of the elite before the deal could be closed, Kazimier returned to siphon off what little was left of the family fortune after the Russian Revolution. He explained that he'd made tons of money with their initial investment, but financial regulations in the United States were slowing down the process of moving that money overseas. He was confident those issues would be resolved soon, but in the interim he'd received a hot lead on an investment that would make them rich beyond the dreams of avarice. With their funds tied up in the banking system, he would need the rest of the family money to buy in before it was too late.

They said they would need time to think it over, and more time still to sneak the money in from accounts they had set up in Prussia when the Bolsheviks came to town.

We were told that while he awaited their decision, Kazimier met a young woman named Sophia, fell in love, and got married.

The truth is that Kazimier began a clandestine affair with his niece Sophia, daughter of his brother Jan and eighteen years his junior. Sophia had long dreamed of becoming an actress in America, where her many qualities—invisible to everyone else, but perfectly obvious to her—would at last be recognized. But not only did her father refuse to let her immigrate alone, she discovered that he intended to marry her off to a local merchant. Her only way out was through Kazimier, who she believed had the connections and the money to make her dreams real. So one night, fueled by desperation, greed, and enough vodka to liquefy the brain cells in charge of good judgment, she revealed the incestuous relationship to the family and announced (falsely, it turned out) that she was pregnant.

As staunch Catholics, her family couldn't allow Sophia to be an unwed mother, but none of them wanted to live with the scandal of her marrying her blood uncle. Their solution was Solomonic in its wisdom: *Get married then get the hell out.*[*]

We were told that Kazimier's blushing bride returned with him to make a life of marital bliss together.

The truth is that after the wedding, Kazimier returned to the United States ahead of her, allegedly to make preparations for her arrival, and promised to send money for her passage when all was ready. Instead he went radio-silent the moment he was safely back on American soil, hoping she lacked the resolve needed to undertake such an arduous voyage alone. But Sophia refused to be deterred and borrowed money for a ticket to America. Her white-hot fury upon discovering that the riches Kazimier had laid claim to were utter fabrications was matched by his own anger when she revealed that her claim to pregnancy had been simply a means to secure their marriage.

Snared by their mutual lies, in a family that would never countenance divorce, they moved into a small apartment in Paterson, New Jersey, a haven for Polish and Russian immigrants. In July 1927 Sophia gave birth to a son, Joseph, who passed away of pneumonia three months later. She never recovered from the loss and each year on the anniversary of Joseph's death made a grim pilgrimage to leave flowers on his grave.

Determined not to let tragedy derail her dreams of stardom, Sophia began bedding down directors, photographers, producers,

---

[*] On the plus side, marrying her father's brother meant she wouldn't have to change anything that had been monogrammed or etched with her last name.

and anyone else she thought could help her career. But her efforts were hindered by her thick, muscular silhouette, typical of Russian stock, and a face hardened by mood and circumstance into a look of perpetual disapproval. When her efforts hit the wall of her talent and her cervix, she became deeply embittered, and would sit for hours on the front stoop of their apartment, drinking and shouting curses at neighbors. If the name of someone she didn't like was mentioned, she would spit on the sidewalk and grind it under her heel. She was not, in short, a people-person.

By contrast, Kazimier grew into a soft, sullen echo of a man. Whenever Sophia flew into one of her rages he would seek refuge at local bars, then tiptoe back into the apartment only after she was asleep. Having come within inches of marrying into a rich family and achieving the successful future that he believed was his rightful destiny, he spent his days and nights in the boozy, soft-focus intersection between his overly romanticized memories of a past he had been forced to flee and the paralysis of a present that seemed utterly beyond his control.

On October 2, 1929, Sophia, then twenty-five, gave birth to another son, unimaginatively named Kazimier after his father and subsequently Americanized to Charles. To make ends meet, she took part-time work bartending at a tavern on River Street. The job was more than an escape from being a wife and mother: it was her stage and she was a star, performing for an audience eager to applaud anything if it meant getting a free drink out of the bargain.

A second child, Theresa, was born July 11, 1931. Rather than objects of affection, Sophia's children were a constant reminder that her life had not turned out the way she'd planned. Her pride prevented her from admitting any of this to her family in Eastern Europe, however, so her letters home were filled with wild tales of wealth and success, each more outrageous than the last, until finally her relatives began to question the veracity of her accounts.

Puffed up with indignation like a pouter pigeon, Sophia announced that she was taking the children for a three-month visit to Poland and Russia to prove that she was successful, happy, and living in America, only one of which was actually true. She then ransacked Kazimier's bank account to buy expensive clothes that would impress her relatives, many of whom were suffering under Soviet rule. She wanted to provoke them into asking her for money just so she could tell them to go to hell. Say what you like about Sophia, the woman knew how to plan ahead.

When everything was ready, she and her children embarked upon their goodwill tour of Eastern Europe, from Hoboken, New Jersey, on the liner *Batory*.

We were told that after arriving at the port of Gdynia, Poland, Sophia took the children to museums and monuments from the Great War, eating at fine restaurants and generally having a wholesome, good time.

The truth is that within days of arriving she began having an affair with a member of the Polish national police, an officer who was sympathetic to the Third Reich, which had just annexed Czechoslovakia and was eager to flex its muscles farther east. Sophia believed that as the Nazis grew more powerful, her lover's fortunes would prosper, and thus her own. To clear the decks for this new relationship, she planned to return to the United States, hand off the children, say nothing of the affair, grab whatever was left in the bank, then return to Poland.

On September 1, 1939, they boarded a train in Lodz, Poland, that would take them to the port of Gdynia and, from there, back to America. Inconveniently, this was *also* the date set by the German air force for the blitzkrieg and invasion of Poland. Sophia and her children had just taken their seats when the Luftwaffe began bombing the station and strafing passenger cars in the opening salvo of what would shortly become World War II.

Barely escaping the attack, they made their way to the United States consulate only to be turned away because the suitcase containing the papers needed to prove their US citizenship had been destroyed in the attack.

We were told that as German troops and tanks poured into Poland, Sophia and her children somehow made their way unimpeded across seven hundred kilometers of war-torn countryside to a train station in Bogdanov in the Minsk region of Belarus, where they were put to work as little more than slaves by the German railway officers who now commanded the station.

The truth is that Sophia turned for help to her lover, who had made his loyalties known to the Germans and switched sides. Despite his newly won connections it was obvious that in the heat of the invasion anyone with missing papers would be subject to arrest, so he put them on a train that would take them far into the countryside and gave Sophia a letter of introduction to the head of the local *Bahnschutzpolizei*, the German railway police. Upon arriving at the Bogdanov train station they were given food and a comfortable place to live above the station, where Sophia would work as live-in housekeeper, cook, and assistant for the ranking officers.

When her lover was killed in the sporadic fighting that was still going on in Poland, Sophia pivoted into having affairs with some of the German officers. On weekends she traveled with them to Valozhyn, a part of Belarus controlled by the German army, where they bought her gifts and expensive clothes. It would have been an altogether comfortable arrangement except for the fact that the station and the German soldiers living there were often targeted by the Resistance, who were apparently really good shots. Fearing that she might eventually be caught in the cross fire, she convinced some of the soldiers to smuggle out letters to Kazimier in hopes of securing safe passage home. Her letters went unanswered for *six years*. Given the vicissitudes of wartime correspondence it's possible that Kazimier never received her letters and in that vast silence concluded that she had been killed in the blitzkrieg, a sign from God that his marital suffering was at an end. It's also possible that the letters were received but ignored in the fevered hope that she might catch a stray bullet while stuck behind enemy lines. But the most likely scenario is that the letters reached their destination only to be lost in the course of Kazimier's inebriated battles with the forces of gravity.

We were told that while they lived at the railway station, some of the soldiers looked kindly upon her son, Charles, and helped guide him toward manhood.

The truth is that Charles quickly developed a fierce appreciation for all things Nazi. With his mother's temper, his father's sense of entitlement, and their mutual inability to take responsibility for their actions, the Nazi philosophy gave him a focus for his anger, and he embraced a strong anti-Semitic ideology that would stay with him the rest of his life. He read *Mein Kampf*, took photos of the soldiers, smoked German cigarettes, and cherished a small collection of SS daggers.

The soldiers approved of his increasingly pro-Nazi sentiments, and began treating him as one of their own, even presenting him with a German uniform replete with swastika armband that became his proudest possession. According to comments made by his sister, Theresa, shortly before her death in 2009, he often tagged along with German soldiers and members of the SS on "hunting expeditions" to nearby Jewish ghettos and villages under German jurisdiction.

"They'd go out looking for Jews caught outside after curfew and beat them with rubber pipes like it was some kind of game," she said. "He'd come back covered in blood then spend hours the next day washing his shirt and shining his boots so he could go out and do it all over again."

Then, in 1942, an incident occurred so terrible that no one in the family would speak of it for decades. In a family based on the withholding of information, the truth of what happened the day Charles embraced the most horrific aspects of Nazi ideology became their Mount Everest of secrets.

The details of what happened that day, and how many died as a result, will have to wait, because this is also a murder mystery, and one never reveals the details of the crime in chapter one.

After Germany surrendered in 1945, the soldiers who had been Sophia's protectors were now on the run from partisans eager to settle scores. With their help she and her children escaped to Valozhyn, where many Nazi loyalists still remained, but they were soon forced to keep moving or risk being identified by other refugees fleeing east. With railroad lines destroyed, cities flattened, and most lines of communication cut off, they made their way to Moscow and took refuge in a Red Cross shelter while their identities were confirmed. Finally, in June 1946 they were cleared to travel to Odessa and booked passage home on the American Merchant Marine ship *Norman J. Coleman*.

During the voyage they learned that reporters in America were eager to interview them about the seven years they had spent behind enemy lines. There were even whispers of book and movie deals. For years Sophia had dreamed of being the center of attention, a star surrounded by people hanging on her every word; now, for the most unexpected of reasons, she was about to get her wish. They spent weeks posing for photos and being interviewed for radio broadcasts and newspapers about their adventures during the war, carefully skewing the events to show them in a sympathetic light. Confident that at any moment producers would show up bearing contracts and vast sums of money, they argued over dinner about who should play them in the movie. Sophia, of course, would play herself. In her interviews she encouraged people to send her money, most of which she spent on clothes, confident that the flow of cash would never stop. But the war-weary public soon lost interest in their story, and by 1947 the phone stopped ringing. Her dreams of stardom dashed once more, Sophia reluctantly reunited with Kazimier. Pooling their funds, they bought a small apartment building on Graham Avenue in Paterson, living in one apartment with the other set aside as a refuge where Charles could live rent-free. Sophia also leased the River Street bar from its ailing owner with an option to buy.

Once they were settled, Charles entered St. Mary's College seminary, the only institution that would accept him without a high school diploma or a clearly defined moral center. He often said that the best thing in the world was to be a crooked priest; there was easy access to church funds, and plenty of women eager to have affairs with dashing young priests with dramatic wartime stories. But by the end of the first term he was booted out for drunkenness, leaving him with no choice but to work for Sophia at her bar. The humiliation and debasement reflected in this turn of events almost certainly proves the existence of God, which to be fair is a pretty solid achievement for a first-year seminarian.

Like Sophia, Charles treated the bar as his own personal fiefdom, holding court late into the night, dispensing free booze to his friends, and sneaking money out of the cash register to pay for expensive aftershave, clothes, and prostitutes. Despite these shenanigans, the bar brought in enough money for Sophia to make a down payment on a house at 275 Dakota Street with a backyard big enough to plant sunflowers, vegetables, and raspberry bushes, the latter of which she fermented with potatoes into a uniquely lethal brand of vodka.

Kazimier took little joy in their new home. Disillusioned and homesick, he hired local artist Victor Rafael Rachwalski to paint two murals in the living room, one depicting his overly romanticized memories of Russia, the other a montage of the day he arrived in the United States, optimistic and full of dreams. Victor was two years younger than Sophia, soft-spoken and gentle, with an artist's sensibility that Sophia found attractive. Given her freewheeling notions about fidelity it was inevitable that they would begin having an affair. It was arguably the best thing that ever happened to her. Victor softened Sophia's worst qualities, and she enjoyed having someone creative and sensitive in her life.

When Victor's landlord raised the rent beyond his means, she convinced Kazimier to let him move into the basement as a boarder. This made the affair simpler to conduct but more difficult to conceal, and when Kazimier discovered the truth he packed up and moved to Los Angeles, determined to put as much distance between them as possible. This left Sophia and Victor free to live together full-time, though for the sake of appearances he kept the basement flat, which also functioned as his studio.

Having failed to master any useful skills, Charles joined the Air Force in 1948 and began training as a military police officer at Camp Gordon, Georgia. He liked the authority of being able to tell people what to do, and the freedom to rough them up when they didn't do it, but mainly I think he just really liked the armband. He rotated through several bases as part of the Fifth Military Police before ending up at Fairfield-Suison Army Air Base in California, where he became a regular customer at several brothels in nearby Vallejo and Benicia. Some of the brothels used underage prostitutes, including Evelyn Dolores Pate, who was fourteen when Charles began seeing her in and out of the brothel. Evelyn always looked older than she was, with frizzy, home-permed hair above a round face that never quite lost its baby fat, and brown eyes set too closely together, as if she was always squinting at something. Their relationship was built on exploitation, power, and his penchant for inflicting pain on someone who could not legally retaliate.

Whenever his drunken violence became too much to bear, Evelyn took shelter in the Vallejo trailer home of her mother, Grace Ross, only to be lured back by promises of money, gifts, and good behavior, none of which materialized. When Evelyn became pregnant, Grace told Charles that if he didn't do the right thing she would expose his activities to the base commander. Rather than face court-martial, Charles married Evelyn on March 15, 1951, in Reno, Nevada. She was fifteen.

Six months later, Charles learned that he was going to be shipped off to the front lines of the Korean War, and decided that this would be a good time to get the hell out of the air force. There are several stories concerning how he made that happen—in one version he let himself be caught cross-dressing; in another he began firing at possible Martians while guarding a definite atomic bomb—but since Charles was an inveterate liar, there is no way to know what actually happened. Either way, on October 17, 1951, the air force kicked Charles out with a general discharge, given in cases of misconduct not *quite* egregious enough to merit a dishonorable discharge.

He returned to Paterson with Evelyn and moved into the Graham Avenue apartment while he looked for work. These searches usually ended at various bars, where he would get drunk then come home to beat and sexually assault Evelyn, incidents that almost certainly contributed to her miscarriage. Once she recovered, she tried on several occasions to run away, only to be caught and dragged back. To preclude further attempts Charles imprisoned her in the apartment, padlocking her in the bedroom and nailing the windows shut. One night, after being badly beaten and raped, she slipped the phone into the bedroom before being locked in for the evening, hiding the long cord behind the dresser and praying he wouldn't discover what she'd done. That morning, after he left for work, she called her mother and said that he'd threatened to kill her when he came home. Frantic with worry, Grace convinced the police to enter the apartment and escort Evelyn off the premises and onto the first train to California. The events surrounding her escape are best described in documents filed in the Superior Court of the State of California on September 30, 1952.

> . . . after said marriage and prior to said infant's[*] attaining the age of sixteen (16) years, and more specifically in the months of April and May of 1951, said infant suffered abuse at the hands of defendant and attempted to separate herself from defendant with the intention of having said marriage relation terminated. That defendant threatened to injure and harm said infant and even to kill her if she left him. That on many occasions defendant beat and struck the said infant and kept her constantly in fear of her life. That said force prevented said infant from separating herself from said defendant and said infant was forced to continue against her will the relationship of husband and wife with defendant. That on or about August 11, 1952, defendant released said infant and she did then and there absent and separate herself from defendant and has not lived with defendant as his wife since. That defendant has continuously and is still threatening to do said infant and plaintiff great grievous bodily harm.

After reviewing photos of her injuries, the court ordered the marriage annulled and issued a restraining order against Charles

---

[*] The document refers to Evelyn as an "infant" because at the time of the events in question she was still a minor under the law.

that would prevent him from entering California to try and retrieve her. Believing herself safe, Evelyn returned to her previous place of employment at the Vallejo brothel. But as far as Charles was concerned, she was his *property*, and he always got back what was his. When he learned that Evelyn had rotated to a brothel in Seattle, Washington—and was thus outside the jurisdiction of the California restraining order—he paid another prostitute to lure her to what was supposed to be a meeting with a wealthy client. When Evelyn arrived, he beat and kidnapped her back to New Jersey, saying that if she ever tried to leave again he would kill her *and* her mother.

To cap off his carefully planned humiliation, Charles did not remarry her, believing that this would deny her any legal standing in court. She would have no access to his bank accounts, no claim to anything he owned, and any property he forced her to put under the name Evelyn Straczynski could be held over her as evidence of fraud, further tightening his grip.

Shortly afterward, Evelyn discovered that she was pregnant, and gave birth to a son on July 17, 1954. Given the timing, Charles wasn't sure if the baby had been conceived during the period when Evelyn was working as a prostitute or later.

"I don't even know if you're my son," Charles often said in the years that followed, an allegation that culminated in two letters he sent in 2003. The first demanded that his son take a DNA test because he had been "conceived in a whore house your mother was employed in Seattle Washington either by the pimp she slept with or one of the pimp's clients. She forgot the pimp's last name and for sure did not know the name of the clientele." He argued that under the circumstances his son "could have been born a black. After (your mother) viewed your pictures on the internet she agreed that there is no resemblance to me, and who should know better than the mother." His goal was to ensure that his alleged son "cannot inherit any of the estate because I am not your father."

The second letter, from Evelyn, elaborated on the situation. "When I was 17 I was in Seattle Washington and unfortunately I wound up in a house of prostitution . . . I am not sure if you were born 8 or 9 months later."

You were conceived in a whorehouse.

That would be me.

CHAPTER 2

Strange Relations

Rather than deal with the needs of a newborn, my father spent most of his time "queer baiting," luring gays to private areas and beating them up. Left alone with Sophia, who regarded her with open disdain, Evelyn soon fell into a severe postpartum depression exacerbated by her isolation and her almost total lack of experience when it came to taking care of an infant.

I was told by Evelyn that because my nose was rather flat at birth, she was worried that my father would accuse her of having had me through sex with a black man, so she began pinching my nose as hard as she could in an attempt to re-form it without understanding that noses don't work that way. This seemed curious to me, even as a child, but I accepted the story since I lacked any other explanation as to why I constantly sniff and snorfle.

The truth, which came later courtesy of Sophia and my aunt Theresa, is that the foregoing story was the alibi Evelyn gave when my aunt found her pinching my nose closed with one hand, the other pressed tightly over my mouth. She used so much pressure to cut off the flow of air that she damaged the still-malleable structure of my nasal passages, causing lifelong problems.

Option One is that my mother honestly believed she could pinch my nose into a different configuration.

Option Two is that she was trying to suffocate me to death.

Option Two might seem fanciful except for what happened later.

When Evelyn became pregnant again, her depression roared back, punctuated by dangerous mood swings. Crying, furious, she said repeatedly that she didn't want to go through with the pregnancy, that she didn't want *any* children. Concerned that she might try to harm me or terminate the pregnancy herself, my aunt and grandmother left her alone as little as possible. Sophia would even take us along when she had to work at the bar, propping me up on the pool table or the cold bar, where I would slide around, nearly naked, in puddles of alcohol.

After giving birth to a daughter, Vicky, Evelyn's depression spiraled into violent outbursts and fits of rage. Then, just weeks after her birth, Vicky abruptly passed away. Years later, when I asked my father what happened, he would say only, "Crib death. Suffocation."

No one in my family ever said to me, point-blank, *Your mother was responsible for Vicky's death.* I know only the whispers that followed Evelyn the rest of her life about what she tried to do to me and what she might have succeeded in doing with Vicky. On several occasions I heard Sophia say that Charles threatened to turn her over to the police for what happened if she ever tried to run away again. Since by now Evelyn knew exactly what my father was capable of doing to her, and what he would *continue* to do, I can't imagine any reason that would compel her to remain in Paterson as his personal, lifelong punching bag other than raw, naked fear over such an accusation. That terror gave my father a level of control over Evelyn that he probably considered a fair trade for Vicky's death, since he never really cared for or about *any* of his children; like his suits and his car, we were simply props whose purpose was to show that he was a successful family man.

And after all, she could always make more children.

Unable to escape my father's increasingly sadistic violence in any conventional way, Evelyn made her first attempt at suicide. To punish her for this act of rebellion my father had her committed to an institution and continued to recommit her for nearly a year.* *Let someone else worry about her moods*, he said. It was the best of all possible worlds: Evelyn would remain in the asylum as long as he wanted, and he would be free to see other women. Her absence would let him present himself as a successful, unencumbered candidate, thus improving his chances of scoring. By contrast, having a kid around would crimp his style, so I was sent off to live with my grandmother.

Most of what happened to my mother while she was institutionalized was kept from me. If I asked where she was, Sophia would ignore the question; if I inquired a second time, she'd lock me in an upstairs bedroom until I stopped asking. One day, tired of my constant questions, she ordered Charles to drive me to where I would finally be able to see my mother.

My father was careful to always present the appearance of success, and rarely left the house without wearing a suit, tie, and a starched white shirt. At five foot eight he weighed over two hundred pounds, and often used his girth to intimidate people who might not be impressed by his height. After taking the time to dress appropriately and slick his black hair into a pompadour, we drove across town, the smell of his cologne stinging my eyes as I peered through the windshield.

When we arrived, he pointed across the street to a wire-mesh window on an upper floor of a plain, whitewashed building. "She's

---

* She would eventually be committed five times, three involuntarily, twice of her own volition, per court documents filed later. During these hospitalizations she was frequently subjected to electroconvulsive (shock) therapy.

up there," he said. I could just make out the silhouette of someone waving at me through the smeared glass. I asked why we couldn't go in to see her.

"They won't let you in," he said.

"Why? What is that place?"

He shrugged. "A nuthouse. She's crazy."

Living with my grandmother was preferable to being with my father, but there were definite drawbacks. Having been reared in rural Eastern Europe, Sophia preferred the parts of chickens, cows, sheep, and lambs that no American would touch on a bet: feet, knuckles, gristle, intestines, udders, and head cheese. Tripe was a particular favorite since it could be purchased by the acre. Her proudest accomplishment, the centerpiece at every meal, was a thick jelly the size and shape of a birthday cake in which pigs' feet, back fat, and other unidentifiable bits of meat floated in a translucent, gelatinous gray mass. It tasted like the gristled end of a chicken leg left out in bad weather for several weeks, and was served alongside horse-radish strong enough to kill your taste buds so you wouldn't throw up whatever the hell you just ate.

Though Sophia was living in America, amid grocery stores laden with fresh food, she still hewed to the Old World belief that if meat looked too fresh, it probably came from a diseased animal. So she bargained with butchers for whatever was about to be thrown out as unfit for human consumption. If the green on the meat could be scraped off, then it was good enough to eat. If it was especially dubious looking, or the green wouldn't entirely come off, she'd grind it into sausage.

Sausage was her solution to everything. She'd sit at a meat grinder bolted to the kitchen table, smoking and drinking as she shoved in whatever bits of meat were too horrific to be used in the rest of her cooking, cigarette ash drifting unnoticed into the grinder. The finished sausages would then be boiled for at least an hour, killing whatever germs might remain and ensuring that the flavor was gone. Her logic was airtight: If you were comfortable with the history of the meat, you would want to experience its flavor. But if its origins were uncertain, the less you could taste it the better, because by this point any piece of meat that could still provide flavor would almost certainly kill you on the spot.

Whenever my grandmother got tired of having me underfoot she sent me to stay with my aunt Theresa and her husband, Ted Skibicki. Theresa was a slender woman with short permed dark hair, sharply defined features, thick glasses, an even thicker New Jersey accent, and a habit of constantly clearing her throat when she was nervous, a tendency I somehow inherited. She was also the only marginally normal member of the Straczynski clan, despite her sincere claim that her dog could talk.* She enjoyed drinking but never to extremes, and where Sophia and Charles were shouters, Theresa would lie back until the right moment then slip in a sly and lethally accurate observation.

Ted was a freelance contractor, a genuinely nice guy who seemed baffled by the violent, psychopathic behavior of Theresa's side of the family, and he always made me feel welcome in the home he had built on Haledon Avenue. He was utterly in love with Theresa, and in defiance of the absence of affection practiced by our family often put her on his lap, snuggling and showing attention. Another frequent guest was Ted's younger brother Frank, who had lost a leg at age five during an Allied bombing of Frankfurt. With matching ducktail haircuts, Ted and Frank stood foursquare for stability and the value of hard work, a stark contrast to the Straczynski tendencies toward lying, larceny, and laziness.

As the date of my mother's release from care approached, my

---

* I once asked her how and why she started talking to her dog in the first place. She said, "Because there are things I know about your father I can only tell to a dog." Odd as this statement was, it would become important later.

father's escapades became bolder, and on several occasions he brought prostitutes back to the Graham Avenue apartment. One night, when Sophia confronted him about his behavior, he made the mistake of hitting her. Her eyes wide with anger, she punched him in the face hard enough to draw blood then threw him out into the street, followed immediately by his clothes and personal belongings. The next day he borrowed money from Ted to rent a small apartment on Van Houten Street, just a few blocks away. Despite all the fighting and multiple moves, most of our family's drama took place within a two-mile radius.

After Evelyn was discharged, her doctors suggested a waiting period before bringing me home, but Theresa would quietly slip me in for occasional visits while my father was out. I would find my mother sitting by the front window, heavily medicated, blinking absently against the sunlight, brow furrowed as if trying to remember something she wanted to say, but which had just that moment slipped away. Though she was nearly oblivious to my presence, I discovered that if I brought in the neighborhood cat and held it out, her face would soften and she would pet it.

Once when she was petting the cat, her hand accidentally brushed mine. It's the only time I can remember her touching me with affection. So at every visit I would hold out the Decoy Cat for as long as I could, even when it started clawing deep welts into my skin, turning it one way then the other so my mother's hand would continue to touch my own.

It was not lost on me that her affection wasn't actually directed at me.

But for those moments, I was okay with that.

I can't remember exactly when it happened, but at some point I realized there was a man living in my grandmother's basement:

Victor Rafael Rachwalski (I called him Pan Rafael, pronounced *pahn*, a term of respect, like mister), the artist with whom Sophia had begun an affair years earlier. Despite being told not to bother him, I would sneak down to his studio and watch him paint. He mostly did commissions: nature scenes and the occasional portrait. I'd sit silently on the basement steps then run upstairs whenever he glanced in my direction, afraid that I'd get in trouble. Finally, he offered a deal: if I'd pretend not to be there, he would pretend not to see me. Our contract sealed, I would spend hours watching him work while a phonograph in the corner played big band music on carefully tended 78s.

At the end of each day he'd wash up, put away the strong-smelling paints, and we'd walk up into the backyard to the blue pedal car he'd given me for Christmas. Using a rope tied to the front bumper, he'd pull the car to the corner store for ice cream, stopping along the way to talk with people who always seemed genuinely pleased to see him. You could troll a child in a pedal car up and down Dakota Street for *days* without finding anyone willing to say a kind word about the Straczynskis, but everyone liked Pan Rafael.

Two incidents give the true measure of the man.

Every Easter a rogues' gallery of family, friends, and hangers-on gathered at Sophia's house for dinner. The menu consisted of turkey, ham, roast beef, pierogi, stuffed cabbage rolls, sauerkraut, whiskey, wine, beer, four kinds of bread, a canning jar containing freshly fermented raspberry vodka, Sophia's trademark sausages, and other, even less savory items Frankenstein'd from leftover parts of dead livestock.

Alcoholism started early in my family, so even though I was only four, vodka was constantly being put in front of me. Whenever someone made a toast, a small amount of vodka was put in a shot glass and I was told to drink, drawing laughter as I screwed up my face and coughed at the fire racing down my throat. I couldn't refuse because it was considered rude not to drink when everyone else did; my only recourse was to try and ditch the vodka when no one was looking. It wasn't a moral decision; I was too young for such opinions. I just didn't care for the taste of it. But this particular Easter my father caught me ditching the booze and blew his stack. He said I was wasting good vodka, and trying to show that I was too good for the rest of the family. So he made another toast and this time goddamnit I was going to drink with the rest of them.

As I reluctantly reached for the glass, Pan Rafael raised his camera and took a picture of the group. I can't say that I was intentionally looking to him for help, but his artist's eye must have caught the truth of that moment, because when the next toast came he made it a point to pour in my vodka himself, then handed the shot glass across with such great flourishes and grand, sweeping gestures that by the time it got to me the glass was virtually empty. Rather than ratting me out, he joined the conspiracy. At last, I had an ally.

That winter Pan Rafael received the biggest commission of his career: a painting based on photographs of the client's ancestral home in Poland, destroyed during the war. He worked for over a month on that canvas, painstakingly rendering every leaf, branch, and brick. From my perch on the stairs I hardly breathed as I watched him work. I'd never seen him as proud as when he finished the last stroke. Eager to show Sophia the result, he trotted past me up the stairs.

I approached the canvas. It was beautiful, the best he'd ever done. He was rightfully proud.

Then, on closer review, it occurred to me that it lacked something.

A cat. That's what it needed.

So I picked up his brush, dipped it in black paint, and drew a big ol' black cat right in the middle of the canvas. I'd barely finished when I heard Pan Rafael and Sophia coming down the stairs. I turned and stood proudly before my work. When my grandmother saw what I'd done, her face turned a shade of white usually only seen in coroner's offices before spiraling into bright red. She let fly with a thundercloud of obscenities in three languages then started to lunge for me, murder in her eyes.

Pan Rafael put out a hand to stop her. Without saying a word he approached the canvas and studied it, angling it one way then the other to catch the light. "It's good," he said. "Obviously he thought it needed a cat, and you know, he's right."

He set the painting on the floor. "This one is mine," he said, "because the work is now much too fine to give to anyone else. I will hang it on the wall where I can see it every day."

He turned and patted me on the head. "For the client, I will make another."

Then he pulled out a blank canvas, put it on the easel, and began again.

Later, as though nothing had happened, he pulled me and the blue pedal car to the corner store and we had ice cream.

Those moments have stayed with me as the most perfect examples of what it is to be a human being. In his actions I could sense, if only on a cellular level, that this was the way grown-ups were *supposed* to treat children; that there should be compassion, affection, and patience; that every day shouldn't be a recurring nightmare of blood and horror and a perpetual sense of *You're not wanted here.* But in my case, it was too little, too late.

During the first few years of a child's life, it's important to form normal emotional attachments with adult family members and other children. But during that crucial period I was constantly being shuttled between a distant grandmother, a dangerous father, and a clinically depressed mother from whom I had also been separated for a year. There was no room for me to just be a kid, no place where I felt *safe*. My early memories are highly detailed because my environment was constantly changing, forcing me to become hypervigilant and self-reliant, meticulously logging everything around me in order to learn the rules that would let me adapt to wherever I was being dumped that week.

Under normal circumstances, when a child falls or hurts himself, he knows there's at least one person he can run to for help and comfort. By contrast, I would not cry out when in pain because at best those pleas would be ignored; at worst, they would summon more trouble. I learned to assess the situation and do what I could to fix it without asking for help. Saying or doing the wrong thing while living in a violent, neglectful environment invariably led to abuse or confinement, so inch by inch I withdrew into silence. I would sit for hours without talking, to the point where people would forget I was in the room. When I did talk, I spoke more like an adult than a child, emotionally at arm's length from everyone around me.

The contemporary term for this is the inhibited version of reactive attachment disorder (RAD). Add in post-traumatic stress disorder caused by these and later incidents, plus a dollop of Asperger's syndrome, and the result was a lifelong inability to create stable attachments, express my feelings, or connect with people on the most basic, emotional level. The hardest part of that equation is that I've always been very much aware of those limitations. Many with these disorders are so deep inside their own perception that they don't really understand what they're missing. But I could always feel the distance between myself and other people, as if I was peering through the bars of a cage that only I could see. As I grew up and watched other people holding hands, hugging, laughing, or playing without reserve, I desperately wished I could experience that freedom for even a single moment.

But that moment never came.

It didn't help that I was kept away from kids my own age. My grandmother hated having children in her home, and I couldn't seek them out on my own because she was constantly feuding with her neighbors and I wasn't allowed behind enemy lines. So whenever I *did* find myself in the presence of other kids I felt as though I was looking at alien beings, and they probably felt the same about me.

The one incident that most firmly locked me into a lifetime of emotional isolation, the shibboleth that denotes the moment when I realized there was absolutely no one I could trust, came when my mother became pregnant again in 1960. As before, she fell into a deep depression and spent whole days in bed, sleeping, crying, or staring angrily at nothing. Her mood became darker still after my sister Theresa was born, leading Sophia and my aunt to keep close watch on the infant to make sure nothing went wrong. Unfortunately, this left nobody to keep an eye on me. Having made it this far, the rest of my family assumed I was safe. So when our washing machine broke down, no one was overly concerned when Evelyn took me along as she carried a bag of diapers to an adjacent apartment building with a working machine.

Once the clothes were washed, my mother and I climbed the stairs to the third-story roof, where a clothesline was stretched across to a nearby telephone pole. Nervous, agitated, crying one moment, angry the next, she pinned up the diapers then shoved them down the line as if slapping an unseen face, moving faster and faster, almost manic as she attacked the symbols of her captivity. Then suddenly she stopped and grew very quiet, looking off into the distance as if coming to a decision.

She pointed past me to some trees behind the house. "Look at the birds," she said.

I turned to look but didn't see any birds. Then I felt her hands lifting me from behind. For a moment I thought she was helping me see the birds, or that she might turn me around and hug me for the first time. My heart leapt at the prospect.

She dropped me over the edge of the roof.

I shrieked as I tumbled into a tangle of electrical and TV antenna wires that kept me from falling to the concrete below. As I screamed in terror Evelyn paced frantically back and forth, looking around nervously and telling me to be quiet. Finally, afraid that people would be drawn by my cries, she yanked me back onto the roof and shook me hard. She told me that what happened was an accident and that I was not to mention it to my father, *ever*, or he'd be angry at me, and *did I understand?* I nodded, crying and scared, snot running down my face.

That night, as my father raged drunkenly around the apartment, my mother wailed, and my grandmother yelled obscenities, I sat on the bathroom floor using a nail clipper to pick splinters from the roof out of my legs. Every time I thought about what happened I would start to cry, only to force it back down again; if I let myself cry, I wouldn't be able to see the splinters. I let the tears come only after the last one was out, not from pain but from the knowledge that there was no place in my life where I was safe, and no one I could trust or talk to about it.

CHAPTER 3

Faster Than a Speeding Bullet

Worn out by constant vigilance over my sister, Sophia and my aunt insisted that Charles bring in Evelyn's mother to help out, believing this might also have a mitigating effect on her depression. My father hated the idea, having crossed swords with Grace over the annulment and restraining order, but he was no match for the two of them. Bitterly unhappy, he called Grace and asked her to come to New Jersey.

This was an extraordinary development, because until now my mother's side of the family had always been something of a mystery. As far as Charles was concerned, only his side of the family mattered, and he often belittled Evelyn's relatives as little more than hillbillies. Charles was so adamant about erasing any connection to Evelyn's side of the family that he ordered her to destroy all her personal photos. She tore up a few in front of him, then secretly sent the rest to my aunt for safekeeping.

Since nobody ever talked about her, I didn't even know I *had* a maternal grandmother until the day she arrived on a bus from California. It was as if the casting department suddenly realized they'd forgotten to hire an actress for the role and shoved someone out at the last minute in the hope that no one would notice she hadn't been there earlier.

One of five children from itinerant, dust-bowl roots, Grace and her daughter had drifted through mining towns in Wyoming and worked on farms in Texarkana and Arkansas before moving to Vallejo and the beat-up trailer that became their home. From the first day she walked into our lives to the last time I saw her, Grace looked to be about two hundred and forty-seven years old, but was probably no more than two hundred and nine. Her skin was the texture of aged parchment, a tracery of fine wrinkles that were always turned in the opposite direction to whichever way she was leaning, as if looking for an opportunity to run off and leave her behind. Her face showed the consequences of too much sun and *far* too many cigarettes. Every morning she would grab a cup of coffee, plant herself in a corner of the living room, pull out her crocheting kit and a pack of Camel cigarettes, then proceed to chain-smoke the room into a perpetual haze. My father also smoked, but he was an amateur next to Grace. Charles smoked for punctuation; Grace smoked in an attempt to modify Earth's atmosphere into something more suited to her species.

Grace and my father despised each other, and kept their distance as much as possible, circling one another like scorpions trapped in a bottle. Her presence forced my father to dial back the nightly beatings because he knew that if he tried it, she'd wait until he was asleep then jab her crocheting needles in his eyes.

Whenever Charles was out of the house, Grace lobbied my mother to come back with her to Vallejo and get another restraining order. She wasn't married, so why *not* leave?

"Once Charlie finds a job, he'll be okay," she'd say, then add, "Besides, where would I go? What would I do? It's better here."

It's better here. It was her mantra, and a source of profound anger for me. I heard it as *Doing nothing is better than risking change*. Inertia was the path of least resistance. Seeing her refuse to take even a single forward step inculcated in me a horror at the idea of settling for what *is* rather than taking a chance on what *might* be. I swore to never settle for *It's better here, it's safer here.* I would take chances, and if my world burned down as a consequence, then it had it coming.

Television provided the only escape from my family, and I fell in love with science shows about space or dinosaurs, and made friends with Bugs Bunny, Soupy Sales, and Captain Kangaroo, *Planet Patrol* and *Colonel Bleep*. For those brief moments I was somewhere else, far from Paterson. But when the TV was switched off, I was right back where I started. None of it stuck. None of it *mattered*.

Then I found it.

Found *him*.

Superman.

Faster than a speeding bullet . . .

More powerful than a locomotive . . .

Able to leap tall buildings in a single bound.

I was oblivious to the fact that behind Superman stood actor George Reeves, or that the *Adventures of Superman* was just a TV show. Superman was *real*, and unlike my father he was kind and honest and fair, and he never hit anybody who didn't hit him first.

The episode that broke me in half was "The Birthday Letter," in which Superman agrees to take a crippled young girl to the county fair for her birthday. Before he can get her there, he's attacked by mobsters. But no matter what they threw at him, you *knew* that he would protect her, that he would never, *ever* back off until he took her to the fair.

I couldn't stop crying. If Superman was my father, he'd never let anyone or anything hurt me. But he *wasn't* my father. I was alone and powerless, and nothing would ever change that.

Then I stumbled upon Max and Dave Fleischer's *Superman* cartoons. They were beautiful, even on a small black-and-white TV. The scene that lit up my brain like a Christmas tree showed Superman using his cape to protect Lois Lane from a cascade of molten metal. Rather than being angry at her for getting in trouble, he was gentle and brave and *saved* her. I imprinted on that moment like a baby duck, and my child's mind folded around a sudden understanding.

No, Superman was never going to be my father, but if I worked at it really hard, maybe one day I could *become* Superman. The idea didn't seem improbable given an *Adventures of Superman* episode about a guy who found Superman's impenetrable costume; putting it on made him nearly as invulnerable as Superman. No, I didn't have a Superman costume (though a kid down the street *did* have one, and it annoyed me greatly that he failed to understand the power of the thing), but if I closed my eyes, I could see myself wearing it, and that's the next best thing, right?

If I was Superman, nobody could hurt me, I thought, *and I could protect my mom and she wouldn't get mad at me and try to throw me off the roof again. But even if she did, it wouldn't matter because if I was Superman, I'd just keep on going, right up into the sky.*

That fall, once Evelyn's depression had diminished enough for her to function, Grace returned to Vallejo and I entered Blessed Sacrament School to begin my training as a Catholic. For the first time I was surrounded by kids my own age, a rite of passage that included an introduction to bullies. The nuns rarely policed the playground since in this part of town their youthful charges were almost certainly destined for lives of crime, so why bother? They probably saw it as a form of vocational training. I would spend most of my free time sitting quietly in a corner of the schoolyard while everyone else played, so the bullies ignored me until the day three of the older ones started punching one of the girls. The more they hit her, reflecting what I saw at home, the angrier I got. Finally, remembering how Superman stood with his cape over Lois Lane, I planted myself like a tree between them, fists on hips, legs slightly spread in his classic pose, imagining myself in his costume, cape rippling in the wind. The bullies were twice my size, but I was sure they would be so intimidated by the ferocity in my eyes and my heroic stance that they would turn tail and flee.

They pounded me into the pavement.

Now that they had my measure, they continued to beat me up over the next several weeks, until I finally lost my mind.

They were waiting for me on the playground at lunch, and as soon as the nuns went inside to eat, the biggest bully tackled me. As I fought back I saw another kid's lunchbox nearby: hard, bright metal with sharp edges and corners. I grabbed it and swung as hard as I could, catching the bully squarely across the forehead and opening a long gash. He fell to the ground screaming. As the nuns raced out, I looked at the blood gushing like a bright red geyser—

—and for all intents and purposes blacked out.

The next thing I remember is being in Mother Superior's office, crying and scared. I tried to explain what happened, but the words kept disappearing into sobs. All I could remember was the blood. Desperate to calm me down, she picked up the nearest random object, a stapler on her desk, and gave it to me as a gift so I'd understand that I wasn't about to be murdered. She said that the kid I'd hit had been taken to the hospital and would have to get stitches. I didn't know what stitches were, but I figured it wasn't good.

When my mother and aunt showed up, Mother Superior said

that since I hadn't started it, I wouldn't be tossed out of school provided it never happened again. But that night my father lit into me. He said some part of me was sick the way my mother was sick, that my head was screwed up. But I knew he was wrong because at that moment it wasn't *my* head being stitched up across town.

When the bully came back to school a few days later, he cried out in terror when he saw me and hunched against a wall, afraid I was going to hurt him again. Remembering the gift Mother Superior used to calm me down, I dug into my pocket for a dinosaur trading card I'd gotten earlier that week. A stegosaurus. I'd torn through bubblegum packets for weeks looking for that card, but I wanted to show him that he was safe. He took it and calmed down, but for the rest of my time at that school, which wasn't long, he never came near me again.

It was my first lesson that at their core, all bullies are cowards. But that didn't diminish my shame at hurting someone, and I vowed never to do anything like it again. I was sickened by the incident and couldn't understand why my father actually *liked* hitting people.

CHAPTER 4

Death as a Lifestyle

In addition to being hooked on every form of alcohol known to modern science, the Straczynski family was addicted to death. Whenever anyone we knew died, the gory details would be dissected and embellished upon for days, especially if the deceased was on my family's rather lengthy shit list. Sophia, a death junkie par excellence, was obsessed with funerals. She not only attended ceremonies for people she knew, she often went to funerals for *total strangers*. She would wail along with the other mourners, then go to the reception and take home as much of the catered food as could fit in her huge purse. She said she liked funeral food because it contained only the freshest ingredients— nobody wanted to add to a grieving family's sorrow by using cheap substitutes—but I think she liked the idea of sneaking food off Death's plate.

My introduction to funerals came when my father took me to the service for a kid my age who had been playing in a gravel pit and suffocated when it collapsed. He didn't know the kid or his family, but that didn't stop him from driving around until he found the right address from an article in the newspaper. He wanted me to see a dead kid in his casket as a warning not to play in gravel pits.

Not that I had any plans to play in gravel pits.

Not that there *were* any gravel pits within a ten-mile radius of where we were living.

But just in case I *might* think about traveling across town to play in a gravel pit, it was important that I see the result: caskets, flowers, and a church filled with mourners, none of whom were my grandmother, who I can only assume had her eye on a better-catered reception. But seeing my first dead body—stiff as a mannequin, pale cheeks warmed by obvious makeup—had little impact because I didn't know the kid in the box, and I was still too young to understand what death was.

That knowledge came a few months later, when Victor Rafael Rachwalski passed away unexpectedly at the age of fifty-three.

The funeral service was packed with people who had known and loved him. This time my grandmother's cries of grief were real: no pretense, no drama for the sake of attention and a platter of take-home pierogi. At one point, out of her mind with sorrow, she tore at her clothes then collapsed to the floor.

While everyone was distracted with Sophia, and still being unclear on the whole death thing, I approached the open coffin. I couldn't understand why my friend Pan Rafael was just lying around. There were canvases to be painted, and ice cream waiting at the other end of a journey in the blue pedal car. I reached into his coffin and tugged at his sleeve.

"Come on, Pan Rafael," I said, "wake up. We have to go."

Someone behind me cried out. My father ripped me away from the coffin, mortified by my actions. My grandmother fainted.

And Pan Rafael remained resolutely in his coffin.

Later, I stood in the back of the room and watched as they closed the lid and loaded him into a hearse for the long ride to the cemetery. I waved as they drove off.

As the days passed, I began to understand that I would never see him again. My friend was gone. Now only the monsters remained.

The Year of Death was not quite finished with me.

On a cool, blustery afternoon, Sophia took my mother and me along on her annual pilgrimage to the grave of her firstborn son. Carrying a white Styrofoam cross with red and blue flowers, she walked with practiced familiarity to where the grass was broken by a rectangle of marble. She crossed herself, knelt, and laid the wreath on the hard ground.

She finished her prayer, crossed herself again, then pulled me over and pointed to the headstone. "Do you know what that says?" she asked.

Of course I knew what it said. I had just turned six, and like most kids the first thing I'd learned to write was my own name.

The words engraved in marble read **Joseph Straczynski**.

"That's your name," she said. "That's *you*."

I don't remember any of what happened after that until we walked back into our apartment. I can only assume that a part of my brain slammed shut all the doors of perception to keep my mind from going too far down the path of *That's you under the ground there*. But from that day on I had a profound sense of my own mortality. I knew that I would only be here for a brief flicker of time and had to make the best of it. I had to *do* something with my life.

A few mornings later, I got up to find my parents waiting for me in the front room. My father had just been fired from his latest job. This in itself was not unusual. What *was* surprising was what he said next.

"We're moving to California."

CHAPTER 5

Pigeon Dinner with a Slice of Watermelon

Without telling Sophia, my father had reestablished contact with my grandfather, who had been regaling Charles with stories of his success. There was serious money to be made in California, Kazimier explained, land that could be bought cheap and turned into vineyards or housing tracts. My father responded with equally wild tales of the vast resources and business acumen he could bring to bear in such an environment. It was an echo chamber built of lies and desperation since both men were actually flat broke. My father wanted to weasel his way into my grandfather's confidence to extract his alleged fortune, and Kazimier hoped that his successful, long-lost son would take care of him in style during his declining years. When Kazimier offered to fund whatever ventures my father wanted to pursue, Charles agreed to move to Los Angeles, where they would build an empire together.

We never owned much furniture, just a handful of pieces that could be folded quickly and thrown into a trailer when creditors came calling, so we were ready to go the next morning. I was allowed two cardboard boxes: one for clothes, the other for toys. If something didn't fit, I had to give it away or see it tossed out, which is why I possess nothing I owned as a child. Everything was ditched at roadsides and trash bins across America, sacrificed to expediency when there was no more room in the box.

The drive to California in my father's old Studebaker turned into a grueling campaign to see how many miles we could rack up before exhaustion set in. We ate in the car, slept in the car, used restrooms at gas stations, and made it to Los Angeles within a week. We lived in the car for several more days while my father tried vainly to meet up with my grandfather. Kazimier had promised we could stay at his house upon arrival, but now he was unexpectedly busy with meetings and suggested we get a place on our own, just for a little while of course, until his schedule calmed down.

We moved into what can best be described as a collection of shanties on South Clarence Street a few blocks off Skid Row: one- or two-room clapboard and cinder block structures that were perpetually covered by a fine, white dust. The area was surrounded by abandoned industrial buildings, heavily barred liquor stores, open lots where transients lived out of cardboard boxes, and SRO (single-room occupancy) hotels that could be rented by the hour and were mainly used by prostitutes.

When my father and Kazimier finally connected, the lies on both sides were revealed in the bright daylight of mutual inconvenience. Charles threatened to go back to New Jersey, but even I knew he was bluffing since that would mean admitting he'd made a mistake. So for the next few months we lived in the shanty, eating once a day at charity kitchens run by the Salvation Army and the Volunteers of America Service Center. Stomach distended from lack of food, I slept on a mat on a concrete floor infested with roaches and bedbugs. Constantly covered in bug bites, I would frantically comb the lice out of my hair every morning only to have them move back in again that night. I became nearly pathological in my attempts to get rid of them and could feel them squirming around on my scalp even after the last one had been found and squished.

Kazimier's command of English was slightly better than Sophia's, but he rarely spoke more than a few sentences before lapsing into silence, quiet in the way of someone whose present thoughts kept crashing against the unrealized hopes of his past. Melancholy and distant, the cuffs of his suit frayed, he would sip from a bottle of vodka inside a paper bag, eyes fixed at a spot deep inside his memories: a sad, small island of a man adrift in a world beyond his comprehension. He rarely said much to me, so I was surprised when he offered to take me out for the afternoon. We rode the bus to a nearby park, where he set an open paper bag on the ground, then pulled a slice of dry bread out of his pocket and laid a trail of crumbs into the sack. He said we were going to play a game. My part was to wait for a pigeon to wander inside the sack then grab it before the pigeon could escape.

I thought it was a strange game, but this was California, and I'd come with an open mind.

After a few failed attempts, I finally caught one of the pigeons. "Now what?" I asked.

"We take it with us," he said, "but we can't let the bus driver know or he'll throw us off."

Once we were on the bus the pigeon started pecking at the bag, trying to tear its way free. To keep the other passengers from figuring out what was going on, Kazimier chided me as if it was *my* fault. "Sit quiet, you're bothering the nice people. Stop rustling that bag."

We arrived at an ancient, four-story walk-up hotel, then climbed up a narrow stairwell past transients sleeping on the bowed wooden steps. The acrid smell of urine, vomit, and booze hung thick in the air. The second floor was unusually dark. Sheets covered the windows at either end of the hall, and most of the lights had been removed. Those that remained cast soft pools of light on women standing alone or talking in small groups. I thought it was strange that they were all in their underwear and wondered if they'd just gotten out of bed.

"What a pretty boy," the nearest of them said, ruffling my hair. "Did you bring me a present, sweetie?"

Kazimier muttered something rude under his breath and kept climbing.

"Come back when you're a little older," she called, laughing as I raced up the stairs.

When we reached his room on the next floor, he took the bag and went in alone while I waited in the hall. A few minutes later he reappeared, gave me a nickel for the bus, and sent me off to make the ride home alone. The women on the second floor laughed and waved good-bye as I ran past the perfumed shadows and faux silk.

The game became our weekly ritual. I never understood why he wanted the pigeons or what he did with them, but assumed they were eventually set loose. This changed the day we reached his apartment and I asked to use the bathroom. He reluctantly opened the door, revealing a one-room flat with a bed, a single chair, and a dresser bearing a hot plate.

Emerging from the bathroom, I glanced behind the dresser and saw what at first appeared to be a jumble of small sticks. Looking more closely, I realized that they were bones.

Pigeon bones.

I don't know if they'd fallen there earlier, or if he had brushed them aside so I wouldn't see them, but it was at this moment that I began to understand just how poor my family and I really were.

A few weeks later, after catching a pigeon at another park (we changed hunting areas regularly to avoid scrutiny), he remembered that he had left his glasses at the shanty, and we had to swing by to get them. I was worried that the extra trip would be too much for the paper sack to bear but he waved away my concerns, anxious to get in and out before Charles returned from his daily perambulations between possible jobs and definite bars. When we got off the bus half a block down, he saw my father's car parked outside.

"Wait here," Kazimier said and went inside.

I tried to stay out of sight, but my father saw me lingering around the corner and ordered me inside. As I stepped through the door the frayed bag ripped and the pigeon escaped. It spiraled around the room, slamming into walls and windows until Evelyn herded it out the door with a broom. When my father realized what was going on, he began screaming at Kazimier, not for sending a seven-year-old home on the bus alone through Skid Row, or because the pigeons were being abused, but because *he* was embarrassed. Then he grabbed Kazimier by the scruff of his neck and propelled him out the door, delivering a kick for good measure. Denied both his dignity and his small portion of meat for the day, Kazimier picked up his hat, glanced back to where my father was still yelling at him from the doorway, and limped out of sight.

That was the end of the pigeon game.

While I was attending the nearby Utah Street School, some of the kids discovered that we were living in what was essentially a homeless shelter and declared me trash. To reinforce my status, they would wait for me by a row of refuse bins near the shanty and throw garbage at me as I ran past. Watermelon rinds were a particular favorite since they could be thrown a long distance and had a good heft when they hit. They were also cheap and could thus be found in abundance, making it easy to load up. Upon arriving home covered in dirt, stickiness, and black seeds, I tried to explain to my mother that I'd been pounded by watermelon rinds, but she didn't believe me. She thought I was just being careless.

So one day I told some of the kids that my folks were gone for the afternoon and that I'd been locked out and would have to wait on the front porch until they got back. News of this quickly reached the Goon Squad, and as soon as the school bell rang they ran ahead of me to the trash bins to load up. I walked to where I knew they'd see me, then started running. They took off after me, throwing the watermelon rinds then picking up the fallen, dirt-encrusted pieces to reload. When I reached the shanty, I jumped inside and slammed the door, waited for a second, then cracked it open to peek outside. Watermelon rinds pelted the door. I slammed it shut again.

As hoped, my mother heard the commotion and ran over to me. "What's going on?" she asked.

I shrugged. "Look outside."

When she opened the door, she was pelted by enough water-melon rinds to fill a five-gallon garbage drum, which was where they'd been found in the first place. They nailed her head to toe before realizing they'd hit a grown-up, then ran like hell, my mother in hot pursuit, cursing loudly.

All things considered, it was a fine day.

When my father found a job working sheet metal in a garage, we were finally able to move out of Clarence Street, but the new loca-tion wasn't much better: Grape Street in the Watts District, one of the most dangerous parts of the city. I attended St. Aloysius Catholic School on East Nadeau Street, my third school in as many years.

After the birth of my youngest sister, Evelyn Lorraine, in Febru-ary 1961, my mother fell into another depression, her mood swings punctuated by outbursts of incoherent rage. Trapped in a perfect postpartum storm, in a city and a life she'd never wanted, she made another suicide attempt, chugging half a bottle of sleeping pills be-fore being rushed to the hospital where her stomach was pumped.

After her release, we moved upstate to a small house on Pine Street in Napa, half an hour south of Vallejo, close enough for Grace to help out but far enough for comfort when Charles didn't want her around. The house had been only partially completed; the shell was there, but the walls and ceilings were unfinished, showing nails and exposed wires. The owner had run out of money to finish the job, so Charles offered to fix up the place in exchange for free rent. Naturally he never did any of the promised work, and I spent the next two months sleeping on raw floors and playing in a yard strewn with debris and broken glass.

As the days passed, Evelyn's depression grew darker and more violent. When my father was gone she would rage around the house, screaming at nothing and throwing clothes around. She would walk out to the street as if determined to leave, pace back and forth, then come back in again, red-faced and talking fast under her breath. It became increasingly apparent that not even Grace's presence would be enough to turn her around this time.

I still don't know what happened the day everything blew up. I know only what I saw.

I'd spent the afternoon out in the dry woods behind our house playing with a cat I'd adopted. By this point, it was my tradition to rescue an abandoned cat every time we moved because we could be loving and playful with each other, emotions I could not safely express anywhere else. I could probably connect my appreciation for cats with the only time my mother's hand touched mine with affection. One could stretch that connection even further to suggest that I liked saving cats because I was incapable of saving my mother.

And maybe I like cats because they're cats. Sometimes a tabby is just a tabby.

I returned to the house to find a scene of total chaos. Dinner plates were shattered on the floor beside an upturned table. One of the window shades had been torn off during a struggle, and blood dotted the walls. Charles sat on the sofa, shirt torn, forehead cut just below the hairline, carefully pulling apart cigarette stubs from an ashtray and tapping the leftover tobacco onto a piece of paper torn out of the phone book. It took him a moment to register my presence, and when he finally glanced up, it was as though he was looking past me rather than at me.

My mother was nowhere to be seen.

The hypervigilant part of my brain started screaming at me. *He's killed her. He's killed her and you need to run away, as fast as you can, right now!*

I pushed down the thought and edged closer, careful not to get more than a few feet from the door. "What happened?" I asked.

He shook his head, rolled the piece of paper into a makeshift cigarette, and lit it. "I don't know," he said, and repeated it several times. "*I* did something bad, and *she* did something bad, and now she's back in the hospital."

"When's she coming back?"

He took a long drag on the cigarette. "I don't know," he said. "I don't know if she *is* coming back."

That night he drove me and my sisters to Grace's trailer, where we stayed while my mother was again institutionalized. When we returned home several weeks later, Evelyn was heavily medicated and in considerable discomfort, moving only when necessary. My father said she'd had an operation, but wouldn't elaborate. One night I pretended to be asleep while he was talking to Grace and heard him give a name to the procedure: hysterectomy.

There would be no more children.

That summer, out of work and facing eviction, my father had no choice other than to return to Paterson, so we began loading up a small trailer for the long drive east. My father had always promised that I could bring along whatever cat I'd adopted if it was there when we moved, but they never seemed to be around when needed and I was forced to leave them behind. I didn't think about the practicalities of bringing a cat on a cross-country road trip because you don't think about those things when you're eight. I knew only that I liked my cat, so as we finished packing I reminded my father about his promise. He said we could make it work.

But when I went into the backyard to get the cat, it was nowhere to be seen.

I was about to start searching the woods when my father came to find me. He said that the cat had gone to sleep behind one of the car's rear tires and had been run over when he backed up. I ran to the car to find most of the cat's body undamaged; only the head had been crushed. Wiping away tears, I carried his remains to the backyard and buried him in the shallow, dry ground. Still crying, I climbed into the car and we drove off.

As Napa melted away behind us, I wondered why the cat hadn't been startled away from the tire when my father started the car. Stranger still, I'd never even seen the cat sleeping there before; she had always been *afraid* of the car and would run from the noise it made. Why would she pick *this* day to decide that she *liked* the car?

And why had only the head been crushed?

I would eventually discover that the Pine Street cat was not the first to be sacrificed to my father's convenience, nor would it be the last.

CHAPTER 6

The First One's Always Free

It was furnace-hot as we passed through Oklahoma crammed into a car whose windows were designed more for appearance than the free passage of anything as frivolous as air. We sat as far as possible from the un-upholstered doors, the bare metal sheeting and handles too hot to touch. When my father stopped at a gas station we piled outside, desperate to catch a breath of air that wasn't superheated beyond the limits of human endurance. We must've been a pretty grim-looking bunch, because when the attendant learned we were driving cross-country with nothing more to occupy ourselves than thoughts of suicide, he took pity on us.

"Wait here," he said and hurried into the station as the gas pump counted gallons. He emerged moments later with a two-foot-high stack of comic books. "These're my nephew's. He was here visiting last month, then left 'em behind when he went back east. I was gonna throw 'em out, but if you want 'em, they're yours."

This was my first exposure to comics, and while most of the books were of the silly sort—*Archie* and *Jughead*, *Sad Sack*, *Mighty Mouse*, *Donald Duck*, and *Casper the Friendly Ghost*—salted in among them were *proper* comics: *Classics Illustrated*,

Batman, *Combat*, *Rip Hunter*, and best of all, *Superman*. I carefully stacked the books, straightened the bent corners, organized them from least interesting to most interesting based on the cover art, and began reading.

By the time we reached New Jersey my appreciation for all things Superman had extended to a love of comic books in general, less for the action and flashy costumes than their sense of morality. The books emphasized the importance of standing up for others, even if doing so meant putting yourself at risk. That ethical core meant everything to a young kid trapped in a family that operated without any sort of moral compass.

Sophia took great pleasure in pointing out to Charles that he had traveled cross-country twice, duped by Kazimier's lies, only to return with his tail between his legs to ask for money while he looked for work. Any pleasure I might have taken from my father's distress was erased when I discovered that he had thrown away the comics. They'd kept me occupied during the drive, and as far as he was concerned they had no greater value. I dug out the few books not totally spoiled by garbage and snuck them into the house. In the months that followed I traded comics with other kids and used whatever small change I could safely liberate from my father's dresser to buy my own. Collecting comics became an act of rebellion against my father, and a means of defining who I was as a person.

Funnily enough, that's *still* how I see them.

Charles had made an art of lying his way into apartments, but that fall pickings were slim in Paterson; few landlords were willing to take a chance on a new tenant with anything larger than a one-bedroom apartment. That wasn't much room for five of us, so I was once again routinely sent off to live with my grandmother or my aunt, the latter of whom realized that the best way to keep me quiet was to have a stack of comics waiting on the hallway table when I arrived. I'd settle in on the couch beneath the living room window and read straight through to bedtime, which was also on the couch. Sometimes she'd sit and talk with me about the stories in the comics, and her comments were often surprisingly specific.

"We always suspected she was reading them herself," her brother-in-law Frank Skibicki said much later. "She'd never admit that of course, because at that time it wasn't something a grown-up should be doing, but I think she liked the stories."

With her help I acquired a healthy collection, including the first appearances of Spider-Man in *Amazing Fantasy* #15 and Thor in *Journey into Mystery* #83, and a full run, starting from issue one, of *The Fantastic Four*, *The X-Men*, *The Incredible Hulk*, as well as Silver Age titles from DC: *Superman*, *The Flash*, *Blackhawk*, *Atom*, *Green Lantern*, *Aquaman*, and *Metal Men*.

But Superman remained my chief focus, and his depiction by Curt Swan became the true, iconic image against which all later versions would be measured. Other comics of the time featured a relatively small cast of characters, but the Superman comics had a large cast of bad guys, friends, and allies, supported by extensive world-building and elaborate histories. It was my first exposure to the process of creating a consistent universe. I loved reading about the Phantom Zone, the Jewel Mountains, the Scarlet Jungle, and the Fire Falls. Krypton was as real to me as Paterson. More real, in some ways. I worried for Clark's safety whenever Brainiac or Lex Luthor appeared on the cover, learned the names and properties of all the various forms of Kryptonite (green, red, gold, jewel, blue, and white), and embraced even the dopiest supporting characters of the Superman universe except for Beppo the Super-Monkey because honestly, who would?

I would read the issues through once as just a fan, to enjoy the story, then over and over again to study how the action and dialogue had been laid out across the pages to tell that story. It never occurred to me that I might one day want to write comics for a living, I just wanted to peek under the hood and figure out how the engine worked.

My own story took an unexpected turn when my father announced that we now had another last name: *Stark*. He said it was common for people to have a *real* name and a *business* name, and I believed him, not knowing anything about aliases at the time. Henceforth, when answering the phone or talking to people who might come to the door, I was to ask who the person wanted to speak with before identifying myself, and under no circumstances should I answer to the wrong name. This would make it more difficult for bill collectors, police, lawyers, and landlords to find him when he skipped out on his obligations.

Our latest ill-gotten refuge was a small two-bedroom apartment nobody else wanted because the oil heater didn't work and we were in the midst of one of the worst winters in New Jersey's long history. The snow drifts were taller than I was. It was so bad that my mother stole a few dollars out of my father's wallet to buy me a bright red cap. That way even if the rest of me was buried in the snow, they could still find me. Or they could at least find the cap.

My latest school, St. Stephen's, was home to the angriest, most dysfunctional nuns I'd ever encountered. In a system where corporal punishment was not only permitted but encouraged, St. Stephen's was the ne plus ultra of student abuse. We were routinely slapped, pushed, punched, and struck with whatever objects were nearest at hand. One afternoon, during a test, I realized that my fountain pen—ballpoints were strictly forbidden—was out of ink, and I didn't have a spare cartridge.

I raised my hand, approached the dragon at the front of the room, and stammered out my dilemma. She looked up from her papers, met my gaze levelly, and backhanded me across the head so hard my ear rang for an hour. She then ordered me back to my desk where I was to wait until one of the other boys (classes were segregated by gender) was finished with his test so I could borrow his pen to finish my work.

The first offered pen came shortly before the end of class, so I was only able to scribble down a few answers before the bell rang. I received an F.

When they weren't teaching Catechism and Introduction to Blunt Force Trauma, the nuns at St. Stephen's worked tirelessly to extract money from the families of their students. Everything had to be purchased from the church or from stores endorsed by the school: uniforms, books, pens (blue fountain pens were preferred, green was acceptable, but only blue or black ink), composition notebooks, and pictures of saints and popes. It was no secret that the stores kicked some of the money back to the church. I may have been just a kid, but even I knew a racket when I saw one. *Nice immortal soul your son's got there, be a real shame if he burned in hell for all eternity 'cause you didn't buy this here sweater. You get what I'm sayin', or do I gotta make a call to Mother Superior?*

Then there was the Pagan Baby Incident.

As the worst blizzard in years roared across Paterson, I arrived at school on a Monday morning grateful to be inside anything that offered four walls and warmth. I hurried into the cloakroom, shucked off my wet coat, then turned to see the homeroom nun approaching on an attack vector, her face an angry red.

"You *didn't* take a *chocolate* box," she said, so furious she was shaking.

The previous Friday, crates of World's Finest Chocolate had arrived, the sales of which helped raise money for orphans and pagan babies. I never understood *why* pagan babies were so important to the Catholic Church, but we were constantly being encouraged by Sister Mary Fisticuffs to *think* about the pagan babies, to *pray* for the pagan babies, to be glad we *weren't* pagan babies (which seemed odd since apparently pagan babies were always first in line for *every*goddamnthing), and if possible, to *buy* a pagan baby.

In 1962, admittedly a more robust economy, you could buy a pagan baby for five bucks.* This entitled you to a certificate of ownership as your "souvenir of the Ransom and Baptism of an Adopted Pagan Baby." You could name your pagan baby whatever you wanted, regardless of the local language, and rest secure in the knowledge that you had saved your pagan baby from whatever pagan babies were being chased by that day. Given my own impoverished conditions, as far as I was concerned if a pagan baby needed five bucks that badly, he could try to steal it off my father's dresser like the *rest* of us.

Not to put too fine a point on it, fuck the pagan babies.†

The chocolate bars were narrow slabs of brown awfulness wrapped in white-and-gold foil, sent by the truckload to be sold by children to friends, neighbors, family members, and anyone else you held a grudge against. You could only consider them to be the World's Finest Chocolate if you were, in fact, a pagan baby, and a 1960s pagan baby at that, because even the most isolated twenty-first-century pagan baby—a pagan baby that had never even *tasted* chocolate before—would take one bite, throw up, then use the box to beat you to death.

Since no one I knew had even *seen* a pagan baby, it was pretty obvious that this was just another scam. But I wasn't about to say that to Sister Mary Cthulhu as she stood before me red-faced and

---

* Adjusted for inflation, that's about thirty-eight dollars in 2019 currency, a good value by any standard, proof that the market for pagan babies is still strong and should be offered on the Nasdaq Stock Market at the first opportunity.
† The Pagan Baby fund still exists today, though it's now called the Missionary Childhood Association. I can only assume that *buysomepaganbabiescheap.com* was already taken.

wide-eyed, her expression prophesying imminent murder or a myo-cardial infarction.

"You *didn't* take any of the *boxes*," Sister Mary Thrombosis said again, so angry that she bit off the words in a staccato rhythm. "You were *supposed* to take them *home* and *sell* them over the *weekend* and bring the money *back*."

I told her that I'd been under the impression that the fund-raiser was voluntary.

"Do you think the *orphans* have a choice in their lives? Do you think the pagan *babies* have a choice in their lives?"

Since I was screwed no matter what I said, I decided for the first time to mouth off to a nun. I started to say "I don't know, why don't we call some pagan babies and ask them?" but halfway through *call some* she slapped me hard enough to ping-pong my head against the cloakroom wall. Then she grabbed my coat and hat, shoved a box of World's Finest Chocolate into my hand, propelled me down the stairs and out onto the snow-lashed sidewalk.

"You will *stay* out here and *sell* these and you will *not* come *back* inside until you've sold *all* of them," she said, then stalked back inside, slamming the door behind her.

The snow was so thick I could barely see to the end of the block. There was no one else around, not a shopper, not a passerby on his way to work, *no one*. I considered walking down the street in search of other life-forms, then abandoned the idea, afraid of what might happen if Sister Mary Botulism discovered that I had deserted my post. I was soon covered in so much snow that the only thing you could see from a distance was a kid-shaped pile of snow topped by a red cap. I looked like a decapitated snowman. An hour passed. Then another. I couldn't feel my face, feet, or fingers.

Finally, an old man dressed in the fashion of the Hassidim appeared through the snow like an apparition. He tottered down the street carrying a bag of groceries, black coat snapping at his legs, head bent low against the wind. When he was within range, I staggered forward to ask if he wanted to buy some chocolate bars, though what came out of my frozen lips sounded more like "Wanna buh suhchoklutburrs?"

He raised his face to look at me, glanced up at the school rising above us, then back at me again. "They shoved you out here to sell those?" he asked.

I nodded. Shivering.

"Terrible people," he said, then sighed and pointed to the box. "I guess I can take one. You got any plain? I don't like almonds, they're not good for my teeth."

I glanced at the box. Almonds.

He sighed again. "I suppose I can eat around them." He handed over the money, shoved the bar in his pocket, and continued away, vanishing into the cloud of snow.

After another hour, the door opened behind me and Sister Mary Goebbels reappeared. "How many?" she asked.

I held up one frozen finger, hoping it wouldn't snap off.

Her face tightened, and for a moment I thought she might hold to her threat to keep me outside until they were all gone. But as she looked up and down the empty street even she was forced to accept that there were simply no customers to be found, and stepped aside to let me in.

"Useless," she said as she followed me upstairs. "You are a useless, *useless* child."

I bet you wouldn't say that to a pagan baby, I thought but, wisely this time, did not say.

Our sketchy living conditions and zero preventive care made me easy prey for viruses, so as the blizzard dragged on I kept getting sick. Making matters worse, the two bedrooms of our unheated apartment had been allocated to my parents and my sisters, leaving me to sleep on the living room couch under a window that offered little resistance to the cold air.

"It's not that bad," my father said as the freezing wind seeping in through the seams rattled the blinds above me. "He's just exaggerating."

This was my father's modus operandi: whenever difficulty arose, it was never his fault; the real problem was people trying to make him look bad.

When a recurring flu turned into bronchitis then blossomed into pneumonia, my father opted against taking me to a hospital because he had outstanding bills at most of them, forcing me to try and tough it out. Too sick to go to school, I received occasional house calls by doctors (paid for by my aunt) who would end their examination by saying, *He really needs to be in a hospital.* Sunlight helped during the day, as did ambient heat from the kitchen when my mother used the stove to cook dinner, but with each cold night I got progressively sicker.

One evening, feverish and shivering beneath a thin blanket, I decided I'd had enough. I crawled into the kitchen, turned on the oven, and lay in front of the open door for warmth. To make sure my father didn't catch me I stayed awake until I could see daylight coming through the window, then turned off the oven, crawled back to the sofa, and passed out.

I did this every night for a week, sleeping during the day when the sun warmed the room. Gradually I began to feel stronger. But there was one unexpected side effect. Prior to this I'd been a morning person, getting up early to read or watch cartoons. Staying awake every night in front of the warm stove, rewarding myself in an almost Pavlovian way for not sleeping, flipped my day/night cycle upside down. I became a night person, and have been ever since, rarely getting to bed before three or four A.M.

When the fever broke, my father said this was proof that I hadn't really been that sick in the first place. It was one of the earliest moments when I realized how lovely it would be to stand on a sidewalk beside him on a warm, sunny day and knock him into the path of an oncoming truck.

In 1964 my father found work in a plastic extrusion factory that paid enough for us to move out of the unheated apartment into something a tick nicer on Butler Street. By now we were changing addresses almost every six months, so I was constantly worried about getting lost. To compensate I would walk each new neighborhood as soon as we unpacked to memorize the surrounding streets. But this time we didn't unpack until late in the evening, so there was no time for my usual reconnaissance.

The next morning my father dropped me off at Our Lady of Lourdes Catholic School, my fifth school in four years. I entered through an open side door and trotted down the hall to wait outside Mother Superior's office, where I would be briefed about the school and my classes. After a few minutes I looked up to see her striding briskly down the freshly waxed hall, eyes down, lost in thought. When she hit a slick patch of floor her legs shot out from under her and she exploded into human shrapnel, her feet, hands, robe, and rosaries flying in four different directions at the same time. I'd seen people fall before, but this was an unparalleled, five-star acrobatic performance so breathtaking that under other circumstances I would have stood and applauded, weeping openly and without shame.

After the ground stopped shaking, she sat up in the tent of her habit, stunned but unhurt, and caught me staring at her. I didn't know what to do. Part of me was horrified on her behalf, another was astounded by the sheer spectacle of it all, and the rest of me knew that if this had happened back at St. Stephen's, I'd be clobbered if I allowed even a smile.

She looked past the cowl of her headpiece, which was tilted at a rather rakish angle, and said, "It's okay to laugh."

The craftiness of her statement told me that this school was going to be a very different experience than I was used to. By giving me *permission* to laugh she removed the *desire* to laugh. It's no fun to laugh at someone who says it's okay to laugh at them.

These were *clever* nuns and had to be regarded with respect and wariness.

At the end of the school day the tide of escaping kids carried me downstairs and out the main entrance, a different way than I'd come in. I looked around, thought I recognized the street that led to our new apartment, and started walking. I've always been a daydreamer, and since I thought I was on the right street I didn't pay attention to where I was going as the maze of streets merged then angled away from each other. After a while I looked up and realized that I had no idea where I was. Absent the landmarks I would've familiarized myself with the day before, I was utterly lost.

I forced myself to calm down. If I could just make my way back to the school, I was sure I could find my way home from there.

But which way was the school?

I asked passing adults if they could point me in the right direction, but they either didn't know or were too busy to stop. (A lost boy in 2019 would attract far more attention than in 1964, when kids were expected to be more self-reliant.) One adult pointed down an intersecting street and said it was *overthere* somewhere. It wasn't much to go on but it was more than I had, so I started off in the suggested direction.

Twenty minutes of walking brought me to an abandoned area nothing at all like the residential neighborhood that bordered the school. I didn't know where I was *or* my new address because my parents hadn't thought to mention this crucial piece of information. I walked faster, fighting panic, desperately searching for an adult or a landmark that would lead me home. But the streets were deserted, industrial and ominous. I'd go halfway down one block to see what was past it, then back up and try the next street, hoping to eventually stumble onto the right path. I started crying.

Then I heard someone call to me.

A car pulled up to the curb on the otherwise empty street. A man sat behind the wheel, a woman in the passenger seat beside him, with another man in the back. The woman had dirty-blond hair. I couldn't make out much about the men.

"There you are," she said.

I hesitated, not sure what was going on.

"Your mom sent us to find you," she said. "She's worried sick about you."

The guy behind the wheel nodded. "Your dad's been in an accident, they told us to find you and bring you to the hospital."

"Get in the car, sweetie," she said. The man in the backseat popped open the door.

I didn't like the look of them and backed up a pace.

She leaned out of the window, waving at me to come forward. "Hurry up," she said.

"What's my mom's name?" I asked.

"This isn't a time to play games," she said firmly.

"What's my mom's *name*?"

The man in the back leaned out the door. "Look, your dad's hurt, now stop screwing around and get in the damned car!"

I didn't.

He started to climb out of the car. "I said come here, goddamnit!"

I took off.

I ran as fast as I could, jetting down alleys and between dumpsters, his footsteps pounding the sidewalk as he chased after me. When I reached a street crowded with traffic, I dashed into the river of cars without waiting for the light, terrified he'd get me if I stopped. Horns roared and drivers yelled as they swerved around me. I hit the other side and didn't slow down for three more blocks. Breathing hard, legs throbbing, I risked a look back to see if he was still behind me. The street seemed empty, but I didn't want to take any chances so I hid between two parked cars and waited until I was sure he was gone.

It was getting dark when I finally stepped back out into the street. I had to find my way home before nightfall, but how? What would Superman do if he couldn't see to find his way home?

He'd use his super-hearing, I thought, and went to the corner, closed my eyes, and listened. I couldn't hear much traffic coming from the way I thought I should go, so I took a chance and struck off toward the area where I could hear the most cars. After a few blocks I spotted a police officer directing traffic, ran across the street and told him I was lost. I didn't tell him about the car or the blond-haired woman, afraid that somehow *I'd* get in trouble. With his help I was able to retrace my steps and return to the apartment.

That night, when my father learned what had happened, he was furious that the police had brought me home. Rule Number One was that we should never do *anything* to attract the attention of anyone with a badge, and how stupid does a kid have to be not to know his way home?

Later, as I tried to fall asleep on the living room sofa, the memory of the car and its ominous passengers kept going through my head. To this day, I wonder what would've happened if I'd started running just a *second* later?*

Our Lady of Lourdes was more than just a welcome relief from the slap-happy antics of the Sisterhood of the Closed Fist at St.

---

* Years later, that scene, with only a very few small changes, wound up in a little movie called *Changeling*.

Stephen's; it changed the trajectory of my life through their participation in the Scholastic TAB book program. Written expressly for children, the books were often about kids who were worse off than any of us but persevered and made good in the end. They included such titles as *Miss Pickerell Goes to Mars*, *The Janitor's Girl*, *The Plain Girl*, and *What's for Lunch, Charley?*

To keep prices down, the books were produced using coarse, brittle paper, cardboard covers with the barest of illustrations, and were written under an assortment of house names. Ironically, the methods used to make cheap, expendable literature for children were the same as those used by publishers of pornographic novels: coarse paper, house names, cardboard covers, and simple illustrations. If not for the presence of lingerie on the cover, you would be hard-pressed to tell a TAB book from *Rubber Dolly*, *The Family That Eats Together*, or *Twilight Girls*. One could even migrate the TAB titles (*The Janitor's Girl*, *The Plain Girl*) to the adult line. To make *What's for Lunch, Charley?* work you'd only have to move the question mark up by one word.

TAB books cost between twenty-five and thirty-five cents each, and had to be paid for up front in cash because there's no such thing as a line of credit in the Catholic Church. I wouldn't start getting an allowance for another year or so (ten cents per week until I turned thirteen), so I continued my habit of pilfering spare change from my father's dresser when he was too drunk to notice: seventy cents exactly, just enough for two TAB books. I studied each month's catalog with an intensity normally reserved for jury rooms because these were *my* choices, books I *wanted* to read rather than the ones forced on me by teachers.

It was while reading one of these TAB books that something magical happened.

At one point in the story, a young boy with only five cents enters an ice cream parlor on a supremely hot day, planning to spend that money on a chocolate ice cream cone. But as he steps back outside someone bumps his arm and the ice cream falls to the hot sidewalk.

Reading this, I started to cry. As a kid with no money I understood what that felt like, how awful it was, how—

Waitasecond, I told myself. *Why are you crying? This didn't actually happen, it's not real. It's just a story somebody made up. There's no reason for tears.*

I shook it off. Closed the book. *Of course it's not real. It's just a story.*

I opened the book and reread the passage.

And started crying again.

I was stunned to realize that it was possible to make up things that had never happened but which *felt* as if they'd happened. The church had tried to convince me that there was only truth and falsehood and nothing in between, but the nuns and priests were wrong; the story in front of me was false, but in the *reading* of it my heart accepted it as true. I turned over the book to reveal the writer's name. I hadn't previously paid much attention to the names on book covers, but by god *somebody* sat down and *wrote* that story.

Wouldn't it be amazing if I could do that? I thought.

And with an electric thrill I felt a key turn deep inside me.

Ever since learning to read I'd been instinctively studying the storytelling process because some part of my brain knew this was important. Only now did it finally possess the information needed to explain itself to the rest of me. In that moment I knew with absolute, rock-solid certainty that I wanted to tell stories. Nobody in my family thought I had anything of value to say because I was too young or too stupid. Telling stories would give me the voice I lacked at home, allowing me to talk about things I cared about.

Clark Kent could have been anything he wanted. He could've been the best athlete or the best scientist in history. But he joined the *Daily Planet* because he knew that the ability to write, to tell stories that could touch people, was a way for him to *change* the world, not just *save* it. And if that was good enough for him, then it was good enough for me.

I wanted to pick up my pen and start writing immediately, but I knew I wasn't ready. If this was really what I wanted to do with my life, then I would have to learn everything I could about writing. That meant no longer thinking of school as something to survive but rather as a launching pad for my ambitions. I didn't know how long it would take before I was ready to start writing, but given the mushroom cloud that was still expanding in my head I was pretty damned sure I'd recognize it when it happened.

CHAPTER 7

The Face Behind the Mask

I spent most of the following summer with my aunt Theresa and uncle Ted, a skilled roofer who sometimes took me with him to work. This was a new experience; I'd never seen where my father worked because he was rarely ever working. Ted would roust me off the living room sofa before dawn and we'd drive to one of the houses he was building or fixing. I'd fetch and carry things he could have easily fetched and carried himself but it gave us something to do together, and at the end of the day I felt I'd actually *accomplished* something. He was trying to instill in me the same work ethic that he and his brother Frank had honed to a fine art.

One afternoon he had me on ladder duty to hand up tools and other supplies. When some of the shingles proved difficult to remove, he asked me to come up and give him a hand. I zipped up the ladder and stepped onto the roof. It was the first time I'd been on a roof since my mother tried to hurl me off one just a few years earlier, and when I made the mistake of looking over the edge, that moment came back with the force of a physical blow. Once again I felt myself being picked up, then falling. The roof tilted beneath me.

Look at the birds!

Ted saw me starting to fall and grabbed my arm, dragging me to the middle of the roof. I sat shaking for several minutes, unable to talk. My eyes were open but the world had vanished. All I could see was that moment playing over and over in my head.

Ted held on to me until my brain returned from wherever it had retreated. "Are you okay?"

I nodded.

"What happened?"

I didn't know how to tell him about the incident with my mother, so I told him I just got dizzy for a second. I don't think he entirely believed me, but he let it go and started leading me toward the ladder. I pulled away, determined to continue the task that had brought me up there in the first place. On some level I knew that if I didn't finish what I'd started I would always be trapped by the fear of that memory. He let me stay but kept close watch the whole time. I was okay as long as I kept away from the edge and didn't look down.

When we were done, he offered to help me down the ladder, but I declined and made it on my own. Later, as we drove back to Ted's house, where my father was to pick me up, he said I'd done a good day's work and deserved a good day's pay, then handed me a five-dollar bill. It was more money than I'd ever seen, enough to buy forty comic books *and* have enough left over for a candy bar! I'd never been as excited about anything as I was for that five-dollar bill. Best of all, it wasn't a gift, it wasn't charity, there were no strings attached, I'd *earned* it. I'd *worked* and I'd been *paid* and the money was *clean*.

This is incredible, I thought. *I can do this again next time and get* another *five dollars! Holy smokes! Does the rest of the world know about this?*

When my father arrived, I showed him the fiver, expecting him to be proud of my accomplishment. Instead he became furious, yelling at Ted and demanding to know what the hell he was thinking.

He said I shouldn't expect to be paid for doing things for the family, even if it constituted actual work. The real problem was that *he* didn't want to worry about paying me if he started putting me to work, as would eventually happen.

At my father's insistence I handed Ted back the money, then we got in the car and headed home. I refused to cry or show that I was upset. I'd learned never to show my emotions to anyone, especially my father, who always found some way to turn them against me. That was his pattern, one of many I was starting to understand.

If dinner wasn't ready when he got home, he'd beat my mother for her laziness, creating an excuse to go out drinking. If dinner *was* ready, he'd announce that it wasn't to his liking and smash the plates of food against the wall then blame her for the mess, threatening that if it wasn't cleaned up by the time he got back, there would be more of the same. If my mother complained or looked like she *might* complain, he'd punch her. I don't mean he'd slap, backhand, or shove her. He would *punch* her, repeatedly and at full strength, in the face, head, shoulders, chest, and back, driving her to the floor then kicking her. If there was anything at hand that he could use as a weapon—a pan or his shoe—he'd hit her with it as hard as he could. If she wept, he'd declare that he would give her "something to cry about" and then proceed to do exactly that.

The point wasn't just about getting off on violence, it was about inflicting humiliation. If there was spoiled meat in the refrigerator, he'd smear her face with it; if the milk had turned sour, he'd pour it over her head as punishment for trying to give him food that could make him sick, even though the food was often bad because he sometimes waited weeks before taking her shopping. Nor could she go on her own if the store was too far because he refused to let her drive, effectively imprisoning her.

Most nights he came back from drinking well after midnight, and would drag us out of bed to make us watch as he beat her. He wanted us to see the grief *she* was causing *him*, so we'd understand that she was a despicable human being, that the beatings were *her* fault, that she *deserved* to be treated this way. I was now ten. My sisters were four and three. We had spent almost the entirety of our lives being forced to watch him beat and brutalize her, exposing us to the worst kind of violence on a weekly, sometimes daily basis. Knowing what she had tried to do to me on that long-ago roof, I had no love for my mother. There was no love *anywhere* in our family, for each other or for ourselves. But for what he did every week, for the blood, the screaming, and the drunken violence, I *hated* my father.

The only break in the routine came when he returned home in a drunken soft focus, bearing cold pizza that had been sitting in the car for hours. We had to eat it or risk giving offense, which would start the violence all over again. When he was in this state he was manageable but sloppy, and would try to win us over with wild, extravagant promises about forthcoming vacations, trips, and presents. His promises were always forgotten by the next day, and if we were foolhardy enough to bring them up, he would deny having said anything of the kind, then start yelling about how we were draining him dry. He said we should be grateful just for having food on the table rather than being out on the street, and blamed the cost of feeding and clothing us as the reason we had to keep moving. In truth we had few clothes, mostly from secondhand stores, that would only be replaced when they fell apart.

By contrast my father's closet was stuffed with expensive suits, ties, and shirts. Preserving the illusion that he was successful and that we were a happy family was the only thing he ever really cared about. So we were trained to never tell anyone what *really* went on inside the house, not to teachers, relatives, or each other. As my sister Theresa would say later, "It seems like there was some unspoken code from back then that kept us from discussing, even amongst ourselves, what we were experiencing."

If asked, we were to say that everything was great; if a camera appeared, we were to smile and look happy. Doing otherwise invited dire consequences. But for all his efforts there is not a single photograph across three generations of Straczynskis that shows even a hint of genuine affection. No hugging, no kissing, no spontaneity, only frozen smiles and distant eyes. We stood *beside* each other, but not *with* each other, backs straight, at attention, like a police lineup. For one of us to say to the other, *I love you*, or to offer a hug was unthinkable. It would have seemed weird and unnatural.

To convince us that our life of violence and brutality was normal, he kept us isolated from the outside world so that we would have nothing to compare it against. We never went on vacations and were discouraged from attending neighborhood parties or social events that might lead us to discover that most people led lives very different from our own. Like most alcoholics my father was all about control, and our constant moves tightened his control while creating a state of conditioned helplessness among the rest of us. Had we stayed in one place for a prolonged period we would have developed relationships with friends or teachers we could confide in, or who might figure out what was happening on their own. Skipping town every six months removed that threat. We were trapped inside the bubble of my father's control, with no one we could turn to for help.

If I was Superman, I could just fly away, I thought more than once. That was the part of the comics and the TV shows I loved the most: seeing him fly. But the appeal was about more than just escaping my surroundings. Everything on the ground died sooner or later: people, animals, trees, whole civilizations. But the stars went on; the sun and the moon went on. They lived forever because they were *up there*, like Superman.

If I wanted to escape, if I wanted to Be Somebody, if I wanted to live forever, then I had to find a way off the planet.

I would have to learn to fly.

A sickness ran deep in my family's DNA, and it sometimes popped up in unexpected places.

It was one of those humid, superheated New Jersey scorchers that make you want to peel off your skin and put it on the line to dry. I'd been sent to stay with my grandmother for the weekend and rather than remain inside, where the hot air was stifling, I went into the backyard to sit in the shade and read. As the shadows lengthened, Sophia called out to say that my parents would be arriving in a few hours to pick me up, and I should take a shower so I didn't "smell like a bum."

I must now make an embarrassing admission. Having been raised like feral animals, my sisters and I were never given much instruction on hygiene. We were told to wash our hands before dinner and brush our teeth before bed, but that's all. Our clothes were only occasionally washed, my first visit to a dentist was still years off, and the three of us rarely bathed, partly because we didn't know any better, but mainly because where we lived there was usually just one bathtub or shower, and that was the exclusive domain of my father.

So I was a little puzzled by my grandmother's insistence that I take a shower—it was the first time I could remember her suggesting it—but dutifully went to the second-floor bathroom, stripped down, turned on the water, and got into the shower.

A moment later, I heard the bathroom door open and close.

Then the plastic shower door slid open and my grandmother got into the shower with me.

Naked.

I didn't understand what was going on, but it freaked me out and I shrank back. She tried to calm me down by acting very casual, as if this sort of thing happened every day, and why was *I* making such a big deal of it? Her tone was friendly and conciliatory and not at all like she was the rest of the time, which only made things weirder. On the pretext of helping me wash she began running her hands up and down my body and between my legs. Then she suggested I do the same for her and put my hand on one of her breasts.

When I turned away, she wrapped her arms around me from behind, the back of my head jammed between her breasts as she groped my genitals. "Turn around," she said and put her mouth on places it was never meant to go.

What she didn't know was that my parents had arrived early. When they came upstairs to look for us, my father saw what was happening and went completely out of his mind. He screamed at her in a mix of languages, his voice high pitched and hysterical as she scrambled out of the shower and pulled on a robe. She tried to explain that she was just making sure I was properly clean, but her words only drove him further over the edge.

Red-faced and furious, he turned to my mother as she led me out, screaming *"She's trying to do to him what she did to me!"*

I didn't understand what had happened, and as I hurried to get dressed I thought maybe *I'd* done something wrong. But by the time we got home nobody wanted to talk about it, so I considered the matter closed. Over the next few months the storm died down, tempers cooled, and relations between Sophia and my parents returned to something approaching normal.

But they never let me stay at her house alone again.

It was only much later that I began to assemble the pieces into another pattern. At sixteen, Sophia had married her blood uncle, with my father, Charles, and my aunt Theresa born out of that incestuous relationship.* Having developed an appreciation for such things, at some point she apparently seduced and molested her son Charles.

And then she came after me.

"She's trying to do to him what she did to me!"

It's amazing how much data, how much horror, how deep and revealing a secret can be contained in a single sentence. Eleven words that explain much, but forgive absolutely fucking nothing.

---

* Following this genetic cul-de-sac to its inevitable conclusion, I am my own second cousin.

CHAPTER 8

The Wind Took Away His Name

On September 25, 1964, my grandfather Kazimier Straczynski passed away at the age of seventy-seven in Vallejo, California. He'd been out drinking and fell off the sidewalk, cracking his skull on the curb hard enough to cause a stroke. The man who had come to America pursuing dreams of riches literally died in the gutter.

My grandmother was unmoved by his passing. He'd been dead to her for years, and if the facts had finally caught up with her feelings, well, that was just fine. My father grabbed the first plane to California in hopes of claiming anything of value in his estate, but returned with just some Russian currency, a few photographs, and the fifteen dollars Kazimier had in his possession when he went curb-diving.

Other than through his children, Kazimier Straczynski left nothing behind to show that he had been here; it was as if the wind had taken away his name. His death reinforced my determination to leave behind a mark that would say *I was here, I lived, and before dying I tried to do something of value with my life.*

The wind would not take away my name.

The following summer my father was fired from his latest job as a machinist at a plastic extrusion factory in Paterson. With all the local shops staffed to capacity, our only option was Newark, where several plastics factories had recently opened. We moved into a tenement in the Central Ward, a slum area also known as the Projects, anonymous buildings of concrete and despair.

The halls echoed day and night with the sound of raised voices, and the buildings were so close together that even with the windows open there was no moving air. Below lay a narrow no-man's-land of dry, dead weeds, broken glass, rusted shopping carts, and piles of garbage. Drunks and druggies used it as a latrine. The smell was beyond description. If you were lucky enough to have a fire escape, you climbed out onto the hard metal at night to try and escape the heat, the wail of police sirens punctuated by street fights, and the car-horn symphony that never seemed capable of finding a concluding note, even at four in the morning.

As awful as the place was, it took nearly all our remaining money to move in, leaving little for food. We were hungry all the time. Bread dipped in milk constituted breakfast, and in the evening catsup mixed with hot water was offered as tomato soup. The eggs and bacon in the fridge were reserved for my father, who needed to be fortified before going to work, and he was rarely there for dinner, preferring to eat at bars with cheap happy-hour food.

There was a palpable tension in the streets of Newark as African Americans fought for their civil rights against a runaway police force determined to put down anything that might turn into organized resistance. The previous summer, our neighborhood in Los Angeles had erupted into violence during the Watts riots, resulting in thirty-four deaths, thousands of arrests, and $40 million in property damage. The incident sparked fears that more violence could ripple out across the country, and the Newark police were determined to do whatever was necessary to stop that from happening.

An avowed racist, my father openly professed hatred for all minorities, from Asians to Hispanics, African Americans, and Jews in particular. Now that we were one of only a few white families in a neighborhood that was otherwise black and *really* pissed off, my father's racism spiraled straight up into the mesosphere with no stops in between. When we came home from school, we weren't permitted to go farther than the front stoop. My father was convinced that at any moment we were all going to be murdered in our sleep, and he bought a semiautomatic rifle that he kept in the bedroom closet beside a loaded clip ready to be slapped in at the first sign of enhanced melanin at midnight.

I had been told by teachers and comic books that the police were to be respected, that they were on the side of all that was right, that they were our *friends*. But now I began to understand that while that might be true in other places and times, it was *not* true in Newark, where every night brought new evidence that the police were out of control. I had been operating in a world of absolutes: good guys on this side, bad guys on the other, and the uniforms made it easy to tell who was who. But the shelf life of that status quo was expiring fast.

There was a vast gap between the world I was seeing in the streets and the one portrayed on television. The country was tearing itself apart over escalation in Vietnam, civil rights marches were being met with horrific police brutality, but the most popular shows on television were *Bonanza*, *The Andy Griffith Show*, *The Beverly Hillbillies*, *Bewitched*, and *Gomer Pyle*. Films like *My Fair Lady*, *That Darn Cat!*, and *The Sound of Music* were the darlings of a film industry that denounced the Beatles' *Help!* as vulgar trash. The media celebrated Julie Andrews singing "Chim Chim Cher-ee" while rivers of blood and fire roared through Selma, Watts, and Montgomery.

In less than a year, Newark would join that list, further traumatizing a nation that had no business being shocked when the fruits of its racism came home armed and angry.

Determined to understand the social changes whirling around me, but lacking teachers or family who could explain it, I turned to the smartest voices I could find: science fiction writers. I figured that somewhere in all those books predicting shifts in future societies somebody must've had something brilliant to say about this one. I wanted stories with meat and heft and social relevance, but the school library only stocked titles they deemed safe for young minds, the public library refused to let me check out books that were considered inappropriate for my age, and I didn't have the money to buy them.

So I turned to a life of crime.

Several stores in our neighborhood sold paperback books in spinner racks at the back; mostly romance and crime novels, along with an assortment of adult science fiction novels and anthologies. So I carefully scoped out each store to figure out what could be seen in the security mirrors from behind the cash register, looking for blind spots. If the mirrors covered the place too thoroughly, I'd wait until the owner was ringing up a purchase then climb onto a box, tilt the mirror to create a gap, and hope the adjustment wouldn't be noticed.

I could then step into the blind spot, slide a book into my jacket, and walk out. To throw off suspicion I'd sometimes buy a nickel candy bar on my way out, and I never hit the same place twice in a row. These stores became my personal libraries, offering books by such cutting-edge writers as J. G. Ballard, Brian Aldiss, Norman Spinrad, Roger Zelazny, and Philip K. Dick. It was the dawn of New Wave Science Fiction, which turned its attention from starships to social issues and pushed the envelope of what was considered acceptable by the literary establishment. They were exactly the stories I needed to read.

The only problem was my conscience. I could reconcile myself to *taking* the books since that was the only way to read them, but the idea of *keeping* them was more than I could bear. Certainly Superman wouldn't go around stealing paperbacks. Unless of course Red Kryptonite was involved, but then he'd put them back as soon as he recovered.

So that's what I decided to do.

I would read each book gently, careful not to break the spine, then press them flat under my schoolbooks until it was impossible to tell they'd been opened, return them to the store using the same blind spots, and exchange them for new books. My greatest fear was that I'd be caught, not while taking a book, but while returning it. Who in his right mind would believe I was putting it *back*?

Given the risk involved, every book I "borrowed" had to be worth the risk of getting turned over to the cops. The only thing worse than the prospect of being sent to Juvenile Hall for stealing *books* was being sent up the river for stealing *shitty* books. But I was unfamiliar with the history of the genre, and most of the writers' names were new to me, so I didn't know where to begin. After a while I noticed that the books I liked best were marked *Hugo Award Winner*. A little digging revealed that the Hugo was science fiction's highest honor, given annually at the World Science Fiction Convention. It said *Pay attention, this is important*.

To avoid being caught with the merchandise, I would stash the books under the living room couch that was my bed, and read them at night after everyone else was asleep. The stories were edgy and sophisticated, shifting the emphasis of science fiction away from wars in space to what William Faulkner described as "the human heart in conflict with itself." I was awestruck by the depth of what I was reading, and hoped that one day I might write something worthy of a Hugo.

Among the writers I discovered during this time was Harlan Ellison. Reading *Paingod and Other Delusions* and *Gentleman Junkie and Other Stories of the Hung-Up Generation* was like having molten steel poured directly into my brain. I would read them over and over, trying to figure out how he did what he did. The writing was hard-edged, the language precise and evocative. Where other books offered introductions written in an aloof, antiseptic fashion, Ellison's intros let you feel what it was to live with a twelve-story brain clicking along at ten thousand revolutions per second.

Eager to read more of his work, and having exhausted the liquor store inventories, I scrounged through used bookstores until I found his anthology *Ellison Wonderland*, which I bought for fifteen cents. Leaving aside the TAB books, which were written for kids, this was the first grown-up book I owned outright and it became one of my prized possessions.

Prior to encountering Ellison's work, I believed that writing was an Ivory Tower profession practiced by artists with rarified sensibilities from good schools and supportive families in Boston or New York. They wore elegant smoking jackets and wrote while reclining on Macassar fainting couches. *That* world didn't touch *my* world at any two contiguous points. Kids like me didn't become writers, we became mechanics or gas station attendants or ended up dead or in prison. But Ellison came from humble beginnings in Painesville, Ohio, ran with street gangs and had done time in the infamous New York Tombs.

If a guy from the streets like Ellison can make it as a writer, I thought, *maybe I can, too.*

It gave me hope, and there wasn't much of it going around Newark that year.

When my grandmother came to visit that Christmas, she was accompanied by Walter Androsik, a quiet, introspective man from the Old Country who kept his hand on Sophia's arm to make it clear that they were an item.* As the evening wore on and the drinking got heavier, Walter waved me over to where he was sitting, a gift-wrapped box in one hand, a glass of vodka in the other. Looking at me through booze-softened eyes, he said, "I buy this for you," his accent thick and blurred. "I buy this for you because he was great man, so you be great man too one day."

Inside the box was a chalk bust of John F. Kennedy that had been painted a flat gold.

Let me revise that sentence: it was a chalk bust of JFK that also functioned as a bank.

To revise further: it was a JFK bank that had been made prior to the assassination, and the way it worked was that you dropped coins through a slot *in the back of his head* right where Oswald popped him. Worse still, there wasn't a coin door at the bottom of the bank; once it was filled the only way to get the money out was by *smashing his head into a million pieces.*

Walter pulled out a nickel, dropped it in the slot at the back of JFK's head, and shook it. The nickel rattled back and forth inside his throat.

Later, when the sea of vodka reached high tide, I found Walter sitting with the bust in his lap, right hand folded into the shape of a gun. He put his finger to the coin slot in the back of JFK's head and pulled the trigger, making a *puffffft!* sound.

"*Puffffft*, gone," he said, then did it again. "*Puffffft* . . . gone."

We were living in a tenement in one of the most dangerous cities in America, I was engaged in a life of crime, and the man who was on a fast track to becoming my step-grandfather was repeatedly assassinating the bust of a dead president.

There was absolutely nothing about my life that made *any* kind of goddamned sense.

---

* My grandmother was not one to let the grass grow under her feet. Or any other part of her anatomy.

CHAPTER 9

Being Invisible

One aspect of Superman that I related to deeply was his position as an outsider, an alien who had to learn what it was to be a human boy. Sort of a Kryptonian Pinocchio. To survive our constant moves I employed a similar tactic. In addition to memorizing the geography of each new location I would study the local kids, their mannerisms, slang, attitudes, and the things they talked about. The more I could successfully mimic them, the more invisible I became; when they looked at me, they saw only their own reflection. Over time I accumulated a catalog of behaviors copied from other people that I could slide in and out of as needed. This was a great resource for a writer, but that pattern of concealment may explain why I've always felt less like an actual person than a Lego set in human form.

What I couldn't adapt to as easily were the class curriculums that often varied wildly between schools. By the time I finally caught up, we would move somewhere else and I'd have to start the process all over again. This was further complicated by my inability to see the blackboard. For as long as I could remember, blackboards had been a distant, blurry mystery, especially since I usually ended up stuck in the back of the room. I was dreadfully nearsighted but didn't know it because I had nothing to compare it against. I assumed everyone saw the same as I did, and that the smarter students were seated up front to give them a better view. At the end of each class I'd run up to the blackboard to try and copy down the Secrets of the Universe only to see them erased in preparation for the next class.

I'd been working doubly hard to catch up at school and was pretty sure I could make up the grades when one of my teachers sent home a letter saying that if my work didn't improve soon, there was a chance I might be held back a year. When my father saw the letter, he went into full rage mode.

And out came the belt.

I haven't mentioned the belt previously because I didn't want to talk about it. I'm mentioning it now, just once, because something different happened this time.

Most parents in the '60s considered corporal punishment a last resort, not the first. My father did it whenever the opportunity presented itself because he *liked* doing it. Any infraction, no matter how small—coming home late, not finishing dinner, complaining there wasn't enough food, even an impertinent look—was grounds to pull out the belt. The lashings were neither brief nor moderate. As early as age three he would whip me as hard as he could across my back, butt, and legs with a heavy leather belt, producing welts, bruises, and, on occasion, cuts. My sisters got the belt rarely and never as hard because he already had a female to beat in my mother. I provided variation to the menu.

Sometimes when I was just sitting on the floor watching television he'd loop the belt then yank it at both ends so it made a loud *snap!* He wanted me to know the belt was there and could be used at any moment. I would be reading, doing homework, and in the background:

Snap.

Snap!

Snap!

After reading the letter, he looped the belt and swung it at me, hard. The first lash caught me up along the rib cage. I instinctively turned away, and the next blow hit square against the small of my back. My eyes stung with tears but I refused to cry out because he *liked* it when I yelled, and I would rather die than give him that satisfaction. The belt struck again. My sisters hid in their bedroom as my mother stood in the kitchen, head down, eyes averted. Silent.

He wound up for another blow. Swung the belt—

—and I snagged it. Grabbed it and wouldn't let go.

His eyes went wide and wild with fury. How *dare* I try to stop him from beating me?

He pulled back. I wrapped my arm through the loop and held on tight.

He yanked harder, hurling me across the room.

I held on. This time, this *one time*, I wasn't going to let him do it to me.

He spun me around and cocked back a fist.

I cannot say definitively that he knocked me out. All I remember is a blur of motion, his fist coming at me, then looking up a moment later from the floor.

"Think you're too big for the belt, you little prick?" he yelled. "You don't want the belt anymore? Fine. You just remember that next time. *Remember* that."

And he stormed out to get drunk.

I learned later what he meant by *the next time*. Henceforth my reward for impertinence would be the fist, not the belt. But in that moment, I'd won. I'd beaten the belt.

When he returned that night, he went to the sofa where I was pretending to be asleep and dragged me into the kitchen. There was a mean smile on his face that I'd seen before, a self-satisfied, dangerous smirk that was equal parts booze and malice.

"I know what your problem is," he said, a slyness in his voice. "I know why your grades stink. Why you think you're a man all of a sudden. Bad influences. I'm going to fix that."

I didn't know what he was talking about until I glanced into the living room and saw that the Box had been opened. The Box was a small, cheap, pot-metal cabinet I'd found in a trash bin. The Box was where I kept my comics. To make sure it wasn't inadvertently thrown out I drew a circle on one side and wrote *JOE'S COMICS* in the middle with a black Sharpie. The books were in pristine condition, kept from sunlight, stacked alternately so the stapled ends wouldn't curl. They looked as if they had come out of the store that day. It never occurred to me that they might have value one day, I was just really anal about my comics. And I would never have left the door open.

My father reached under his chair, pulled out the comics, and set them on the table. He said comics were responsible for my falling grades and bad behavior. It wasn't *his* fault—it *couldn't* be him, or the nights of drunken excess or cold midnight pizzas or changing schools every six months or the fact that *I couldn't see the freaking blackboard*—it *had* to be the comics. True, they had a bad reputation in some circles, but that wasn't the point. He just knew I loved my comics and wanted to hurt me in the soft places where the belt and the fist couldn't reach.

Before I could move, he grabbed a handful of comics and ripped them in half. Then another. I cried out despite myself, because this wasn't about me; it was about watching him turn full runs of *The Amazing Spider-Man*, *The Fantastic Four*, *The Incredible Hulk*, *Iron Man*, *The Flash*, *Green Lantern*, and *Superman* into confetti. He kept going until the last comic lay on the floor in multicolored shards.[*]

---

[*] Had those comics been kept in the condition they were that evening—and believe

"This is for your own good," he said, without meaning a word of it, "because you'll never make a living with *that* crap."

"Now clean up this mess," he said, then walked into the bedroom and slammed the door shut behind him.

I'd refused to cry when he was beating me, but now I was hysterical with grief as I sifted through the mountain of shredded paper, eyes stinging at the sight of familiar faces and insignias. A fragment of Reed Richards's uniform. Part of the key to the Fortress of Solitude. Krypto. I piled them into two grocery bags, walked down the hall, dropped them into the slot marked *TRASH*, and went back to the sofa. As I lay there crying, I tried to push down the rage and the pain in my heart because it was a school night; there was a test waiting for me in the morning, and I needed to sleep.

I failed at both.

When Walter Androsik married my grandmother, the reception at her house was more than a little awkward. Walter had a large party of well-wishers, but all of Sophia's relatives were in Europe and most of her neighbors wouldn't show up for anything less celebratory than her funeral. The rest attended out of fear of retaliation or the lure of a free dinner.

Later that night, after the last of the guests had departed, Sophia and Walter went upstairs to change while my father and Aunt Theresa sat at the kitchen table speaking in a mix of Polish and Russian. I was settled in at the far end of the table, trying to look disinterested while actively trying to follow the conversation. One of the few ways I could learn anything interesting about my family was by listening

---

me, they would have been—at the height of the comics boom they would have been worth nearly three hundred thousand dollars. Just my pristine copy of *Amazing Fantasy* #15, Spider-Man's debut (current value: $27,000) would've covered tuition at the best university in the country.

in on discussions I wasn't supposed to hear or understand. By now I had acquired a smattering of both languages, and sometimes my aunt would lapse into English when there wasn't a foreign corollary, so while I couldn't always catch the subtleties I usually got the gist of what was being discussed.

Hunkered over his vodka, drunk and sullen, my father suggested that if Walter *really* knew what he was marrying, he would run out the door and never come back.

Theresa slammed her palm on the table. Who the hell was he to talk about her that way?

My father's mood got darker as he fired another salvo at my absent grandmother. I recognized one of his words from the way he talked about the women he saw on the streets in Newark: *kurwa.* Or in English, *whore.*

Theresa jabbed a finger at him, yelling angrily. She'd had enough to drink, and enough of *him*, that she didn't care what she said or what he thought of it. Besides, Ted was in the other room; if Charles lifted a finger against her, Ted would nail his head to the table.[*]

"You don't talk about her like that!" Theresa said. "She did everything for you, for *us!*"

"I ought to go up there, tell him who she is, what she did—"

My aunt leaned in, eyes drilling into his skull, her voice low and cold. "You're not the only one here who can talk about things that someone has done."

And her words came back to me from years earlier: *There are things I know about your father that I can only tell to a dog.*

He lit a cigarette and waved away her comment. "What're you talking about?"

She said just one word. It sounded like *Vishnevo.*

Before this night I'd seen my father exhibit every kind of emotion,

---

[*] And the craftsmanship would be *impeccable.*

but this was the first time I ever saw him afraid. The blood rushed from his face as he started to stammer out a protest. She cut him off with a look, then stood, spat on the floor, and stormed out, throwing back that word again: *Vishnevo!*

Visibly shaken, my father walked out to the backyard and stood there for a very long time, his Lucky Strike cigarette glowing red in the night.

I wondered what *Vishnevo* meant. I assumed it was a curse word but couldn't figure out why it had such a sobering effect on my father. I mentally filed the word away in case it ever came up again in context so I could add it to my growing collection of Russian and Polish profanity.

Without realizing it I had glimpsed the tip of an iceberg that contained my family's most horrific secret. At the time, I just figured that she had called him a dick.

Which I could totally support.

With each passing month the violence and despair in our Newark apartment grew worse. As my sister Theresa would write much later, "The earliest memory I have from Newark was walking out of the bedroom to find Mom with her head in the oven. Of course I was too young to know what she was doing. She yelled at me to go back to my room and then we heard Charles come home and he beat her up."

Then my father convinced a businessman he met at the plastics factory where he worked to fund an extrusion business that they would own together, purchasing the machinery and collecting the profits while my father ran the physical operation. If things went well, in time my father could buy him out. Charles's partner offered to set up the business in Matawan, a small town in central New Jersey, and pay for our relocation.

Not long after we moved out, large swaths of the city went up in flames during the Newark uprising, one of the largest riots in the nation's history. When the fighting finally bled to an end, the country went back to watching *Lassie*, *Gentle Ben*, Disney's *Wonderful World of Color*, and *Bonanza* as though nothing had happened. Certainly very little changed, and less still was learned. Each side seemed incapable of understanding the other.

And I thought, *Someday I want to write about people forced to experience how others live, and think, and act, so they'll understand that we're not really that different. We all want the same things: to be happy, to find love, to have our lives* mean *something. There has to be a story in there somewhere.*

There was, but it would take several decades before it was written—and titled *Sense8*.

CHAPTER 10

Targets of Opportunity

B y now I had formulated the Weird Shit hypothesis, which held that in every town there were usually only one or two really Weird Shit things going on, because it's hard to support more than that. To illustrate by the opposite: in the Collinsport of *Dark Shadows*, the Weird Shit Index would be off the scale because it would include vampires *and* werewolves *and* witches *and* ghosts *and* time travel *and* the Frankenstein monster *and and and and and.*

The average kid growing up in an average part of the average town might get Killer Nuns from Space, *or* Catching Pigeons for Dinner, *or* Skid Row Freaks, but he wouldn't get *all* of them. Moving so often to so many vastly different places, each with their own Weird Shit, meant that I was being exposed to a cumulative WSI many times the normal range. It didn't help that we could only afford to live in the sketchiest parts of town, where Weird Shit tended to settle, putting us dead center for whatever local nuttiness was looking for someone to eat. So I couldn't *wait* to see what lay in store for me next.

A small rural town with a population approximately 90 percent white, Matawan, New Jersey, was a considerable culture shock after

Newark. It was the embodiment of middle-class suburbia, with broad lawns fronting single-family houses and newly constructed garden apartments that catered to young families; a tight-knit community where girls joined the Brownies, boys joined the Boy Scouts, the town emptied out for Little League softball games, fireworks, and church, and everybody knew everyone else.

Our apartment on Sutton Drive was at the end of a tree-lined driveway that led past flower beds and a carefully manicured lawn to a white columned entry. It had air-conditioning and electric heat, and for the first time I had a bedroom of my own. Having spent years living in shanties, tenements, and houses without heating, we looked at it with the kind of awe usually reserved for Soviet refugees newly escaped to the West. It was nice. *Too* nice. I kept waiting for the local Weird Shit to leap out of the shadows at me.

"You should be happy," my mother said, noting my concern. "Why aren't you smiling?"

I didn't answer. She wouldn't understand.

I might have been just twelve, but even I knew a Venus flytrap when I saw one.

During the day, as my father and his partner set up their factory at the edge of town, I went on extended walks through the thick woods and gullies that bordered Matawan. Church Street and Aberdeen Road led to a small cluster of downtown businesses: a hamburger stand and a pizza parlor and, best of all, a store that sold records, comic books, and secondhand science fiction books for a dime apiece! Unfortunately, my father had finally figured out that his loose change had a way of disappearing off the nightstand, so to feed my book habit I began scavenging around town for used soda bottles I could return for the two-cent-apiece refund. I didn't care that people might see me digging through garbage cans or searching for castoffs beside the road. All that mattered was that for every five bottles I could buy access to the stories of Heinlein, Ellison, Bradbury, or Asimov; a dime for every new world, every *universe*.

I also began rebuilding my comic collection, covertly at first, then more openly when I realized my father no longer cared about it. But the most amazing day of all was when a manila envelope arrived with the membership material I'd purchased for the Supermen of America Fan Club. After years spent watching and reading about Superman, I now had a certificate with my name beneath his picture, and an official badge. Since Clark Kent wore his Superman uniform under his regular clothes, I pinned the badge to the inside of my jacket, where no one could see it, steal it, or give me a hard time about my nascent secret identity. No, I hadn't yet achieved my goal of becoming Superman, but now I was one of the Super*men* of America, which put me just *thismuch* closer to my goal.

Out of a sense of fairness I also joined the Merry Marvel Marching Society and received a similar packet filled with character posters. Our frequent moves had denied me the chance to make lasting friends, but as I covered the walls with posters of Superman, Thor, Iron Man, Captain America, Spider-Man, and the Hulk, everywhere I turned, the face of a friend looked back at me.

Nineteen sixty-six was also an amazing year for genre television: *Lost in Space* then *Star Trek* took me to distant worlds, Batman slugged it out with bad guys to the on-screen accompaniment of *BLATT!* and *POW!*, and courtesy of *The Avengers* and Emma Peel I finally began to get a rough idea of what testosterone was all about. The inspiration was dizzying, and since my goal was to become a writer, and writers often worked for television, I wondered if one day it might be possible to have my own TV show, maybe even a *science fiction* show. True, I hadn't written anything yet, but that was a deliberate choice. There was a lot of work ahead of me before I'd be good enough to commit anything to paper, so I kept the stories in my head, mentally editing them while in bed or at my school desk, sanding them down until they were smooth. I looked forward to the day when those stories would finally say *Okay, now we're ready for you to write us down.*

Keep the lid on, I thought. *Let the water come to a boil.*

In the hope that we might actually stay put for a while, I risked getting to know some of the neighborhood kids, including a Jewish girl my own age who lived in the same apartment complex. I knew nothing about Judaism, so she offered to teach me some of the rituals and songs, a little Yiddish, and even some Hebrew. Her religion seemed friendlier and gentler than the one I'd been born into, so I asked if it was possible to switch sides. She checked with her mom, who said Judaism didn't go out of its way to convert people, unlike a certain *other* religion, and that I should wait until I was older to think about such things. Meanwhile, she said that under *no* circumstances should I mention this to my father.

At first we met only at her parents' apartment under their eagle-eyed supervision, but eventually I won their trust enough to invite her to our apartment while my father was working and my mother was out with my sisters. Being a nerd I had nothing salacious in mind, I just wanted to show her my room and my comics. But she never got that far once she saw my father's framed collection of Nazi paraphernalia proudly displayed in the living room.

Did I not mention the Nazi paraphernalia before now? Oh.

It's important to remember that my father wasn't a historian, a World War II buff, or a soldier who brought back German artifacts as trophies. These were his *personal* mementos from his time with German soldiers who taught him the value of Nazism and took him along to beat Jews. The display included his swastika armband, Nazi cigarette coupons, photos of the soldiers who were his friends, and a German military hat proudly set on the bar. It wasn't just Nazi stuff, it was *his* Nazi stuff, cherished and revisited as one might page through a high school yearbook, with nostalgia and something very close to reverence.

And in his bedroom closet, safe in a plastic dry-cleaning bag, was the German uniform jacket made for him by his pals in the unit, which he had secretly held on to in defiance of orders from Sophia to destroy any incriminating evidence from that time. Quoting my uncle Ted's brother Frank years later, "I was told by Theresa that Charles buried it after he saw that partisans annihilated totally a family suspected of collaborating with the Germans."

My father would take it out of the plastic, slip the swastika onto the arm, hang it on the closet door, and just *look* at it for a long time before resignedly putting it back in the closet again.

Had I been smarter, I would have figured out that there was more going on under the surface when it came to my father and Nazis, but it was just His Stuff from the War that I walked past on my way to another room. But when my friend saw the display, she paled visibly and ran out of the apartment. After she told her parents about my father's altar to all things Nazi, they didn't let her hang out with me anymore.

"They told me to tell you it's not because of you," she said, "they say you're okay. It's your dad. They think there's something not right about him."

They *knew*. From just her ten-second glimpse into my father's dark heart, they knew there was *something* wrong with him. But it would be many years before I figured out just *how* wrong.

The veneer of paradise began to crack when my father's business partner realized that not only was Charles clueless about how to set up a company, he had a tendency to show up drunk or hungover, hiding bottles of vodka around the shop so he could imbibe during work hours. As his days grew more tense, he spent his nights prowling the bars of neighboring towns, ranging farther afield in search of whatever the hell he was searching for. His increasingly tenuous position at work made him even more determined to convince the rest of the family that we were happy and that everything was fine, just *fine* goddamnit.

The most disturbing aspect of this pathology was the Dance.

Using an eight-millimeter film camera he had obtained,* my father began documenting family dinners and gatherings. We had already been trained to look happy whenever photos were taken, but movies added another dimension. Like everything else in my father's life, the film camera was a propaganda device whose purpose was to reinforce his image as a good father, and he decided that the best way to convey this was to show his kids dancing. Didn't matter where we were. Didn't matter if dancing was appropriate. Didn't matter if the people looking on shook their heads at the weirdness, or that *there wasn't even any music*. The order came: dance.

By now I was starting to exhibit a stubborn streak so I refused to take part. But my sisters, younger and more vulnerable, had no choice, nor did they understand the fiction they were being asked to create. So they danced. Silently. Pretending for the camera, inside the house, on the front yard, outside Sophia's house or a local park. The same moves. The same silent dance.

For years afterward, Charles would play those films at family gatherings as his personal, paternal validation, his eight-millimeter Potemkin village. His alibi.

Look how happy everyone is . . . look . . . you're dancing . . .

And those movies *did* record the truth . . . just not the one he

---

* More accurately: after my father confiscated the film camera I'd earned by selling a buttload of greeting cards door-to-door in the belief that I might one day make movies . . .

wanted. A snapshot requires only a second of pretense, but film catches wary glances, fractured smiles, and haunted eyes that might elude single images. I began to understand that movies could be a gateway to Revealed Truth.

If God were to write the Bible today, He would write it on film.

When my grades fell again due to my father's drunken mayhem, I was given a choice: attend summer school and continue on to high school in the fall, or be held back a year. If I were held back, my comic collection would be back on the chopping block, so I opted for summer school.

When I told my father the news, he hauled back and punched me in the mouth hard enough to send me to the floor. He said I was lazy and stupid and I'd goddamned better finish summer school without giving him any more problems or there'd be more of *that* in store. Tasting blood, I felt grit in my mouth and spit out a bit of white enamel. I ran to the mirror and saw that my front right tooth was chipped and felt loose. Panicked, I asked if it could be fixed— even at this late date none of us had been taken to a dentist—but he said that if my tooth was broken, it was my fault; it wouldn't have happened if I hadn't provoked him and he was goddamned if he'd spend his good money to get it fixed.

The damaged front tooth gradually turned a mottled gray and was always slightly loose, a defect that left me extremely self-conscious. I was ashamed of how I looked, and from then on avoided smiling or laughing openmouthed.

A few weeks later I returned from summer school to find Charles nursing a bump on his head, his mood black and angry. He said that a worker at the factory had hit him with a claw hammer for no reason. Knowing my father, the employee had probably struck back in self-defense against his drunken aggression. Either way it was the breaking point for his investor, who dissolved the partnership; my father could run the factory by himself, provided he paid back the initial investment. That meant moving the factory to a cheaper location and firing the employees, who he could no longer afford.

He made up the difference by forcing me to work without pay each day after school and on weekends at the new location in an industrial warehouse, producing tubes that would be inserted into golf bags to protect the clubs. The manufacturing process began with plastic pellets that were melted in a big bin and extruded into a long tube before being pulled through water troughs and hardened so another machine could cut it to the proper length. My job was to grab the tubes as they came off the cutter and slide one end up a drill bit that was spinning fast enough for the friction to melt the end outward, forming a lip. It was important to hold the tube really hard because if it slipped or there wasn't enough oil on the bit, it would smack you across the head hard enough to send you to the floor.

Suffice to say this happened a lot.

The warehouse had been designed to keep crates of merchandise safe from weather, so there were few windows. To avoid having to heat the place in winter my father sealed all of them except for the one in his office, saying that the equipment would provide plenty of warmth. That was technically true, but sealing the windows also kept the plastic fumes from venting, so by the time I was done each night I was dizzy and barely able to stand.

To further cut back on expenses we gave up the Sutton Drive apartment with its central heating and lush lawns and moved into a drafty, broken-down old house on the other side of town. My father continued his boycott against high-priced heating oil, so we slept in double layers of clothes in freezing cold rooms. When morning came, we'd rush downstairs to dress in front of the open stove for warmth. The house didn't have a refrigerator, and my father didn't want to buy one, so he stored our food on the back porch, which was left open to the wind and snow outside.

"That's how we kept meat cold in Russia," he said.

But New Jersey was not Russia; the temperatures often rose above what was safe to store meat and milk so we were constantly coming down with food poisoning. Rather than admit his mistake my father blamed my mother's cooking, which had the added benefit of giving him another excuse to beat her then go out to eat with his drinking buddies, leaving us to pick through whatever looked least spoiled on the porch.

For a brief moment, we had lived just like other people.

Now it was gone.

Stephen King once wrote, "There's little good in sedentary small towns. Mostly indifference spiced with an occasional vapid evil—or worse, a conscious one."

For me, the nexus for that evil was Matawan Regional High School. With a population of eighteen hundred students, MRHS was an insular, narrow-minded world hostile to newcomers or anyone who seemed strange, and I was both.

High school is all about cliques, about who you know and who you don't, who you sit with and who you most emphatically *don't* sit with, who's at the top of the food chain and who's at the bottom. Once you're locked into that hierarchy there's nothing you can do to change it. The kids at Matawan Regional had grown up together, with parents who had good jobs and could afford decent clothes for their offspring. I wasn't just the new kid, I was the *poor* kid: skinny, physically awkward, and painfully shy; the snaggle-toothed loner who owned one pair of beat-up old shoes and wore secondhand shirts and cheap gray work pants that I had long ago outgrown.

I was the perfect target.

It started when two seniors said I dressed like a retard and jumped me on the way home. I managed to get away without being pounded too badly, but when I saw some of the other kids cheering on the ambush I knew this was just going to get worse.

Here's how it would happen.

A collection of jocks and bullies, thick-necked and towheaded, cheeks flushed with free-floating testosterone in need of expression, would wait outside the school and follow me to the Little Street Bridge that led across Lake Matawan. It was a choke point, the only way to get home without going miles out of my way on foot. First came the names. "Hey, Cosmo!" they'd yell. (Cosmo, short for Cosmonaut, since I had a Russian last name.) "Hey, Shitski!" Then they'd start throwing rocks, small ones at first, then bigger, followed by whatever they could find on the road: lug nuts, chunks of brick, anything that could be thrown a good distance and land hard. Sometimes a rock would hit my head hard enough to send me to my knees.

I'd get up and keep walking.

The bigger kids would run up behind me, shoving and punching me in the back, then stick their feet between my legs to trip me. When I went down, that was the signal for the rest to swarm in, kicking and punching me while I was on the ground. Sometimes they'd dangle me off the side of the bridge, trying to throw me into the dark waters below. I didn't know how to swim so I hung on to the railing as hard as I could while they pummeled me. They'd leave only after they decided they'd done enough damage, laughing and tossing around whatever was left of my stuff as I picked myself up.

They did this every day.

For *months*.

Telling the teachers was pointless because the incidents happened off school property and thus weren't their problem. Besides, if it got back to the bullies that I'd talked, they'd beat me twice as bad. So I learned to be patient, to absorb the pain, get back up, and keep going. I have no memory of my classes or teachers during that time. I made a couple of casual friends—guys who, like me, were at the bottom of the totem pole—but remember almost nothing of what we did or where we went.

I couldn't figure it out. Why me? Was I doing something to attract this? Was there a KICK ME sign on my back that everyone else could see but was invisible to me? Seriously, what the hell?

Since writing is all about seeing things from someone else's point of view, I looked at it from the perspective of the bullies, and the answer became very clear. High school is as primal and vicious as the African veldt. Most of the animals are in the center of the bell curve, big enough or fast enough to avoid getting eaten. At one narrow end of the curve are the predators that prowl the tall grass, looking for easy prey; at the other are the wounded, the sick, the slow, and most attractive of all, the solitary, those who walk alone, outside the herd's protection.

The bullies needed targets they could attack in order to demonstrate their strength, but they could only go so far in beating up local kids whose parents knew *their* parents. But no one knew my family, and my father was happy to keep it that way, so there would be no consequences for coming after me. I also lacked a posse of friends who could ride in on my behalf, which was why it was important not just to hurt me but to humiliate me in front of the other kids. They wanted to scare off anyone who might want to help me by making it clear that if they befriended the goat, they would *become* the goat and get the same treatment. So when the bullies jumped me, the other kids just walked past, eyes averted, looking anywhere but at me. I felt shame, violation, and a sense of being utterly alone.

At five foot three I was smaller than most of them, skinny and malnourished, but I fought back anyway. While I was still on my feet I had a chance, but once they swarmed and I went down all I could do was ball up with my back to the curb to protect my kidneys and endure the blows until they got tired of it. Most of the bullies were just mean and spiteful and wanted to show off. But for some of the others, the pathology went far deeper. They beat me up because they *liked* it. They had the same look in their eyes my father did when he beat Evelyn, as dark and dead as a shark.

Though I finally understood why I was a target the knowledge did me no good. There was no way for me to win against kids who were older and bigger than me.

Then I realized that while I couldn't win, I *could* refuse to *lose*. All I had to do was change the rules of the game.

So the next time they beat me to a pulp I waited until they started walking away, laughing and high-fiving each other—

—and mouthed off at them.

They stopped and looked back at me, scarcely believing that I was telling them to fuck off. Not just them: their sisters, their mothers, their whole families. By now I had developed a solid vocabulary of profanity and I used every bit of it.

Furious, they ran back, pummeled me back into the ground, and started away, exhausted from the effort.

I mouthed off at them again.

They beat me again.

I mouthed off again.

I kept doing it, no matter how badly they bloodied me, until they realized that the only way to shut me up, the only way to *win* was to kill me, and none of them were prepared to go that far. I didn't care if I ended up as little more than a smear on the sidewalk; what mattered was denying them a victory, and thus their power.

From that day on, whenever they came after me, I would ball

up to ward off the blows, the Supermen of America badge inside my jacket pressed up against my chest, eyes closed, waiting for my chance to mouth off. I pretended that I didn't feel the blows, that I was invulnerable, that I was Superman.

And I learned just how much I could endure.[*]

Secrets were my family's currency, so I was always looking for new ways to learn some of them. This led to the habit of eavesdropping on phone calls via the extension in my parents' upstairs bedroom when my mother was on the phone with my aunt or grandmother, since those were the most likely to produce useful information. One afternoon, during an otherwise uneventful conversation, I heard my aunt pause, as if trying to decide how to ask something, then decided the hell with it and just asked.

"Does Joey know about his sister?" she said.

My mother's voice rose sharply. "Oh, no, Theresa, he doesn't know. He can *never* know about that. It's just . . . no, he can't ever know."

Then she said she had to go and hung up.

I did the same, then tiptoed back to my room and sat heavily on the bed.

Does Joey know about his sister?

He doesn't know . . . he can never *know about that.*

It was clear from my aunt's voice that she wasn't talking about Theresa or Lorraine, because she would have identified them by name. *Does Joey know about his sister?* What the hell did *that* mean? Was it something to do with the death of my sister Vicky, or something else entirely?

I'd started listening in on conversations in the hope of unraveling

---

* And *that*, ladies and gentlemen, is how I trained for a career as a television writer.

some of my family's secrets, and in return I'd been hit in the face by one I hadn't even *known* about. So I stopped the practice that day. Best to quit while I was ahead.

By now I was old enough to look past the violence and tears, the threats and recriminations, to see a larger and infinitely more disturbing pattern to my parents' behavior, and began to understand how we were being manipulated by *both* of them.

When Charles would go out for the night after beating our mother, she'd show us the bruises and abrasions to solicit our affection and sympathy. She almost seemed to *enjoy* the effect they had on us, a satisfied light in her eyes as my sisters cried at the sight of the injuries. I didn't know the phrase *Munchausen Syndrome*, nor is there a direct one-to-one correlation, but the shape is the same: the beatings allowed her to get sympathy from us that she would not have received otherwise given her extraordinary lack of parenting skills. She not only *liked* getting that reaction, I think a part of her *needed* it in deeply troubling ways.

My father played the opposite side of the coin, telling us that he didn't *want* to hit her; it was *her* fault, she kept making mistakes, she was stupid. *He* was the one being driven crazy by her behavior when he had to work for a living, so *he* was the one who deserved compassion and understanding.

The key to my father's pathology was the notion that if he could elicit sympathy from those he had harmed, *even under fraudulent circumstances*, it was equivalent to being forgiven for his actions. Sympathy equated expiation, as though the act had never occurred, and thus required neither guilt nor self-examination.

I could trust neither of them.

CHAPTER 11

Patricide by Proxy

That summer we were booted out of our house for nonpayment of rent and took up residence in an apartment complex on the other side of Matawan. (When moving around inside the same town, my father avoided complications by telling the landlord that he was new to the area, using Sophia's address as his last place of residence.) As we unpacked, my father called me into his room. I found him holding the German jacket that he kept carefully preserved in his closet. "Put this on," he said.

I said I'd rather not.

"It's not going to bite you," he said, "just put the damned thing on!"

I reluctantly pulled on the jacket. At fourteen I was the right size to wear it properly, the same age he'd been when *he* wore it. He studied me for a minute, then pulled out the cap that went with it and set it on my head. The worn leather band scratched against my forehead.

I instinctively pulled away when he started sliding the swastika up my arm. He smacked me on the back of the head. "Stand still, goddamnit."

He got it into the right position, so the symbol faced out. "Now raise your arm, like this," he said and thrust out his hand in a Nazi salute.

"Why?" I asked.

"I want to see how it looks," he said. "I want to see how *I* looked."

I refused. He cuffed the back of my head again. "Raise your arm!"

"No."

Another cuff. "Raise it! Like *this*!" He did it again.

I was determined to refuse no matter what happened. By now I knew enough to realize that this was deeply wrong.

He hit me again. "What are you, some kind of faggot?" he said, believing I'd want to prove I *wasn't* one by doing what he wanted me to do. But I had nothing to prove to him.

"Raise your arm," he said again, cocking back a fist.

"No." I'd been beaten up so much over the years that being smacked around was no longer a threat. "You can hit me all you want, I'm *not* raising my arm."

He turned away in disgust. "Take it off," he said, "before you get yellow all over it. You don't deserve to wear it. And don't tear the lining."

I pulled off the jacket and tossed it onto the bed.

As I started away he said, "And you know what? I'm not even sure I'm your father. What do you think about that, faggot?"

I left without answering, but silently thought, *You shouldn't get my hopes up like that.*

As I continued down the hall, it occurred to me that if I was on the path to becoming Superman, then my father was very definitely Lex Luthor.

None of us had been taken to a dentist yet, so our teeth were in pretty bad shape, leading to frequent toothaches. My mother in particular had ongoing dental problems, but my father balked at spending the money for her care. Finally, tired of her complaints, he said he'd found a dentist who could help. We learned later that the dentist in question had lost his practice and was operating illegally out of his home. My father apparently met him at one of the bars he frequented and made an off-the-books "arrangement."

She went to the appointment hoping that he would finally be able to help her.

She believed that even as he put her under.

She woke to discover that all her teeth had been extracted, even the healthy ones.

"What's wrong?" my father asked. "I said he'd make sure you don't have a problem with your teeth anymore, and now you don't."

For days afterward, she cried every time she saw her reflection in a mirror.

My father made fun of how she looked and the way she lisped around her swollen, empty gums. "Say *she sells seashells by the seashore*," he'd tell her, and laugh.

A week later a pair of ill-fitting plastic dentures arrived in the mail. They had not been properly fitted and whenever she wore them or tried to chew, tears of pain rolled down her face. My father just laughed.

And I stopped mentioning toothaches.

My biggest medical problem was that I still didn't realize that I was nearsighted. This changed the day I found myself sitting on a school bus behind a kid with glasses. When he turned to look out the window I caught a glimpse of the street through his glasses, and for the barest flicker of a second everything was crystal clear!

I tapped him on the shoulder. "Can I see your glasses?"

He looked warily back at me, afraid I would throw them out the window or play keep-away. I asked again, even more earnestly, and he handed them over.

When I slipped them on, I saw the world with a sharpness I had never imagined. Leaves, tree branches, street signs, faces! All this time I'd been wrong about the world. It wasn't that the teachers were keeping me from the blackboard so the more popular or smarter students could read what was there, the problem was that *I needed glasses*!

I could be fixed!

I got off the bus and ran home, eager to tell my father what I'd discovered.

"Bullshit," he said. "You're just trying to get attention. No kid of mine is going to walk around a four-eyes."

I tried to revisit the subject over the next few weeks, but he refused to listen and finally told me to stop talking about it. Reluctant to incur his wrath, I let it go until the next time I was dispatched to my aunt's place.

"Did your father take you to an eye doctor?" she asked when I told her about the incident on the bus.

I shook my head, no.

"Has he *ever* taken you to an eye doctor?"

Again: no.

"So how does he *know* you don't need glasses?"

When I told her what he said, her jaw tightened. She didn't say it, but I could see her thinking: *What an asshole.*

"Come with me," she said, and took me to her optometrist.

"Joseph is tremendously nearsighted," he said at the end of the examination, "but with the right prescription, his vision can be corrected to almost 20/20."

My father was furious when she told him about the diagnosis. "He doesn't need goddamned glasses! He's *pretending*, trying to get attention. He wants glasses because *you* wear glasses, that's all!"

"Then *you* take him to the doctor!" she yelled back. "See for yourself! I'll pay for it."

With his pride on the line we went to a local optometrist in Matawan. My father conferred privately with the doctor in his office
before the exam, and again right afterward. When the doctor came
out to talk to me, his expression was grim. He said that my eyes
were in a state of extreme decline and that I would be blind within
a year, maybe less. He gave me a prescription for glasses that would
let me see for the time being but warned that I should prepare myself for what was to come.

I felt as though a knife had been driven through my heart. I
couldn't sleep, couldn't focus on schoolwork or reading or much
of anything. I would lie in bed crying, then force myself to stop,
irrationally afraid that the extra saline might cause further damage. Determined to step outside my fear and start dealing with the
problem while there was still time, I began counting the steps from
the street, and walking through every room with my eyes closed.
I learned where things were and what they felt like, and I started
teaching myself Braille from a library book. After a while I began
to feel confident that I could get by living where we were. But what
would happen when we moved? How would I deal with being blind
in a new place?

I went through this for *two months*, until the day my father saw
me pacing the hall, measuring the length of my stride to see how
much ground I covered with each step, and asked what the hell I
was doing.

"Preparing," I explained to him.

"Preparing for what?"

I explained.

"Jesus Christ," he said, disgusted with my stupidity. "You're not
going blind."

"But the doctor said—"

"I didn't believe your stupid aunt. All she does is stir up trouble.
So when the doctor asked if I'd ever taken you to get your eyes

checked before, I said yeah, every year, and your eyes were always fine. Wasn't any of his fucking business. He figured if your eyes went from normal to this bad in just a year that you were going blind."

My jaw hung there for a moment as I inwardly screamed my rage about having lived with this terror for so long.

"Why didn't you *tell* me?"

He headed past me to the refrigerator for a beer. Shrugged. "You wanted glasses, you got fucking glasses. So what's the problem, four-eyes?"

Once I knew I wouldn't be spending the rest of my life in darkness, I decided that now was the time to buckle down and start learning as much as I could about being a writer. I read everything I could find by the best in science fiction, fantasy, and other genres. I'd pick a story at random by Samuel Delany, Mark Twain, or Poe, and copy every line by hand so I could feel the decisions hiding behind every word and turn of phrase. I even tried mixing and matching styles from different writers to see if that might lead me to a creative style of my own.

What would it sound like if Poe had written Jack London's White Fang *in the style of "The Bells"?*

"The howling and the growling of the wolves, wolves, wolves, wolves, wolves, wolves, wolves, the biting and the tearing of the wolves."

I also fell in love with Rod Serling's *The Twilight Zone*, enthralled by the clockwork precision of his words, the trademark of a consummate writer. By the '60s, anthology television was a lost art form with no sign of coming back any time soon, and I lamented that I would never have the chance to write for a show like *The Twilight Zone*.

When the other kids in our apartment complex learned that I wanted to become a writer, they would ask me to create scary stories on the spot based on their suggestions. I never wrote down any of them—I still wasn't ready for that—but the efforts were good enough to merit repeat performances. One of the kids even offered to pay for my services with cigarettes. His dad was a chain-smoker and there were always plenty around the house. At sixteen he already had a half-pack-a-day habit.

"You want to be tough, you gotta smoke," he said.

I tried it a few times but didn't like it any more than I liked drinking. Besides, I told him, my dad smoked, and that was reason enough for me not to do it.

Later that night, as I lay in bed, that sentence kept coming back to me, and by morning it led to the most important decision of my life.

I desperately wanted to kill my father. Sometimes just the *idea* of killing him was enough to keep me going. I would imagine him at the receiving end of an Edgar Allan Poe horror story, that it was *his* heart buried beneath the floorboards in "The Tell-Tale Heart," *his* body tied to a table as the blade descends in "The Pit and the Pendulum" or walled up for all time in a dank basement in "The Cask of Amontillado." *"For the love of god, Montresor!"*

But Poe's protagonists rarely got away with their murders, so I decided to go another way: rather than killing him, I would *negate* him. Whatever he was, I would be the opposite. He drank, so I wouldn't touch the stuff. He smoked; I wouldn't. He was brutal to women; I would strive to be chivalrous. He never kept his promises; I would always keep mine. He blamed others for what he did; I would take responsibility for my actions. With each choice I would try to balance out the meanness and suffering he brought into the world.

The realization that I didn't have to become my father was

electrifying. Kazimier, Sophia, and Charles all believed that they were the inevitable product of their circumstances, that they had no choice other than to become what they were. But negating my father would allow me to decide what *I* wanted to do with my life. Suddenly I had a superpower so great that my father could never destroy it because it was outside his reach.

I had the power to choose, and the will to back it up.

And one can go far on that.

The most important aspect to negate was my family's sense of victimization. Given my circumstances it would have been easy to feel like a victim, but that was the first step on the road to becoming what they had become. They believed that since they had been mistreated, they were entitled to do the same to others without being questioned or criticized. *It's not my fault that I'm like this, I am what I was made, I'm the victim here, so* you *have to put up with me.*

To be a victim is to be forever frozen in amber by *that* person's actions at *that* moment. Victimization only looks backward, never forward, which is why my family was incapable of moving on or redefining themselves. If I allowed myself to be defined by what my father did to me, it would put him at the center of my identity. He would have control over me for the rest of my life, even once he was gone. Yes, I was stuck in a box with a monster, but wallowing in indulgent self-pity wasn't the solution; the task before me was to *survive* the monster without *becoming* the monster.

In a way, I was lucky that my father was as awful as he was. He had no good qualities to negate. Had he been a better human being, I would have become a worse one.

When I was fifteen, we again moved across town to a worn-down, ill-kept house on Main Street whose most charming feature was a broken septic tank that leaked into the backyard. You could locate the house by the smell if you couldn't find the address. It was here that my long-delayed growth spurt started. As if trying to make up for lost time, I would grow from five foot three to six foot three in less than a year. Whenever I reached for something, it wasn't where my body-memory said it was supposed to be, so I was constantly breaking things and tripping. My clumsiness gave my father something new to mock, and the thugs at school one more reason to come after me.

But growing tall enough to loom over the bullies began to have a psychological effect on them. For the first time I saw hesitation in their eyes. It was as if Nature said, *We better give this guy some protective coloration or he's going to get killed. Let's make him taller. No, six inches isn't nearly enough. Ten? Still not enough. Let's give him an extra foot. No, not that kind, he already has two left feet, let's not complicate things.*

My anchor through these moves was Midnight, a black cat I'd found under a bush shortly after moving to Matawan, very sick and waiting to die. I nursed her back to health and we became inseparable. She'd lie on my bed as I did my homework, or sit with me at night, just watching. Had I been smarter, had I been able to see a bit further down the road, I would have tried to find another home for her, but I was too caught up with the joy of having her around.

That's no excuse. I should've seen what was coming. Maybe I could've saved her.

In June 1970 my father's factory went under after months of poor management and overdue bills. The equipment was repossessed, creditors were calling nonstop, and this time they were asking for Stark *and* Straczynski. Having worn out his welcome in New Jersey, he told us to be ready to leave the next night under cover of darkness, our destination: Los Angeles, the only place he knew well enough to make a fresh start.

As usual, my sisters and I were allocated only two boxes each. But with my comics, records, toys, and clothes, I had four. I asked my father if the extra load was okay, and he said yes. I then reminded him of his promise that if Midnight was around on moving day, she could come along.

"Not a problem," he said.

He was being reasonable. I should've suspected something.

To make sure Midnight didn't stray, I kept her in my room all night as I packed, only taking her out the next morning to use the backyard. As I watched her play, my father called over from the garage to say he couldn't fit all four of my boxes into the U-Haul and told me to narrow it down to three. I raced upstairs and divvied up the comics, putting some in with my clothes and others in a box with my books, then dumped my few toys, most of which no longer had any appeal to a fifteen-year-old.

As I finished repacking, I became aware of Midnight behind me in the door to my room. She always liked to sit and watch me, but this felt different. She was looking at me with a strange intensity, as though trying to burn the image into her head. When I called her name, she turned and headed downstairs, moving slowly and with difficulty. I followed her outside, and within moments she began spasming, pushing her face into the cool grass for comfort. I ran to her, petting her and calling her name. She was shaking, muscles tense, eyes focused at a point somewhere past me. Strangely, she was purring, as if self-medicating against the pain. I was sobbing into her fur as she fixed on my face.

Then the light went out of her eyes, and she was gone.

I turned to see my father standing on the back porch, where he had watched the whole thing. His eyes were dull, his voice flat. "I was moving boxes out of the garage and found some rat poison," he said. "I put it off to the side so I could throw it out. She must've found it." Then he went back inside.

I sat on the grass, crying and rocking Midnight back and forth in my lap. As the daylight faded I backhanded the tears, got a screwdriver, and tore at the hard ground to make a grave. When it was deep enough, I wrapped her in one of my T-shirts so she could have my smell with her, covered her with soil, and returned to the house.

As I went upstairs to get my three boxes, the tears were replaced by cold rage.

This was not the first time a cat I'd adopted had disappeared or unexpectedly died on moving day. That was not, *could* not be a coincidence. Midnight was a finicky eater, she *never* would have eaten rat poison out of a box. She would only have eaten it if someone put it inside a piece of meat or fish while I was upstairs.

Correction: while my father *sent* me upstairs. It was the only time I'd left her unguarded.

And in that moment, he'd poisoned her.

I cursed myself for my stupidity. I should've given her to someone else, should've known better than to try to hold on to her. But I'd been selfish, and she paid the price.[*]

A few hours later we hit the road, heading west. After an hour of driving, my father told me that he had to leave one of my boxes behind, since there wasn't room for it in the truck with all of *his* stuff.

I asked him which box he'd ditched beside the road.

"The heavy one," he said.

It was the one with most of my comics and other books.

Thinking of Midnight and my lost comics, I turned my face to the passing night, determined not to let him see me cry.

---

[*] Years later, I would write a tribute by proxy to Midnight in the pages of *Superman: Earth One*.

CHAPTER 12

Discovering Words, Worlds, and Estrogen

When we hit Los Angeles, we lived in the car for several days until Charles found a cheap apartment in Inglewood. It wasn't until we moved in that we learned the reason for the low rent: the apartment was at the ass end of one of the main runways to Los Angeles International Airport. Planes roared overhead all day and most of the night, drowning out conversation.

But it beat sleeping in the car, and we never had much to talk about anyway.

The only thing I knew for sure about the writing profession was that there was a lot of typing involved, so when I started at Lennox High School as a junior, I signed up for introductory and intermediate typing classes concurrently and discovered in the latter case that I was the only boy in the joint. Even in the '70s girls were still expected to take typing classes to prepare for career paths as secretaries to powerful men, while boys took physical education courses that would somehow qualify them to give dictation. Girls were a mystery to me, as alien and unknowable as the surface of Mars.

I'd never been on a date and was painfully shy. The idea of walking up to a girl and starting a conversation was more frightening than anything Lovecraft had ever written. So I was understandably terrified when some of these life-forms crowded around me on the first day of class and actually started *talking* to me, asking where I was from and what was I doing on their planet? Was I hoping to become a male secretary?

Encircled and outgunned by miniskirts, perfume, and pheromones, I inadvertently defaulted to the truth and stammered out that I was training to become a writer. Rather than ending the conversation, my explanation only piqued their interest further and now there were more of them and *they kept talking to me*!

"What have you written so far?" they asked, leaning in, over, and around me.

Cheeks flushed, I looked down at the typewriter keys and muttered something noncommittal. Would the spiral of madness never end?

They asked if I could show them something I'd written.

"No!" I said, louder than intended in a voice that had not yet changed from falsetto into something more manly. When I tried to explain that I hadn't yet committed anything to paper because I wasn't ready, the circle of girls lost interest. Deciding that I was either faking it or just weird, they returned to their planet and left me to my keystroking.

I'd been saying for years that I wanted to become a writer, but my father always ridiculed the idea, saying that I was speaking above my station and trying to be a big shot. He hadn't changed his opinion, but when he found out I was taking typing, he saw a skill that he could use.

"You want to be a writer?" he said. "Good. I've got something for you to write. You're going to write the story about how I was stuck in Russia during the war."

Swell.

Decades had passed since his return from Europe, but my father was still convinced that he could have sold his story for untold riches had the press simply delved more deeply. Now that there was a writer in the house—or at least a damned fast typist—he had another chance. So every day after school I was pressed into writing my father's story, using an old 1930s Royal American typewriter he'd purchased from a local tavern for ten bucks. It had been sitting on a mantel over the bar for years, more a prop than a working machine, and had not been cleaned or fixed in all that time. The keys stuck, the lines were ragged, the tab worked only intermittently, and the platen was badly dented. I had to push down on each key with all my might to convince it to strike the page, after which it would slowly float down to rejoin its brethren for a well-deserved rest.

His awful title for the story—which I wrote under his name, even though I was doing all the actual work[*]—was "The Vacation I Am Trying to Forget." I would take detailed notes as he described each step of his journey, then retire to my room to start writing, adding what I thought were writerly touches but which made the text feel desperately overwrought. I didn't understand the difference between *drama* and *melodrama*, between *succinct description* and *purple prose*, and the work too often fell into the latter categories.

This is how the story started, reprinted verbatim, with footnoted color commentary:

When mother told us that we were going to Europe, my sister and I were in a maze of excitement[†] for several days.

---

[*] And it's ridiculous that this still bugs me. Arguing over writing credits on this piece of nonsense is like fighting over who had the better suite on the *Titanic*.

[†] A "maze of excitement" couldn't be more incorrect. A whirl of excitement, per-

Finally the day of departure arrived. Although it was only going to be a three-month trip, we packed enough clothes to last us a year.[*]

I was a boy of ten[†] and since my eight-year-old sister was suffering from polio, our doctor suggested that the trip abroad might help our spirits.

It was on the evening of June 6, 1939 that a small group of friends gathered on the pier in Hoboken, NJ to see us off as we boarded the Polish liner *Batory* that was to take us to Poland to visit our relatives.

For us, life aboard the ship was one of constant delights journey.[‡] Most of the time we sat on the deck enjoying the ocean breeze, and on the fifth day out we encountered the liner *Batory*'s twin sister ship, *Pilsudski*. The ship was returning from Poland. Both ships greeted each other with a handful of hoots from the foghorns and as the ships passed by we noticed a crowd of people waving to us,[§] so we waved back.

The voyage lasted ten days and on June 16, 1939, we arrived in Gdynia, Poland. The entrance of the ship to the port[¶] was greeted with bands playing, people singing and dancing. It made us all feel very welcome.

---

haps, or even a haze of excitement, but not a maze. A maze is a physical object, while excitement is conceptual. They have no business being in the same sentence with each other.

[*] A typical amateur writer's mistake, overstating the case in an attempt to create importance or drama.

[†] Unless the author has changed genders since the title and credit, "I was ten" would suffice.

[‡] I have no idea what the hell happened to this sentence.

[§] Given the political situation at the time, they were almost certainly saying "You're going the wrong way."

[¶] More poor writing. One doesn't have to enumerate every aspect of an action. For this, "The ship's arrival" would have sufficed.

Today when I think of it, I realize that we were very
blissful and excited on that day. We had no inkling of what
horror was soon to beset us.*

The writing was awful. One can almost hear the musical sting at
the end of the last sentence: *da-da-da-dummm!* My only defense is
that I was sixteen and working with inferior material from a dubious source on a badly wounded typewriter.

The more he talked, the more loquacious he became, delving
deeper into the details. Then a curious thing happened.† We'd
reached the point in the story where he, Theresa, and Sophia were
living at the Bogdanova train station occupied by German soldiers.
Then he paused for a moment, as if trying to decide how to say
something without giving too much away.

"This is the part about Vishnevo," he said at last.

I sat up straighter. *Vishnevo* was the word my aunt had used to
put him in his place. Finally, I was going to discover what it meant.

He said that toward the end of August 1942, SS soldiers arrived
by railcar at the train station. After joining up with elements of the
Gestapo, they moved into the countryside, heading for the village
of Vishnevo.

The pertinent excerpt from the document, transcribed from his
own words:

I followed behind at a distance. They marched past the
Orthodox Church then made a right turn on the road
where the Jewish cemetery was located. I cut across the
field and hid in an old first world war bunker across from
the cemetery and waited. When the Jews arrived a few

---

* Horror does not beset anyone. Something horrific can befall someone, and a person can be beset by problems, but horror does not beset.
† *Da-da-da-dummm!*

minutes later the Gestapo and police prodded the Jews towards the hole that had been dug previously. There were shouts, I could not hear very well what was being said, but I assume that they were ordered to line up in front of the holes. Some moved very slowly and reluctantly. Others were shoved towards the hole. A signal was given. The guns fired loudly piercing the still air. The prisoners slowly slumped and fell into the open holes. It looked like some tried to escape, but I don't know if any made it. From the bunker where I was hiding I could plainly see that some were still alive but already they had a crew ready to cover them up with dirt to smother and die.

My father then described another incident at Vishnevo that took place soon afterward:

In August of 1942 my mother's helpers[*] reported for work very early in the morning. Edmund Lang[†] confided to my mother that he had information that something was going to happen in Vishnevo. My mother was telling my uncle who was visiting us of what she heard; I overheard this and the next thing that happened I was on my way to Vishnevo. I got there about an hour later and found that a lot of commotion was going on near and at the square. There were trucks and some gunfire and a German truck that was blocking the road would not let anyone pass through.

I asked a man standing nearby what was going on and he replied that they are taking the Jews out of the ghetto and moving them up the street where the ghetto ended. They

---

* These "helpers" were young Jewish girls who were apparently forced to work for Sophia.
† A German railway soldier at the station.

were taking them there by foot and the ones that were too
old, sick or too slow were driven by truck. I got as close
as I could. I heard terrifying screams above the gunfire. I
knew that someone was being hurt, but I did not go to find
out. I remembered what had happened at the cemetery and
I didn't want to see something like that again. Instead I
decided to leave and return to the station.

The story raised more questions than it answered. How did
Charles end up at both events, which by his own account were half
an hour's drive from the station on bad roads?

I followed behind at a distance.

On *foot*? Pacing trucks and soldiers on a forced march? For *five
miles*?

*I overheard this and the next thing that happened I was on my
way to Vishnevo.*

The next thing that *happened*?

Happened *how*? Did he sneak onto a truck? Dematerialize and
rematerialize outside the village? He refused to explain. He *happened* to be there and that was as far as he'd go. It was the sort
of evasiveness my father resorted to when he wanted to avoid
specificity for his own protection, which under the circumstances
seemed odd.

I also thought it strange that a German soldier would give Sophia, supposedly little more than a housekeeper, tactical information about a coming attack; and stranger still that after the second
incident, another German officer would tell her to get out of the
area or be branded a collaborator because they worked at the train
station. Lots of people worked at the station, many against their
will, so why would *they* be singled out?

He refused to elaborate. "Just write it up," he said.

Later, as I passed my parents' bedroom, I saw that my father had laid the German jacket out on the bed and was looking at it with an expression that was wistful, almost nostalgic. When he saw me, his expression hardened and for a moment it wasn't him looking at me; there was something darker peering out through his eyes as he closed and locked the door. For just a moment I felt a flicker of sympathy for my father. Witnessing such a crime must have been traumatic for him. Scores were murdered. This was important. He had been a witness to history. But I couldn't shake the feeling that there was more to the story. He'd chosen his words too carefully for me to think otherwise.

There was *something* he didn't want me to know.

In February 1971 one of my father's job applications bore unexpected fruit. International Telephone and Telegraph (ITT) was looking for people with experience in plastic manufacturing for their Cable Hydrospace facility in National City, just south of San Diego.* After selling them a bill of goods about how successful his plastics company in Matawan had been, they hired him and paid all expenses to relocate our family to San Diego.

We moved into an apartment at 1250 Fifth Avenue in Chula Vista, a bedroom community south of San Diego. I would complete the last half of my junior year at Chula Vista High School, my twelfth school and our eighteenth move in just under seventeen years.

Since I had no idea what the town's Weird Shit Index might be, I kept my usual distance in case the locals turned into flesh-eating zombies and came after me. The teachers knew me as a name on a roll sheet, my test scores generated neither praise nor alarm, and in

---

* In later years, ITT was successfully prosecuted on a range of criminal charges, including helping conduct coups in Brazil and Chile, and for violations of the Arms Export Control Act. My father was *perfect* for this place.

time I knew a handful of students well enough to nod to in the hall or sit beside at lunch.

I took advantage of the town's well-stocked library to broaden my reading habits beyond science fiction and fantasy to include historical texts, biographies, and college-level textbooks on writing, history, science, psychology, and political affairs. It was as if there was a black hole in the middle of my head: the more I fed it, the more it wanted. There was an eagerness stirring inside me, like a coiled spring ready to . . . what? To write? Was I nearly there? I couldn't tell if the writing impulse was making itself known or if the rest of my hormones had finally kicked in.

Every time I thought I *might* be ready to start writing I ran afoul of my inability to distinguish between a writer's *style* and his *voice*. I could *feel* the difference but couldn't quantify it in any useful way. A Ray Bradbury story felt soft and warm, like a pile of leaves on a fall lawn; a Robert Heinlein story was as hard-edged and unforgiving as steel gears. That's who those writers *were*, that was their style.

But wasn't that the same thing as their voice?

The breakthrough came the summer after the end of my junior year, while reading *The Colour Out of Space*, a collection of short stories by H. P. Lovecraft. There are many laudatory things one can say about Lovecraft's fiction—that it's imaginative, colorful, surrealistic, and high-flown—but what it's *not* is subtle. He comes at you with adverbs and adjectives blazing, little caring who might get caught in the cross fire, tossing off one overburdened phrase after another, describing alien cities as *cyclopean constructs of an eldritch race*, using words like *squamous* and *noisome* and others that sent me dictionary-diving for relief. His stories took place in ancient, sleeping cities of bronze and gold, where gibbous (*there goes the dictionary again*) creatures caparisoned (*and again*) on great beasts far beneath the sea under the watchful gaze of vast, space-borne entities whose true magnitude could only be glimpsed through the lens of madness.

He was so over the top that suddenly I got it: *style* was the pacing and flow of one word to another to create a melody that would carry the images, characters, and narrative straight into the brain, a specific, practiced rhythm that could be slowed or quickened depending on the mood or purpose of the story. *Voice* was who the writer actually was beneath it all: their attitude, point of view, and personality. A writer might move between a variety of styles—hard-boiled noir, gothic, baroque—but the same intelligence informed the story at every step. Literary styles can pass in and out of favor, or be shared by different writers at the same time (as Lovecraft borrowed stylistic tools from Lord Dunsany and Arthur Machen), but a writer's *voice* is distinctly his or her own; it's a one-off.

Style was the clothes; *voice* was the body.

The instant I hit that realization I felt a circuit close inside me, switching on an engine in my brain. Suddenly all the little unrelated things I knew about writing (or brashly thought I knew) arranged themselves into a pattern so clear and precise that it knocked the breath out of me.

I threw down the Lovecraft book, picked up a notepad, and frantically began writing a short story. The words rushed out in a jack-straw tumble faster than I could scribble them down. A few hours later, breathless and excited, I had finished my first (very) short story.

But the machine wasn't done. *Another!* it said.

I started a second story and finished it shortly after midnight.

More! it said.

I couldn't stop. The words were just *there*. I could choose to write them down or let them go past me to find another writer, but they would keep coming regardless. I wasn't able to shake loose of its teeth until dawn, when I collapsed into bed and slept for almost twelve hours.

My first thought when I woke up was *What the hell was THAT?* I felt as though I'd been mugged. But the truth was something infinitely more profound.

For the first time in my life, I was *awake*.

I spent the rest of that summer experimenting. I'd write stories in Lovecraft's style because it was the easiest to see. Besides, he was a professional writer, so that must be how a writer writes. Then I'd read a Harlan Ellison story, and decide, *No, wait,* that's *how a writer writes*, and write a story in that style. Studying Bradbury or Hunter Thompson, I shifted gears again. *Yes, that's it,* that *must be what a writer sounds like.*

What I wouldn't fully understand for many years is that writing is nothing more or less than speaking on the page in your own natural voice. Writers write the way they talk and talk the way they write. You have to get out of your own way enough to say only and exactly what you *mean* to say without second-guessing yourself. Like most neophyte writers I was prettying up the language to make it sound "literary," which was *exactly* the wrong thing to do.

By summer's end I'd written eleven short stories. I held off rereading them until a few weeks before school was to begin, then settled back for what I expected to be an evening of greatness. But the stories were absolute crap. Total, unmitigated awfulness.

I couldn't understand it. Had the brilliant, Earth-shattering, Nobel Prize–worthy stories I'd written earlier been stolen and replaced with the wretched, malformed creatures before me? The answer, of course, was that the stories had been written as well as could be expected *given the tools I had when I wrote them*. Every writer starts with the same toolbox, which at most might contain a screwdriver and a pair of rusty pliers, and there's not much you can make with that. Each finished story adds a new tool to the box that assists in the construction of better stories going forward, and reveals the strengths and weaknesses of the prior work.

Absent the occasional annoying prodigy, all writers, artists, and musicians suck at the beginning of their careers, which is why so many of them fall early and easily by the wayside. *You're not very good at this*, the naysayers declare, and the awful thing is that they're not wrong, and we *know* they're not wrong. But that's not the same thing as a lack of talent; that particular speed limit hasn't yet been established. The flaws in one's early work reflect nothing more than the artist's lack of experience. The struggle is to keep going, incrementally acquiring more tools until the work begins to improve, *as it inevitably will.*

The horrific part is that well-meaning friends and family will often say *Fine, give this writing/acting/music thing two years, and if you don't make it big by then, drop it and do something else.* Art is progressive; the more you do it, the better you get. I defy anyone to write fifteen short stories and not have story #15 be at least marginally better than story #1. It's simply not possible. Setting a date-certain for surrender often results in giving up just as you're starting to get good at your craft.

Of the eleven stories I had written, eight through eleven had given me just enough tools to know that stories one to seven were shit, but not enough to know how to fix the damned things. Similarly, writing stories twelve to sixteen would make eight to eleven *also* look like crap. The flaws in my work were so painfully obvious that I wondered if my stories might be better suited for lining litter boxes than literary magazines. Only the slight improvements in the last few stories gave me any hope. I began to understand that learning to write is like drilling for oil: before getting to the good stuff, you first have to pump out vast quantities of mud, water, dinosaur bones, and general, garden-variety ick. So I set out to write as much as I could, as quickly as possible, to drill past the *ohmygodthisiscrap* stage. In a burst of ego

I thought it might take a year, maybe two, before I had this whole writing thing figured out.

As I write these words I am sixty-four, and still waiting for that day to come.

As I began my senior year, I signed up for two classes that would alter the trajectory of my life in profound and unexpected ways. One was a class in satire taught by Rochelle Terry; the other was my first creative writing class, led by Jo Ann Massie. When I confided to them my ambition to be a writer, I assumed they'd respond with the same ridicule as every other adult. Instead they went out of their way to encourage me, and I began flooding them with short stories. Where other students struggled to turn in assignments of four or five handwritten pages, I'd turn in twenty or more typed pages at a shot. Mrs. Massie included one of my short stories in that year's senior magazine, and Mrs. Terry encouraged me to write short satirical plays that we produced for other classes. Yes, I was a wretched writer, but they saw promise in my work, and with their guidance I hoped in time to become slightly less wretched.

It has become a cliché that the right teacher, in the right place, at the right moment can change someone's life. But in this case the truth behind that cliché cannot be overstated. They invested time, effort, and belief into me at a time when nobody else even had me on their radar. They went through my stories line by line, word by word, and comma by comma, showing a very defensive young writer that it was possible to be critical of the work while still supporting the effort behind it. Everything I've ever achieved as a writer can all be traced back to the moment these two teachers entered my orbit.

Every year the local high schools held a joint Career Day that brought together their best writers, artists, musicians, and actors in a showcase that the teachers hoped would encourage them to pursue those passions into college. Noting my shyness, and eager to get my work out into the world, Massie and Terry invited me to the event, which would take place in the spring. Based on their recommendation, a teacher from one of the other schools invited me to an earlier, smaller, and more informal gathering in November 1971 at nearby Southwestern Community College.

On the appointed day, I took the bus to Southwestern and made my way to where the other invitees were gathered at a clutch of tables near the cafeteria. Painted canvases had been set out for viewing while other students played guitar or sang in the shade of nearby trees. It was festive and friendly, but also very ad hoc; other than a few flyers tacked to bulletin boards there had been no publicity, so most of the students and faculty walking by had no idea what we were doing or why we were there. Some paused to glance at the artwork or listen to the music, but there was no way to sample the written work without actually stopping to read, and few felt so inclined.

As the shadows lengthened, most of the participants packed up and left. Since the bus home wasn't due for another hour, I was one of the few still at my table when a man approached out of the twilight. His face was tanned and weathered beneath a shock of salt-and-pepper hair that was combed in a pompadour several times higher than seemed possible. He looked familiar but I couldn't place him out of context. He scanned the remaining manuscripts on display until he reached where I was sitting, then picked up one of my science fiction stories and, without a word, sat on a nearby lawn chair, reading in the light spilling out of the cafeteria. When he was finished, he came back, got another, read it, and returned to the table, studying me from beneath heavy eyebrows.

"You have a substantial talent for someone of your age," he said.

His voice was strangely familiar, but I still couldn't place it. "Let me give you two pieces of advice. First, cut every third adjective.* Second, never let them stop you from telling the story you want to tell."

Then he checked his watch, wished me a good day, and left.

A microsecond later one of the teachers raced over to ask what he'd said.

When I repeated his words, she beamed proudly. "Don't you know who that *was*?"

"No," I said. "I figured he was a teacher. I mean, he looked familiar, but—"

"That was Rod Serling! He's here to give a talk tonight at the college. He must've gotten here early and decided to take a walk around the campus before—"

I have no idea what she said after that because I ran off to try and catch him, but he was already gone, vanished like an apparition from one of his stories. I couldn't even afford to buy a ticket to his speech that night about working on *The Twilight Zone* and *Night Gallery*. But that didn't matter. A writer—a *real* writer, hell, one of the Gods of Writing—said I had talent! It was a transformative moment that would sustain me for a long time to come.

Years later, I had the opportunity to work with Rod's widow, Carol Serling, on an attempted revival of *Night Gallery*. We spoke more than once about this chance encounter and agreed that sometimes the world is smaller and weirder than even Rod could have imagined.

---

* I'm still working on this one.

CHAPTER 13

The God Thing

During the early '70s, Charismatic Christianity exploded into mainstream churches. Its adherents practiced prophecy, ecstatic singing, ritual healing, spoke in tongues, and in some cases engaged in the kind of ascetic communal living described in the Book of Acts. The Jesus People Movement proved extremely popular with high school and college students searching for meaning. Christian coffeehouses and youth centers used folk music to bring biblical messages to listeners used to hearing Bob Dylan or Joan Baez sing about their hopes for a better world. Sporting linen pants or jeans, denim or tie-dyed shirts, leather sandals and Christ-length hair, they could be found singing and praying in parks, or gathered on street corners handing out leaflets inviting young people to social gatherings and religious concerts. The most popular venues were coffeehouses like the Living Room in San Francisco, the Way Word in Greenwich Village, the Catacombs in Seattle, I Am in Spokane, and His Place, on the Sunset Strip in Hollywood.

The ecclesiastical epicenter for Jesus People activity in Chula Vista was the First Baptist Church at the corner of Fifth and E Streets, where Pastor Ken Pagaard operated a Christian coffeehouse* called the House of Abba out of a small utility building adjacent to the church. Every Friday night scores of young people crowded into a space not much bigger than a three-car garage. The only furniture consisted of a few chairs on a stage reserved for the musicians, so everyone else had to sit cross-legged on the floor, prompting calls of "If you can see carpet in front of you, you're a sinner, move up!" Members prayed, read from the Bible, and listened to Christian folk music performed by various groups, of which Hebron was the primary band in residence.

Speaking of the House of Abba years later, Tim Pagaard, Ken's son and a member of Hebron, said, "We were kind of the only gig in town, so for all the kids that wanted some kind of a way-hip thing, there was nothing else going on in Chula Vista."

Even so, he was astonished by how quickly the group expanded. "Here we've got this place where there are some kids playing guitars on Friday and Saturday night, and one week there's fifty kids (in the audience), the next week there's a hundred and fifty, and the next week there's five hundred, and you're just going, really?"

The music was a delivery mechanism for soft-sell conversion. Floaters patrolled the parking lot or worked the coffeehouse in search of prospects. Those who found Jesus were invited to join the congregation, where they would be instructed in the Christian faith by Ken Pagaard and members of the church hierarchy known as the Elders. From his modest appearance and soft-spoken manner, Ken could easily be mistaken for a simple businessman, but behind the pulpit he was a charismatic speaker who inculcated a fierce loyalty among his followers. The church also operated several religious communes, collectively referred to as Community, each housing twelve or more full-time residents who turned their possessions over to the church and submitted their lives to the authority of Ken and the Elders.

The House of Abba's reach extended into Chula Vista High

---

* Coffee was never served, so why they called it a coffeehouse is anyone's guess.

School, where members gathered on the lawn at lunch to talk and pray and witness to others. Several of these students were in my classes, including another senior named Cathi Williams. She was smart and creative, with a sly sense of humor that crept up behind you, playfully smacked you on the back of the head then ran off laughing. She was bigger than life. She was trouble. She was glorious.

My schedule put me in the same classroom twice in a row. Due to the quirks of alphabetized seating, in Class One I sat at the same desk that Cathi occupied during Class Two, while I sat one row over. Like any bored student I sometimes tuned out whatever was being discussed and doodled on a sheet of paper or on the desk-top. One day, I was sufficiently bored in Class One that I affixed a sticker bearing a pentagram to the rear of the seat facing me. (My writing was still in its Lovecraftian supernatural period and I thought stuff like that was cool. I was an idiot.)

When I was back in the same desk the next day for Class One, I noticed that she had written *Jesus Saves* next to the pentagram. She had no idea who had put it there, she just needed to respond. So I wrote a rather rude and highly anti-Christian response next to her comment to see if I could provoke a reaction.

She replied. I did the same. She countered. It amused me that we were having a theological discussion via the back of a desk seat, and that she had no idea who I was. After we ran out of room on the wooden backrest, we began leaving lengthy notes hidden under the desk. The more she tried to pull me in, the harder I pushed back, my position becoming more extreme with each new letter; some were real fire-breathers. In Class Two I would watch her unfold the latest salvo and laugh with her friends about this jerk she was try-ing to convert.

Though I was still too shy to talk easily to girls, I could appar-ently write to them without problem, with Satan as my Cyrano.

This went on for about a month before I decided to end the charade and left a note extending an invitation to meet after school. As she waited for her unknown correspondent, ready to do spiritual battle, I approached and said hello. She nodded distractedly, searching for the dark and terrible figure who had sent her those awful notes and would be there at any moment, cloaked in shadows and smoke. I waited. After a moment she turned to me and the light of realization went on in her eyes. She reddened in embarrassment then hauled back and slugged me.

After that I became Cathi's special project. Her tireless efforts to convert me turned into a group effort as other members of the House of Abba joined in. If one of them saw me walking across town, they'd offer a lift. Every day at lunch they invited me to sit with them, to talk or to say nothing at all, if that's what I chose.

And then there were the gang hugs.

To this point in my life, no one—not my parents, my siblings, my other relatives, *nobody*—had ever told me *I love you*. Nor can I remember ever being hugged or embraced; physical affection was alien to me. So for a group of my peers to hug me and say they loved me was overwhelming. The first time it happened I excused myself, found a place behind the gym where I couldn't be seen, and just cried. *Is this what affection is like?* I wondered. I'd grown up like a tree in the desert, twisted and bent from lack of water, and suddenly found myself being love-bombed several times a week.

I refused to yield, convinced that they were living in a fantasy world. I needed that conviction to keep from shattering under the weight of what seemed like genuine affection to someone who was in no position to know better.

One afternoon I was pulled out of class to meet with CVHS principal Raymond O'Donnell. "Mrs. Terry and Mrs. Massie tell me you're a writer. They say you're really good."

I nodded but said nothing. Could be a trap.

"Here's the thing," he continued. "We want to institute a new tradition where a senior is chosen to write a satirical play about the school and its teachers. Nothing too extreme, mind you, all in good fun. The play will be staged in the gym in front of the entire student body. If it works, it'll become a yearly tradition.

"Based on your teachers' endorsement, I want you to write the play. You'll have two weeks to write it, pull together other students to act in it, and rehearse. It needs to be funny, but if you go too far in making fun of the staff, we won't do it again and you'll have destroyed the student body's only chance to fire back at their teachers. So don't screw it up."

I walked back across campus utterly at sea. I'd worked for years to become invisible. Taking on this task would thrust me into the spotlight before the entire student body. If my writing was safe but not funny, they'd eat me alive. If it was funny but too *truthful*, the school would never do this again and the other students would *still* eat me alive. I'd be putting my neck on the line in *exactly* the way I'd been fighting so long to avoid.

On the other hand . . .

Mrs. Terry and Mrs. Massie tell me you're a writer. They say you're really good.

It was a challenge, but instead of coming from someone eager to fight me, this time it came from people who *believed* in me.

It was as though the universe was saying *time to stop hiding*.

I spent the next week writing the play, which included some sharp jabs at the Jesus People, but you can't make an omelet without breaking a few Christians. I enlisted the aid of several students to help out, one or two of whom added their own material, and we got in a few rehearsals.

On the day of the production the gymnasium was packed with eighteen hundred students. The lights dimmed, the show began . . . and the humor was every bit as awful as could be expected: juvenile, forced, crude, and derivative. It was a baseball bat swung wildly by someone who had never held one before in the hope of connecting with anything that might accidentally wander over the plate. But the shock factor saved us; the students roared as the same snide comments they made among themselves were echoed in front of the very teachers being lampooned. For the finale, a student playing Principal O'Donnell stepped onto the stage and demanded to know who had written this nonsense.

This was the moment I had chosen to literally and figuratively step out of the shadows, in full view of the jocks who had ignored me, the cheerleaders for whom I didn't exist, the class officers, the Jesus People, *all* of them.

My name is Kal-El, I come from Krypton, take me to your leader.

"I wrote this!" I said defiantly.

He pulled out a gun. We'd only been given permission to use a cap gun, but a starter's pistol from the gym class lockup had somehow managed to find its way onto the stage.

I ran. He fired. I went down in a spray of fake blood.

The place went nuts. They applauded, shouted, and stamped their feet on the bleachers, shaking the gymnasium so hard that it rattled the rafters and vibrated up through the floor.

It wasn't the opening of a Broadway play or a TV program beamed to a million homes; it wasn't much of *anything*, really, it was a *high school assembly* for chrissakes. But it was the first time I got applause for something I'd written, the first time I felt genuinely appreciated, and it solidified my conviction that I was meant to be a writer. Over the following days, whenever I walked across campus, students who still didn't even know my *name* would see me and yell out, "Hey, writer, way to go, good job!"

Yeah, I was hooked, all right.

With graduation looming, Cathi knew she might lose her last chance to convert me, and prevailed upon me to come with her to the House of Abba. She said that I'd taken some pretty substantial shots at the Jesus People in my play so it was only fair that they have their turn. She was right, of course, and being also rather smitten with her I agreed to attend that Friday night. Normally it would have been difficult to get out of the apartment, but my father was spending increasing amounts of time out of town on business. I didn't know what those trips entailed and was too relieved by his absence to give it much thought.

The coffeehouse was packed. Cathi and I sat cross-legged on the floor, squinching forward as more people arrived until everyone was locked in knee to knee. Definitely not the place for someone with an uncertain bladder. The air inside was so hot that a regular procession of the fainthearted made their way to the parking lot. The house group, Abba's Children, played gospel songs in contemporary folk arrangements, preached, led the audience in song, and told personal stories punctuated by jokes.

It was unlike anything I'd seen in formal Catholicism.

At a pause in the music, they asked if anyone wanted to offer testimony describing acts of God that had occurred in their personal lives. A young woman raised her hand and I noticed that she was sitting with one of the students who had taken part in my play.

"You know that show they did at school that made fun of us?" she asked.

"Sure do," some of them called back.

"Well, I brought one of the guys who played us, he's right here!" Rather than booing or giving him a hard time, the crowd applauded, welcoming their visitor.

When the noise died down, Cathi straightened. "I can beat *that*," she said proudly, wrapping an arm around me. "I brought the guy who *wrote* the thing!"

The place erupted in laughter and gentle barbs aimed in my direction. If I could've found a weak spot in the carpeting—if I could've found *carpeting*—I would have burrowed through the floor and disappeared into the earth. Instead I muttered something about it being nothing personal, then sank back, hoping not to draw further attention.

There was more testimony, witnessing, and singing. Then someone behind me started chanting in a way that sounded like singing but wasn't. Her voice rose and fell in a hypnotic rhythm, the sound unrecognizable as any language. Others joined in, a rush of voices crying out. I recognized the sound as something I'd read about in a magazine article: *glossolalia*, speaking in tongues. But it's one thing to read about the phenomenon and quite another to be inundated by it. I could feel myself being caught up in the tide of ecstatic joy that filled the room. I didn't have to believe in the religion to be mesmerized by the moment.

Then Cathi was talking to me, asking me to pledge myself to God. Others around us lifted one hand in prayer and pressed the other to my back, encouraging conversion. The logical part of my brain wasn't buying it. *You're being manipulated, don't fall for it.*

But the emotion and peer pressure was ferocious. It wasn't a quiet conversion moment, it was an ecclesiastical mugging.

"Do you feel Jesus inside you? Do you believe he wants to save you?" she asked, her face inches from my own. "Do you?"

I closed my eyes. I wasn't sure *what* I thought. In the heat of the moment it's possible that a part of me did believe, or at least *wanted* to believe. As the voices of the faithful washed over me, I opened my eyes and looked at Cathi, her face flushed, beautiful, the first girl who ever gave me the slightest attention, eager for my response . . . and my heart overwhelmed my head.

Even now I can't say with certainty whether I believed or didn't believe, if I felt God or if I felt nothing. I knew only that after a lifetime of misery I wanted to be part of something joyful. I wanted to be *happy*.

And I wanted *her* to be happy.
So I told her I believed.
And she hugged me.
They *all* hugged me.
I was doomed.

The graduation ceremony for Chula Vista High School took place Thursday, June 15, 1972; its theme was "Perhaps It Is Because He Hears a Different Drummer." (It was the '70s and we were apparently incapable of embarrassment.) Ken Pagaard gave the commencement speech, a controversial choice for some who were concerned about the communes Ken operated around town. Afterward, Cathi and everyone else went to parties to celebrate with friends. I had no such option. My father said he had something special in mind to mark the occasion. I hoped it might entail a trip to Disneyland or dinner someplace nice followed by an envelope containing cash. It was neither.

There was to be a party at our apartment, with only two guests, both friends of my father. The first was a drinking buddy from a local tavern; the other was Irene (not her real name), a hairstylist who was pushing fifty but dressing thirty. One of my father's "bar friends" from Paterson who had recently come to California with his assistance, her trademark was a black beehive wig so old and ratty that it never sat properly on her head. It looked like a beat-up cat with one eye forever on the lookout for stray dogs. Whether she was an outright hooker (as some speculated) or simply my father's convenient go-to source for casual sex (as most believed) I cannot say. But she spent many late nights out on the town with Charles and often came to the apartment to see him. If my mother had any feelings on the subject, self-preservation obliged her to remain silent.

The three of them proceeded to get as drunk as I've ever seen three humans get and not die.

With growing anger I realized that this was my *father's* party, not mine, as if *he* was the one who had graduated.

His friends.

His achievement.

His drunken celebration.

"You never woulda got this far if I hadn't been pushing you," he said repeatedly, oblivious to the fact that I'd managed to graduate *despite* his drunkenness and the difficulty of constantly changing schools. "You'd be out on the street starving if it wasn't for me!"

As bottles of whiskey and vodka disappeared I tried several times to retreat to my room only to be dragged back, a prop in my father's big day. Around midnight he turned to Irene and, with dramatic flourishes of his empty glass, said, "We need more booze. Go get us more booze."

He looked at me. "Go with her. Make sure she doesn't plow into anything."

I wanted to say no, but he was at that sloppy drunk stage that could turn dark in a second, so it was easier to do as instructed. As we headed out she leaned on me for support, wobbly and knock-kneed, reeking of alcohol, cheap perfume, and stale body powder, her beehive wig tilted at an angle that defied the laws of gravity. In the stark glow of the parking lot lights, I fixated on the fact that her black dress, torn more than once, had been stitched with the wrong color thread.

I helped her into the car then got in on the passenger side. She fumbled with her keys, trying several times to figure out which end went into the little slot before getting it right. Then she leaned over me, very close, revealing smeared red lipstick on thin lips. Her makeup, two shades too pale and Kabuki thick, failed to conceal the heavy lines beneath, the skin's signature from a lifetime of drinking.

She put her right arm around my shoulder. "I want you to know we're all very proud of you, Joey," she slurred.

"Thank you," I said, thinking, *Can we just go now?*

"And I want you to know that I'm here for you."

Then I noticed her left hand moving up my leg.

"If there's anything you *want*," she said, her hand continuing its journey up my thigh, "anything I can *do* for you, anything at *all*, just let me know."

Oh, shit.

Trying to act casual I folded my hands across my lap, creating a wall between her hand and the good china. "We better get going or the store's going to close," I said.

"Liquor stores are open late, baby."

"Yeah, but I think this one closes early."

She peered out at me from under heavy lids, her eyes darkening as she realized this wasn't going anywhere. "Okay," she said resignedly and we drove off.

When we returned with fresh supplies, I was debating whether to say anything about the incident when I saw my father give her a quizzical look, a raised eyebrow. *So?*

She shook her head. *No.*

He looked away with an expression of disgust.

With a horror I cannot begin to describe I realized that *this* was what he had intended as his big "surprise" for my graduation. In his controlling way he wanted to make sure that the first time I had sex it was with his bounce-buddy, this (and I recognize the meanness of this, but it's how I felt at the time) worn-out, dried-up, overly made-up refugee from a twelve-step program.

As she sat heavily on the sofa beside him, he leaned in, one hand over his mouth in a stage whisper he knew full well I could hear, that he *wanted* me to hear, and nodded in my direction. "Faggot," he said.

I went to my room, pushed my small fiberboard desk against the door to preclude any further surprises for the night, and went to bed.

I emerged shortly after dawn to find the three of them passed out. Irene was on the living room floor, dress hiked up around her hips, while my father's bar friend was unconscious on the sofa in a stew of his own vomit. I found Charles face-down on the kitchen table. I called his name. No response.

I thought about how easy it would be to get a meat cleaver from the kitchen and bring it down on his neck from behind, severing his spine and killing him instantly. I could then put the bloody knife in his friend's unconscious hand to soak up the appropriate fingerprints, wash my hands, and go back to bed until my mother emerged and screamed at the sight.

I stared at that exposed neck for a very long time before finally going back to my room.

With my father spending increasing amounts of time out of town, I had no trouble slipping off to the House of Abba every Friday night, then attending Sunday services at the First Baptist Church. When Cathi invited me to a beach party, it was a first for me. I'd never gone to the beach with friends my own age, or watched a log burn in a fire pit, talking about life as the sun dipped beneath the horizon. But a few hours later there I was, sitting with my back against a seawall as they laughed and sang and chased each other along the beach. *Is this how normal people live?* I wondered. *Is this what I've been missing all this time?* I fought back a wave of resentment. Yes, I'd lost the first eighteen years of my life to living in a cage, but better to have found such small joys now than never to have known they existed.

At the end of the evening we crammed into the back of an open pickup truck for the drive home, good-naturedly jostling each other and exaggerating the car's every turn, bodies slamming bodies. I realized I was grinning like an idiot. By now I'd been in Chula Vista for almost a year and a half. I had friends, stability, and a place where I could experience the kind of affection that had always been denied me. I'd even started making inroads as a writer, and while I couldn't afford to attend San Diego State University, the journalism, writing, and theater departments at Southwestern College were well regarded. Besides, most everyone I knew planned to attend SWC, so I'd have friends there.

That was the most amazing part. I had actual *friends*! I felt exhilarated, excited to be alive.

At last, I was *happy*.

As I entered the apartment my father was waiting for me, a half-empty bottle of vodka on the table in front of him.

"You better get packed," he said. "We're moving to Illinois."

CHAPTER 14

The Weed of Evil Bears Strange Fruit

This time it wasn't my father's drinking that was forcing us to move. ITT had slowed their plans for a new hydrocable division, resulting in layoffs and vague promises of being rehired once things geared back up. The company had given everyone notice of what was coming, and my father had used that time to scope out other opportunities. This explained his prolonged trips out of town. His search led to a company in Kankakee, Illinois, and now that the layoffs had begun, he was ready to go.

I wasn't. I wanted desperately to stay in Chula Vista. This was my *home* now, and there was a part of me that believed, foolishly in retrospect, that I might actually have a chance with Cathi if she ever ditched her boyfriend. I asked the Elders if they could take me into Community but the households were restricted to members who had belonged to the church for a while. There was nothing left but final farewells, and as we drove off I was sure that I would never see Chula Vista again.

We'd barely unpacked into a small rental house at 310 North Convent Street in Bourbonnais, north of Kankakee and south of Chicago, when the new job evaporated after a follow-up call to ITT by his prospective employers revealed that my father had been less than straightforward about the extent of his training. I was furious. If there wasn't a job to be had in Illinois, then we should go back to San Diego. But he'd invested too much time and money in getting there to turn back, so for the next several months he worked during the day as a consultant for various plastics companies, and at night dissolved into his usual pattern of drunken violence.

I enrolled at the recently opened Kankakee Community College. Much of it was still under construction, the handful of finished buildings outnumbered by trailers housing classrooms and labs. There were no theater or journalism departments, no on-campus radio or TV stations, and only one rudimentary class in creative writing. Since most students who majored in writing ended up as teachers rather than writers, I decided to major in psychology in the belief that it would help me get into the heads of my characters. Naturally my father declined to help pay for my education, so I took out loans, grants, and hardship assistance, and worked part-time in the Adult Education office, typing forms and filing papers.

Desperate to break the monotony, I looked for anything that might resemble the House of Abba, but the Jesus Movement had not yet penetrated into Kankakee. A lively contingent had taken root in Chicago, but for a nondriver that was impossibly out of range, so I decided to try and create a coffeehouse on my own. I'd barely started discussing the idea with pastors at local churches and youth centers when I was contacted by members of the Chicago Jesus Movement. They explained that the areas south of the Windy City were under the jurisdiction of one of the group's leaders (his name long since forgotten) and nothing could be done without his blessings. This felt more like a McDonald's franchise than a religious one, but I didn't want to cause trouble so I made the pilgrimage by bus to meet with him.

The leader was a large man with a long, thick beard who spoke slowly and sonorously, as though trying to give each word importance by how he said it. He asked about my beliefs, and where I had found Christ. I answered politely, then described what I had in mind. He seemed perturbed that I was bringing a California vibe to Chicago.

"What's the name you want to give to the coffeehouse?" he asked.

I leaned forward, very proud of the name I'd chosen. "The House of the Risen Son."

He shook his head. "That's not it."

"That's not what?"

"The Lord revealed to me the name of the coffeehouse that is to rise down there, and that's not the name."

"Okay, so what *is* the name? I can always change it."

"I can't tell you."

"Why not?"

"Because the Lord told me not to tell anyone the name. That way I would know when someone else said it that *this* was the right coffeehouse to support."

I'd seen my father con enough people to recognize one when I heard it. Since the information was only in his head, he could say *no, that's not it* forever and there was no way to prove he was lying. But I decided to play it out anyway. *Let's see where this goes.*

"Did you write the name down anywhere so this could be confirmed?" I asked.

"The Lord told me not to write it down, because faith does not require proof, and if it was written down, the Devil could get it and use it."

"To form a Christian coffeehouse."

"Yes."

"Does he do that very often?"

"The Devil comes in familiar clothes."

"What if I said the Lord told me that he didn't give you the right name, that he gave *me* the right name?"

"That isn't the Lord."

"Why not?"

"Because the Lord *told* me it's not him."

"Just now?"

"Yes."

"But isn't my hearing the Lord as valid as you hearing the Lord?"

"No."

"Why not?"

"Because the Lord told me *first*."

Cornered by his ineluctable logic, I took the bus home and let the idea slide.

During the long and lonely months that followed, I stayed sane through a series of letters and, later, phone calls with Cathi in Chula Vista. But when my father saw the phone bill, he flew into a rage, even though I was giving my mother money to cover the charges. The cost wasn't the issue; it was that I was calling *anyone* without his permission. He demanded I stop at once.

I refused. I was in college, earning my own money, and there was no *way* I was going to stop calling Cathi.

Enraged at my defiance, he punched me in the face hard enough to hurl my glasses across the room and put a vertical fracture in my right lateral incisor, next to the tooth he'd damaged earlier. (It would later break lengthwise, leaving me with two-thirds of a tooth for many years because I couldn't afford to fix it.)

As I walked across the room to pick up my badly bent glasses I didn't yell back at him. Instead I got very quiet. Everything inside me grew cold. When I turned to face him, my voice was low and deadly serious.

"I want you to understand that if you *ever* hit me again, I'm going to kill you." It wasn't a threat. It wasn't anger. It was a statement of fact, and he could see it in my eyes.

"You can't talk to me like that! I'm your father!"

"Maybe you are, and maybe you're not, according to you. But I'm telling you again, straight up: if you hit me one more time, between now and forever, I will kill you."

"You wouldn't dare."

"Then try me, right now," I said, my anger coming out in every syllable. "Maybe I won't kill you this second. Maybe I'll wait until you're asleep or passed out. You sleep ten feet from my door. Wouldn't take much to put a pillow over your face and say you choked to death on your own vomit. Today, tomorrow, a week from now. I don't even care if I go to jail. I'll kill you."

I meant it. I meant every *inch* of it.

And he *knew* it.

"Try me," I said again, getting right up in his face. "*Try me!*"

He backed away, yelling and cursing and throwing things around the room.

But he didn't hit me. He didn't fucking *dare*.

That was the last time he *ever* hit me.

Under other conditions I would have left home and found some way to earn a living while going to school, but for years I'd been the only thing standing between my father and my sisters and, to a degree, my mother, taking whatever came when he was drunk and violent. Though I'd given him cause to hold back on hitting me again, he would still come home each night full of rage, profanity, and psychological abuse. If I walked away, my sisters would inherit the brunt of his behavior which would sooner or later turn to violence, and that I could not allow. So I stayed.

By the end of the semester my father announced that we were

moving to Texas, where several new plastics companies were starting up that might need experienced workers. There was nothing to hold me to Illinois, so for once I was actually okay with the move.

Our apartment on West Spring Valley Road in Richardson, Texas, was right at the town's border: cross the street and you're in Dallas, cross back and you're in Richardson. This is what passes for a good time in Richardson.

I was delighted to discover that Richland Junior College crackled with an energy and creativity that KCC lacked. Twice a week beat poetry was performed in the common area just abaft the cafeteria, and the experience of hearing words slammed together in ways that emphasized the sound as much as the content led me to fall in love with the works of Lawrence Ferlinghetti, e. e. cummings, and Allen Ginsberg. Poetry helped me understand the power and the *precision* of language because it allowed for no margin of error: you had only a few lines to make your point, so every word had to be the right word in the right place.

Since I was still paying my own way through college I began hitchhiking to school to save money. The hardest part was standing in the blistering Texas heat, thumb out, waiting for a car to bleed out of the distance. I was matchstick thin and clearly not a threat to anyone, so most of my rides came from elderly women concerned for *my* safety.

Then I saw an ad on the campus bulletin board from a young woman who wanted someone to drive to school with, not even a paying carpooler, just someone to share the ride.

"My name's Donna," she said when I called, "and I drive a gunmetal-gray Toyota with a black top that looks like a stolen car. I drive fast, so if you're not there when I pull up, I'm gone."

I liked her instantly, and over the next few months we became friends, logging miles and confidences. One afternoon she said, "So, you ever do grass?"

I shook my head. The tactics used by government and teachers had done a good job of scaring me, especially in Texas where being caught with a single joint was a felony charge that would get you sent to prison.

"You want to try some?" she asked.

I demurred. She let it go, then asked again a few days later, suggesting that it would make me more creative. Since every writer has to be open to new experiences, and I was always looking for new ways to explore my creative side, I finally said sure, why not?

That night we drove up into the hills above Richardson. The throaty engine of the souped-up Toyota roared through the darkness as we cut down dusty switchback roads barely wider than the car. To make sure we weren't being followed she killed the lights and drove by instinct down a dirt path to a cutout that overlooked the city. She switched on the radio, reached under the dashboard, and came up with a joint; she lit up, took a long drag, and handed it to me. I studied it, hesitated, then took a puff. It seared my throat and I coughed most of it out before trying again. As we passed it back and forth I gazed out at the city, and a soft, fuzzy calm descended over me. The music on the radio sounded clearer than usual, and the warm air held the scent of night-blooming jasmine. It was a really terrific view, and "I just noticed that the streetlights down below seem to float if you look at them the right way, green, red . . . and man, it's taking them a *looooong* time to change . . ."

Donna laughed up smoke. "You're stoned," she said.

"I am?"

She nodded. "First time lucky." This was when weed was still fairly gentle, before the arrival of later strains strong enough to blind a police dog at thirty paces. I turned my attention back out the window. It *was* a beautiful view, and if that's what being stoned meant, taking the ordinary and making it beautiful, well, what's wrong with that?

She handed back the joint as Gregg Allman's "Midnight Rider" drifted up from the speakers. There is no more perfect song to hear the first time one does grass in a car overlooking the moonlit Texas hills than "Midnight Rider." That song was stoned before we got there.

None of this reconciled with what I'd learned about religion in Chula Vista, but this wasn't Chula Vista, I was learning to take chances as a writer, and frankly, what the hell had Chula Vista done for *me* lately?

The only nagging question I couldn't avoid was: What would Superman think about this?

I don't know, I thought, staring out at the night. *I'm lost. I don't know where I am or where I'm going or much of anything anymore. I'm in the Phantom Zone. And if grass exists anywhere in the Superman universe, it's definitely in the Phantom Zone.*

I emerged from the apartment one morning to find my father slumped over the steering wheel where he'd passed out the night before. I tapped on the window. He looked up, too drunk to register it was me, then passed out again.

As I walked off, I fantasized about dragging him into the trunk and leaving him there to suffocate, and an idea hit me: rather than shoving my father into the trunk, what if the job he was looking for could be shoved into something the size of a car trunk?

An extruder is a massive piece of machinery: six feet tall for the heater and grinder, plus another three feet for the bin holding the plastic pellets that were melted then pushed into a four-foot-long heated metal barrel. Add the cooling troughs and the whole thing was about nine feet tall and twenty feet long, necessary for producing golf tubes, landscaping pipes, and other heavy-duty plastics products. But you wouldn't need a machine that big to make something small, like dental rings for braces. If the machine could be scaled down small enough to be carried in the trunk of a car, my father could work anywhere he wanted, which for my purposes was Chula Vista.

When I suggested the idea, he did a few sketches and decided that, yes, in theory it would work and he could have his own company. But machining something this precise was expensive and he could never afford to hire the guys who did that kind of work in Dallas.

I'd been lying in wait for this exact argument, and reminded him that in Chula Vista he'd worked with several good machinists at ITT who were out of work and could do the work cheap.

He shook his head. Better to stick with his plan to find local work, which had so far resulted in absolutely nothing.

I was furious. I'd come *thisclose*. In my head I told the universe that if it wanted me back in California, then it had goddamned better get moving.

Apparently the universe heard me, because a few days later he received a letter from personnel manager Paul Komara at ITT in National City to say that they had finally begun rehiring. He offered my father the position of production superintendent, and how soon could we be back in Chula Vista?

CHAPTER 15

The God Thing, Redux

The Villa Seville Apartments at 555 Naples Street marked our twenty-first move in nineteen years, for a total of eleven schools, including four high schools, and as of the most current move, three community colleges. Two decades spent taking off in the middle of the night and roaring cross-country in an alcohol-fueled haze of drunken violence. If there is anything remarkable about my life, it is that I did not come out the other side a serial killer.

I picked up where I'd left off with my friends at the House of Abba, including Cathi, who as I'd hoped had ditched her boyfriend (yay!) only to replace him with the youth minister at First Baptist, who she eventually married (nuts). By now Cathi and most of my other friends were living in the church's communal households, and suggested that I consider doing the same. I'd pursued the idea earlier out of desperation, but over time the idea of me living in a commune became increasingly improbable. Besides, I still wasn't sure what I did or didn't believe when it came to the God Thing.

There was much to commend Sunday services—everyone was friendly, the music was great, and Ken was a terrific speaker—but it troubled me that the congregation was willing to accept the most outlandish statements when offered up as testimony or witnessing. One guest speaker allegedly from a small Polynesian island whose talk was entitled "Like a Mighty Wind," told those assembled that his prayers had brought a man back from the dead. Not a single person in that audience questioned it.

So I cornered the guy in the foyer afterward and asked for the name of the deceased.

"Why do you want to know?" he asked, already offended.

"Well, if he was dead then there has to be a death certificate. If you have that and you have the guy walking around, then that's bona fide proof of a miracle."

"I don't have a *death certificate,*" he said. By now he was getting visibly angry and speaking in italics, which I hadn't seen anyone pull off successfully since Sister Mary Psychosis at St. Stephen's. "It's a small *island* and we don't *do* death certificates and God doesn't *require* proof, or *provide* proof, and if you're *demanding* proof of God's works then you're not of God! You have to *believe!*"

It was High Priest logic: *it's true because I say it's true so just accept it.*

I was troubled by his response, but didn't pursue the subject further in case he might resort to boldface, because in a room that small someone was bound to get hurt.

I was also concerned that the group seemed to be taking on the trappings of an authoritarian cult. Members of Community were expected to submit every aspect of their lives to men whose authority was absolute. Pastor Ken Pagaard and the Elders could never be wrong because they spoke for God; to disagree was to risk being labeled a "Rebellious Spirit." I liked the idea of being part of something that resembled an actual family, but the rest of it gave me the willies. Besides, I was still needed at home as a buffer until my sisters were old enough to leave.

As I started classes at Southwestern I doubled down on my writing efforts, setting a minimum of ten pages per day, finishing a short story every week. Eager to shovel out the bad stuff as quickly as possible, I would write until two or three A.M., collapse for a few hours, go to school, write in the library or the cafeteria between classes, come home, eat, and keep writing.

Having attended college in three different states, my credits were literally all over the map. To make up the difference I began taking twice as many classes as those around me, twenty-one units the first semester alone. I also took full advantage of the other opportunities available at SWC. The drama department under creative director William Virchis staged free one-act plays every Wednesday for students who then critiqued the performance. Most of these were written by professional playwrights, but they were also open to works by local authors, so I wrote a one-act play and dropped it off at the department. Virchis liked it and gave it to his students to perform. It went over well enough for them to stage four more of my one-acts. Rather than focus on the applause at the end, I made a point to note the audience's reaction to every failed characterization or false line, learning where I'd screwed up or was being lazy in the writing.

It was at Southwestern that I met Sandy Richardson, who was also a member of First Baptist. Thin, with dark blond hair above an angular face, she had a laugh that sounded like she'd just heard the best dirty joke ever. When we realized we lived within a few blocks of each other, we began carpooling together. This led to having lunch every day, going to the park for free concerts, stopping by her parents' place to hang out . . . and I slowly realized that we were dating. Sort of. I'd never dated anyone before so I had no idea of the protocol involved or what was required to create a functional relationship. I didn't reach out to hug her unless she did it first, and even after we started formally going out, I never tried to kiss her. Not for lack of desire, I just didn't know how to make that move. So one night she planted herself in front of me and said, "Look, Joe, it's real simple: either you kiss me or I'm going to scream."*

After the Elders gave the relationship their blessings, we talked about getting married after college. Once I had my degree in psychology I could work as a counselor while pursuing my writing and she could continue studying for her master's in social work. I saw us sharing a small house with a corner office where I would work after dinner on science fiction novels and short stories. We would have cats, teaching positions at a respectable college, and ride the years out together.

And maybe that's how my life would have turned out had things gone differently.

When my father's job at ITT ended with the usual allegations of drinking and abusive behavior, I was afraid that this would trigger another move, but by now even he was tired of the constant back-and-forthing. He used his severance pay to build the micro-extruder I'd mentioned back in Texas—which was now suddenly his idea—and set up shop in a grimy storage area, manufacturing dental supplies under the most unsanitary conditions imaginable. In the months that followed he used the excuse of having his own business to travel around the country and "consult" with buyers. We all knew what was really going on. Taking a page from Kazimier's book, my father had a number of women on the hook in various parts of the country, none of whom knew he was married with a family.

To help pay for my college tuition and expenses, I took part-time

---

* My social awkwardness never really faded. I once overheard a woman I knew tell her friend, "This is how you flirt with Joe: you start taking his clothes off, otherwise he hasn't got a goddamned clue."

work at the Chula Vista Public Library, stacking books and *shush-ing*. On school nights the library was a hangout for jocks trying to pick up girls. If they started getting loud or making trouble, my job was to *shush* them and, if necessary, boot them out. Yeah, I was a bouncer at a library. I'm bad that way.

I was six foot three but pencil thin, so playing security to foot-ball jocks was ridiculous on any number of levels. Every time I tossed them out there were threats—"You better watch your back when you leave tonight, asshole!"—but nothing came of it until the night I bounced four guys out for smoking grass in the back while trying to get the attention of several young women who wanted to be left alone.

After the library closed, I walked to an all-night diner to wait for the bus home. As I ordered coffee at the counter I noticed the same four guys sitting in a booth at the back, eye-fucking me and mak-ing remarks. I ignored them and kept an eye on my watch, intent on timing my departure to the arrival of the bus to minimize the pos-sibility of trouble. When the bus was ten minutes away, I went to the restroom; when I came out they were gone. I checked the street in case they were waiting for me outside, but the coast was clear. Relieved, I chugged down the last of the coffee.

As I put down the cup I saw a tiny square piece of blotter paper at the bottom, where it had obviously been dropped by the guys in the back on their way out.

By now I had enough friends in the counterculture to recognize windowpane acid when I saw it.

Windowpane was LSD applied to small pieces of gelatin-sealed blotter paper. One of the cheapest but strongest forms of acid, it was often laced with strychnine to increase the physical effect. I'd done grass a dozen times but had never touched anything stronger, and I had no way to know how much LSD was on the blotter; this could be a mild trip or something that would blow the back of my head off. The latter was the most likely since the user's mood affects the trip and I was as terrified as I'd ever been. If I asked for help, the police would be called, and I was pretty sure they wouldn't believe my story since the guys were gone and I didn't have their names. Lacking proof of my innocence, the cops would arrest me for drug use and that was definitely *not* on my agenda.

I figured I had maybe twenty minutes before the acid kicked in. The bus was due in five. I would be home in fifteen. My sisters would be asleep, my father was away, and my mother had begun using sleeping pills to get through the night; she wouldn't hear an F-16 landing on the roof. I was pretty sure I'd be okay if I could just get home in one piece.

As I walked into the apartment I noticed that my arms were several times longer than they should have been. Everything was brighter, the colors more intense. Suddenly there were four *me*'s in my head, each trying to have a conversation at the same time: a logical voice, a scared voice, a "whoa, look at that" voice, and a very dark, very cold "you're going to die" voice that was *really* making things tough for everybody else. Thanks to the strychnine every muscle in my body was tensing up and spasming, further adding to my panic.

I closed my eyes and tried to concentrate, but that only made matters worse. Thousands of paranoid thoughts began ping-ponging back and forth inside my head like coherent light trying to build up enough strength to fire out of my eyes as a laser. I couldn't sit still. I wanted to tear my skin off except I wasn't sure what I might find inside.

Drawn by the sound of my distress, Theresa emerged to see what was going on. "The hallucination you were having that sent you into extreme panic was that your eyelids were wrapping around your eyes," she said much later. "You were screaming that you couldn't open your eyes, but they were wide open and staring into space. It was pretty scary to watch."

Terrified but not wanting to involve Sandy, I called Cathi and explained the situation as best I could. She couldn't come over but offered to send someone ASAP. Meanwhile, she said it might calm me to read from the Bible. It fell open to 2 Samuel 12:31, describing the massacre by torture of the men, women, and children of Ammon.

"And he brought forth the people that were therein," I said, reading aloud, "and put them under *saws*, and under *harrows* of iron, and under *axes* of iron, and made them *pass through the brick kiln*—"

"*New Testament!*" Cathi yelled over the phone as my voice spiraled up several octaves into hysteria. "New Testament, New Testament, don't go into the Old Testament!"

Every word had a hundred meanings. To read the word *blue* was to know it's a color but also to feel the *intensity* of blue, the context of a clear blue sky, the emotion of a blue day or a blue mood. I would be struck by the richness and varied meanings of one word only to be blindsided by the next as it exploded into my head and changed the *meaning* of the first word, which ricocheted right back again to alter the *intent* of the second word. Every sentence was a kaleidoscope illuminating constructs of context and metaphor so elaborate that I had to stop after each word to absorb it all before moving on to the next.

When Cathi's friend arrived, he used music and questions like "hey, so what does *that* look like to you?" to distract me from what was happening. This was important because if I started to think *I'm on an acid trip*, I'd panic; but if I could be induced into thinking *What actually* is *the inside versus the outside, I've never thought about that before*, then I was okay for a while.

Gray light was coming in the window by the time I felt sufficiently back in my own body to say I could take it from there and collapsed into bed for twelve hours straight. A few days later I was studying in the Southwestern College library when everything started to go all twisty-turny. Realizing that I was having a flash-back, I waited it out behind the bookshelves in the advanced phys-ics section on the assumption that few students at a junior college would venture into that area except at gunpoint.

As awful as the experience was, it helped me understand how the mind can turn on itself during a psychotic break or schizo-phrenic episode. Just one acid trip permanently alters the way the brain works, which is why some artists seek it out to enhance their perception and their work. I cannot say with certainty that my writing improved thereafter because the mechanism I would use to make that determination has also been altered, but I *could* sense a difference. In the past I'd written superficially, but now I began drilling down into ideas and theoretical concepts more deeply, dis-covering new and unexpected layers of meaning.

That part of it was fascinating.

The rest, frankly, sucked.

I'd hoped that having a successful business would mitigate my father's rage, but every time he returned home from his cross-country perambulations, the drunken violence was worse than ever. I think he was mentally comparing my mother to the other women he was seeing, and the beatings became a way to reinforce her alleged stupidity and make him feel better about the affairs.

It was during one of those visits that I realized I had to get out.

From the moment he walked in the door he was ready to back-hand her for the wrong word. He said she was useless and better off dead, that he deserved more than a stinking cow like her. He ordered her to make dinner, but as she started cutting up vegetables he slammed her face into the counter hard enough to draw blood, then knocked her to the floor and began kicking her in the ribs. She screamed, sucking back tears and blood and snot as he grabbed her by the neck and slammed her head into the kitchen table, leaving her dazed and semiconscious.

I was convinced he was going to kill her.

And I snapped.

I'd had as much as I could take. I had to try and stop it, stop *him*, once and for all.

There was only one way to do that. I had to kill him. Right then, right there. Not metaphorically, not by negation, *literally*. Given the extent of his drunken rage there was no question that if I tried to stop him by any means other than killing him, he would kill *both* of us.

I walked toward the bedroom closet where he still kept the rifle he had purchased in Newark, fully aware that after this my life would be different from what I had imagined. A very cold part of my brain was already laying out what to tell the police: I would argue self-defense, or at least her defense. But even with ample proof of violence to back up my statement, they would still file charges of manslaughter or second-degree homicide; either way it would end any hope of having a career as a writer. But in the fury of the moment I was committed. I was going to walk into the kitchen, shoot him as many times as needed to stop him from hitting her anymore, and take the consequences.

I found the long box at the back of the closet, yanked out the rifle, then reached to the top shelf where he kept the cartridge and bullets. They were gone. I tore the closet apart, desperate to find the clip that should have been there. Nothing.

Then I heard the front door open and slam shut again as he went out. Having worked up an appetite brutalizing my mother, he left to get dinner and booze it up for a while. He wouldn't come home again until dawn, just long enough to grab some clothes and leave for the airport and his next "consulting" job.

I have no doubt that I would have killed him if I'd found the clip.

I know it now, I knew it then, and I knew it was insane. I had to get the hell out of there. If I didn't, sooner or later I would *find* that clip, and that would be the end of him *and* me.

I put my case before the Elders, telling them just enough to explain why I needed to leave home without revealing just how *much* of a dangerous nutjob my father was, since that might make them hesitate to take me in. A week later they gave their blessings and assigned me to a household on Mitscher Street in Chula Vista. It wasn't my first choice. Often referred to as the Island of Broken Toys, Mitscher was home to disciplinary cases and guys who had been in trouble with cults or drugs, or were otherwise damaged goods in need of therapy. But by this time most of the Community households were becoming known for blurring the lines between counseling and Christianity.

"Through the last half of the seventies, the ministry kind of took a wrong turn," Tim Pagaard said later. "My dad became connected with a man named Frank Lake, who was a British psychiatrist and minister, who had developed this theory—and this sounds almost obscene—called clinical theology, where he applied Christian ministry to psychotherapy. Our church, and Community in particular, began to more and more address people who had really serious emotional and psychological problems. You basically had people who needed professional help who were getting amateurish help, for all the best motivations."

Ken dubbed this process *inner healing*.

A charismatic leader with full control over the lives of his followers, using barely understood psychoanalytic techniques to drill down into their deepest secrets and insecurities . . . how could this possibly go wrong?

Previously, I'd only seen how the communes worked from the

outside, but now I was living with nearly a dozen people under the biblical authority of the head of the household, Elder Larry Clark, and his wife, Joyce. Whatever money we earned from outside work was turned over to the household in exchange for an allowance of five dollars per week. Those in college could remain there as long as Larry deemed it appropriate, but that could change in a heartbeat.

One of the first things we learned about each other was that I had zero skills for living with actual human beings. I rarely spoke at meals, and after school would go straight to the corner room I shared with two other residents to study or write, only emerging when summoned. Despite the safety of the house, I jumped at the slightest noise and was constantly on alert, sure that something bad was about to happen. The survival instincts I'd developed to cope with my father were now working against me. Over the course of several late-night conversations they slowly drew me out about just how bad things had been. It was the first time I'd talked to anyone about it, and from their reactions I began to think that maybe I *did* belong on the Island of Broken Toys.

My father had been out of town the day I moved into Community, and none of us had any idea when he might return. But I knew that if he heard about my departure over the phone, he would return and take out his anger on my mother, so I told her not to say anything. I wanted to tell him myself, in person; that way whatever he did in response would be done to me and no one else. But she told him on the phone anyway, and when I heard he was racing back in white-hot fury, I told Larry that I had to be there to face him. He and another member of the household volunteered to come along. They felt that their presence might keep the situation from turning violent, and I was in no position to decline their offer.

My father entered in a screaming rage. I'd committed the most unpardonable offense imaginable, removing myself from his control, and that could not be permitted. When he started to get violent, Larry said that if he touched anyone, the police would be called. The warning slowed my father but didn't lessen his fury. He refused to listen to anything we had to say, shouting profanities and declaring that if I walked out the door, I was dead to him.

With nothing left to say, I walked out the door.

What happened next I did not know until 2016, when my sister Theresa sent me an email after reading this section for fact-checking purposes. It took nearly forty years for her to break our family's code of silence to tell me what happened on the other side of the door after I left.

I had imagined there was nothing about my father that could still shock me.

I was wrong.

"Before Charles got there, I was in full-on panic mode," she wrote, "nearly hysterical, because I knew it was going to be really, really bad. Mom's solution was to give me 3 pills, it may have been 4, but I'm not sure. They were probably sleeping pills or heavy duty sedatives. Now as amped up as I was, the pills probably weren't going to knock me out, but as she's giving me those pills, she is telling me that when I wake up in the morning she will probably be dead, she was probably going to have to kill herself. Once she told me about her plan, there was no way I was going to let them knock me out, but they made me very groggy. So I don't recall all that went on while you were there. But after you left all hell broke loose. He dragged Mom into Lorraine's and my bedroom by the hair, she was on her hands and knees. He was definitely going to have an audience. He proceeded to pummel and kick and choke her. Now no doubt, my perspective was tainted from being so groggy, but it had to have been one of the worst, if not the worst beating she ever had and it seemed to go on for hours.

"Now I don't remember if this next part is a memory because I saw it or because she told me about it later, but at some point she broke free and ran to her bedroom and grabbed the rifle from the closet and stuck the dangerous end in her mouth. He told her to go ahead. She did. No ammo.* He grabbed the rifle and proceeded to beat her with the butt of the rifle, in the stomach and sides and back. Later, I demanded that she show me the bruises from the rifle butt beating. The whole of her midsection, front sides and back, was a horrible mass of bruises.

"At some point, I retreated back to my room with the sound of her beating still going on, the pills or exhaustion or mental self-preservation had kicked in. I fell asleep. When I woke it was dead silent, the sun was just coming up. I crept down the hallway from my room to see if Mom was still alive. I heard some noise coming from their bedroom. The door was open a crack and I peeked in. He was raping her and whispering sweet nothings to her, like 'you cocksucker, whore, how could you do this to me?'"

I had naively assumed that by moving out I would become the focus of his rage since I was the one defying him, not my mother or sisters. I thought that knowing he could not keep us in a box forever might even serve as a shot across his bow, moderating his behavior.

Had I known what happened that night I would have come back and killed the son of a bitch, regardless of the consequences.

---

* Now I understood why the clip was missing; my mother had attempted suicide before, so he probably thought she might try something like this.

Blood in the Street

L arry Clark, the head of the Mitscher household, wasn't sold on my dream of becoming a science-fiction writer. Like many evangelicals he considered the genre just a few inches shy of being demonically inspired, the work of C. S. Lewis being the obvious and oft-cited exception. When he suggested that I reconsider my career choices and throw out the SF books I'd brought with me, I argued that I needed them for school. After much discussion he finally relented, but not before reminding me that I was only being allowed to attend college because it served the household's interests to have college graduates, permission that could be revoked at any time. Meanwhile, I was not to write any stories without submitting the ideas to him first to ensure that I didn't write anything of a non-Christian nature.

I acquiesced, but it was consent in name only. I would write what I needed to write, even if that meant doing so secretly.

Such difficulties aside, there was much good to be said about Larry. He was always willing to talk, and in the early days he worked hard to help me fit in.

And then there was the night I awoke to the familiar sound of my father's car roaring up in front of the house.

I dressed quickly and bolted outside as my father throttled the engine up and down. "Get in the car," he yelled drunkenly, "or I'm gonna ram the fucking house!"

He hit the gas and the car lurched forward a few feet. I jumped out of the way and yelled at him to stop. As other members of the household raced outside, we surrounded the car, trying to pen him in, but he kept jumping the car forward, driving us back then slamming on the brakes again, inching closer to the house.

Then I heard the ga-*thump* ga-*thump* ga-*thump* of Larry's slippers on the sidewalk. Roused from bed, half asleep and wrapped in a robe, he asked "What's going on?"

"My dad says he's gonna ram the house unless I get in the car."

He looked at the car, at my dad, at the house, and back at the car again.

"Let him," he said. "We're insured."

"But . . . no, we can't—"

"He won't ram the house," he said, then gestured to the others. "Everybody go on back inside, morning comes early you know."

We looked at one another, hesitated . . . then started back inside.

Larry patted the hood of the car. "Go for it," he said, "we could use a new kitchen."

Shouting obscenities, my father backed the car down the street to build up speed, then floored the pedal. The car roared forward then screeched to a stop at the curb, tires smoking.

"What the hell's wrong with you assholes?" my father yelled. "You *want* me to get killed? Is that it?"

Rather than reply Larry closed the front door and padded down the hall to his bedroom. Ga-*thump*, ga-*thump*, ga-*thump*.

My father remained outside for a while longer, throttling the engine up and down menacingly before finally driving off into the night.

As I lay in the upper bunk of our room, I kept running Larry's actions through my head. My father had come to instill terror. But

Larry beat him because he didn't show even a flicker of fear. *Go for it.*

Never let them see you're afraid, I decided. *Ever.*

Though I had shared my short stories with friends and teachers, I hadn't yet dared to submit them anywhere for publication, fearing the rejections that would inevitably follow. But now that I had a new credo, *Never let them see you're afraid*, I began sending my stories to various magazines, using a friend's address for the submissions. I soon had shoeboxes full of rejection slips from *Analog* and *Fantasy and Science Fiction* as well as *Playboy* and the *Saturday Evening Post*. I even submitted to the *New Yorker* on the theory that if you're going to fail, fail big.

And I was failing *spectacularly.*

As months passed without selling anything I began to wonder if I simply wasn't good enough. I'd finish a short story, read it, tear it up, and start something else, hoping that this time I'd get it right. The stories felt empty because I lacked a firm sense of identity as a man and as a writer. I'd spent my life defining myself as everything my father wasn't, by being his opposite, or by being invisible. But now that I was on my own, who *was* I? What did I want to say as a writer? Did I believe in God or did I simply *want* to believe? Did I belong in Community or was it simply a convenient escape route? I was riddled with doubt, and there weren't any other writers in my life to whom I could turn for advice.

Then I remembered that one of Harlan Ellison's essays contained what he said was his home phone number. I agonized over whether or not to try it. What if it was just a gag or a wrong number? Scarier still, what if it really *was* his phone number? Harlan was legendary for his inability to suffer fools gladly; he could dissect me and hang the innards out to dry before I even knew what happened. He was a gunslinger, I was the town fool. This was *not* the best-case scenario for first contact.

Screw it, I thought, and dialed the number.

The line rang for what seemed like a very long time, then *click!* a voice came on the line. "Yeah, what is it?"

I stammered for a moment, then managed, "Is this . . . I mean, is this Harlan Ellison?"

"Yeah, what do you want?" Only he said it *"yehwhaddoyou-want!"* as in *stop wasting my time*.

I realized I was sweating heavily. "Uhm, Mr. Ellison, my name is Joe Straczynski and—"

"Yeah, and?"

"—and I'm a writer, but the work hasn't been coming out right and it's not selling and I thought you might have some advice." For the record, that is the stupidest question anyone can ask a writer because generic advice given without actually seeing the work is useless. And every writer *knows* it's a stupid question because they get it all the time from idiots like . . . well, like me.

"Your stuff's not selling?" he said.

"That's right."

"And you want my advice, is that it?"

"Yes, sir."

"Okay, then here's my advice: stop writing shit."

"Yes, sir."

"Because if it *wasn't* shit, sooner or later somebody would buy it, right?"

"Right."

"So if your stuff isn't selling, then it's shit. Consequently: stop writing shit."

"Yes sir, Mr. Ellison," I said, my voice thin in my ears. "Thank you."

Click!

I hung up and prayed for the earth to open up and swallow me whole, leaving not a trace behind.[*]

Sandy's birthday was coming up in July, and I wanted to buy her something nice. She had a fondness for Russian lacquer boxes sold by a small shop in La Jolla, but the cheapest was eighty dollars, which was more than I could afford on an allowance of five dollars per week, so I sold some of the books I'd brought with me when I moved into Community. When Larry found out what I'd done, he told me to give him the money because the books and any money that came from their sale belonged to the household, not to me. After confiscating the cash, he imposed a bunch of penalties for doing this in secret, even though he only found out about it because I told everyone else in the household about it because *I didn't know I was doing anything wrong.*

It was profoundly unfair. But on the other hand, the situation pissed me off just enough so that I didn't look away a few days later when everything exploded.

Since some of the participants are still alive, I will only say that when I came back to the household earlier than usual one day, when the house was supposed to be empty, I discovered that Ken Pagaard was using it to facilitate affairs with several women at the church. The indiscretions had grown out of Ken's inner healing ministry, during which he would meet with women alone and encourage them to share their feelings about personal and sexual matters. As the sessions became more intimate, he crossed the line into physical contact, then sexual activity.

I wasn't sure Larry would believe me given our strained rela-

---

[*] Years later, after Harlan and I became friends, I reminded him of this exchange. As it happened, he remembered the conversation very well. "Were you offended by what I said?" he asked. I replied, "Had you been *wrong*, I would have been offended, but you were right."

tionship, so I told the head of the Elders, Emery Fryer, what I'd discovered. I assumed he would intervene once he knew what was going on. Instead he said that *I* was the problem, that I was possessed by a spirit of rebellion to spread false rumors designed to tear down God's servant. He knew that I had come to him instead of Larry because of the bookselling incident, and seized upon this as evidence that I was trying to get back at the church for being disciplined. The only way I could exorcise this rebellious spirit was to cease my defiance, submit to authority, and admit that I'd made the whole thing up.

It had been a long time since I'd felt the Superman symbol burning beneath the skin of my chest, but now it roared back to life. I knew what I'd seen and wasn't about to back down. Truth, Justice, and the American Way were on my side and sooner or later that would make a difference. To encourage me to admit my error he assigned me to clean-up duties, including hand-washing the church floors and toilets. When these tactics failed, I was reminded that not only could the church revoke their blessings for my relationship with Sandy, they could also block my imminent transfer to San Diego State University. I just dug in deeper. Finally came the ultimatum: if I recanted, I could remain in Community with the people I had come to care about. If I refused, I would have to leave under a cloud of spiritual rebelliousness, meaning that every friend at the church, the only friends I *had*, would be told to break off contact with me in order to minimize the risk of contamination. I would lose *everything*.

What the Elders didn't understand was that I'd spent my entire life systematically losing whatever I owned, so the threat held no fear. I think that to get *anywhere* we sometimes have to go back to *nowhere*, that to achieve *anything* we have to be willing to let go of *everything*.

So the next day I left Community with nothing more than

the clothes on my back and two grocery bags of science fiction books.

Friendless and broke, I had no choice but to return home. My father treated this as a personal victory and took every opportunity to ridicule my decision to leave home in the first place. But by moving out I'd demonstrated that he couldn't control me, and that I was capable of making other people aware of his violent tendencies. This triggered his well-honed instinct for self-preservation, and he dialed back the beatings, at least when I was around.

Depressed and angry over everything that had happened, I began taking long, late-night walks around Chula Vista. The night suited my mood. During one of these excursions I decided to check out *The Golden Voyage of Sinbad* playing at the Fiesta Theater. The film was bloated, portentous, and dull, but there wasn't a lot of competition for my attention so I stayed to the end, around ten thirty. On any other night I would have walked up H Street to Broadway to catch the bus home. But it was now over a month since I'd left Community, and I was feeling lonelier than usual, so I decided to walk by First Baptist in case I ran into anyone willing to acknowledge my existence. The closer I got, the more foolish the idea became. Nobody was going to listen to me, it was over. So one block shy of the church I turned left and went up F Street from Fifth Avenue.

Before continuing, I must make clear that I do not believe in the supernatural. I'm not a woo-woo kind of guy. I believe in what I can see, hear, and touch. I believe in science. That being said, quantum mechanics suggests that we perceive time as a straight line only as a matter of perception, that all of those moments are happening simultaneously. *Right now* I'm hanging onto the roof after being thrown off by my mother; *right now* I'm standing in the snow trying to sell chocolate bars; *right now* I'm moving into the Mitscher household; *right now* I'm writing this book. Though I don't have any evidence to back it up, I believe that the veil of perception between those moments is gossamer thin, and sometimes one bleeds over into the other.

Which is the only way to explain the fact that as I started up F Street, an urgent thought bubbled up from somewhere deep inside. The thought was: *Right, let's get this over with.*

I was so intent on trying to figure out what that meant that I failed to notice six guys crossing the street half a block in front of me, coming my way. As the nearest guy came abreast of me I looked up just as he slammed a fist into my face.

They swarmed me as I fell to the ground, kicking and punching as hard as they could. I put my back against a fence, instinctively balling up to protect my internal organs, arms crossed over my head. A light switched on in a house across the street. I yelled for help. A figure came to the window, saw what was going on, then turned off the light and disappeared into the shadows, choosing not to get involved.

The attack escalated. One of them pulled out a belt with a buckle honed to razor sharpness and used it as a whip. A knife flashed and my ear was cut in half. I put my hand in front of my face to block a steel-toed boot and bones snapped. Another whip of the buckle tore through the back of my head. There was blood everywhere. I fought the instinct to flee. They *wanted* me to try and run because as soon as I stood I'd expose my organs and I'd be dead in a minute. I'd learned a long time ago how to bite back the pain and endure, but even with that experience I couldn't take much more. If I moved, they'd kill me; if I stayed, it might take longer but they'd *still* kill me.

A boot caught me hard across the forehead and the world kicked slantwise, then turned to a soft blur. I felt myself blacking out. Then a porch light went on in the house behind me as the owner came outside. Believing someone was trying to break into his car he yelled that he was calling the cops, and the attackers took off.

Lying on the sidewalk, blinking back blood, I drifted in and out of consciousness, barely aware of the wail of sirens and the faces of onlookers, washed in red and blue light, circling the scene now that it was safe. Then: a floating sensation as I was lifted up onto a gurney. IV tubes and compression bandages moved quickly at the edge of my vision.

From far away I heard the voices of the ambulance attendants. "Goddamn, he's lost a lot of blood."

I struggled to move my jaw. It didn't seem to line up properly. "How much blood?" I managed to ask. He looked away and didn't answer. I was shivering, in shock.

The ambulance screamed through the streets as he radioed ahead. "Multiple lacerations, possible concussion, torn right ear, broken bones in right hand, probable internal bleeding . . . Christ, another few minutes and they would've beat him to death."

The world turned soft and insubstantial. I closed my eyes.

He shook my arm. "Don't fall asleep, okay? Stay with me.

"What religion are you?" he asked.

Okay, this is bad, I thought.

"None," I said. It felt like I was talking in my sleep. "Not now."

As they wheeled me into the hospital I thought about the randomness of the attack. *Another few minutes and they would've beat him to death.* And I got angry. I began fighting the anesthetic, the pain, even the nurses trying to hold me down. I'd been through too much to get this far, I would *not* lie down. I had too many stories in me to let this get in the way.

Then a needle found a vein and the world went away.

The next thing I remember is waking up to see a nurse standing over me. "How do you feel?" she asked. "Can you hear me okay?"

I nodded, heavily medicated to cut off the pain. That would come later.

"Can I get you anything?"

"Pen . . . paper."

She stepped down the hall and returned with both. My right hand and arm were in a cast, so I forced the pen between my index and middle fingers and touched it to the notepad, writing a few words that would later become the first line of a short story. A down payment on work yet to come.

As I lay there, the anger that had been building during the last few months spiraled into a black, destructive rage. I'd lost my friends, my communal home, my faith, the woman I thought I would marry, and after spending most of my life getting pounded by bullies, six guys I didn't even know had just tried very hard to *beat me to death*.

Enough, I thought. *Enough. I've had it. I've had it with* all *of you.*

If the only way to get through life was to be stronger and meaner than whatever the world threw at me, then that's what I would do. I wasn't going to let anything stop me from being the writer I believed I was meant to be: not this, not the people who had turned against me, not my father, *no one*.

In that moment, all the gentle things I'd ever believed in or cared about went away.

Only the rage remained.

As soon as I was released from the hospital, I went back to the spot where I'd been attacked. I knew I had to go immediately or I'd be too afraid to go later. They'd tried to wash away the blood, but some had dried into cracks in the cement. Across the street the same figure who had looked out at the scene and done nothing came to the window to peer out again.

Face swollen, one eye shut, arm in a sling, I met his gaze hard. *I saw you.*

He retreated into the shadows.

I went back every night for a week to stand on that spot. Part of it was proving to myself that I wasn't afraid, but on another level I was hoping to run into the guys who had done this. I didn't care if it ended up again as six against one, *this* time they wouldn't catch me by surprise. *This* time I'd be ready, and while I might still go down, I would not go down easy and I would *not* go down alone. But they were gone without a trace.

The police suggested they were aspiring gang members looking for someone to kill as part of an initiation, which was not uncommon in San Diego at that time. A fatal shooting or stabbing would get you in, but beating someone to death showed you were seriously tough and you came in with more respect. More than the violence it was the sheer randomness of it that horrified me the most. They didn't know or care who I was, they just needed a body on the deck that would let them check off one of the items needed to join a gang. It was like some kind of goddamned scavenger hunt. *Get out there and bring back a chicken leg, a basketball pump, a Ping Pong ball, and oh yeah, kill some random guy. Annnnnd . . . go!*

The attack was so violent that some of the local newspapers got involved to try and find the guys responsible. In an editorial published August 3, 1975, the *Chula Vista Star-News* said, "Joseph Straczynsky[*] of Chula Vista is a pretty quiet 21 year old student. He's been on the Dean's List of Southwestern College for years and now he's going to San Diego State. That's why, as his bloody, broken body lay across a gurney in the emergency room of the Bay General Hospital Wednesday night, he couldn't figure out why six hoods beat him so furiously."

---

[*] Yes, they misspelled it.

Rather than being sympathetic, my father was embarrassed by the incident. He'd spent years going out with drinking buddies to beat up "queers," and couldn't process the idea that someone could be attacked without cause. When he demanded to know what I'd done to make them mad, I became too angry to speak and stormed out.

The library where I worked asked me to take a few days off. "Your face looks like five pounds of ground round," one of the librarians said, trying to be gentle.

But the *best* reaction came when I ran into someone from church. "Everybody is saying you got beat up because God's punishing you for spreading lies about Ken Pagaard."

It was as if the universe decided to take a year of my life and kick the shit out of me, emotionally, spiritually, and literally. I went into a downward spiral: beyond anger, beyond reason. I couldn't eat or sleep. If anyone even *looked* at me wrong, I would shake with rage, going from calm to fury in a second. I was already prone to taking long midnight walks around Chula Vista, but now I ranged farther afield, going into the worst parts of downtown San Diego when it was still the tenderloin district, home to addicts, drunks, and muggers. I think I was *looking* for trouble, hoping somebody would take a swing at me so I could come back with everything I had at someone who meant to hurt me.

Sometimes I would stay out all night and greet the dawn sitting at a bus stop by Horton Plaza as the drug dealers, hookers, and homeless faded into the shadows, replaced by secretaries, businessmen, students, and others on their way to work. It was as though there were two different worlds, two San Diegos switching places in front of me. *There's a story here*, I thought, but it would take decades before I figured it out.

Lacking a clear target for my rage, I turned on anyone unlucky enough to come within range. Eventually I realized that I was reacting the way my father would, acting out against people who had nothing to do with what happened. So I turned my anger inward, going radio silent rather than inflict civilian casualties. But it was still there, tearing me apart from the inside. I had to do *something* with it or lose my mind.

I decided that if I couldn't fight my way out of it, then I'd write my way out, and funneled my rage into the work. Until that moment I'd *played* with the writing, I'd *enjoyed* the writing, but never used it as a way to express what I was feeling: my hopes for the future, my anger at my past, and my doubts about the present. Emotion was the final ingredient that had been lacking in my work, *that's* why it was shit. Having never been able to adequately express my emotions, my stories were cool to the touch, more about the plot and the gimmick than what the characters felt. But now my emotions were pouring out, with rage at the head of the line, and I was totally fine with that. A writer can be motivated as much by fury as by love, as much by anger as affection, as long as there's *something* driving him to tell *this* story at *this* time about *this* character. And rage I had in abundance.

I continued to accumulate rejection letters, but now that there was more meat to the stories I started receiving personal notes from editors suggesting changes, or saying that while the story didn't fit their current needs I should come back to them again with something else. It was *just* enough to keep me at the typewriter while I burned through everything that was going on in my life.

Sooner or later, things *had* to get better.

Right?

CHAPTER 17

When the Light at the End of the Tunnel Isn't a Train (For a Change)

'd intended to get my bachelor's in psychology by twenty-one, but I'd fallen way behind due to the difficulties in transferring credits between schools, my limited funds, and the crater left in my life by recent events. So I once again began taking ridiculously heavy course loads. Students weren't allowed to take more than twenty units during regular registration at San Diego State University, so I resorted to crashing classes and asking the instructor to add me to his roster à la carte. That way no one in administration would know what I was up to until I was already doing it. Where most students took twelve to fifteen units per semester, I took twenty-one hard-core academic classes my first semester, hit twenty-seven credits in the second semester, then dropped to twenty-two in my third semester when an academic adviser discovered what I was doing and told me to knock it off.

One of my classes was a writing workshop taught by Richard E. Kim, one of the few members of the creative writing department with actual published novels to his credit, as well as a Guggenheim Fellowship and a Fulbright Award. Knowing that a working writer would be critiquing my work, I ratcheted up my writing regimen, turning in a new story every week.

One day, after dropping off my latest salvo for his review, Kim said, "Thanks," then added as I turned to leave, "you're a real word machine."

I was halfway down the hall when I stopped, turned, and walked back to find him sitting at his desk, smiling.

"Was I just insulted?" I asked.

The smile broadened. "That you can recognize that means there's still hope for you."

I got the message: better to take the time to write one good story than three adequate ones.

The only student in Kim's class who could go toe-to-toe with me on the volume of material was Mark Orwoll. Mark was really good, and most classes turned into a shoot-out between us. He'd write something amazing, which challenged me to write something even *more* amazing, in turn forcing him to work even harder. He was so talented that by all rights I should've been conspiring to drop arsenic in his water, but I was excited to have someone to push against. Besides, it was impossible not to like Mark. Where I was quiet, mumble-mouthed, and skinny, he was bigger than life, gregarious, and classically handsome. As our fierce competition turned into friendship, he began dragging me to parties and bars. Determined to Hemingway-up my life, he was horrified to discover I didn't drink, and more horrified still when he learned that I didn't drive because of depth perception issues. I'm fine when traveling on foot, but in a car going at speed I can't tell if I'm two or two and a *half* car lengths behind the vehicle in front of me, which is crucial if one doesn't want to end up in the backseat of a stranger's car.

"This whole depth perception thing is a crock," he said. "You just haven't had the right teacher." So we drove to a secluded part of town where he put me behind the wheel. By the end he was as pale, and terrified, and neither of us ever tried it again.*

---

* Mark went on to become the international editor at *Travel + Leisure* magazine,

My other liabilities—shyness and a pronounced lack of social skills—came back to haunt me when my instructor in science fiction writing, Elizabeth Chater, assigned us to write a short story that we would read aloud to the class. Terrified by the prospect of public speaking, I wrote the shortest short story I've ever written, just five pages. If I could've just typed a period on the page and called the story "Dot," I would've done it.

When my turn came, I stood before the class, cheeks flushed and sweating profusely, and began to read. I stumbled over my words, reading faster to try and make up for my incoherence, which only made things worse. Someone in the back called out *Louder!* I kept trying to push down the fear only to become even more incomprehensible.

Halfway through the reading, Mrs. Chater put her hand on my arm. "It's okay," she said, putting me out of my misery, "that'll do. You can sit down."

I was humiliated and angry at myself. There were things I wanted to do with my life that could only happen if I was willing to do what scared me. I'd returned to the street where I was attacked because otherwise the fear would have had power over me. This was no different.

So that summer I signed on with the university's orientation counseling program, which put incoming students through a grueling faux registration and counseled them about their academic choices. At the end of the day the students would break into groups of twenty or thirty and each of us would take our group on a walking tour of the campus. I was so terrified at the prospect of talking to large groups of strangers that for the first three weeks I threw up almost every morning. But you can only throw up for so long; after a while you run out of ammunition. By week four I was able to

---

spending twenty-nine years on their masthead, the longest in the magazine's fifty-year history.

speak in public well enough that the fear no longer had power over me. I was still nervous in front of groups, and remain so to this day, but that's okay; I didn't have to do it *perfectly*, I just had to *do* it.

By fall '76 I had burned through enough classes to qualify for my bachelor's in psychology, but the achievement felt anticlimactic since the term would end in November and there wouldn't be a graduation ceremony. Worse still, I was dead broke. I hadn't made a single sale for money, and my father took full advantage of this to grind down my ambitions of a writing career.

If you were going to sell something, you'd have done it by now.

Do you want to end up starving out on the street, begging for money?

When are you going to stop this nonsense and focus on getting a real job?

And the ever-popular *You're just another kid from the streets. Who the hell do you think you are, Hemingway?*

It was a valid question. Who the hell *did* I think I was? *Was* I kidding myself?

Worse still, my father insisted that I get a master's degree once I knocked down the BA so he could show off to relatives. But the time, energy, and money necessary to get a master's would preclude me from doing the volume of writing necessary to become good at it. A master's in psychology was of limited value in any event; to make the effort worthwhile I'd have to go into the PhD program, for a total of five years where my writing would have to be done piecemeal if at all.

By now my student loans and library work had allowed me to move into a tiny apartment on Cherokee Avenue in El Cajon, but my sisters were still living with my father. If I refused to get another degree it would raise the temperature in ways that could rebound badly onto them. I had to figure out a way to stall long enough for *something* to happen with the writing.

Then a solution hit me. My father wanted me to get a second degree, but did it have to be a master's? Doubling up on my course load had given me nearly enough credits for a second BA in sociology, philosophy, or literature. While I liked the idea of a degree in philosophy, it would be easier to justify a second bachelor's in an allied field. But even if I managed to sell him on the idea, it would provide only a brief reprieve; the coursework needed for a second BA could easily be covered during the next semester, after which I'd be facing the same dilemma all over again.

I don't know what I thought would happen in the next six months that hadn't happened in the previous four years, but I had to try, and with some effort convinced my father to sign off on a BA in sociology. Shortly afterward, I got a message from Bill Virchis at Southwestern College asking me to stop by his office. I assumed he wanted to know if I had any more one-act plays that would, like the rest, be produced for free.

I was wrong. He wanted to *hire* me to write a play.

For several weeks each summer, Southwestern College produced a full-length children's play for an audience of kids bussed in from schools across San Diego County. This year, Bill wanted to mount a version of *Snow White* that would be evocative of the Disney movie while telling a funnier and more hip story, and would I write the play on commission?

I asked what the gig paid.

He shrugged a smile. "Joe, I got a hundred bucks in the budget. That's it."

One hundred dollars was 100 percent more than I'd made on anything I'd written before, so I responded with an enthusiastic "Yes!" As we shook hands I realized I was shaking. At last somebody was actually going to *pay* me to write something! A week earlier I'd despaired that in twenty-two years nothing like this had ever happened. But what had never happened before *had just happened*! Holy shit!

As I walked back across the chilly, deserted campus, I passed a bulletin board where a flyer announced that Israeli psychic Uri Geller would be performing there in a few nights. I'd heard about Geller's alleged ability to bend spoons with his mind and was curious to check it out. It would be a great way to celebrate my very first assignment. Best of all, I still had a Southwestern ID that would let me get in free.

Given the vicissitudes of bus schedules, I arrived early for his performance on a wet October night. Rather than stand out in the rain for an hour I managed to talk my way into the theater, where I overheard a publicist tell a reporter with a local radio station that Geller would be available for an informal press conference and interviews after the show.

Press conference? Interviews?

Waitaminnit . . . didn't people get *paid* to write that stuff?

Summoning my courage, I introduced myself to the publicist as a freelance reporter with the *San Diego Reader*, a free weekly newspaper that catered to the college crowd, and asked if I could interview Mr. Geller. I was sure she would see through the lie at once but with the rest of the audience waiting to be let in she was sufficiently distracted that she didn't ask to see my credentials. "Come around back after the show," she said, "and he'll give you twenty minutes."

After the performance, which did little to convince me of his abilities, I went backstage and interviewed Geller, jotting down his answers on the back of the program before hurrying home to write up a five-page article.

The next day I visited the offices of the *San Diego Reader* in hopes of talking to an editor, but the receptionist wouldn't let me past the front door. She told me to leave the article with her and one of the editors would get back to me. I dropped the manila envelope on a pile of mail and headed home, figuring that was the end of it.

They called the next day to buy the article for the princely sum of fifteen dollars. But the amount was irrelevant. After years spent fruitlessly trying to sell my work, I had now been paid as a writer twice in a two-week period. I didn't cash the check from the *Reader* for months because I needed to hold that rectangular validation in my hand for a while.

This means something, I thought, staring at the check. *This is where it starts.*

It occurred to me that if I could turn my skills to journalism, I might be able to earn a living while working on my prose. Unfortunately, all my training to this point had been in fiction and live theater; I lacked the training, the experience, or the ego to think I could go from a standing start to working full-time as a journalist. I had a *lot* to learn.

But if Clark Kent could become a reporter, then by god so could I.

So get started, I told myself. *You know what you want, you have the momentum, go and get it.*

Great, I thought. *How?*

A few weeks later, at the start of the spring '77 semester, the weekly humor columnist for the *Daily Aztec*, the official newspaper of San Diego State University, announced in print that he was quitting on the grounds that he wasn't funny enough, an opinion few students would have disputed. And one columnist walking *out* the door meant there was room for another columnist to walk *in*.

You wanted to learn how to write for newspapers, well, here's your chance.

I skipped class, commandeered a library typewriter, and banged out three columns. It was typical college humor: sophomoric, simplistic, and self-indulgent, but it would have to do. Eager to beat out any competitors, I ran to the *Daily Aztec* offices—crowded and loud with the clatter of typewriters, telephones, and chatter—and introduced myself to entertainment editor David Hasemyer. When I said I wanted the humor column, he stared at me like something unpleasant he'd just found on the bottom of his shoe. It was an understandable reaction given that I was trying to leapfrog the meritocracy. Reporters start at the bottom of the ladder by writing individual articles; only after proving themselves over time are they given the prestige of a weekly column. But he reluctantly agreed to read the columns then booted me out the door.

Several days later he called me in for a meeting. As expected, others were angling for the job, but he was inclined to give me the Friday humor column. He said he liked my style, which was surprising because I didn't know I had one.

"Have you ever written anything on a weekly schedule?" he asked.

When I said no, his lips pursed sourly, worried that I'd flame out after one or two installments and they'd have to find somebody else. I assured him that hitting deadlines wouldn't be a problem. He was still dubious but agreed to give me a shot and asked how I wanted my credit to appear. For the *Reader* article I'd used J. M. Straczynski, but that felt too anonymous, as though I were still hiding. Joe Straczynski looked lopsided, a whisper of a first name ambushed by a last name big enough to scare a cat, and Joseph Straczynski was too hard to say. So I went with J. Michael Straczynski: a single letter, followed by a friendly two-syllable name that would give readers a moment to work up their courage for the final assault on that Mount Everest of a three-syllable last name.

My column, "A View from the Rabbit Hole," premiered in the *Daily Aztec* on February 11, 1977, and I hit every goddamned deadline for as long as I had it. Dave was thrilled to receive each new installment, not so much for the quality of the writing, which was fairly dreadful, but because many of his other writers tended to flake out, forcing him to fill the gap with stories from wire services. This taught me the most important lesson about being a writer: get the damned thing done well enough to print and turn it in on time, because others won't. So when Dave once again found himself stuck after another reporter failed to deliver, I offered to fill the hole with an updated version of Ambrose Bierce's "The Devil's Diction-ary" to be called "A Modern Cynic's Dictionary." He agreed, and I pounded out the piece in about twenty minutes. It went over sur-prisingly well and became my second weekly column.

Then Dave called to say that a writer who was supposed to re-view a local concert had fallen ill, and could I go in his place and write the review?

I said I'd love to but didn't have tickets to the show and couldn't afford to buy them.

"You don't have to buy a ticket," he said. "Reviewers *never* pay for tickets. The guys who review plays, books, movies, and music for the *Aztec* get *all* their stuff free, it's just that half of them never turn in their fucking reviews."

It took me several seconds to process this information. I'd as-sumed that reviewers paid for everything so they wouldn't be be-holden to the subject of their critiques. The idea that they could go to plays and shows and get books for *free* had never occurred to me.

When I broke out of my paralysis, I said, rather loudly, *"Why the hell didn't someone tell me about this before?"*

"I thought you knew."*

I immediately began writing reviews of movies, books, and plays.

---

* After graduating from SDSU, Dave Hasemyer would go on to a stellar career as a journalist, eventually winning a Pulitzer Prize for his reporting on climate change.

Access to every theater in San Diego proved particularly helpful to my own writing. I learned about dramatic structure from the Old Globe's Shakespeare festival; understood the value of silence via Harold Pinter; and developed a passion for nonlinear, modernist theater from Ibsen and Beckett.

With no one to stop me, and dozens of column inches in need of filling, I expanded my reach into editorials and feature articles, as well as profiles of local actors and other celebrities. Writing so much so quickly helped me burn through the crap in my system and taught me how to produce on demand. I'd roll into the *Daily Aztec* offices around noon, find out what holes needed filling, grab a typewriter, shut out the noise, and just fly. I learned how to write anywhere under any conditions. Some weeks I had an article or column in every issue of the *Daily Aztec*, prompting some to nickname it *The Daily Joe*.

This exposure allowed me to experience what it was like to be popular, or at least visible, as students and professors recognized me on campus or wrote letters to the editor to praise (or roundly condemn) something I'd written. Then there was the afternoon a stunningly beautiful red-haired woman named Liz entered the male-dominated, sweaty, testosterone-filled offices of the *Daily Aztec*. All work stopped as she said, "I'm trying to find someone."

Every male in that room prayed to whatever deity he worshipped that she was looking for him.

"J. Michael Stra—Icantpronounceit."

The receptionist pointed to my desk and the woman walked toward me, oblivious to the staffers staring daggers in my direction. Without introduction or preamble, she asked, "Have you ever seen *The Rocky Horror Picture Show*?"

I allowed as how I hadn't.

"Good," she said, "because I love your work, I love the way you think, and I'm taking you on a date. There's a midnight showing

Friday night at the Strand Theatre in Ocean Beach. Meet me there at eleven thirty."

Oddly enough, this was how most of my dates happened since I was usually far too shy to ask women out. I justified it as being chivalrous and respectful to avoid admitting that I was still bricked up behind the wall of my inability to form normal relationships. I didn't know how to ask a woman out without looking ridiculous, and on those rare occasions when I managed to gird up my loins enough to make the attempt, instead of just saying *hey, you want to go out sometime?* I'd spend twenty minutes laying out all the practical, logical, non-emotional reasons why someone should go out with me before getting to the actual question, as if I was in a job interview. For some women this was justifiably off-putting; others found it charming or, even more horrifically, thought it was cute.

The issues that made it hard for me to seek out a relationship also made it difficult to sustain one. When they wanted things to go deeper, I couldn't get there. I was desperate to find those deep emotions and share them with someone else, but they weren't anyplace where I could reach. One of Zeno's paradoxes suggests that there's an infinite number of points between you and your destination, and since you can't transverse infinity, you can never actually get anywhere.* No matter how fast or how long I ran toward them, my emotions were always just on the other side of an infinite horizon.

So I went where and when invited, and the night I showed up for *The Rocky Horror Picture Show*, Liz was already in line, wearing a heavy fringed coat over a dress. It was a balmy evening, so the coat seemed an odd choice, but this was my first introduction to the fetish-and-stockings world of *Rocky Horror* fans, so it took

---

* For this reason Zeno's Greek philosopher peers considered him a troublemaker, and a pain in the ass.

me a while to cycle through several levels of social anxiety before I thought to ask her about it.

"Oh, this?" she said. "I like to wear it because I cut out the bottoms of the pockets, see?" She pushed her hands through the coat pockets to show them coming through to the inside. "This way I can diddle myself during the movie."

During the on-and-off-again relationship that followed, Liz took great pleasure in my shyness, naiveté, and lack of experience. One night we were sharing a banana split at a Farrell's Ice Cream Parlour when a woman walked past our table to the restroom. After she was out of earshot, Liz nodded in her direction and said, "Nice tits."

"I didn't know women noticed that about other women," I said.

She smiled. "I also like women."

"That's good," I said as the meaning flew past me, "I mean, that you don't feel competitive with other women and—"

She leaned across the table, her eyes saying *Idiot* before she even got to the words. "No, I'm *saying* I like *women*, too."

And it *still* took thirty seconds before I got there. "Oh . . . OH!"

On another night she invited me to a party with some of her friends in Imperial Beach. When we arrived, I noticed that there were mattresses on the floor of all five bedrooms. *Must be still moving in*, I thought.

Later, as we were chatting in the living room, I noticed something amiss out of the corner of my eye and leaned in to whisper to Liz. "Okay, don't panic, but that little guy in the corner just took off all his clothes."

"Of course he did," she said. "Oh darling, don't you know? This is an orgy."

My social anxiety skyrocketed up through the middle of my head in a display of fireworks that could be seen from space. She laughed at the look of unbridled terror in my eyes and took me by the arm. "It's okay, we don't have to stay," she said.

And what I *thought* she whispered into my ear on the way out was, "I want to get you home as fast as I can so I can radish you."

I ran that sentence through my head over and over as we drove back to her place. Radish me? *Radish?* What the hell did *that* mean? Maybe it didn't mean anything, but then I hadn't known about the orgy either.

"You okay?" she asked.

And in a tumble of words: "You told me you wanted to get me home and radish me and I don't know what that means and maybe that means shoving a radish up my ass or it's code for something else and I don't know the code because I don't hang out in the same crowd as you and I just wanna know what you're gonna do to me when we get back and—"

By now she was laughing so hard that she nearly drove off the road and had to pull over. Barely able to speak, tears of laughter rolling down her cheeks, she said, "Not radish, ravish! *Ravish!*"

A few weeks later she left to visit relatives out of state, and we lost track of each other for several months, both busy with our own lives. Then one afternoon as I was leaving campus, heading to the bus stop, I heard a car honk at me. I turned as she roared up to the curb and waved. "Hi, how are you?" she asked.

"Good," I said.

"What're you doing?"

"Heading home. Gotta get some writing done."

"No, no, no," she said, "you're *supposed* to say you've just run into a friend you haven't seen in far too long and you're going to get in the car, drive to my place, and spend the rest of the day making love to a beautiful redhead who thinks you're terribly sexy."

I looked up to see the bus approaching, then back at Liz. I could either spend the day frolicking with a beautiful redhead, or go home and pound on a typewriter.

Redhead or typewriter. Frolicking or writing.

That was the moment I knew I *had* to be a writer, because otherwise I was out of my goddamned mind.

"I wish I could," I said, shaking my head. "Can't, gotta write."*

"Okay, sweetie, love you!" Then she put the car in gear and roared off down College Avenue.

I never saw her again.

Today we're friends on Facebook.

Go figure.

On August 19, 1977, I received my bachelor of arts in sociology, which, added to my BA in psychology, qualified me to be unemployed in two directions at the same time. But by now I'd written scores of articles for the *Daily Aztec* and felt I was at last ready to leave school to try writing full-time for local newspapers and magazines. Besides, I'd technically fulfilled my part of the bargain with my father by getting a second degree. It was time to go.

When I told him my decision, he bristled angrily. "Who the fuck do you think you are?" he yelled. "You're nobody. Nobodies don't become writers. You think you're *special* or something? Bullshit. You're just too goddamn big for your britches. All this writing shit and what've you got to show for it? A dollar here, a dollar there. You think you're gonna make a living at this? Horseshit. I don't care if you get a master's in psychology, sociology, or any other goddamn thing, but you're gonna get one. Any loser can get a bachelor's. I want to make sure everybody knows that I pushed you to get a master's."

It was my high school graduation all over again. It didn't matter what *I* wanted, or if the degree would actually be of assistance. He just wanted to be able to tell everyone that *he* made this happen, this was *his* accomplishment.

---

* And if there was a T-shirt representing my life, that's what it would say.

"You're going to get a master's," he said, "because if you *don't*, then I have to ask why I should support your sisters going to college, since they're even stupider than you are. And if your mother can't convince you to do what I tell you, well, then she's gonna have to pay the price."

Success by proxy wasn't his only reason for trying to force me to get a master's. I was twenty-three and living on my own, and he was determined to keep me from breaking away from his influence any further. Forcing me to stick around for a useless degree was his last shot at keeping me answerable to him; we both knew he wouldn't contribute a dime to my education, so I'd have to take out more loans, going further into debt, a weakness he would exploit later. *You want help to pay off those loans? Then do what I say.*

I wanted to tell him to fuck off, but I couldn't risk hurting my sisters' chance to go to college, so I enrolled in the master's program in mass communications and wrote freelance articles when I had the time, which wasn't often.

Though I'd made an art form of concealing my emotions, there was still a very dark and dangerous rage in me left over from the God Thing, the Losing All My Friends Thing, and the Nearly Getting Beaten to Death Thing; the added prospect of having the next two years of my life taken hostage was more than I could bear. I tried to exorcise the anger while I was writing but failed miserably. When journalists finish an article, they type *-30-* at the bottom of the page to signify the end of the copy. I might as well have substituted *That'll show you* at the end because every article I wrote was a punch in the face of one of the people who had hurt me. Rather than taking pleasure by seeing my work in print, it was all subsumed by anger.

I was savvy enough to know this was poisoning the work, but too lost to figure out how to stop it. Since I was stuck at SDSU for the foreseeable future, I looked for classes that would feed the writing part of my brain and keep me from going insane, and found two scriptwriting courses being taught that semester by distinguished visiting lecturer Norman Corwin. Considered a writer's writer, Norman was the most respected radio drama writer of the 1940s, bigger than Orson Welles and Arch Oboler combined. The press proclaimed him "the poet laureate of radio," and actors like Humphrey Bogart, Rita Hayworth, Elsa Lanchester, Walter Huston, Groucho Marx, and Charles Laughton lined up to be in his radio plays. When he was commissioned to write a radio drama to celebrate the German surrender on V-E Day, the program was broadcast on all three networks, the first and only time this happened.

I was frantic to take his classes, but they were restricted to students majoring in telecommunications and film (TCF). Registering for restricted classes meant physically walking into the department office where the receptionist would check your name against their list of majors. If you were on the list, they'd give you the corresponding computer control card; once you had your cards, you had your classes. In Norman's case, not only were his classes restricted to TCF majors, even they could take only one of his classes, not both, *and* students had to submit a writing sample for his review. I had a good sample—a one-act play called *Death in Stasis*—but there was no way to get the cards during registration.

Unless I showed up early. *Real* early.

Like the night *before* registration, when the cleaning crews had the department door open. In theory, one could slip inside, find the packets of control cards, remove two, put everything back, and get the hell out before being discovered by campus security. The writing sample could then be dropped off at Corwin's office along with the rest of the submissions because nobody would be checking the pile against the list of majors.

Not that I would ever actually *do* such a thing, of course.

I have no idea how those cards found their way into my hands.

I was foolish to think I could get away with it, but I convinced myself that the university bureaucracy was so screwed up that no one in authority would notice a name on the roster that shouldn't be there. On the first day of class I took a seat in the back of the room, trying not to draw attention.

Then a tall, elegant figure with leonine gray hair appeared in the door.

"Is there a Joe Straczynski here?" he said.

Crap, I thought. *Crap, crap, crap, crap!*

I held up my hand.

"Can I see you in the hall for a moment?"

Crap!

I stepped outside and he closed the door, regarding me with serene, curious eyes. "I understand from the TCF Department that you're not actually supposed to be here," he said.

"Technically, yes, that's correct."

"I further understand that not only are you not supposed to be in *this* class, you somehow managed to get into *both* classes, even though not even TCF majors are allowed to do that."

"Yes, sir."

"How?"

As I described my nighttime raid on the TCF office I could see him fighting a smile. He seemed pleased and a little flattered that I'd gone through so much effort.

"Breaking and entering, well, that's quite an achievement," he said. "May I inquire why you would do all this?"

"I know who you are, sir. I've read your work. I want to learn from you."

He gazed absently at the floor for a moment then folded his arms and looked up at me. "You should know, they want you gone. Today. Right now."

"I understand."

"I'm not just talking about this class. They would very much like to kick you out of the university."

I nodded but said nothing.

"Here's the thing, though," he said. "I read your play, and it's really quite good. Far better than the samples provided by the other students. So I was wondering if you could stay on, not specifically as a teacher's assistant, just to help me out a bit. Perhaps the others can learn from you while you're learning from me."

It took a second before I realized what he was saying. "So . . . I can stay?"

He smiled and nodded. "Yes."

"In *both* classes?"

The smile broadened. "Both classes. I imagine the head of the department will be a bit miffed with me, but I think it would be best for everyone if you remained here."

After class, Norman walked me to the office of the department head—a gruff, garrulous, blustery sort of fellow—who argued loudly against letting me stay. Norman simply nodded and kept saying, very softly, but very firmly, "I understand, but I want him to stay so he's staying."

Over the next five months Norman taught me more about writing than I had learned in the previous decade. He could do things with words that I'm *still* trying to figure out. In the past I'd fired wildly at the dictionary rather than taking the time to pick my targets; Norman taught me how to gauge sound, meaning, and rhythm for maximum effect. He showed me the supple elegance of language, how to think carefully and strike with precision.

It was in one of his classes that I met Kathryn Drennan, a talented writer and one of the top students in the TCF department. She was tall, slender, and ramrod-straight, with long dark hair and a brilliant, steel-trap mind. I wanted to ask her out on several occasions but ran into my usual shortcomings. It didn't help that at the end of each class she would jet out the door, striding across campus with surprising speed.

I never mentioned my attraction to Norman, but he apparently figured it out and decided it was time to start moving things along.

I'll let Kathryn tell this part of it.

"When Norman arrived at the classroom [one day], he called me up to his desk, said he had forgotten a film canister in his car, handed me his car keys, and asked me if I would go get the film so he could show it in class that day. I worked part-time in the TCF office and one of my jobs was to assist distinguished visiting lecturers with small errands like this. Norman then called you up to the desk and asked you to accompany me and carry the heavy film canister. I didn't think anything of this other than if Norman thinks this is a two-person job, then that's fine with me, and off we went.

"So I was rather puzzled when you spent the whole trip to Norman's car, and back again, basically reciting your résumé to me.* It took me a while to realize you might be working up to eventually asking me out. I thought it was all rather charming.† Later on, when Norman made an obvious point of speaking well of you to me while I was helping him with paperwork in his TCF office, I thought, 'Okay, if Joe does ask me out I will say yes.' But though we talked many times before and after class you didn't actually ask me out until near the end of the semester,‡ and it was to some evening event, a play, as I remember. This was a problem, because you assumed I had a car, I assumed you had a car, and neither of us did.§ Hilarity ensued, but not a date, and as I was about to leave for a summer visit home there was no time to make plans for a non-

---

* Applying for the job.
† Told you.
‡ Dork.
§ Big dork.

car-related date. So you gave me your phone number and suggested maybe I could call you when I returned for the fall semester. I did, and we finally went on that first date: lunch, at one of the campus restaurants."

Kathryn shared my love of science fiction, did volunteer work with KPBS-FM, SDSU's affiliated radio station, and would later host her own show, *Science Fiction Omnibus*, on the station's sub-channel for the blind, KPBS-FM/SCA. This, along with Norman's work, led me to consider writing radio drama. The subchannel was eager for original material so I submitted a half-hour radio play about a warrior losing his sight on the eve of his last battle. The station assigned it to a producer/director who was, himself, totally blind. He ran the audio board by touch and never commented on the subject of the drama until the last day of mixing. As we listened to the part where the character describes how it felt and what he saw as his sight finally failed, the producer said, quietly, "That's exactly what it was like for me."

Norman was very proud of the program, and earning his regard meant a great deal to me. In one of his essays, Harlan Ellison declared that "writing is a holy chore," but it wasn't until meeting Norman that I encountered one of the high priests of this particular religion. Harlan and Rod Serling excited me, but Norman *humbled* me, and that's exactly what I needed at that moment. He also *fixed* me, not by instruction or cajoling but by example.

At the height of the 1950s red scare, a fascist little rag called *Red Channels*, published by the owner of a supermarket chain, decided that Norman was a little pink based on a series of radio dramas he'd written during World War II designed to strengthen our alliance with the Soviet Union against the Nazis. The publisher decided that Norman had done *too* good a job and was therefore almost certainly a Communist, despite the fact that the Soviets were our allies at the time and that the dramas had been commissioned in part *by our own government*.

Norman was never formally blacklisted or asked to appear before the House Committee on Un-American Activities, but being named by *Red Channels* killed his career in radio. At the exact moment when his writing was at its greatest strength, every door was suddenly closed. When he spoke of those days, which was rare, he said, "Radio had been like this great horse that had carried me very far, very fast, and was suddenly shot out from under me."

If I'd been in his position, I never would've gotten over the rage. But Norman never showed a flicker of bitterness, anger, or resentment over what happened. There was simply no acrimony to be found in him, and that shamed me. I realized that if he could go through so much and come out the other side with that degree of gentleness and equanimity of spirit, what right did *I* have to complain about *any*damnthing?

He showed me that words can do more than tell stories, they can heal, and that as long as you live inside the dignity of what you write, no one can take away that which matters most. Those who hate you can kill you, but they cannot destroy you or the ideals that matter to you. To be a *decent* writer you had to give yourself over to the power of words and a love of storytelling. To be a *Norman Corwin*-level writer you couldn't look at it as a career or a way to get famous; you were entering a monastery to dedicate yourself to a lifetime of writing as prayer.

Having lost my religion, I needed something to believe in, and Norman provided it. I walked out of his classes not just a better writer but a better person, calmer and stronger, an eager novitiate in a church made up of words in place of stone and stained glass. The anger was gone, and I could hear more clearly than ever the voice at the back of my head that told stories. No longer would the right words be drowned out by the background noise of my unsettled heart.

In later years, Norman and I became friends, though I could never quite bring myself to call him by his first name. He was Mr. Corwin, period. He didn't correct it. I think he wanted to see how far I would carry this. Finally, after *ten years* of "Mr. Corwin," he pulled me aside and said, "It's okay, Joe, you can call me Norman."

Norman passed away in November 2011 at the age of 101, and he had been writing right up to the end. There will never be another like him, and there is not a day that I don't think of him and miss him.

I've always known I didn't want to have children. Given my upbringing it's pretty obvious that my parenting skills are zero. But conventional birth control methods are never 100 percent effective 100 percent of the time, and I couldn't justify rolling the dice now that I was in an ongoing relationship with Kathryn. Taking responsibility for my choices meant that vasectomy was the only option that made permanent sense.

Since I was still in my early twenties the Planned Parenthood staff urged me to reconsider my decision. Unlike contemporary procedures, which leave room for reconsideration, vasectomies at that time were irreversible. Doctors didn't just cut the vas deferens, they took out a chunk to ensure it could never grow back together, so most men only underwent the procedure late in life, after having all the kids they wanted. But I was determined to see it through. It was the responsible, ethical choice. And there was one ancillary benefit. If my sisters had kids, those children would bear the father's last name. It was only through me that any kids in our branch of the family would bear the Straczynski name. Taking steps to prevent that from happening meant killing my father's name and, in a way, killing him.

"Just a heads-up," the doctor said as he prepped for the surgery, "after the incision we pull the vas deferens out so we can cut it.

That's the hardest part. Just remember: it's not pain, it just feels like pain."

Last stand for the Last Son of Krypton.

Up yours, Dad, I thought as the cutting began. *I win.*

It's not pain, it just feels like pain.

CHAPTER 18

The Big Con

In May 1978 my step-grandfather Walter Androsik abruptly died at the age of seventy. My father muttered something about natural causes but turned vague when pressed for details. My aunt implied that he had taken his own life, but again there were no details. The wagons had circled; something was going on.

My uncle Ted's brother Frank said later that "Walter's death was rather quick. I was just told that he died. He was fine one week, then gone."

It was not until after Sophia died many years later that my mother finally told *me* what my grandmother had told *her* about what happened the day Walter passed away.* After spending the day grocery shopping for the least-green meat available, she returned home to find Walter standing precariously on a chair, a rope around his neck. Sophia said he revealed for the first time that during World War II he had collaborated with the Nazis, and that recent events had led him to believe that his past was about to catch up with him, and he might soon be arrested.

---

* It should be mentioned that despite repeated efforts over the years to verify this story one way or another, nothing definitive has emerged.

"I can't go through this alone," he allegedly said. "So I'm going to kill myself unless you're willing to stand with me. If so, then I'll come down and we can face this together."

My grandmother considered this gravely for a moment, then told him that yes, she would stand by him; they would see this troubled time through as man and wife. She talked to him for fifteen minutes, giving him every reason not to kill himself. She gave him *hope*.

Grateful for her words, cheeks wet with tears, Walter reached for the rope—

—and she kicked the chair out from under him.

Sophia then poured a drink and waited twenty minutes before calling the police to make sure he was dead. She went on to say that she convinced the attending physician to change the cause of death from suicide to natural causes to avoid a scandal that would needlessly upset the rest of the family. After all, Walter was seventy and in poor health so it wasn't like anybody was going to ask for an inquest.

No one in my family ever really knew for sure if she was telling the truth, but all of them were absolutely willing to *believe* she had done it because it was absolutely in keeping with her personality. If she'd simply wanted to spare herself the grief of a trial, all she had to say was "I won't stand by you" and let him step off the chair into a newer and better incarnation.

But leaving that step to him meant there was a chance that he might change his mind at the last moment and *not* kill himself. If that happened, she'd have to deal with the messiness of an investigation and public trial. The simplest way to keep him from backing out would've been to say nothing and just kick the chair out from under him. But that wasn't her style. Better to give him a reason to live, to give him hope, *then* kick the chair out from under him as a sign of her displeasure at being ambushed by this crucial piece of information.

If the story is true, Sophia's actions might have been motivated by more urgent reasons than simply avoiding a scandal, like making sure no one looking for Nazi collaborators started poking around the rest of the family.

But if the story was false, if she hadn't ushered Walter to the other side, why would she say that she *had*? Given information that came along later, it's altogether possible that she wanted to scare the rest of the family into greater vigilance about the risk of any such revelations striking close to home.

Either way, the strategy worked. In the years that followed, not even Frank was safe from scrutiny.

"One time Theresa asked me a question about my father," he said later. "'Are you sure he wasn't working with the Germans?' I said I was absolutely sure, there's no record, nothing to indicate he was even remotely connected. I was curious why she would ask about my father. It really got me wondering, why such a question?"

Why indeed?

That fall, the SDSU Telecommunications and Film Department decided to stage my play *Death in Stasis* as part of their TV production program, the first time anything of mine had been committed to videotape. A few weeks later one of those involved asked me to write a half-hour sitcom pilot that would be produced by the department and KPBS-TV Channel 15. After I agreed to do the job, without payment of course, he said that he needed the finished script in twenty-four hours. They were up against a hard deadline because the writer he'd originally chosen to write the script flaked out at the last minute, reinforcing the lesson learned at the *Daily Aztec*: get the damned thing done. I would be starting from scratch, the only stipulations being that it had to be about an advertising agency, and that the main character should be named Marty Sprinkle, the producer having come to the conclusion, against all evidence to the contrary, that this would be a swell title for a TV show.

Despite knowing nothing about television writing, advertising agencies, or anyone who had the bad taste to name their son Marty Sprinkle, I got to work and turned the script in the next day. After some last-minute tweaks the pilot for *Marty Sprinkle* went before the cameras and was subsequently aired by KPBS to a resounding and well-deserved silence.

It. Was. Awful.

The direction was painful, the acting self-indulgent, and the dialogue that had seemed reasonable while safely on the page was revealed as amateurish and heavy-handed when spoken aloud. In a weird bit of synchronicity the SDSU liaison assigned to the pilot was Robert McKee, who would later write one of publishing's best-selling (and in my view least useful) books on screenplay writing. In the middle of the taping, and against my wishes, he revised the only joke in the entire half hour that actually worked and utterly destroyed it.

I'm still not over it.

I deeply resented every hour I spent in class pursuing a master's degree that I didn't want, time that could have been better spent working on my craft, and began to subconsciously sabotage myself. I would go into the college library to study then fall asleep at a desk, waking hours later to discover I'd missed another class or forgotten to take a test. It got so bad that an academic counselor pulled me in to say that if my grades didn't improve soon "we'll have to let you go, because our computer system isn't set up to handle a GPA in negative numbers."

Leaving aside the fact that this was probably the funniest thing ever said by an academic adviser, I knew there was no way to get my grades high enough by the end of the semester to avoid being kicked out, and my sisters would suffer the consequences. But what else could I do? It wasn't like I could fake it.

Or could I?

My father had no idea about the level of work that was involved in getting a master's degree. He didn't know from thesis papers or GPAs. He only cared about graduation photos and a piece of paper that would give him bragging rights over the rest of the family.

So the solution was to give him exactly what he wanted.

Step one was to forge a master's degree.

I made a copy of my bachelor's degree in psychology, whited out the major and the date, used matching Old Gothic press-on letters to lay in the new information by hand, recopied the document using a machine that produced versions with raised letters, and finished by coloring in the seal for the state of California. The work was painstaking and slow, but the final product was good enough to survive any but the very closest of inspections.

Step two involved getting my name into the computer program used to print the graduation booklets. This was tricky because in order to be added to the program you had to file forms with the ad-ministration office that were checked against the lists of graduating students. Only after the information was verified would your name be added to the roster. There was no other way to do it . . . unless one just *happened* to find oneself in the administration office when there was no one else around and entered the data directly into the system.

Beyond that, on advice of counsel, deponent sayeth not.

That left step three: renting a cap and gown and hoping for the best.

My parents reacted with awe at my dedication when I told them I'd completed my work and was going to graduate a year early. "Now aren't you glad I pushed you?" my father asked.

I smiled and said nothing.

I arrived early on graduation day, clad in cap, gown, and the appropriate tassel, to check the booklets in case someone in administration had noticed there was one entry too many. But my name and degree were right where they should have been. Soon afterward my family showed up, a caravan that included Sophia, flown in at my father's expense not out of familial affection but to show her what *he* had achieved. Photos were taken, and I joined my classmates on the greensward. Due to the size of the ceremony, diplomas were not handed out individually; as each major was called, the students would stand up as a group, wave, then sit down again.

My category was called. I stood. Waved. Sat back down. Then scurried away as quickly as discretion would allow, unspeakably proud of myself.

Later that day, for one of the very few times in my life, I asked my mother for a favor, something to note the occasion. "Everything I did as a kid and everywhere we lived is a blur because there's no sense of continuity, there's nothing to connect the dots," I said. "So give me one thing. Give me my past: dates, addresses, whatever you've got."

She agreed, and went through copies of old bills, letters, and other bits of paperwork to put together a rough chronology of all the places where we'd lived since I was born, a document that became essential to creating this book. Even with those resources she was a little fuzzy on some of the dates, but when she was done, I finally had my past in my hand.

Now we stop looking backward, I thought. *Now we build the future.*

A Brief Authorial Intrusion

I have dwelled at length on this section because most creative people flare into existence when they hit college. The artist you are *now*, you became when you were the most excited about your newfound abilities, and the most vulnerable about your prospects; caught in the nexus between *Everything I write is great* and *Everything I write is shit*, between *I know I can make this work* and *I'll never make this work*.

That's why it's desperately important for those still in college to use every resource at their disposal to learn their craft: you'll find college newspapers, magazines, theaters, audio labs, websites, and radio and TV stations eager for material. This will allow you to burn through the crap in your system at light speed, see your words produced or in print, and have the quality of your work challenged at a time when the consequences won't hurt you. I started out as a writer of short stories who never even considered that I might one day make a living writing articles. That's what college is *for*: to experiment, try new things, fail and fall and laugh and get back up again, to be dangerous, to be glorious, to take risks and push yourself, to have fun and go on absurd adventures that will provide years of stories and decades of material.

For those reading this who have just received your degrees in creative writing or film studies, you will soon find relatives and friends asking why you aren't making a living at it, questions fueled by media-hyped expectations of overnight success. When that doesn't happen, as is almost always the case, it's easy to become discouraged. But there are no portents to be drawn, no deeper meanings to be derived from the time required to find your footing.

Writing is an art more than a craft, and failing to understand that distinction is pernicious. Once you've learned how to make a dovetailed joint in carpentry* class, you're done with that part of it. You may make bigger or smaller dovetailed joints, using different

---

* And yes, I know that there is an art to carpentry just as there is a craft to writing, just in case there are some really tough but artistic carpenters in my neighborhood reading this. Doesn't change the essential point.

materials, but the math is the same. By contrast, no two sentences are alike. Getting a degree in art or music does not guarantee an instantaneous Rembrandt or a Mozart, so why put that expectation on writers? The degree marks the *beginning* of the process, not the end, so all parties must understand that the goal of earning a living at writing will come slowly and with ridiculous amounts of pain.

Be patient with yourselves, and with each other.

End of Authorial Intrusion

Now that I was free to write full-time, I put everything I had into selling reviews and feature articles to every publication in town, including *San Diego City Lights*, *Tuned In*, the *Daily Californian*, and the *San Diego Reader*. But such short pieces only brought in twenty or thirty bucks apiece; even if I managed to sell two per week that barely covered rent on my small apartment. So I branched out into news stories and longer investigative pieces that would generate more money, greater recognition, and on occasion, a fair degree of controversy. When I went undercover at a recruitment camp run by the Moonies cult to do a cover story for the *Reader*, members of the group responded by trying to confiscate all copies of the issue the day it came out, only to find themselves confronted by editors and staffers who showed up at key newsstands armed with baseball bats.

I was having more fun than should legally be allowed.

In December 1978 the *Los Angeles Times* launched a San Diego edition under editor Dale Fetherling, and let it be known that they were looking for local writers. The *San Diego Union* and *Tribune* (which later merged) didn't like the *Times* intruding on their turf and word got around that anyone who worked for them would be blackballed from the other two dailies. But I was prepared to take that chance when Dale asked me to come on board. I was still new to journalism, so the idea of working for the *Los Angeles Times* was too exciting to refuse. I would be a "special correspondent," meaning I'd write regularly for the paper but wouldn't be salaried. Given available space, he could only give me a few articles per month, but they paid a hundred bucks apiece so I could make that work. Writing for the *Times* had the added benefit of increasing my visibility as a writer, prompting KSDO News Radio—a CBS affiliate—to bring me aboard as on-air entertainment editor working pro bono.

This led to a meeting with an individual who identified himself as an independent film producer and asked me to write a movie for him. He offered the princely sum of one thousand dollars against a full Writers Guild screenplay fee should the movie be produced. I didn't have an agent and knew nothing of contracts, but a thousand dollars was a lot of money so I eagerly signed the paperwork.

Around this same time Kathryn noticed a small advertisement in the *Los Angeles Times* soliciting writers for *Alien Worlds*, a half-hour science fiction radio drama series about a research station in Earth orbit that frequently found itself caught up in alien invasions and other interstellar nuisances. I'd heard a few episodes of *Alien Worlds* and thought the stories and production values were terrific, so I couldn't understand why they were putting ads for writers in the newspapers when there were probably lots of talented writers in Hollywood eager for the opportunity. When I contacted executive producer Lee Hansen, he explained that television writers had become so used to relying on visuals that they found it difficult to transition to radio. I had only a modest background in radio drama, but that work—along with having studied under Norman Corwin—was enough for Hansen to send me a series bible, sample scripts, and several finished episodes.

A week later I fired off a spec script entitled "A Question of Conscience." He bought it for several hundred dollars—more than I'd ever earned for a single piece of writing—and invited me to Los Angeles for the recording session. This was the first time I'd flown on an airplane, and as I stepped into a chauffeured car waiting at Burbank Airport it all felt very Hollywood. The studio session was great fun and the cast were exemplary. Pleased that I'd turned the script around in a week, Lee invited me to write as many episodes as I wanted.

For a moment, I allowed myself to think that this writing thing might actually work out.

Then everything all fell apart.

The flameout started with the *Times*. By July 1979 I'd been working with the paper for six months, and was just finishing up an article about a local religious theater group called the Lamb's Players. During the interview the head of the group said that they were getting financing from the State of California. I quoted this in my article and noted that some people would consider this a breach of the separation of church and state.

When I stopped by the *Times* office to check the copy prior to publication, I noticed that the line had been cut. "This is supposed to be a feature story," Dale explained when I inquired, "not a news story about a group receiving financing in violation of various laws."

"But that's as much a fact as where they're performing next. Why is one fact okay to mention and the other fact *not* okay to mention?"

"Because that makes it a news story. You're a feature writer, not a news writer; this is the features department, not the news department."

"So you can only publish the article if it doesn't say anything important?" I asked, getting cranky.

"That's not the point and you know it. Everyone here understands that we have to color inside the lines."

For me it was a question of right and wrong; for Dale it was a matter of editorial policy. In a way we were both right, just fighting from opposite sides of the desk.

"Here's the deal," he said. "If you're willing to let the line go, I can publish it and give you another assignment. If you insist that the line stays, the article will not see print. I'm not spiking the article, just holding it in abeyance. But I can't give you a new assignment until this one is resolved one way or the other."

I was sure he'd eventually change his mind, and he doubtless assumed the same about me. It was just one sentence in an otherwise lengthy article. I should've let it go. But neither of us was willing to budge, and true to his word he never gave me another assignment. The article would sit on the shelf for almost a year before finally being published, minus the offending sentence, so in the end I'd fought for nothing. Losing the *Times* was a huge blow because I'd taken the job knowing I'd be blackballed by the other San Diego dailies, so I couldn't go to them for work, and the *Reader* was cutting way back on freelance assignments.

Desperate for income, I finished the movie script and asked to be paid the one thousand dollars promised by the contract. The "producer" pointed to a clause stipulating that this was a kill fee that would only be paid if he stopped making "best efforts" to get the script produced. In practical terms, it meant he could avoid paying the thousand dollars forever by saying he was still making best efforts.[*]

That left *Alien Worlds* as my sole source of income, and the hammer fell again when the show was canceled due to a misunderstanding between the producers and the sponsors about how many

---

[*] *Thirty-five years later*, the thousand dollars has still not been paid. A recent email to this individual led to his reply that he was still making "best efforts" to produce the script and thus wasn't liable to pay me a dime.

people were actually listening to the show. My first produced episode would never be aired, and none of the three new scripts I'd started would be purchased.

I tried to get KSDO to pay a token fee for my on-air reviews, but there was nothing in the budget to cover it . . . and suddenly I had no source of revenue. To make rent I sold my modest comic collection and stopped leaving the apartment because I couldn't afford bus fare. Since food was the only expense I could control I cut back to just one packet of beef jerky and one can of Mountain Dew per day. The jerky provided protein and gave my stomach something to digest during the day while the Mountain Dew gave me a sugar spike to keep writing late into the night. On Sundays I allowed myself a few pieces of chicken and mashed potatoes at Kentucky Fried Chicken. What little money I had left over each week was spent on writing supplies and postage. I sent queries, résumés, and articles to every magazine I thought I could write for, desperate to sell something to someone.

Nothing sold. *Nothing.*

I spent my nights writing, sleeping only when the hunger got to be too much, and my days dumpster-diving for anything I could sell or recycle. I'd always been thin, but now the drop was precipitous; at six three I weighed only about 140 pounds, with a twenty-eight-inch waist. Friends, alarmed by my appearance, urged me to go on welfare. I refused. I'd make it as a writer or crash and burn trying. There were no other options. There *couldn't* be, not if I was going to get where I needed to go.

To further stretch my already limited funds I began fasting one day per week, then twice weekly. My hands shook from hunger as I tried to type. My weight continued to drop, clothes hanging off me like clown pants. I was unable to sleep and too often unable to write; all I could think about was food and failure. I started wearing long-sleeve shirts in the dead of summer to hide how frail and thin I'd become. Every night I told myself that sooner or later I'd write my way out of this mess, but every morning looked more hopeless than the one before.

One afternoon, out of money, desperate and half starved, I wandered into a bookstore in search of magazines or books on writing that might have listings for new markets that I could copy down before putting them back on the shelf. But there were only a couple of out-of-date books on scriptwriting, more theoretical than practical, penned by academics instead of working writers. (This was before the glut of scriptwriting books that would later crowd the market.) I was disappointed to find nothing new or useful in any of the arenas I'd worked in: playwriting, TV, radio—

Waitaminnit, I thought through a haze of hunger. *Hold on a second.*

I have a background in all those areas! I may not have enough experience with any one of them to write a full book on the subject— just television writing, for instance—but I can write a book that covers all of them in broad strokes. I can pad out each section by writing about the history of each medium, delve into the art and craft of the actual writing, and finish with a look at the current state of the market. No, I don't have a lifetime of experience, but I have a lot more than any of these other people who've written books on scriptwriting, and that didn't stop them.

I hurried home, wrote a fifteen-page outline for *The Complete Book of Scriptwriting*, and sent it off to Writer's Digest Books with a prayer to the gods of writing to let this work out.

A few weeks later they sent back a letter commissioning the book for three thousand dollars: one-third payable on signing the attached contract, one-third upon completion, and the last on publication. I signed the contract and mailed it back the same day.

When the check for one thousand dollars arrived, I considered it no less than a bona fide, no-kidding-around, saved-at-the-last-minute miracle. It would cover two or three months' worth of food and rent, and then I could—

I stopped. And then I could *what*, exactly? I was still persona non grata at the local newspapers, and none of the other gigs in my life were paying anything.

Then it seemed I heard a voice whispering in my ear, as intimate and familiar as the quiet turning of my considered conscience. *You're done here*, it said. *Time to move on.*

I loved San Diego, but it held few opportunities for writers and I had burned through all of them. The town had been as generous with me as it could. If I wanted to write for bigger newspapers and magazines, or even—and this seemed an impossible dream at the time—for television or movies, I would have to move to Los Angeles.

The check for one thousand dollars had not come to provide security, three months' rent, and a chance to maintain the status quo. The universe had just bought me a ticket out of town.

Moving to LA would be terribly risky. After initial expenses, cleaning deposit, and first and last months' rent, the money would be gone almost immediately. If I ran out of cash in San Diego, there was at least the possibility of seeking help from friends, but I knew no one in Los Angeles and had no connections or waiting opportunities. If I didn't get something going almost immediately, I'd be out on the street.

But I had to take the chance.

The hard part would be telling Kathryn. While I had been busy burning every bridge I could find, she had prospered, graduating from the SDSU Telecommunications and Film Department as Outstanding Graduate with Highest Honors, then taking work with KPBS-TV as an associate producer, then full producer on documentary programs. Her career path in San Diego was clear, and I couldn't justify asking her to walk away from all that into the uncertain future I saw for myself. By now we had been dating on and off for two years. I liked her a great deal; respected and admired her even more, but neither of us were terribly demonstrative in our emotions, so in many ways we always felt more like friends than lovers. In recent months we'd started drifting apart, but neither of us had moved to change anything because nothing had happened to break the inertia. Now I had to confront reality for both our sakes.

The day I went to tell her my decision she came racing out of her apartment with news of her own. After learning that ABC was going to commission a new TV series from Carl Sagan—*Nucleus*, a sequel to his groundbreaking PBS series *Cosmos*—she had sent her résumé to his production company in Montrose, a northern suburb of Los Angeles. The letter was their reply, offering her a job as administrative assistant.

On hearing my news, she suggested that we pool our resources and move to LA together, no commitment, sharing space and expenses. If things worked out for us, great; if we went our separate ways, that was fine too. We all do what we do for the same reason: it seemed like a good idea at the time, so I said yes.

Moving to LA didn't seem like a good idea to everyone else, however. Even my friends weren't convinced. *You don't know anyone up there. You'll be starting from nothing.*

What if it doesn't work out?

What if you fail*?*

I came to call this the Tyranny of Reasonable Voices. Those closest to us abhor the idea that we might get hurt, or be disappointed, or fail, because in contemporary American culture there is no greater peril or embarrassment than public failure. But sometimes failure is the only way to identify the flaws in our plan to get over the wall; if we don't risk failure we never learn those things and thus never get over the wall. But that rarely diminishes the desire of those close to us to protect us, so they four-wall us with concern and gentle discouragement. *Don't take the chance, it's not worth it.*

The voices were right, the risks were huge. But we went anyway, and on April Fools' Day 1981 we moved into a one-bedroom furnished apartment in Glendale, California, twenty minutes northeast of Hollywood. By the time the paperwork was signed, the one thousand dollars was gone.

I couldn't sleep that first night, equally excited and terrified. We were making a new start in a city where the frontiers of possibility were as wide as we chose to make them. *Anything* could happen. We could succeed spectacularly, or fail just as spectacularly.

It scared the shit out of me.

CHAPTER 19

God, Death, and Harlan Ellison

One of the first things we did upon arriving in Los Angeles was to unpack the radio so we could listen to *Hour 25*, a science-fiction-themed talk show that had been running since 1972. Hosted by Mike Hodel and Mel Gilden, the show aired every Friday from ten P.M. to midnight on KPFK 90.7 FM, a Pacifica radio station. Kathryn had heard about *Hour 25* for years but the signal wasn't strong enough to reach San Diego.

It was a delight. Mike ran the show with a thoughtful, casual ease that encouraged even the shyest guests to open up. Broadcasting out of a coffin-size booth at KPFK's studio on Ventura Boulevard in Studio City, the show's roster of guests included Ray Bradbury, Robert Bloch, Philip K. Dick, George Clayton Johnson, and Robert Silverberg, along with genre producers, directors, prose editors, and publishers eager to discuss the art and craft of their work. My long-distance role model Harlan Ellison was another frequent guest, answering questions and reading aloud from some of his more recent works. Hearing Harlan transition from conversation to reading one of his stories aloud solidified the connection between the way a writer *writes* and the way he *speaks*. Harlan sounded like his stories, and his stories sounded like Harlan; it was *who he was*. I'd known that intellectually, but the experience of hearing it was a revelation.

Mike took calls from the show's listeners during the last half hour, and I sometimes summoned up the courage to call in with a question or observation, but never when Harlan was on the air. He was a powerful speaker and not to be trifled with. Still, I hoped to tell him one day how much his work had guided me over the years.

My opportunity came a few months later on a hot summer day during a strike by the Writers Guild of America. As a WGA member—courtesy of the still-unpaid feature I'd written—I was required to march on picket lines outside studios I had never sold to, whose lofty portals I had never crossed, alongside writers of infinitely greater stature than I could ever hope to achieve. When I saw Harlan, I approached him and stammered out, "Hi, my name is Joe, and you're one of the reasons I'm a writer—"

"I'm not responsible for anyone other than myself, fuck off!" Harlan snapped back.

It took several weeks to rebuild my courage enough to call during one of Harlan's appearances on *Hour 25* to tell him what I'd tried to convey on the picket line: that as a fellow street rat who came from nothing, his work inspired me to keep writing when nothing else worked. Pleased by my words, he invited me to stop in during an autograph party the next day at Dangerous Visions bookstore, named for one of Harlan's stories.

The line of fans eager for his signature stretched around the block, and the tiny store was packed with well-wishers and other writers. When Harlan took a break, Arthur Byron Cover, co-owner of Dangerous Visions, brought me to face the man who had unknowingly been my long-distance mentor. The meeting lasted only a few minutes; Harlan had a limited attention span for anything less than witty or interesting banter, and I was hopelessly inept at such things, so after a brief exchange, he glazed over and went off in search of deeper waters. But that was okay, I was just happy that I could finally thank him for his inspiration over the years, and happier still that he hadn't yelled at me or hit me with a chair.

While Kathryn carried the burden of earning a weekly income I finished writing *The Complete Book of Scriptwriting* and a boatload of short stories, none of which sold. Gradually, however, I began to get traction in other areas. To set the stage for the script book, *Writer's Digest* magazine gave me a monthly column that paid five hundred bucks per issue. I also started selling articles to David Gritten, entertainment editor for the *Los Angeles Herald Examiner.* I liked writing for David because he took the time to point out the errors I was still making in my work.

Then Cathi Williams (now Jamison) called from San Diego to tell me that the congregation of the First Baptist Church, former home to the House of Abba, was blowing apart in a fireball of appropriately biblical proportions.

Years earlier some of the Elders had steamrolled me out of Community to keep me from discussing Pastor Ken Pagaard's sexual indiscretions with some of the women in the church, affairs that had grown out of his "inner healing" sessions. After my departure, and despite knowing *exactly* what was going on, they continued to do all they could to discredit or intimidate church members who saw that something was wrong and dared to speak out.* But the rumors snowballed anyway, leading to an article in *Eternity* magazine by Ronald Enroth entitled "The Power Abusers," in which he wrote that "A well-known charismatic American Baptist church in Chula

---

* To my shame and regret this strategy proved successful in silencing me. When interviewed about the church a year or two earlier by the *San Diego Reader* I voiced my concerns but stopped short of describing Ken's liaisons, afraid of being further harassed or even sued.

Vista, California, continues in a swirl of controversy over the alleged authoritarianism of its leadership, especially the pastor, Ken Pagaard. The church, many of whose members live in communal households, has also been criticized for certain aspects of its 'inner healing' ministry. Some ex-members have claimed that . . . any criticism of the pastor (occasionally referred to as 'our apostle') and elders was interpreted as a 'spirit of rebellion' and hence, the work of Satan. Many have left the communal lifestyle claiming that heads of households are 'on a power trip.'"

Years later, Dan Stolebarger—an Elder who was on the right side of the issue—described the situation for the Koinonia House website. "Ken was always on the cutting edge and eventually got involved in the 'inner healing' ministry. Because of his all-or-nothing approach, Ken took on some of the most needy and broken women in the church. He felt that if Jesus couldn't heal and set these women free, then Christianity had 'limits.'

"Over the next few years, accusations concerning sexual misconduct began to surface. The situation became unbearable and Ken refused to walk away from this ministry . . . and the accusations of sexual misconduct kept coming. Because of Ken's refusal to seek redemption and reconciliation, we had no other choice than to remove Ken from the Community and as pastor of the First Baptist Church of Chula Vista."

The scandal shattered the congregation, drove many to leave in protest, and led to the Community households being disbanded. Those who remained demanded accountability from Ken and the Elders who had looked the other way. Others urged forgiveness, but that required an acknowledgment of guilt and nobody was in a hurry to take responsibility for abusing the trust of the congregation.*

---

* A formal apology from the church wouldn't come until February 2007, nearly *thirty years* after the fact.

I took no comfort from the implosion, deeply aware of the price paid by families that had been torn apart by Ken's indiscretions and the tapestry of lies that followed.

I should've listened to my gut, I thought. *Never trust a father figure who doesn't come from Krypton or Smallville.*

In May 1982 my grandmother passed away after an inch-by-inch battle against the death with which she had once so casually flirted. Always quick to act whenever somebody fell over dead, my father took the first plane to New Jersey to claim as much of her estate as possible. When he discovered that nearly all of it had been willed to my aunt Theresa, he went on a drunken rampage through Sophia's house in the middle of the night, taking anything that wasn't nailed down. My aunt always thought the midnight raid was less about collecting valuables and more about ensuring that certain parts of his past were eradicated.

The day of Sophia's funeral he showed up drunk and spoiling for a fight, pointing at the coffin and yelling "Whore!" until my aunt, Uncle Ted, and other mourners dogpiled him and propelled him out into the street.

The most telling thing about my grandmother's life and death is that she was not buried beside either of her husbands. Sophia (under her nickname Sophie) was interred at Holy Sepulchre Cemetery beside the artist Victor Rafael Rachwalski, the only man she ever truly loved.

In February 1983 David Gritten left the *Los Angeles Herald Examiner* to become editor of *TV-Cable Week*, a new weekly magazine from TIME Inc. set to debut the following April as a competitor to *TV Guide*. David asked me to come along as a special correspondent, and though I wouldn't be on a weekly salary, this time I'd be listed in the masthead. The *HerEx* brass were pissed at David's departure, so going with him would close another market, but I've always put more value on the people I work with than the job, so I told David, "Where you go, I go."

I worked the celebrity beat, interviewing the Smothers Brothers one day, then flying to Mexico City the next to interview Sean Young during filming on David Lynch's *Dune*. The competition for assignments was fierce, so I developed sources around Los Angeles who could tip me off to good stories. Among these was a contact in City Hall who called one day to say I should get down there at once. "We have to burn some old records because there's no room to store them," he said, "and I think you'll be interested in one of them."

I zoomed down to City Hall as quickly as one can zoom when taking two buses from Glendale, and upon arriving was ushered into the archive room. On a table sat a bound book of transcripts containing testimony given before the Welfare Committee of the Los Angeles City Council in 1928 concerning a boy who had been reported missing, then found and returned to his mother, Christine Collins. Case closed. Except the police returned the wrong boy. Rather than admit their mistake, they committed her to an insane asylum to try and force her into accepting the imposter as her own.

It was the goddamnedest story I'd ever come across.

I wanted to copy some of the pages before they took the book away, but they cost twenty-five cents each and I only had five dollars, so I had to be strategic, choosing pages with names, dates, and references to other documents that would allow me to pick up the thread later. As I reread the copies on the bus ride back to Glendale it was obvious that this was a compelling story, but I had no idea what to do with it. Was it a novel? A series of articles? A script? The only way to find out was to keep digging up information until the structure of the story revealed itself. Even then, I knew the process would be a long one.

How long, and how difficult, I would not fully grasp for quite some time.

Over the next several months, David gave me as many assignments as he could spare, but it was a slow season for showbiz news. Rather than launch the magazine in the fall to coincide with the new season of TV shows, the brain trust at TIME Inc. had scheduled our premiere during the dog days of summer reruns, when even *TV Guide* saw its numbers drop. The low sales led to budget cuts, which meant fewer articles per month.

But there was also some happy news: after collecting rejection slips for nearly *ten years*, one of my short stories, "A Last Testament for Nick and the Trooper," was purchased by Charles L. Grant for his anthology *Shadows 6*. Since the first fiction sale is always the hardest, I took it as a sign that everything was going to work out.

By this time you'd think I would know better.

First ABC pulled the plug on *Nucleus*—Carl Sagan's miniseries about atomic warfare—and suddenly Kathryn was out of a job, crashing a trajectory that would have made her an associate producer. She was fortunate enough to pick up a job as researcher for a one-shot TV program, but it was only a stopgap measure. *The Complete Book of Scriptwriting* was out at last, but I wouldn't get any money from the sales for at least six months.

Then in September David informed us that after a staggering investment of nearly $50 million, TIME was shutting down *TV-Cable Week*. The collapse was attributed to massive overhead, bad managerial decisions, and a war of attrition with *TV Guide*. Some even suggested that we had been quietly sandbagged by TIME's other editorial divisions, such as *People* magazine, because we were competing with them for time, resources, and access to celebrities. The finger-pointing was loud, public, and ultimately pointless.

As one of his last acts, David recommended me and several other writers to the editors at *People*, and I spent weeks slugging it out for assignments at staff meetings with infinitely more well-entrenched reporters. During one such gathering, I patiently awaited my turn as another reporter pitched a story about a new national rape hotline that had just opened.

The female editor chairing the session considered this for a moment, then said, "Well, you know, rape's been very good to us, but do you have a new angle on the rape thing?"

On one level, her statement was understandable given the scandals and tabloid-style sex stories that drove sales of *People* magazine in the '80s. But for me, hearing a woman say "rape's been very good to us" was life-changing. I believe there is a trapdoor under all of us that has a single pin keeping it closed; it only takes one nudge, at the right time, to pop it open. With that comment, my pin was pushed, the trapdoor opened, and I fell through.

When my turn came to pitch, I looked at the notes on my lap and said, "I don't have anything that the others haven't already covered." It was a lie.

You're done, a familiar voice in my head whispered at me. *Your career in journalism is over. Move on. Find something else to do. Find something clean.*

I took the elevator to the lobby, walked out, and never went back.

After publishing roughly five hundred articles, columns, and reviews in six years, I was done with journalism. The decision was easy but the consequences were difficult. My modest income as a reporter had helped fill in the corners so we could *almost* make ends meet; absent that, we were now perilously short on cash. My only other source of income was from the monthly *Writer's Digest* column. Kathryn's parents, Tom and Phyllis Drennan—lovely people who believed in me even when that belief seemed misplaced— helped out when they could, but they were retired pensioners of modest means and we didn't want to be a burden.

Unfazed by our predicament, and with her research job at an end, Kathryn took temp clerical work in what she described as "a windowless office putting numbers into tax forms on an old green-on-green computer for a chain-smoking boss who was the only other person in the office, a job I agreed to because I could get to it on the bus." She also sold occasional articles of her own to *Cat Fancy* magazine, *Profiles Magazine*, *SF Movieland*, and the *Foothill Leader* newspaper. They didn't pay much, but even that little bit helped us keep going. Through all the hard times, Kathryn never complained or asked me to get a "real" job rather than stay home writing. That is a singular accomplishment for anyone living with a writer, but it did nothing to diminish my distress at failing to look after her as she deserved. Every time it looked like things were going to work out, the universe smacked me in the face.

I have to fix this, I thought every night. *I have to write my way out of this, somehow.*

CHAPTER 20

An Unexpected Journey to Toon-Town

With our finances and options nearly exhausted, I decided to throw a Hail Mary. As a kid I used to get up early on Saturday mornings to watch *Looney Tunes*, *The Flintstones*, *Jonny Quest*, and other cartoon series without ever giving much thought to the idea that people actually wrote cartoons. Since moving to Los Angeles, however, I'd met a number of writers who worked for such animated series as *Blackstar*, *Super Friends*, *The Smurfs*, *G.I. Joe*, *Fat Albert*, and *He-Man and the Masters of the Universe*.

I was actually quite fond of *He-Man*, a fantasy series from Filmation Studios. The hero, Prince Adam, would use a magic sword to transform into the heavily muscled title character. His greatest enemy was the bone-faced Skeletor, whose plans for world domination were never clearly defined. Despite the presence of a talking green tiger and a legless floating imp named Orko, the science fiction aspects of the show were unusually well thought out, which told me that *somebody* writing the show knew a lot about world-building.

Animation studios at that time paid between eight hundred and one thousand dollars for a half-hour script. Selling even one would save us from disaster for a while, but I didn't have an agent and knew nothing about animation writing. I'd never even *seen* an animation script, which has a very specific format, and when I asked some of the animation writers I knew for a sample they turned to vapor. Competition for assignments was fierce, so the idea of helping create a competitor was counterintuitive. After searching through every showbiz bookstore in Los Angeles I finally found a torn, dog-eared script for the 1979 animated *Spider-Woman* series. With that as a template I was able to finish a spec *He-Man* script in a few days.

To find out who the script should be sent to, I called Filmation and told the receptionist I was returning a call from someone at the studio. "It was one of the producers, I think, but I didn't catch the name before we were cut off, could you connect me to the right person?"

"Well, there are only two producers here," she said. "Lou Scheimer, the head of the studio, and Arthur Nadel, who's producing the *He-Man* series."

"That must be the one," I said. "The name sounded like Arthur but I wasn't sure."

"So who should I say is returning the call?" she asked.

I started to answer, then clicked the line mid-word to make it sound as though we got disconnected.

Armed with a name and the address of the studio, I sent off the script with a release form from my scriptwriting book. It was a cold submission: no prior contact, no work experience, no references, and no agent to vouch for me. I couldn't have done it more wrong if I'd set out with that goal in mind. When a week passed without word, I assumed that whoever opened the envelope took one look at the contents and tossed it in the trash.

Then the phone rang, and the voice at the other end introduced himself as Arthur Nadel. "Listen," he said, "I read your script, and it's very good. Unfortunately, it's too close to a story we're already doing, so I'm afraid we can't buy it."

I tried to say something intelligible, like *I understand, I appreciate that you took the time to look at it* . . .

He kept going. "Anyway, you really seem to get our characters, so I was wondering if you could come in to pitch some more stories, see if we can get something going."

I met Arthur that Friday in Reseda at the industrial-looking Filmation Studios facility that had previously produced *Fat Albert and the Cosby Kids*, *The Batman/Superman Hour*, and the animated *Star Trek* series. *He-Man and the Masters of the Universe* had launched in September 1983 with sixty-five original half-hour episodes, and was Filmation's first massive hit, airing domestically on 120 TV stations and syndicated overseas in over thirty countries.

A tall man, thin and patrician, Arthur was intrigued by the fact that I'd previously been a journalist. The others working for him were either straight-up TV writers or had dabbled in prose fiction, and he thought that someone who had been a reporter could bring a fresh perspective to the show.[*]

I had come armed with three story ideas. The first two were quickly shot down, but the third caught his attention. "Let's start with that one," he said. "We'll put you to outline, and if that works, we'll commission the script."

As he stood to shake my hand I kept thinking there had to be more hoops to jump through before he could just blithely say I had an assignment. But when his assistant began drawing up the paperwork, I finally allowed myself to believe this was actually happening.

With bills overdue and no guarantee that this would go any

---

[*] This was my first introduction to the Prince from a Distant Land Scenario, about which more later.

further than the outline, I turned around the assignment in three days. Arthur was pleasantly surprised to get the material so quickly, and commissioned the script, which I delivered a week later. He had a few small notes but liked the script enough to put it into production. More than the script itself he liked that I had delivered the whole thing end to end in a third of the time taken by his other writers, many of whom were slow to deliver or had a habit of flaking out entirely, a complaint I'd heard since my time at the *Daily Aztec*. I explained that when you're a reporter and a story breaks you can't just wait around for the elusive Muse to show up. You sit down and get it done before another newspaper beats you to the punch. He liked that philosophy, and invited me to come back as soon as possible to pitch another story.

A few days later, at a party attended by other animation writers, I mentioned that I'd sold a script for *He-Man*. Some of them were guardedly positive about the news while others were patronizing, almost to the pat-on-the-head level of, *well, isn't that nice, he sold a script*. Even among those who congratulated me, the consensus seemed to be that I'd gotten lucky and this script was a one-off. But with sixty-five *He-Man* episodes to be produced Arthur quickly bought my next script, which I delivered on the same schedule, and asked for another.

After turning in script number three, I met with Arthur to get his notes, then started to pitch some ideas for another story. He stopped me with a gesture. "Take a walk with me," he said.

We went down the street to get donuts and coffee from a food truck, making small talk along the way. He seemed curious to know more about me as a person, and my goals as a writer. I learned then that Arthur had been a TV producer for many decades, starting with *The Rifleman* in 1960. "So I'm pretty good at spotting writers," he said, as if weighing some decision.

He must've figured it out because as we headed back, he said, "I have some bad news. We're out of money for freelance scripts, so we can't afford to buy any more from you."

I nodded silently, accepting that the job had come to an end. I started to say "I'm just happy to have had the opportunity, it was a lot of fun—"

Arthur kept going. "The point is, we can't afford to have you write more freelance scripts, but we *can* offer you a staff job if you're interested. It pays six hundred dollars a week and your script fees are included in that salary, so there's no over-and-above, you get paid the same amount regardless of how many scripts you write. The job's yours if you want it."

As we walked inside I tried to play it cool as I said, "Yes, I'd love to come on staff," but my heart was pounding.

He pointed to a tiny room down the hall from his digs. "This will be your office. You start Monday." Then he shook my hand and sent me on my way.

I ran to the nearest pay phone[*] and called Kathryn, yelling the news so loudly I was sure I'd blow out my vocal cords. That night I told her to quit her temp job. For three years she had gone above and beyond the call of duty to buy me enough time for exactly this sort of thing to happen, and I was damned if I'd let her suffer one more day. "I give you my word that you will never again have to work in a windowless, airless, soul-killing office," I said, "not now, not for the rest of your life."

And she never did.

The day I showed up to start my job at Filmation I was introduced to staff writer Larry DiTillio, who occupied the office directly across from my own. In his mid-forties, Larry was an expat New

---

* Ask your mom.

Yorker of Italian descent with close-cropped, tight black hair, an affinity for loud Hawaiian shirts, and a fierce sense of humor. While watching *He-Man* I'd felt the presence of someone who knew how to design worlds, and I soon learned that Larry was responsible for much of that mythos; it was his intelligence I had detected.

I got right to work so we didn't speak much until that Friday, when I poked my head into his office to say that I was relieved to have gotten this far. "To be honest, I wasn't sure I could do this job."

"That's okay," he said. "I didn't think you could do it either."

With that we became friends and competitors, each determined to turn in more scripts than the other. Every week was a shoot-out to see who would come in first with a finished draft. When he suggested a race to see who could write a script in the least time from a dead start, I barely beat him, coming in at eight hours to his twelve. To enliven the work and screw with the writing process on the other side of the hall, we would sometimes declare war on each other. One afternoon when he was out of the office for lunch, I stole the platen* from his electric typewriter and hid it, leaving the paper in place so it would take him a moment to figure out what I'd done.

Shortly afterward I heard him return to his office and sit at his desk. The squeak of his chair was followed by the *tap-tap-tap* of his typewriter. Silence. Another squeak. Then Larry appeared in my doorway, surrounded by a plume of pipe smoke. "I want my platen back."

"I know not this platen of which you speak, sir," I said, not looking up from my work.

He pulled out a cigarette lighter and nodded to the cartoons I'd taped to my office door. "Give me my platen back or I'll burn down your office."

"You wouldn't dare," said I.

---

* It's the black rolly-thing the paper goes around . . . ask your grandmother . . .

He clicked on the lighter and ignited the bottom cartoon. Flames began making their way up the door. I counted to ten to see how far he was prepared to take this. He didn't move.

"Fair enough," I said and handed back his platen. He put out the blaze, turned, and left.

Moments later, Arthur passed my office on his way back from a meeting, then stopped. Backed up. Looked at the charred remains of the cartoons. "What happened here?"

I shrugged. "Larry tried to burn down my office."

"Oh," he said and continued on his way. That's just kind of how it was between me and Larry.

Working at Filmation led to representation by Candace (Candy) Monteiro and Fredda Rose, who ran a boutique agency that represented most of the animation writers in town because other agencies didn't think it was worth their time. When Arthur asked me to work with the remaining freelance writers, most of whom were their clients, I found myself giving notes to the same people who had been less than helpful in my early attempts to sell an animation script. Many of them had been hoping to land the last available staff gig at Filmation, and seemed rather annoyed that I was on the other side of the desk.

Working with outside writers was the kind of work normally done by story editors, who received on-screen credit as such, not by staff writers, but at that moment I didn't really care. I was just happy to have my very first full-time job in television.

During the five years Kathryn and I had been living together, we'd rarely discussed the idea of getting married because we were always just scraping by. Now that we had achieved some measure of stability there was a growing expectation among both our families that we would get married.

For years I'd hoped that I would grow out of the emotional distance that stood between me and a healthy, normal relationship; that one day I'd awaken free of past traumas, capable of openly expressing love and affection. But that day never came. If anything, the older I got, the more distant those emotions became. There is a French proverb: *In love there are two kinds: those who kiss, and those who offer the cheek.* With each passing year I was being buried alive beneath the ass-end of that equation, and there was nothing I could do about it.

I wasn't husband material by any stretch of the imagination, but Kathryn was my best friend; I was deeply grateful for her unwavering support and profoundly guilty that she had endured so much difficulty during the time we'd been together. Getting married would allow me to show my appreciation for all she'd done, honoring her sacrifices and our friendship.

Only with decades of hindsight is it clear that those were *exactly* the wrong reasons to get married. That decision also led to a particularly weird conversation with my father shortly before the ceremony.

"Are you sure you want to do this?" he asked.

"I think so . . . she's a terrific person."

"I'm not asking about her, she's fine. The question is, do you really want to inflict *you* on *her*?"

It was probably the only fair question he'd ever asked.

Despite having opposed my writing career at every step, my father saw my job in TV as entirely his doing, and he demanded we gather for dinner every Thanksgiving in San Diego so he could show off. He liked to tell everyone that without him standing behind me, pushing me to succeed, I would've ended up "a bum." By contrast, the years I'd struggled and failed were entirely my fault, he had nothing to do with it. Kathryn and I dreaded those dinners, during which my father would get louder, drunker, and more insufferable.

Finally, my patience at an end, I said that I would only come down for the next Thanksgiving if there was no drinking. "If it happens again," I said, "there will be consequences."

To my surprise he agreed, and when we arrived that Thursday there was no evidence of alcohol in sight. For a brief moment I thought he might actually keep his promise. But as the evening wore on he became noticeably drunk. When he went to the bathroom, I checked the cup of coffee he'd been nursing. It reeked of booze slipped in during his visits to the kitchen. At dinner his eyes glittered darkly, confident that he'd pulled a fast one on me.

During the long drive back to Los Angeles, I finally came to terms with the fact that my family was more than just dysfunctional, it was destructive. My mother, sisters, and I had always been strangers to one another, kept together by threats rather than affection, and my father was never going to change because he saw no *reason* to change. If there was a problem, it was always someone else's fault. There was no joy in my family; our every contact was forced, awkward, and dissatisfying. There was nothing good to be salvaged.

My father ignored my warning because he believed there was nothing I could do to him.

He was wrong.

For the first eighteen years of my life he had subjected me to the worst kinds of physical, psychological, and emotional torture. I could debate endlessly his reasons for doing those things, or try to figure out why his personality had splintered to the point where he needed to inflict pain on others to feel alive, but that didn't alter the fact that those were *his* problems, *his* choices. Like all abusers he wanted me to believe I had no choice but to accept this behavior, that I could never escape him. That had been true when

I was younger, but I was now old enough to walk away from an abusive situation; if I failed to do so, then it became *my* problem, *my* choice. I had no control over my father's behavior, but I had *absolute* control over my proximity. He could only hurt me while I chose to remain within range of the fist and the boot, the lie and the scream. If I wanted to stop the abuse, all I had to do was step outside his reach.

Superman may have been the most patient person on the planet, but when faced with someone he couldn't kill because of his moral code—but who was too dangerous to be allowed to roam free— sooner or later even *he* gave up and exiled that individual to the Phantom Zone.

I'd given my family thirty years of my life. I would not surrender a minute more.

"Let me be really clear," I said when I called the next day. "You will never see or hear from me again. There will be no visits, no phone calls, no letters . . . I'm cutting off all contact, permanently."

Was I running away from the problem? Probably. But when you're in a situation where nothing will change, running away isn't just *a* solution, it's the *only* solution. No one being chased by a bobcat thinks, *Maybe I should stick it out, try to make the relationship work.*

And there are some people in this world who are just frickin' bobcats.

For this to succeed it would have to be a complete break with everyone in my immediate family. I'd waited years for my sisters to get out from under my father's thumb, but Theresa stayed because she thought she was helping my mother, little understanding Evelyn's role in the dysfunctional nightmare that was our family, and Lorraine was induced to stay by Charles's vague promises of financial reward (none of which were kept). If I stayed in contact with my sisters, he would use them to try and drag me back into the snake pit of our family's psychodramas. A clean break would protect them.*

He'll crawl back, my father said.

He was wrong. From Thanksgiving 1984 to my father's death on January 28, 2011, I never saw or spoke to my parents again, not in person, and not over the phone. For months after breaking away, the twelve-year-old boy in me was afraid he would show up and beat me. But that day never came. I began to feel as though I had awakened from the nightmare of a lifetime, and stopped dreading the approach of the holidays, or the ringing phone.

For the first time in a long, long, very long time, I could *breathe*.

That winter I turned my attention back to the Christine Collins pages I'd copied from the City Council transcript. The more I read the more curious I became. Why had her child been kidnapped, and what happened to him? How did the police manage to bring back the wrong boy, and why would they incarcerate then institutionalize her to avoid admitting their error? I would need to do a lot more research before I could figure out the story, but there were no secondary sources (contemporary articles, novels, or nonfiction books) that covered the events. So I began digging into primary sources: original documents, letters, files, and microfiche copies of articles at the Los Angeles Public Library, City Hall, and the Los Angeles County Courthouse. The process was agonizingly slow. Many of the files dating back to 1928 weren't well indexed, so I spent my weekends sifting through mountains of white-on-black photocopies of court records and newspapers for any mention of the case during its earliest stages. It was only later, after news got out that

---

* The only exception to this was my aunt Theresa, who would sometimes back-channel information that she thought I might need to know.

Christine's son was one of several boys kidnapped and presumably killed at a ranch in Riverside, that lurid headlines describing the case splashed across the front page of every major newspaper in Southern California.

The more I dug, the more I realized that I didn't have the tools as a writer to wrestle this beast to the ground. Every time I thought I had it figured out, the story would twist off in another direction. It was like trying to break a horse without reins or a saddle, and always ended up with me face-down in the dirt. So I decided to stop trying to tell the story and just organize the facts into a timeline, hoping that once I could see the whole thing at a glance I'd know where to go with it.

He-Man and the Masters of the Universe generated hundreds of millions of dollars for Mattel and attracted legions of fans, but it also drew the ire of media watchdogs and parents' groups. Church sermons decried the show as "pro-Satan" and offered workshops to help parents protect their children from the evil that permeated every frame. Child psychologists and pressure groups like Peggy Charon's Action for Children's Television pushed the fiction that the show was filled with violence, using numbers that were skewed by designating incidents as trivial as a slammed door as an act of violence.

Despite this backlash, Filmation decided to launch a companion series, and since Larry DiTillio and I were world-builders fascinated by mythology, we were chosen to develop *She-Ra: Princess of Power*, breaking out the characters, rules of engagement, and history of this fictional world. The downside was that we would not get credit for creating the show or receive residuals on the series or the sale of any toys based on our creations.

We bristled further when we learned that we'd be working under new creative restraints. To soften the ire of the pressure groups that were hammering *He-Man*, Filmation enlisted consultants to ensure that our female lead was appropriately maternal, nurturing, and nonthreatening to male authority figures. They also decided that while the *male* characters on the show could use swords or arrows or punch the bad guys, our *female* lead was not free to do the same. So even though she owned a massive sword, she wasn't allowed to actually hurt anyone with it. Instead she would spin like a ballerina and—almost by accident—kick someone out of frame and hope the audience would fail to ask why the bad guy didn't just walk back into frame and beat the crap out of her.

This took much of the fun out of developing *She-Ra*, but Larry and I kept pushing forward because we liked the world we were creating. After finishing the series bible and the arc for the first sixty-five-episode season, we began writing our own scripts and meeting with freelancers.

One of the hardest parts of launching a new TV series is making sure that the outside writers share the same vision for the show that you do. But many of the writers who had no problem writing for *He-Man* or other male-dominated shows hit a wall when writing for a female action lead. Some made her soft, passive, or little-girl feminine, while others wrote her as He-Man with breasts. When we reached a point where we were spending more time editing the freelancers than writing our own scripts, we met with Arthur and studio head Lou Scheimer to ask for credit as story editors. We weren't even looking for more money, just to have the work acknowledged. We thought our position fairly reasonable: give us credit for what we're doing, or we'll just do the work we were being given credit for, writing our own scripts as staff writers.

They were outraged. Filmation didn't allow story editor credits or give their writers created-by credit. As far as the outside world was concerned, Lou was the only creative force guiding Filmation, and he was determined to keep it that way.

After returning to the writers' wing stunned and dispirited, I convinced Larry that we should keep trying to change their minds, but if we didn't get what we wanted by that Friday, we should resign. We were the heart of the *She-Ra* development process; finding someone new at this late date would be expensive and time-consuming. Surely they'd see the sense of that.

The Friday deadline passed.

I walked across the hall into Larry's office. "We have to go," I said.

He didn't want to leave. Neither did I. Nine months earlier I'd been teetering on the edge of financial catastrophe, and now I was going to quit the best job I'd ever had? Worse still, most of the other animated series in town were already staffed and there were no new shows on the horizon. If we quit, we might be out of work for a long time. The logical part of my brain said resigning was the height of foolishness. But the rest of my brain is incapable of backing down from a fight.

"We have to do this," I said, "and we have to do it right now."

Larry chewed on his pipe for a moment, then nodded. "Okay," he said, "but I want you to remember that I'm Italian. If I don't work again because of this, I'm going to hunt you down and kill you."

"Fair deal," I said.

Despite the battle that ended our tenure on *He-Man* and *She-Ra*, the shows took root in popular culture beyond anything we could have anticipated, spawning thirty years of comic books, conventions, cosplay, toys, a *He-Man* feature film in 1987, sequel animated series in 1990 and 2002, and, as I write this, a new version of *She-Ra* on Netflix. DVDs of the series became bestsellers, and featured interviews with me and Larry, as well as digital copies of our original scripts, notes, and the *She-Ra* series bible. Young women saw *She-Ra* as a role model, a female action hero at a time when there were very few of those. Their response validated our struggle to maintain her warrior edge against those who wanted to soften her into a mommy figure.

But we foresaw none of this as we walked out of Filmation. We knew only that we were out of a job, and that if things didn't work out, Larry would put out a contract on my life.

It took a while, but our agents found jobs for us at DIC Entertainment in Studio City on an animated series entitled *Jayce and the Wheeled Warriors*. It was another dumb title in a string of shows whose titles were based on the *He-Man* model of NAME OF HERO + OTHERS: *He-Man and the Masters of the Universe*, *She-Ra: Princess of Power*, *Jayce and the Wheeled Warriors*, *Captain Planet and the Planeteers*, *Captain Harlock and the Queen of a Thousand Years*, and *Spider-Man and His Amazing Friends*. We wouldn't be on a weekly salary, but our per-script fees were decent and we were guaranteed enough assignments to make up the difference in what we'd lost by leaving Filmation.

The show's premise was patently ridiculous: sentient monster plants capable of turning into vehicles would *drive* from planet to planet on massive vines that could literally stretch trillions of miles and create highways between planets *orbiting in different directions in totally different solar systems* where they would wreak havoc for no clearly defined reason.* The science was nonsensical to anyone with a third-grade education, and the characters were derivative in the extreme: a young hero (à la Prince Adam in *He-Man*, or Luke Skywalker in *Star Wars*), a wise mentor (à la the Sorceress in *He-Man* or Obi-Wan), a reckless pilot (about as à la Han Solo as they could get without receiving fire from Lucasfilm's attorneys), and a suit of armor inhabited by an invisible but constantly nervous companion (à la Orko or R2D2).

Since nothing about the show made sense, story editors Haskell

---

* Bad guys in the '80s had a lot to learn about goal management.

Barkin and Jim Carlson had a hard time infusing their writers with any sense of passion. Many of them just ignored the illogic, wrote for the paycheck, and moved on. But coming from a love of world-building, Larry and I were incapable of writing scripts where things happen just because they happen. There had to be *some* kind of rationale. So we fought incessantly against the series' various dumbnesses, making life hell for Haskell and Jim, who just wanted to get this over with so they could move on to something more rewarding. Why were we hammering them with questions about physics in a show about *giant killer interstellar plants with a fetish for all-wheel drives, for chrissakes*? What the hell was *wrong* with us?

In January 1986 the town had barely come back from Christmas hiatus when I stopped by Jim Carlson's office to drop off my most recent script for *Jayce*. He shut the door, his expression grave, and said he'd just received bad news from the head of the studio.

I was to be taken off the show, effective immediately.

CHAPTER 21

Who Ya Gonna Call?

Jim didn't know if I was being fired outright or if I'd simply pissed off someone higher up the food chain, but I was to report *immediately* to Jean Chalopin, the French owner of DIC.

Jean's office was strewn with concept sketches for new shows in various stages of development, including artwork for a new animated series for ABC based on the *Ghostbusters* movie (titled *The Real Ghostbusters* to distinguish it from Filmation's 1975 *Ghostbusters* series about some guys and a gorilla riding around in an old jalopy chasing spooks). *Ghostbusters* was one of my favorite movies and I'd been hoping to write an episode or two once I was done with *Jayce*. The odds of an assignment were small since I'd only worked in syndication and wasn't on the network's list of approved writers, and now even that modest goal seemed out of reach since I'd apparently done something to annoy the studio.

Jean finished a phone call then turned to me and asked, "Do you know Ame Simon and Jennie Trias at ABC?" Since Jean spoke with a heavy French accent, it came out more like, "Du yu gnaw Aaaame S'mon n Jennnie Triaaas at ABC?"

The only part I actually understood was *ABC*, and since I didn't know anyone there I said no, figuring that way I was safe no matter what the hell he'd just asked me.

His reply, translated into English: "The story editors I hired to work on *The Real Ghostbusters*, Len Janson and Chuck Menville, did not understand that they would be working on both the network series *and* the syndicated series we will be producing at the same time. They decided they do not wish to do that much work and will only write their own episodes. So I need a story editor to come in on both series.

"I have told *Aaaame-n-Jennnie** that you are the funny man," he continued. "Do not make from me the liar."

It happened so quickly that it wasn't until leaving his office that I stopped to do the math. DIC was producing thirteen half-hour episodes for ABC and sixty-five for first-run syndication for a total of seventy-eight episodes that would have to be written and story-edited *simultaneously*. By this point I'd written thirty-two scripts—nine for *He-Man*, another nine for *She-Ra*, and fourteen for *Jayce*—and story-edited about two dozen scripts while at Filmation. I'd never written or edited seventy-eight episodes of *anything*, let alone a show that would be launched with as much visibility as *The Real Ghostbusters*. No one had. The only reason Jean offered me the show in the first place was because Len and Chuck, story editors with years of experience, had run screaming into the night rather than even *try* to tackle that number. And while there would be action and supernatural components to the show, at its core *The Real Ghostbusters* was a comedy series, whereas all my experience to this point was in straight-ahead action/adventure.

I have told Aaaame-n-Jennnie that you are the funny man. Do not make from me the liar.

The numbers and the genre were against me. What if I failed?

---

* Which is either *Ame and Jennie* or a river in France.

What's the worst that can happen? I thought. *They can't kill you, they can't eat you, and they can't put you in TV prison. Yes, it'll be embarrassing if you fail, but risking failure is necessary. So let's embrace the nightmare and get this goddamned thing up and on the rails.*

Though Jean had offered me the job, I still had to pass muster with Ame and Jennie, as well as executive producers Joe Medjuck and Michael Gross, who had also produced the original *Ghostbusters* movie. I'd never worked in comedy so the network execs were understandably dubious, but they signed off on me when they saw that I got along well with the producers, who wanted the show to have teeth, telling scary stories with humor and strong characters. The faces of the Ghostbusters were changed for contractual reasons involving actors' likenesses, but everything else had to feel just like the movie.

To extend a 107-minute movie into thirty-nine hours of storytelling, I brought in the best writers I could find, including Larry DiTillio. Then, with the support of a terrific cast (Frank Welker, Maurice LaMarche, Lorenzo Music, Laura Summer, and Arsenio Hall) we produced some of the weirdest stories ever told in a network animated series. We drew upon ancient myths, forgotten gods, and supernatural creatures that ranged from Samhain to the Sandman, ghosts to goblins, Lovecraftian demons to monsters in the closet. No reference was too obscure. In one script we referred to a group of characters trying to defeat a creature plaguing an Eskimo village as "an Inuit minyan." Only three people in the country got that joke, but it was worth it.

The wide palette of humor, horror, and action made it the most rewarding gig I'd had to that point, and I scripted twenty-one episodes, determined to write the hell out of it. Two of the best received were "Xmas Marks the Spot," where the Ghostbusters inadvertently save Scrooge from the three ghosts of Christmas, and "Take

Two," which suggested that the *Ghostbusters* movie was based on the animated series rather than the other way around. Many young viewers actually came to believe that was true, much to the annoyance of the film's producers.

The main difference between the network and syndicated versions of *The Real Ghostbusters* came down to the involvement in the former by censors, also known as Broadcast Standards and Practices (BS&P), whose input was often problematic. Borrowing a page from the old Warner Bros. cartoons, I wanted the show to be written on two levels: with action and humor that was simple enough for kids to follow, and sophisticated ideas behind the mythology that adults could appreciate. BS&P *hated* that approach, especially when it came to death and the supernatural. It was okay for us to have monsters in the show, but we couldn't say they were dead people because that was too scary, even though the show was called *Ghost*busters, not *Monster*busters. The supernatural aspects of the storytelling also led BS&P to suspect us of constantly trying to slip in references to Satanism and the occult, so they scrutinized every line of every script in case I was secretly an emissary of Ba'al out to subvert the children of America and bring about the Apocalypse.

Which, of course, I was. They just could never prove it.

On May 6, 1986, the Los Angeles science fiction community was rocked by the passing of Mike Hodel,* host of *Hour 25*. What he believed was just a sore throat turned out to be a tumor that had crawled deep into his brain. It happened so quickly that Mike was gone before most people even knew he was sick. Before his passing,

---

* In later years, Mike's father, George Hodel, would emerge as one of the prime suspects in the infamous Black Dahlia murder. Apparently both our fathers had something to hide.

he asked Harlan Ellison to take over as host. Harlan obliged and rechristened the show *Mike Hodel's Hour 25*. For Harlan, Mike's death was the latest in a series of body blows that left him stunned and reeling. Five months earlier he had walked off a recent revival of *The Twilight Zone* over CBS's evisceration of one of his scripts; then he ended up on the receiving end of a $2 million libel suit based on an offhand remark made six years earlier about a comic book writer. Harlan refused to settle out of court, but the cost of prolonged litigation was eating through his savings with terrifying speed.

"I'm afraid I'm gonna lose the house," he confided to a mutual friend.

I couldn't let that happen. Harlan and I were only casual acquaintances, but I would never have had the courage to keep going without his example of a working-class writer who made good. So Kathryn and I, along with another writer, decided to throw a roast to raise funds for Harlan's defense.

The event took place on July 12, 1986, at the Los Angeles Press Club, and featured David Gerrold, Robert Bloch, Ray Bradbury, *Twilight Zone* producer Phil DeGuere, journalist Paul Krassner, comics legend Stan Lee, and comedian Robin Williams. We even convinced artist Frank Miller to create a poster based on Harlan's famous short story "'Repent, Harlequin!' Said the Ticktockman" that could be sold along with audiotapes of the event. It was a raucous, obscenity-riddled celebration of Harlan's work that provided both the needed funds and an emotional boost that would let him go on to prevail in court.

By the end of the night Kathryn and I were relieved. We were exhausted.

We were ditched.

Quoting Kathryn: "After the roast, we weren't invited to the after-event dinner, because Harlan assumed that [name withheld] had organized the whole thing, and only much later realized that I had done most of the work and apologized to both of us for leaving us standing there in the parking lot while everyone else went to dinner. But Harlan didn't know us very well at all at that point."

That summer I finished my first pass at a timeline for the Christine Collins story, and while it included most of the essential pieces there were still gaps big enough to drive a starship through. I was annoyed and frustrated at the lack of available information and my own inability to corral the events into a coherent story and working on seventy-eight episodes of *The Real Ghostbusters* didn't leave much time for prowling around dusty archives.

It's just one of a hundred true stories out there that you could be telling, I thought. *Why are you so focused on **this** one?*

The answer, I realized, lay in Christine's refusal to lay down to those in power. The LAPD, the chief of police, and the doctors who helped commit her to an asylum for the crime of disagreeing with the police, hit her as hard as they could, trying to break her will. In her struggle I saw echoes of my own past, getting pounded by bullies or Elders determined to make me recant what I knew to be true. She was a *fighter*, and her efforts deserved to be recognized.

I swore that one day I'd finish the research that would let me tell Christine's story in a way that honored her battle for her son's life.

The Real Ghostbusters debuted on September 13, 1986, as ABC's number one animated series and the highest-rated animated series airing on any network. The series was the darling of critics and viewers, sold millions of dollars in toys, and generated a fan following that persists to this day.

Given that reception, I decided that this was as good a time as any to try and break into live-action television. There was just one problem: before *South Park* and *The Simpsons* made animation respectable, most network executives believed that writers who worked in animation did so because they weren't good enough for live-action. The longer one stayed in animation, the more everyone assumed that was all you could do. I'd been writing animation for only two years, so the usual prejudices had not yet calcified around me, but that grace period wouldn't last much longer, so I had to move quickly. The hard part would be finding a live-action show that would even *consider* a writer with my limited credits.

So naturally I went for the most difficult option available.

During its first season every animation writer in town had tried to sell a script to the new *Twilight Zone*, but few succeeded. When the show was renewed for a second season, the word went out that you couldn't get in the door unless you had at least some experience writing live-action. By all rights this should have left me out in the cold, but that once-in-a-lifetime meeting with Rod Serling had to portend *something*, right?

My agent waved away the idea of trying to get a meeting to pitch stories. "Without prior credits the only way they *might* let you pitch is if you give them a spec script that gets their interest," Candy said, "but even then the odds are pretty slim."

I bristled inwardly; it was the same song I'd heard my whole life. *It's impossible, there's no point in trying, so don't even bother.*

I tucked away my annoyance. "Fine, then I'll write a spec."

She sighed, knowing there was no point in trying to talk me out of something once I'd made up my mind. "Then it had better be *really* good, though I can't guarantee they'll actually read it."

With the gauntlet thrown, I racked my brain for a story that would catch their attention. Since the best episodes of the original *Twilight Zone* were morality plays based on the writer's background or perspective, I thought, *How about a story about a kid from the mean streets of Newark? A fledgling writer who managed to get out in one piece and left his friends behind, some of whom later died in those streets. Guilt-ridden, he never returns until the night his plane is rerouted to Newark for weather. Suddenly he finds himself pursued by the literal ghosts of his past. He thinks they're out to kill him because he ran out on them, only to discover that they're trying to help him let go of his guilt and stop feeling bad about his past, so he can enjoy the life they never had.*

I finished the script a week later, and Candy sent it over without much hope. So we were both astonished when the writing staff called to say that while they didn't want to do this story, they liked the writing well enough for me to come in and pitch some more ideas.

When I arrived at *The Twilight Zone* offices in Studio City, the first person I ran into was science fiction/fantasy novelist George R. R. Martin, who had been brought on as story editor after Harlan's fiery departure. Though he would later write the books that became *Game of Thrones*, George's only prior television credit at the time was a single episode of the *Hitchhiker* series based on one of his stories. In transitioning to story editor on the *Zone*, some writers in town felt that he zealously guarded his status as resident up-and-comer by discouraging any *other* up-and-comers who might displace him. I'd seen George a few times at Dangerous Visions autograph parties and though we'd never spoken he seemed a nice enough fellow, so I didn't put much stock in the stories.

He was sitting by the door as I came in, and offered a tight flicker of a smile at my greeting before glancing away. Then I noticed he had a copy of my spec on his lap. "Yeah, I just now got it," he said, vaguely annoyed.

"What did you think?" I asked, eager for criticism from a writer of his stature.

He shrugged. "It's okay," he said and wandered away.

Oboy, he so doesn't want me here.

I was then ushered into the office of Executive Producer Phil DeGuere. Once the rest of the writing staff had settled in, I began laying out the stories I wanted to tell. Phil was twitchy and distracted, covertly (and sometimes overtly) reading *Daily Variety* as I pitched. George kept glancing out the window in case something more interesting might flutter past. I was sweating bullets. The first two stories were shot down immediately. That left just story number three, the most personal of the bunch.

My family's history had amply demonstrated how the sins of a father addicted to alcohol and violence could be visited upon the son, a cycle continued across generations. The pathology is obvious: you get kicked by someone bigger than you, so you kick down at something smaller than you. I wanted to write a story that would tell people it's possible to break that cycle by refusing to do to others what was done to them.

"The story's called 'Appointment Overdue'" I said, painfully aware of the nervousness in my voice. "A divorced guy trying to figure out what to do with his life brings his ten-year-old son on vacation to the house where he grew up. After a while the son starts seeing what he thinks is a kid from the neighborhood hanging around. We discover it's the imaginary friend his father had as a kid, only it's not imaginary, it's a *genius loci*, a spirit of the place, drawn by loneliness. Resentful at being abandoned years earlier, and determined not to be ditched again, the spirit starts pulling him into its shadowy world. As the father fights to save his son's life he realizes that he's been doing to his son what his father did to him: being distant, short-tempered, and dismissive, forcing him to seek affection elsewhere. By taking responsibility for his actions he's able to release the spirit and rescue his son."

Phil turned another page in *Daily Variety*.

George kept scanning the skies in case a UFO happened by.

But the other staffers liked the idea and jumped in with questions about the relationship between father and son, what the spirit wanted and where it came from. Once their questions were answered, the room turned quiet as everyone looked to Phil, who finally glanced up at me. "Yeah, okay, why don't you go ahead and we'll figure it out from there."

I wasn't sure what *go ahead* meant. Had I gotten the assignment? Or was he asking me to redo it and come back with a new take on the story? My difficulty reading Phil's expression was exacerbated by darkness, since George had sucked all the light out of the room the instant the words had been spoken.

As we walked out the door I turned to one of the staffers. "Did he just buy my story?"

"Yes," he said. "You're approved to outline. After that, we'll see."

On the bus ride home, the knowledge that I'd made a sale to *The Twilight Zone* began to sink in. I allowed a brief moment of excitement then shut it down. I'd only sold the story; there was a long road (and apparently a sea of darkness) between me and a script deal, and a longer road still to seeing it produced. I'd learned by now not to get carried away about how things might work out because television is one of the few businesses where hope can kill you.

Eager not to let their interest cool I delivered the outline quickly and was then called in for a notes meeting. I can't remember whether or not George was in the room, but the other staffers had additional questions and suggestions. Most of them loved the story and were pushing hard to get me approved to script; others, not so much.

A week later, the phone rang. "There's resistance in some quarters to you going to script, but we've thrashed it out and you're good to go," the staffer said. "Everyone agrees we should at least get the script in hand. After that we can figure out what we want to do with it."

My agent couldn't believe it. "This is a great opportunity," she said. "Don't blow it."

I turned in the script two weeks later.

It disappeared into silence.

After two more weeks, my phone rang. "Some of us like it the way it is," the same staffer said, "and some of us don't. Can you come in to discuss revisions?"

When I arrived for the notes session, Phil seemed even more distracted and disorganized than before. He'd hurry to make one point then lose it halfway through and flip to another topic, talking fast. Then I noticed that his pupils had been replaced by giant black basketballs.

Oh shit, he's coked up.[*]

"Here's what you need to do with the script," he said at last. "Reverse the polarity."

I froze, pen in hand, and glanced around for clarification, but the other staff members were busy trying to find something interesting to look at on the carpet.

"Reverse . . . the polarity?" I asked.

"Yeahyeahyeah, it's too much what it is," he said. "And it's too much a morality play."

"But isn't that what *The Twilight Zone* is *supposed* to be? A morality play?"

He shook his head, his expression darkening. "No, that's *Rod's* version," he snapped. "We're not *doing* that version. This is *edgier*. We don't *do* morality stories. So you need to take that out, and reverse the polarity."

I did the best I could to meet the notes I understood, ignored the ones I didn't, and sent back the revision. Silence. A week passed. Another.

Finally, a staffer called me at home. "There's a lot of division over the script," she said. "So those of us who like it are going to make

---

[*] Phil's problem with cocaine was generally known but rarely spoken of until after his death in 2005.

the necessary changes in-house, which we hope will make everyone happy. We're not sure it can be done, but we're going to try."

Over the next month I heard that the script was alive, then dead, then in between. They tried removing the father's guilt about his behavior toward his son, but the structure fell apart because that was the whole point of the story, so they had to put it back. The drafts bounced back and forth between versions that were radically different, others that were virtually identical to my original script, and some that were edgier but emotionally empty.

I'd no sooner reconciled myself to the idea that my script was never going to be produced when they called to say that they'd ended up with a draft very close to my original script, and it had been put into the production pipeline. The main change, made in deference to Phil, was to remove the father's discovery that he was doing to his son what had been done to him. The spirit was just *there*. Having once been the father's imaginary friend, it tries to fill the same role with his son, drawing him into its world, then releasing him for no other reason than that's what being a friend is all about. To fit the new resolution, they retitled the episode "What Are Friends For?"

When the episode aired on CBS on October 4, 1986, the consensus was that the episode was just okay. I couldn't argue the point since much of the reason for telling the story had been obliterated. As it turned out, I wasn't the only one who preferred the morality tales that were a hallmark of the original *Twilight Zone*; the audience vanished, the ratings fell, and the show was canceled.

It would've been so great if I could've kept working on The Twilight Zone, I thought as I stashed away my VHS copy of the episode. *But I guess some things just aren't meant to be.*

A few weeks later, in a twist worthy of *The Twilight Zone*, my aunt called to tell me that she was divorcing Ted after learning that he was having an affair. This was shocking enough, but then she added that my parents—who had been pretending to be married since the annulment in 1952—were about to *get* married. But there would be no wedding ceremony, no public announcement, and no reception. Stranger still, the new marriage wasn't just private, it was *confidential*. Under California law, documents in a confidential marriage are not available in the public record, only through court order or with the permission of the couple in question.

"Why would he keep it a secret?" I asked. "Is he worried that people will discover they weren't married all those years?"

"I don't think he gives a shit about what people think. The real question is: Why is he getting married *now*?"

"He's getting older, maybe he wants her to have access to his accounts if he gets sick."

"He doesn't want anybody putting their hands on his money, let alone your mother. Try again."

It was a frustrating exchange. My aunt had a lot of dirt on my father, but she had been so thoroughly terrorized by his threats of violence and lawsuits over the years that she was reluctant to say anything that could be traced back to her. This left me in the annoying position of having to figure things out from the few little clues she was comfortable providing. I felt like Bob Woodward in an underground parking lot with Deep Throat, being fed just enough information to guide me to the right conclusions.

Follow the marriage license.

"Is he getting married because a wife can't be compelled to testify against her husband?"

"That's part of it. Your father wants to make sure she can't be legally *forced* to talk about things she saw or heard about him."

"But that doesn't stop her from talking to someone of her own free will."

"Getting warmer," she said.

Then it hit me. "He wants her to sign a prenuptial non-disclosure agreement as a condition of the marriage, doesn't he?"

"Took you long enough. He didn't tell her that, of course. He said he was marrying her to make sure she'd inherit his money when he dies, but that son of a bitch isn't going to leave her a dime. It's just bait to convince her to sign the paperwork. He knows that marrying her will complicate his life later, but if there's no marriage, there's no prenup, and if there's no prenup, then he's exposed."

My father had spent decades making sure my mother had no legal standing, no access to his accounts, nothing. For him to suddenly spin the wheel this hard the other way meant that something major must have happened behind the scenes.

"What's he so afraid of people finding out that he'd go through this much trouble to protect himself?" I asked. "And like you said, why *now*?"

"If I outlive the little prick, ask me when he's dead," she said, ending the conversation.

The appearance of another family mystery reminded me just how much I didn't want to know *any* of this. I had neither the time nor the inclination to play twenty questions with my aunt. I understood that secrets were the engine of our family, but if there was something she wanted me to know, then she should just come out and say it. Otherwise why drag me back into the mess in the first place?

Had I known just a little more about my father's past I would have been able to connect the dots between the confidential marriage and news out of Paterson about a pipe bomb that had exploded a few months earlier, fatally injuring a local resident. But getting that piece of the puzzle would take several more decades.

The Real Ghostbusters finished its first season on ABC with an Emmy nomination for Best Animated Series and a renewal for year two. The show was working, the ratings were huge, it was an un-mitigated hit.

So naturally they decided to fix it.

Ever since its debut the show had been attacked by media watch-dogs who accused the show of advancing leftist politics and radical feminism on one side, and black magic and Satanism on the other. (Between this show, *He-Man*, and *She-Ra* I had apparently been in the employ of Satan for nearly three years without knowing it, so there's a considerable back-pay issue that needs to be resolved.) Rather than tell these groups to take a hike, the network censors used the complaints to push for changes that would make the show more acceptable to their rarified sensibilities. This led to a meeting at DIC with producers Joe Medjuck and Michael Gross, Ame Simon and Jennie Trias from ABC, some of our writers, and several "experts" from a consulting firm specializing in children's entertainment.

One of the consultants teed off the meeting by saying "We need to change Janine." Janine was one of our most popular characters, strong, smart, hip, witty, and independent—attributes the consul-tants and censors absolutely hated. They felt that her stylish, tough wardrobe made her "harsh and slutty," an assessment that said more about how they viewed strong women than it did about Janine.

"She needs to be more of a mother to the group," they said, "warmer and more nurturing. She should be put in softer clothes, dresses rather than skirts, no jewelry, and drop her spiky hair and eyeglasses."

Her *eyeglasses*?

"They're pointed at the ends. Children are frightened by sharp objects, so her glasses should be round and inviting."

I asked to see the data supporting their thesis that children were scared of pointy glasses. Rather than answer the question they argued that their research could only be properly deciphered by someone with a degree in psychology.

"I *have* a degree in psychology," I said, "and I want to see your data."

Faced with someone who could call them on their bullshit, the consultants became defensive and looked to the network execs and producers for backup, as though *I* were the one acting inappropriately. It was the return of High Priest logic.

Why don't you just say you brought someone back from the dead on a small Polynesian island and save us all the ambiguity?

"Let them finish their suggestions and we can come back to the details," Ame said. I sat back, chewing the inside of my cheek as I conjured up the image of the lead consultant at the receiving end of a LAWS shoulder-mounted rocket.

"There's also a problem with the main cast because they're all adults," they continued. "Children identify with children more than they do with adults. So you need to introduce some recurring characters who are children, and make them Junior Ghostbusters."

"I absolutely disagree," I said. Everyone looked away, embarrassed by my determination to point out that the emperor was naked. "Most kids don't want to be Robin, they want to be Batman, because if they work really hard, there's a chance they might someday *become* Batman. But Robin is their own age and can already do things that are impossible for them. Kids can look up to the adult Ghostbusters and aspire to become like them one day. Putting kids in the show and giving them proton packs—essentially unlicensed nuclear reactors—destroys any sense of believability. Besides, while we can put our adult characters into realistic jeopardy, BS&P says we can't do that with kids, so you're going to cripple the storytelling."

They refused to debate the question. After all, they were *experts* with *degrees*, and the network supported their work enough to hire them. They knew what they were talking about. I was just the guy who made the show ABC's highest-rated, Emmy-nominated series.

"In keeping with making the show more child-friendly," they continued, "we strongly suggest that the character of Slimer be made more important, because he is the child surrogate for the audience. His inability to articulate himself reflects every child who cannot communicate well. The Ghostbusters should therefore be accepting of him, playful but not harsh. He is your audience personified, and should be as much a star as the rest of the cast. Consequently we suggest renaming the show *Slimer! and the Real Ghostbusters*."

Slimer was not a child surrogate, he was a dead creature, a foil for the cast; kicking him around was half the fun. But I held my tongue, confident that Ame and the others would realize that there was no way we could make him the center of the show.

There was more. "Children like clarity, they want to know who a character is and how he fits in with the others. But the adult characters aren't well delineated. So we suggest eliminating Ray Stantz [the Dan Aykroyd character] because he does not appear to serve the benefit of the program."

"No way that's gonna happen," I said, "but keep going."

They suggested that the role of Winston Zeddemore (our only African American character) was also vague, so to give him a clearly defined position we should make him the driver.

"Let me see if I've got this right," I said. "You want to give all the other characters positive, creative, scientific roles and turn Winston, our only black character, into the *driver*?"

They nodded, quite pleased with themselves.

"And this doesn't strike any of you as racist?"

The consultants went batshit at the suggestion that their notes were fueled by prejudice (much as I considered their suggestions about Janine to be party-line sexism at its worst). There were intimations of complaints to vast, implacable Superiors for the poor way they were being treated. To calm the situation Ame, Jennie, and the producers made soft soothing sounds and eventually the consultants left the room.

"You can't do this," I said. "If you make these changes, you'll destroy the show. You've got the highest-rated animated series on television right now, why would you want to kill it?"

"Their opinions have been very useful to us before," Ame said, though I could see that even she knew what was being shoved down our throats was dubious at best.

"We're all here for the same reason," Jennie said, "we want to improve the show."

"Improve it *how*? You're in the number one spot, there's nothing higher than that. Getting the show to this point was a careful, delicate dance. If you go along with this, you'll destroy the infrastructure that allowed it to become a hit."

They wouldn't listen. Even the producers were willing to go along with the changes, which surprised and unmanned me. I was all alone. They were going to implement these changes whether I liked it or not.

"Then I can't be a part of it," I said, "especially the changes to Janine. She's a strong, smart female character, one of the few on Saturday morning television, and I refuse to turn her into one more cliché mommy character. There are plenty of those out there; we need at least one female character who is witty, independent, and cool. That's how she was in the movie, how she is in the series, and I'm not going to destroy that."

"So what are you saying?" Ame asked.

"I'm saying that if you do this, I'm off the show."

"Joe, c'mon, calm down," Michael Gross said, "you're not going to walk off a number one network animated series."

"Watch me," I said.

My agent was furious when I told her I was leaving the show. "You can't piss off the network like that," she said. "If you quit, you'll never work for them again. And don't forget, you walked off *She-Ra*; if you walk off another show, you'll get a reputation for being difficult. Once you get that rep, it doesn't come off. No one will want to work with you."

God knows I didn't *want* to quit: I'd fought hard to make the show a success, and there weren't a lot of open berths on other shows. It was the same choice I faced back in Community: betray what I knew to be true, or walk away. In both cases my conscience said go, so the next day I packed up my office and left *The Real Ghostbusters* behind.

The blatantly sexist manner in which the consultants interfered in the show galvanized fans and critics alike. The sexism was so egregious that the *Los Angeles Times* ran a story about the contretemps on September 3, 1987. Neither the consultants nor ABC wanted copies of their internal reports to appear in the article because it would confirm the misogyny behind their notes. But somehow excerpts and illustrations taken directly from the reports ended up in the piece.

How this happened I have no idea.

ABC would launch the retitled *Slimer! and the Real Ghostbusters* a year later, featuring the Junior Ghostbusters, a softer Janine, and a Winston who drove the car while everybody else did the cool stuff. As predicted, the ratings plummeted like a cartoon piano: adult fans despised the sappy changes, kids hated the Junior Ghostbusters, both sides rejected the softer, more mommy-ish Janine, and Slimer became the most annoying thing about the show.

The Real Ghostbusters was the best job I'd ever had. But I've always believed that as long as we hold fast to what we believe is true and honest and just, things generally work out in the end.

But that knowledge was cold comfort as I started once again looking for work.

CHAPTER 22

Captain, My Captain

S hortly after leaving *The Real Ghostbusters*, my agent arranged for a meeting with producers Doug Netter, John Copeland, and Gary Goddard, who were putting together a new science fiction series called *Captain Power and the Soldiers of the Future.** As with *He-Man* and *She-Ra*, the show was tied to a toy line from Mattel, but this was a *live-action* series. They needed a story editor with at least one live-action credit and a history of working with toy-based shows. Thanks to *He-Man* and the timing of my one *Twilight Zone* script I fit the bill, and they hired me at once.

The point was not lost on me that if I had surrendered to corporate stupidity and stayed with *The Real Ghostbusters*, I would've been contractually unable to work on *Captain Power*. But I'd followed my conscience, and in return the universe opened the door to the live-action TV gig that I'd been chasing for the past two years.

I don't believe in God. But I do believe in dramatic irony.

Captain Power was set in a post-apocalyptic world where

---

* See the previous section on the stupidest series names in television history for an explanation of that title.

machines hunted humans, a concept that owed much to James Cameron's *Terminator.*[*] There were some key differences—our protagonists wore nanotech uniforms that could transform into battle armor, and there was no time travel involved—but I was still uncomfortable with some of the parallels, so I set about moving the concept as far from *The Terminator* as possible. I changed the emphasis from machines killing humans as an act of war to the idea that our antagonist is digitizing humans in order to *save* them from all the diseases and weaknesses to which flesh is heir until the day when they can be transferred permanently into perfect robotic forms.

It's a not-unreasonable argument, as demonstrated later by Ray Kurzweil's work on the synthesis of man and machine. Given the choice between living in a flesh shell that will one day die, or a bio-engineered form that would live forever, there are many who would opt for the latter, and that's where our antagonist lands. Where he crosses the line is by deciding to digitize the world's population whether they want him to or not. Our heroes, the aforementioned Soldiers of the Future, are trying to stop him and end the war.

Since the show required a lot of world-building, I again brought in Larry DiTillio, who after me would become the series' primary writer. Besides, I wasn't quite sure when the vendetta he'd mentioned upon leaving *He-Man* might expire.

Like all dramatic television at the time, science fiction shows were episodic in structure. Story threads set up in one episode had to be paid off in the same episode, pushing the reset button at *fade out* so the next episode could start clean with nothing left unresolved. Long-form storytelling simply wasn't done because the networks and studios didn't think audiences were capable of following a plot line that went longer than the occasional two-parter.

---

[*] "Imitation is the sincerest form of television." —Fred Allen

Being rather contrarian, I wanted to try something different: a season-long story that would build on events in prior episodes and foreshadow incidents that would play out much later. To further subvert audience expectations, the season finale would turn the premise of the series upside down by destroying the characters' base of operations, transforming a show about a group of heroes operating out of a safe haven into a series about insurrectionists on the run, hunted and alone. I could never have gotten that idea past any network, but we were making the show for syndication, without a network riding herd on us, for a toy company that wasn't quite sure what to do with us. It was the rough beginning of a new approach to episodic storytelling that would profoundly alter the television landscape, but I didn't know that at the time.

I just thought it would be really cool.

As I began working on *Captain Power*, DC Comics editor Bob Greenberger invited me to write an issue of *Teen Titans Spotlight*. I agreed immediately, excited to come full circle with comics from fan to writer. Besides, the form was new to me and would push me out of my comfort zone.

Spotlight featured solo tales of the group's members, so I set Cyborg against Harvey Dent, a character from Batman's rogues' gallery better known as Two-Face. Both men were alike in that they were physically scarred and kept their faces partially covered, but one became a hero, the other a killer. Dent believes that the circumstances of his injury left him no other choice than to become a killer, and that Cyborg would have turned out the same under similar conditions. To test this theory, Dent puts him through a series of horrific events, confident that they will push him to the dark side.

I wanted to make Cyborg's refusal to return evil with evil a reflection of what I went through with my family. Like Dent, my father blamed outside circumstances for what he became, whereas I leaned into the idea that we can choose another path. Every time Dent or my father said "I have no choice," they'd made a choice, they just didn't want to admit it.

Inch by inch I was working more of my personal history into the writing, a process I found both liberating and terrifying.

I was dead asleep when the phone rang at nine A.M. on a Saturday morning. Everybody knows I'm a night writer and to never call before noon, so I figured it was important.

I fumbled for the phone and figured out which part went to my ear. "Yeahwhuddisit?"

I recognized the voice instantly as Harlan Ellison. "I've had it with those fuckers at KPFK," he said and let fly with a string of profanities whose fury was matched only by their flawless construction. In keeping with Mike Hodel's last wishes, Harlan had been hosting *Hour 25* for over a year, only to be worn down by repeated tugs-of-war with the station over content and Politburo-style power struggles over who was in charge of what. The flashpoint was a heated argument over whether or not he would be allowed to read one of his short stories over the air, a piece that contained language permissible in previous years but which was now considered problematic by station personnel. Fed up, Harlan quit the show.

"I want you to take over as host of *Hour 25*," he said.

"What about the guys at the station? Don't they get a vote in who takes over?"

"No, fuck 'em" he said. "Mike gave it to me, I own it, I copyrighted the show in the name of my company, and now I give it to you. You know the genre, the people, you used to be a reporter, you've done radio . . . you're the best guy for the job. Do you want it or not?"

The Rather Scandalous
Wedding of Sophia and
Kazimier Straczynski

Sophia pursues Kazimier to New York (*center, behind life preserver*)

Sophia Straczynski sits with her children, visibly unhappy

Sophia poses with German officer at a memorial

Friends of the family: the German soldiers and workers of the Bogdanova train station

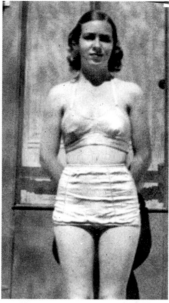

Evelyn, age fourteen (*left*), when she began seeing Charles; brothel photo (*right*) used in the selection process

The License and Certificate of Confidential Marriage noting when my parents, who got married earlier only to have the marriage annulled over his violence, and went decades pretending to be married, actually got married but didn't want anybody to know that they hadn't been married and were now getting married.

My family in Los Angeles, with me holding a "stand still" bribery ice cream, my father holding my sister, and my grandfather Kazimier holding his tongue. My mother was told by Charles to stand in the back because she was "too ugly" to be in front.

Me and my mother, pregnant with Vicky, during one of her bouts of depression

Sophia Straczynski with me
in the River Street tavern

Me visiting my mother
on Van Houten with the
Decoy Cat

The moment Pan Rafael saw my distress at being forced to drink vodka and became an ally

Evelyn, Victor Rafael Rachwalski, Sophia Straczynski, me, and the blue pedal car

Some of my father's framed personal Nazi photos and belongings

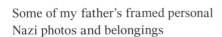

Me in the doorway of our Skid Row shanty, stomach distended from lack of food

Me and my father at the Graham Avenue apartment in Paterson. To keep me from squirming during photos he'd grab my ear and pinch really hard.

Me and my mother on my first day of school. First class: Introduction to Bullies.

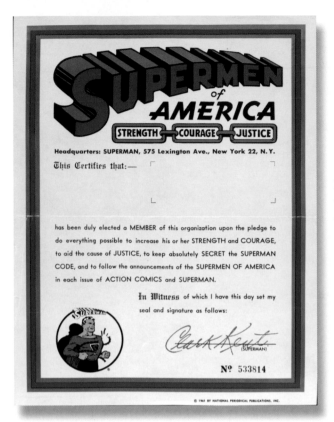

Membership certificate for the Supermen of America, which put me just that much closer to my goal

A promotional poster for the Supermen of America. "Everywhere I looked, a friend was looking back at me."

Ken Pagaard with one of the elders, Clay Ford, a genuinely nice guy who worked predominantly with the House of Abba crowd

Ken Pagaard and some of the members of Community

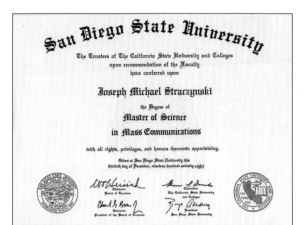

Fake master's degree, fake graduation, allegedly non-fake grandmother and father

The San Diego journalism years: on KSDO (*left*) and interviewing actor/ comedian Irwin Corey (*below*)

Six foot three, about 140 pounds, and putting every penny into writing supplies instead of food

Me and Kathryn, around the time we got married

Working on *The Twilight Zone* with casting director Mary Ann Barton, and producer Mark Shelmerdine, along with a credit I could never have imagined

Story by
ROD SERLING
Teleplay By
J. MICHAEL STRACZYNSKI

Approving prosthetics for *Babylon 5* at Criswell EFX house, which provided prosthetics for the pilot movie

The first gathering of most of the *B5* cast: Me, Jerry Doyle, Mira Furlan, Tamlyn Tomita, Peter Jurasik, director Richard Compton, Michael O'Hare, Johnny Sekka (*left to right*). Seated: Doug Netter, Blair Baron, Patricia Tallman.

Me, Kathryn, and the brain trust from Foundation Imaging the night *Babylon 5* won its first Emmy Award. (The late Ron Thornton is seated to my right.)

One of the proudest days of my life: receiving the Hugo Award for my work on *Babylon 5*

My first check for something I'd written: fifteen dollars for an article sold to the *San Diego Reader* much, much earlier

My first check for one million dollars, paid to my loan-out company, One Ski. One of the most astonishing moments in my life. From small beginnings truly wonderful things can grow.

Colm Feore, Clint Eastwood, John Malkovich, Angelina Jolie, and me during the filming of *Changeling*

In the Icelandic void for *Sense8*

At a Chula Vista High School reunion with teachers Jo Ann Seipel (née Massie) and Rochelle Terry

The story in two photos: a
child with dreams in Paterson,
then much later, attending the
BAFTA ceremony in London,
nominated for a British
Academy Award

"Yeah . . . yeah, I'll take it," I said.

"Good luck," Harlan said, and hung up.

Two cups of coffee later I was sufficiently awake to understand what I'd just agreed to. Hosting a two-hour weekly talk show meant more than just doing the interviews; there would have to be extensive prep work—reading books by guest authors, researching the latest doings in SF, finding and booking guests—all while working ridiculously long hours on *Captain Power*.

And then there was the fear factor. I was not that far from the student who couldn't finish reading a story out loud in Mrs. Chater's class and threw up every morning out of sheer terror at speaking to an audience of thirty SDSU freshmen. I'd done brief, ten-minute review segments for KSDO, but hosting *Hour 25* would mean being live on the radio for *two hours* every Friday night, speaking to thousands of listeners. The very idea filled me with dread.

I picked up the phone to call Harlan back and decline the offer, then put it back down. Yes, the idea scared the bejeezus out of me, but wasn't that the very reason why I should do it, why I *had* to do it? Taking chances was why I'd come to Los Angeles in the first place. Besides, doing the show would let me talk to some of the brightest minds in science fiction, fantasy, and horror, conversations that would be invaluable to my development as a writer.

I could do this. I *would* do this.

Six days later, Friday, June 26, 1987, I throttled back my terror and showed up to host my first installment of *Hour 25*, with Larry DiTillio along as cohost because his sense of humor was a good complement to my own occasional stodginess. During our interview with *Star Trek* actor Walter Koenig, my fear of screwing up kicked my voice a full octave higher than normal, but I got through it and stayed with the show for five years. No, it didn't pay anything—listener-supported Pacifica stations were staffed almost entirely by volunteers—but over the course of 260 broadcasts we interviewed such luminaries as William Gibson, Ray Bradbury, Neil Gaiman, Dean Koontz, John Carpenter, Wes Craven, Robert Bloch, Vonda McIntyre, and Norman Spinrad. Every Friday night was a master class in writing with some of the best in the business.

Since KPFK didn't have the resources to provide aircheck copies of our broadcasts, I used a video recorder wired to a radio to record them, hoping to one day publish the interviews in book form. I didn't know that the recording head was damaged, so the audio could only be played back on that same VCR. After it died, only a few recordings made before the heads blew out could be rescued. Five years of work, over five hundred hours of history, just gone.

You've got a mean sense of humor, Mike Hodel.

Captain Power debuted September 20, 1987, as the number-one-rated kids show in the United States—my third show to earn that distinction—and became a favorite of legions of science fiction fans. Even critic Roger Ebert praised it.

So of course it was immediately dogpiled by media advocacy groups for "excessive violence." There were newspaper editorials against the show, televised tub-thumpings, tarring, feathering, and dead-catting. Even activist Jerry Rubin rode the tidal wave of protest, writing in the *Los Angeles Times* that *Captain Power* "exposed thousands of children to the myth that violence can solve our differences."*

The press uncritically repeated claims that the show subjected viewers to 130 acts of violence per episode, which was patently ridiculous. One hundred thirty acts of violence in twenty-two minutes

---

* It should be noted that Rubin was convicted of battery in 1980. By contrast not a single incident of real-world violence was ever attributed to *Captain Power*.

of airtime would require five violent acts *every minute*, which was inconceivable and far beyond our budget. A little digging revealed that if there was a firefight during an episode, the critics counted *every bullet fired* as a violent incident rather than labeling it as one fight. Some even categorized harsh words or insults as acts of violence. It's easy to start racking up numbers when you fudge the data so violence means whatever you want it to mean.

But the criticisms made Mattel nervous, and they began pumping out notes to minimize the violence. After getting a note that we could no longer shoot robots in the head, I emailed producer John Copeland to ask, "Is there any stricture against kicking them in the nuts?"

In August 1987, after finishing work on the first season of *Captain Power*, Kathryn and I visited Brighton, England, to promote the show at the 45th World Science Fiction Convention, with a side trip to London. In the three years since selling my first *He-Man* episode, I'd written sixty-six produced scripts, along with dozens of outlines and premises for outside writers, story-edited over 150 freelance scripts, *and* had taken on a weekly two-hour radio talk show.

I was beyond exhausted.

"You're not going to do any writing on this vacation, okay?" Kathryn said. "You're going to leave the work behind and just enjoy yourself."

By now I was used to writing ten to twenty pages per day, every day; without a place to put that energy, I was like a border collie desperate for something to do. Within a few days of arriving in England I was vibrating so badly that I bought a pocket-size notebook and began slipping into the bathroom at night while Kathryn was asleep to outline *Demon Night*, my first attempt at a horror novel. By the time we returned to Los Angeles I'd secretly written vast tracts of the book and was able to finish the whole thing over the next month. I'd tackled the book as a writing exercise, to see if I could pull off a story at that length, so I didn't give much thought to selling it; I just put the manuscript away and forgot about it. *Captain Power* was about to gear up for a second season and that would keep me plenty busy for a while. The ratings were solid, the reviews were good, the producers were happy, everything was perfect.

Honestly, by now you'd think I'd see it coming, wouldn't you?

A few days after I was nominated for a Gemini Award, Canada's version of an Emmy, for Best Writing in a Dramatic Series for my work on *Captain Power*, a meeting was convened with Gary Goddard, Doug Netter, and John Copeland to discuss the renewal. They explained that Mattel insisted on having approval over all scripts as a condition of renewing the series. I said I couldn't work in a situation where a toy company had creative control, and suggested they hire DiTillio as my replacement. Larry was a gentler, more collaborative soul and knew the *Captain Power* universe better than anyone else. Overall, it was a very amicable conversation: I knew this wasn't their fault, and they respected my position.

On the other hand:

"What the hell is *wrong* with you?" my agent asked when I told her the news. Her tone left no doubt that she wanted to put my head between two red-hot iron tongs for an extended period. "First *She-Ra*, then *Ghostbusters*, now this? You can't keep walking off shows. You're going to get a reputation for being difficult. What am I talking about, you've already *got* that reputation. Still, it's your decision. If you really believe you have to go, then go, just don't be surprised when no one calls to hire you after this."

She was right. I was almost certainly unemployable by now.

If you hold fast to what's true and right and just, things work out, I reminded myself. *Remember, you only got* Captain Power *because you left* Ghostbusters.

Candy called back a few days later. "Mark Shelmerdine, who runs London Films, wants to talk to you about coming on as story editor for a show he's producing," she said, disbelief in her voice. "How the *hell* do you keep doing this? How do you keep blowing up your career only to end up on something better within a week? I just don't understand it."

I allowed that it was a mystery to me as well. "So what's the show?" I assumed it was going to be an animated series, or another toy-sponsored show.

She let out a long, slow breath, anticipating my reaction, and I heard a smile come into her voice.

"It's season three of *The Twilight Zone.*"

CHAPTER 23

Into the Zone

MGM had made a significant investment in *The Twilight Zone* during its network run, but ended up short of the one hundred episodes needed to be viable in syndication. Desperate to recoup their investment, they commissioned another thirty half-hour episodes to be produced by Mark Shelmerdine.

Mark shared my belief that the *Zone* functioned best when there was a sense of morality at the center of the stories, and that this had been missing from many of the network episodes. I'd only written one produced script, but as Mark scanned through the episodes he could see that I was trying to hew to that tradition. I took great pleasure in knowing that the very aspect that Phil DeGuere had worked so hard to kill in my script was *exactly* what led Mark to hire me as executive story editor.

To balance out the more fantastical elements of *The Twilight Zone*, Mark wanted a show grounded in emotional truth, that would explore our own dreams, nightmares, hopes, and fears. This was exciting but scary; I was still getting used to the idea of exposing my personal feelings in my stories. Doing what he described would require confronting parts of my life that I'd worked hard to ignore.

Find what you're afraid of, and do it.

Having always felt emotionally cut off from the rest of the world, I wrote "Dream Me a Life" (with Eddie Albert) about a reclusive widower in a retirement home who begins sharing the dreams of a catatonic woman down the hall. Alone, neither of them can overcome the loss of those they loved, but together they find the strength to face the world anew. "Rendezvous in a Dark Place" was based on my grandmother's obsession with death and her tendency to attend the funerals of people she didn't know. Refusing to engage with a world she feels has passed her by, our protagonist falls into a dangerous romance with Death personified. The episode starred Janet Leigh (known for her work in *Psycho*) as a surrogate for my grandmother, who was not available for the role on account of being actually dead.

From the "where do you get your ideas?" department: One evening after taking Kathryn and her parents to dinner, the waiter came running after me because I'd forgotten to sign the credit card slip. Embarrassed by the gaffe, I explained that I'd pawned my memory that morning and it was now full of holes. *Wait a second*, I thought, *I can make a story out of that.* The result was "The Mind of Simon Foster" (starring Bruce Weitz), about a pawnshop that buys people's memories of high school graduations, first kisses, and other deeply personal moments that are then sold to collectors.

The hardest episode to write concerned domestic violence. "Acts of Terror" starred Melanie Mayron as a battered wife who gets a porcelain Doberman that becomes her guardian, the literal manifestation of her rage at years of abuse. Born of my desire to see my father get back a little of the pain he dealt out, I was pleased and honored to learn later that several battered women's groups used the episode to help them face their rage.

I'd always heard the term "writing as therapy" but never applied it to myself until *The Twilight Zone*. There was a lot about my life that I couldn't talk about openly, but putting those events into the lives of fictional characters made it easier. I could be more objective while at the same time investing the characters with the emotions I couldn't allow for myself, a process that diminished some of the weight I'd been carrying for years. I felt lighter. I hadn't expected that.

One afternoon, Mark asked if I'd be willing to write a script based on someone else's outline. I hesitated. I'd come onto the *Zone* to tell my own stories, not someone else's. While I sometimes developed stories that were then assigned to freelancers, the river had never flowed the other way. But Mark was a great guy so I said yes, eager to be of service.

"So what've you got?" I asked.

He plopped a sheaf of papers on my desk.

The outline was entitled "Our Selena Is Dying."

The writer was Rod Serling.

"Carol Serling, Rod's widow, found this in his files," Mark said. "It's an outline for a *Twilight Zone* episode he never got around to writing in teleplay form. Would you like to write the script in a posthumous collaboration with Mr. Serling?"

And for the barest flicker of a moment I was back at Southwestern College, in my senior year of high school, looking at a familiar figure in a corduroy jacket. *Cut every third adjective. And never let them stop you from telling the story you want to tell.*

Yes, sir, I'll do my best.

How unlikely was it that I would grow up on Serling's words, meet him without realizing it, then sixteen years later find myself on staff of *The Twilight Zone*, collaborating with him after the fact on *one of his scripts*? Improbable. No: *impossible.* But there it was.

The story—about an elderly woman who invites her young cousin to stay with her in an attempt to draw off her youth and thus avoid death—would not have fallen into Serling's major arcana, like "The Monsters Are Due on Maple Street" or "Walking Distance." But even his minor works were good enough to make me want to get out of the writing business before someone figured out I was a fraud.

Giving the script the correct flavor meant trying to approximate Serling's writing style, which is so distinct that it's easy to spin out into unintended parody, as evidenced by any comedian who's ever said to an audience, "Submitted for your approval." But ignoring the music in his style would produce something that was tone-deaf and inelegant. I thought back to the first day I began to write, when I finally understood the difference between a writer's style and his voice. Comedians could mock Serling's *style* because it was the most obvious part of his work; but his *voice*, the clockwork precision of the mind behind that trademark style, was far more difficult to emulate.

So every night I watched four or more of his episodes, soaking in his words so I could carry his grammar, inflections, and structure with me the next day. I worked harder on that half-hour script than anything I'd ever written and turned it in only when I felt it wouldn't diminish Rod's legacy. The night it aired I saw a title card that the seventeen-year-old version of me could never have imagined that night at Southwestern College: *Story by Rod Serling, Teleplay by J. Michael Straczynski*.

Evolutionary biologist John Haldane was right: "The universe is not only stranger than we imagine, it is stranger than we *can* imagine."

But frankly, I wouldn't live anywhere else.

While working on the *Zone* I was having dinner with Kathryn and my agents when Candy said, "You know, you really should write a novel someday."

I confessed that I had. "It's a contemporary horror novel in the Stephen King tradition."

"Why haven't I seen it?"

"Because it's sitting in a closet. I just wrote it for myself, to see if I could do it."

"Let me read it."

I said that it wasn't very good and not worth her time, but she pressed the point and the next day I sent over the manuscript for *Demon Night.*

Three weeks later, Candy called. "Congratulations, you just sold your first novel."

She'd sent the book via her New York affiliate to Richard Marek, president of E. P. Dutton, who offered to publish it in hardcover with a substantial advance. The book would be published on July 12, 1988, five days shy of my thirty-fourth birthday.

"Now aren't you glad you mentioned it?" she said. "Always tell me these things."

But there was something else I hadn't mentioned to her. For some time I'd been playing with a couple of ideas for an original science fiction series. One was a big, sprawling saga about races from different worlds engaged in a massive war. The story would take years to tell, chronicling the rise and fall of empires, and featured characters who would change radically as they embraced their destinies for good or ill. I loved the idea, but the scale was beyond what could be afforded on a normal television budget. The other story was much smaller, centered on a commercial space station where ships bearing cargo from other worlds could set up shop or continue to Earth after passing through customs.

I couldn't figure out how to make the saga series small enough to be produced for TV or how to make the stakes in the space station show big enough to be interesting over the long haul. I was about to give up on *both* of them when something unexpected happened.

Most days, any story problems I'm working on when I step into the shower are almost always resolved by the time I step out again. So instead of thinking about the *Twilight Zone* script I was supposed to be writing that day, I loaded the two series ideas into my head at the same time . . . and realized that I hadn't been able to make either of them work because they weren't two different series.

They were *two sides of the same story.*

The solution was to put the commercial space station in neutral territory as a diplomatic outpost, where beings from a hundred worlds could work out their differences. When their efforts fail, the resulting war story could be told by reflecting the larger struggle within the smaller confines of the station, much as a World War II story was told through a nightclub in *Casablanca.*

The moment those wires crossed in my head I saw an entire five-year arc, each season corresponding to a year of story time. If my one-season arc on *Captain Power* had been a set of training wheels, this was a Harley-Davidson. A five-year arc would echo the five-part structure of a novel—introduction, rising action, complication, climax, and denouement—allowing me to foreshadow events years in advance. I could also create characters who were polar opposites of each other and put them on parallel tracks, weaving them in and out of each other's lives as counterpoint then *reversing* their roles in the story. The station would go from a place of peace to the front line of a war, then the center of a new alliance heralding an age of interstellar tranquility.

I expanded the story into a treatment and two-hour spec pilot script then took them to Doug Netter and John Copeland, with whom I had worked on *Captain Power.* They agreed to help try to sell the series, which I entitled *Babylon 5,* and thought the process might take at most a few months.

Even now, I laugh.

CHAPTER 24

Blowing Up the World

In March 1988, two months shy of finishing up the writing season on *The Twilight Zone*, the Writers Guild of America voted to go on strike. Everyone knew this was going to be messy. The studios had dug in, the writers were tired of being screwed, and neither side was willing to budge. So for the second time since arriving in LA, I was walking a picket line in what would become one of the most volatile and longest labor actions in the union's history.

The timing couldn't have been worse. Confident that we would be solvent for a while, Kathryn and I had finally paid off a bunch of long-standing bills, including the last of my student loans, so we had little money in our savings. To distract myself from the sudden shock of not going into an office every day, and since the strike didn't preclude writing fiction or hosting a talk show pro bono, I focused on *Hour 25* while outlining my second novel, *OtherSyde*.

On July 12, 1988, E. P. Dutton published *Demon Night*. Holding your first novel in your hands is unlike any other experience. You're hyperaware of the texture of the pages, the heft and smell of a book that actually has your name on it. I'd put it on the table, walk away, come back, pick it up, and just stare at it. It was also a deeply humbling experience. The publisher had arranged autograph sessions at local bookstores, and with each appearance any fantasies I'd harbored of eager fans lined up to buy the book came to a screeching stop. I would sit alone at a table for hours as customers walked past on their way to buy books they actually *wanted*. Once in a while someone would wander up and ask what the book was about. I'd tell them, they'd nod for a moment then toddle off. Selling just one or two copies was a victory, even if it was obvious that they were only buying it out of pity. I felt as if I was back on that frozen Paterson street corner, trying to sell bars of World's Finest Chocolate to people who weren't there.

Despite the rocky start, the book got decent reviews, sold nicely, and was reprinted in the UK, Germany, Sweden, and South America. It was also nominated for a Bram Stoker Award by the Horror Writers of America for Best First Novel, and though it didn't win, I took quiet pride in knowing (by virtue of being the awards counter that year) that Stephen King voted for it.

On August 7, 1988, after five months of bitterness and recriminations that resulted in many writers losing their homes and their careers, the WGA strike came to what many still consider an unsatisfying conclusion. The acrimony would take years to heal, but when I returned to my office at *The Twilight Zone*, Mark dispelled any awkwardness and treated me as the Prodigal Son returned. I buckled down to write as many of the remaining episodes as I could, painfully aware that this opportunity might never come again.

Having grown up rootless, I'd always fantasized about having a proper home, so with the strike over we bought a small house in

Sherman Oaks. After moving in, I was working in my new home office when Kathryn stuck her head in the door. "I just opened a letter from someone, I think you better take a look at it," she said. "You're not going to believe this."

The letter, from a woman named Charlean, began, "You may or may not have heard of me throughout your life, but I am your half sister through your father, Charles. I didn't discover until last year that Charles was my father. All my life it was kept a well-guarded secret in my mother's family until I decided to pursue the truth."

The letter included her address, phone number, and an invitation to call. I looked again at her first name. Charlean. As in Charles.

A circuit closed in my brain as I remembered my aunt's words to my mother: *Does Joey know about his sister?*

Oh, no, Theresa, he can never know about that.

Another Straczynski secret had emerged from the shadows.

"You think it's real?" Kathryn asked.

"Only one way to find out," I said and picked up the phone.

Kathryn shook her head and walked out of the office, throwing back, "Honestly, your *family*."

It was all that needed to be said.

My conversation with Charlean confirmed that she was indeed my father's illegitimate child, eager to find out as much as possible about the family she'd never known.

"Let me give you a piece of advice," I said. "There are some family trees that don't bear shaking. This is one of them. Actually, this is a whole *forest* of them. You're infinitely better off for not having known Charles as you grew up. He's the most evil man I've ever met; if you're smart, you'll keep your distance."

She thanked me for my concern but had already made plans to visit him.

She later admitted that my warning had been exactly on target. *Honestly, your family.*

Yep.

Several months after finishing work on *The Twilight Zone* I was still looking for another gig when a call came from Michael Gross, producer of the rebooted *Slimer! and the Real Ghostbusters*. He explained that the show's ratings had continued to plummet and they needed my help. "Would you be willing to come back and write some scripts for the show, get us back on track?"

"Sure," I said, "but I have some conditions. First, I want the authority to argue with the network censors. Second, the Junior Ghostbusters don't exist. Third, I don't write Slimer as a kid surrogate—he's a ghost, he's a dead thing, and I like kicking the crap out of him. Finally, I want to restore Janine to what she was: an independent, smart, assertive woman, not the submissive, passive mommy character the network turned her into."

I could feel him wince under the weight of those demands. I was basically asking him to shove a grenade up the network's ass and pull the pin. Anticipating the battles ahead of him, he sighed and said, "Let me see what I can do and get back to you."

After I hung up, a part of me said, *Don't be stupid; with the* Zone *over you could use the money, don't piss them off.* But having gotten *The Real Ghostbusters* right the first time, I felt some measure of ownership and was too stubborn to back down. I'd write the show the way it was meant to be or not at all.

Michael called back a few hours later. "Done," he said. "You've got a deal."

Eager to repair the show, my first script up was "Janine, You've Changed," about a demon who, unbeknownst to the rest, had been posing as Janine's fairy godmother the last two seasons. Feeding off her insecurity about her appearance, the demon convinced

Janine to keep changing her look to be more appealing to others. The Ghostbusters help her accept that she's beautiful just as she is, which banishes the demon and restores Janine to her original appearance.

The censors and consultants who had pushed for a softer Janine *hated* the story, but there was nothing they could do to stop it. They were particularly furious that the story equated them with a hell-born demon.

Interestingly, the Union of Hellborn Demons Local 666 voiced similar complaints in the other direction.

To drum up interest in the show, ABC asked me to write a prime-time *Real Ghostbusters* special that would be fast-tracked through the animation process (which normally took up to a year). I said I'd only do it if the daytime BS&P folks had no say in the story. I justified this demand on the grounds that instead of airing on Saturday morning, this would be broadcast in prime time, when programming standards were much more relaxed. They agreed in the belief that I was tired of the constant fights and wanted a break. But that was only partly true. The goal was less about writing a script free *from* the censors and more about telling a story *about* them, and if they saw the script before it was produced they'd howl bloody murder.

"The Halloween Door" told the story of Dr. Crowley, a madman with a machine that would destroy all the scary supernatural books in the world because kids shouldn't be exposed to such things. I even put some of BS&P's comments in the mouth of the censorship-driven madman to illustrate the idea that however well intended, censors can be as destructive as any demonic entity by curtailing independence of thought.

The kicker? After being falsely accused for years of trying to slip in references to Satan, I named the antagonist after Aleister Crowley, a famous practitioner of the dark arts, often referred to as the most evil man in the world, and *not one of the censors caught it.*

Idiots.

Then, as seemed inevitable in my work by now, everything blew up.

One of my last *Ghostbusters* scripts to be produced was entitled "Russian About," an homage to H. P. Lovecraft's Cthulhu mythos. As one of America's foremost writers of supernatural fiction, Lovecraft's legacy includes a rich history of fictional characters, locations, and books that he encouraged other writers to use in their own works to keep that mythos alive long after his passing. One such book was *The Necronomicon*, a guide to the elder gods supposedly written by the Mad Arab, Abdul Alhazred.

Let me reemphasize: The Necronomicon *doesn't exist*. Lovecraft invented it out of whole cloth. Anyone with a thimbleful of knowledge about literature knows this. So I didn't think twice about featuring *The Necronomicon* in my script. Of all the things I'd written for the show that I knew would lead to a fight, this wasn't one of them.

So I was stunned when Broadcast Standards and Practices fired off a memo saying I couldn't reference *The Necronomicon* because "our research has shown that it is a real book associated with Satanism."

I called bullshit. "Show me your data," I said. "I want to see what convinced you that a book that has been publicly acknowledged for over sixty years as fictional is actually real."

The censors blew their collective stacks. By now I'd said they were wrong one time too many, and suddenly I was in a war that ricocheted all the way up to the heads of the network. Their response made it clear that they didn't *care* whether or not *The Necronomicon* really existed; BS&P's statements could not be challenged *whether they were factual or not*. If they let a writer successfully challenge their assertions, it could undermine the entire process. They didn't have to justify their statements *even if they proved untrue*.

When I threatened to walk off the show again, Ame Simon pleaded for understanding. "Let it go," she said. "It's one of the last scripts of the season, and we don't want a fight. This isn't a hill to die on."

As a favor to Ame, who had to live with these jerks, I changed *The Necronomicon* to *The Nameless Book*, because if you said the name aloud, terrible things would happen. That compromise seemed to make everyone happy.

That is, everyone *except* me, and for the second time the voice inside my head that does the actual writing whispered, *You're done with animation. Move on.*

I had to agree: the system had been corrupted by censors and consultants, and it was time to go. But while I may have been done writing animation, I was most definitely *not* done with the Forces of Evil. There was one last battle left in me, so I wrote an article about censorship in network television animation that included some of the incidents described herein. I wanted to blow the lid off the cozy relationship between the censors and con-sultants, exposing a political agenda that I considered sexist and borderline racist.

My agent urged me not to publish it. "If you expose these guys, you'll never work in animation again," she said. "Are you really sure you want to do that?"

She was right, of course. If this article came out, there would be nothing but scorched earth all the way to the horizon. I'd blown up a good gig with the *Los Angeles Times* over my stubbornness at being censored, ended my journalism career over what I felt were ethical issues, and had now walked off several TV jobs. Was I really prepared to burn down my career in animation over this?

Absolutely.

Never let them stop you from telling the story you want to tell.

Truth, Justice, and the American Way, baby.

Yeah, there would probably be difficult times in the future when it would be helpful to have animation writing to fall back on financially, but publishing the article would be worth every lost dollar. Because this wasn't about creative disagreements or wanting my own way; it was about confronting a broken system that put itself above correction. The consultants and censors fudged facts and wrapped their prejudices in jargon presented as scientific fact to exploit the legitimate concerns of parents, all for their own financial betterment. If I didn't at least try to punch them in the nose on my way out the door, I could never live with myself.

When confronted by a decision that may have problematic outcomes, I ask one fundamental question: *What's the worst thing that can happen if I do this?* If I'm willing to accept those consequences, I do it; if I'm not, then I don't.

And in this case I was *more* than okay with the coming blast crater.

Unfortunately, magazines like *TV Guide* were too cozy with the networks to publish anything this critical, and I couldn't come up with any mainstream magazines that might care enough about censors vivisecting children's television to print it. Then I remembered one magazine that had been battling censors for years and might be willing to accept the controversy such an article would stir up.

I sent the article to *Penthouse*, one of the leading men's magazines of the time.

A few weeks later their nonfiction editor called to say they wanted to buy the article. "I just have one question," she said. "Of all the magazines in the world, why pick *Penthouse* to publish an article about children's television?"

"Because when the article comes out, these tight-assed consultants and censors are going to want to see what I said about them. I like the idea that the only way they can do that is by buying a magazine full of racy photos. I like that idea a *lot*."

On and off, she didn't stop laughing for five minutes. I clocked it.

Penthouse would go on to publish my article, "TV's Weirdest Censors: Looking for Satan in Kids' Cartoons," in June 1991. Within twenty-four hours my agent heard from every animation studio in town to say that I would never, *ever* work in animation again.

And I never did.

CHAPTER 25

Things I Learned Dancing with the Fatman

For months, my agent had been bugging me about going in to pitch on *Jake and the Fatman*, a CBS series about a detective and a prosecutor in Hawaii, with Joe Penny and William Conrad respectively assaying the title roles. I didn't want to go because . . . look, it was *Jake and the Fatman*, you don't *need* anything after the word *go*. I felt the show was mind-numbingly formulaic. Other than the money, which I will confess we needed, I couldn't see any benefit to writing for the show, or any reason to do it.*

She eventually prevailed and made an appointment for me to go in and pitch. The process, which until now I've only alluded to briefly, involves coming up with two or three fully fleshed-out stories, with all the act breaks and important moments worked out, along with one or two quick, one-paragraph notions in case the larger stories get shot down. Since I didn't *want* an assignment, I developed three pretty lame stories that I was pretty sure would be turned down. That left just a couple of brief notions to figure out.

In watching the show, I noticed how little William Conrad moved

---

* Pretty haughty for a guy who had barely made his first sale a few years earlier.

around. He'd stand and talk, sit and talk, walk from his desk to the door and talk, but that's about it.

Well, of course, I thought. *He's a massive guy, he probably doesn't like to walk much.* By some reports Conrad weighed nearly three hundred pounds, hence my faux *TV Guide* logline on the show: "Jake and the Fatman: *He* can't act, *he* can't walk, together they fight crime."*

This led to the last brief notion I needed to go in and pitch. My plan was to torpedo the process as quickly as possible, but when I arrived at the *Jake* office on the Universal Studios lot, I was struck by the kindness and generosity of executive producers/showrunners Jeri Taylor and David Moessinger. They were talented, smart, and welcomed me warmly into their office. I began to regret that I wouldn't be getting an assignment, as they seemed like really nice people.

"We've read your work and we both agreed we *had* to have you come in, even though we got into a fight with CBS over it. They don't like most of the writers coming out of syndication and genre television, but we think you could do a great job for us."

Now I was even *more* torn. That CBS didn't think I could do it made me want to prove them wrong. I wished I'd brought better stories but had only the ammunition I'd packed, so I pitched the three big ideas I'd developed. As expected they were shot down in short order.

"Do you have anything else?" Jeri asked, genuinely disappointed that there wasn't anything they could buy. They really wanted to work with me. I felt like an assassin.

"Well, I have two other quick notions," I said and gave them the first one.

---

* At the request of my attorneys it should be stressed that this is simply a joke and not a commentary on the skills of either of these two actors, who are equally remarkable and talented despite one being deceased.

No sale. Two strikes, three foul balls.

"What's the other one?" Jeri asked, her eyes hopeful.

"Well, I thought there might be a story about William Conrad's character being kidnapped by someone he'd arrested years earlier. He's taken hostage and tied to a chair for the entire episode."

David's eyes lit up like a Las Vegas slot machine. "That's great!" he said. "That's terrific! Bill *hates* to walk! He'll love it!"

And *that's* how I got my first assignment on a major prime-time network series since the '85 *Twilight Zone*. I felt terribly conflicted about the whole thing, but figured it would be a moot point. They wanted an outline as the next step, and my outlines always suck.

They loved it and put me to script.

I was now past the point of no return. I couldn't throw the script under a bus by writing a crappy draft because a less-than-stellar performance would hurt me later. I had to write it as well as I could, or at least as well as anyone *could* write a show called *Jake and the Fatman*, I decided at the time.

Because I was a pompous ass.

Two weeks later, at ten A.M. on a Monday morning, I faxed Jeri the script for "Who's Sorry Now?"

At two P.M. she called to offer me a job on staff as executive story consultant.

I'd gone into this reluctantly—rather snottily, to be honest—to write one episode. Now they were offering me a staff job on a network show, which was a better gig and more money than anything I'd done before. I was caught on the horns of my own hypocrisy. If I said no, I'd be thumbing my nose at an important opportunity for reasons that were stupid and juvenile. Saying yes would show that I was willing to set aside what I considered to be my standards when vast sums of money were thrown my way.

The decision came down to two realizations: first, that I was full of myself and behaving like a dick; second, that David and Jeri were excellent writers, and I could learn a lot from them. They were more than just a great team, they were good people who had gone to the mat with a reluctant CBS to give me this opportunity.

So by the end of the week I was reporting to work at the *Jake* offices.

This was my first time working on a studio lot full-time. Universal felt like a college campus, with low-slung bungalows, rows of massive shooting stages, and a big back lot filled with false-front buildings silhouetted against the sun-blasted Hollywood Hills. We spent the mornings spinning out plots, dialogue, and character beats, followed by lunch at the self-serve cafeteria where David would regale us with horror stories about working on *Quincy, M.E.* and *In the Heat of the Night* before returning to the office to write until evening.

Jeri was the earth mother of the *Jake* writing staff: nurturing and willing to go out of her way to engage with everyone, her scripts were generally softer and more character based. David was gregarious and incisive, so his writing was all about conflict. David led the story meetings, growling his way through *who hates who* and *who wants to kill whom* as Jeri lay in wait for *exactly* the right moment to ground the story in emotion and humor. Their strengths balanced each other perfectly, and I liked them immensely.

Until now I had worked alone as a writer or story editor with no creative producers above me, so there was no one to teach me the ropes. Whatever I learned about dialogue, plot, and structure came less through instruction than by bashing my head against the problem until one of us relented. And since all my TV work to this point was for half-hour shows, I was hopelessly tone-deaf when it came to structuring a one-hour drama.

David and Jeri took pity on me and over the coming months taught me techniques I'd never even heard of before. They showed me how to pace a one-hour story for maximum effect, layer multiple threads to create red herrings, and turn the expectations of the audience against itself, so they think you're going *thisaway* when you're actually going *thataway*, but it all makes sense at the end with no cheating involved. They constantly drilled into me the importance of playing fair with the audience. In a mystery all the clues have to be set out in plain sight, so if the viewer backs up the show and watches it again, everything needed to figure it out was right there; they just didn't know how to interpret the clues until the last piece of information was in hand, courtesy of the star's dogged inquiry.

Despite having initially opposed hiring me, CBS decided they liked my stuff, and I went on to write five episodes that season. By my previous standards this wasn't a lot—prior to *Jake* I'd written eighty-one scripts, averaging eleven to twenty per season—but five wasn't bad given that I'd come in well after the start of the season. Just as the *Daily Aztec* editors had relied on me to fill the gaps when a freelancer bailed, David and Jeri often looked to me to rewrite or deliver a draft in days if a freelance script failed to materialize. As a reward they assigned me to write the two-part season finale. The network was going to advertise the hell out of it, so they would likely end up the highest-rated episodes of the season.

Then once again, everything went to shit.

The writing and producing staff of *Jake* were based in Los Angeles, but physical production took place in Hawaii. Regardless of distance, the showrunner of a TV series is the final authority on all production matters, from writing and casting down to the color of the paint on the sets. If local producers or others begin to override their decisions, it puts the showrunner in the position of having to shoulder the responsibility for making a series without the authority to make their decisions stick. The tug-of-war exploded when some on the Hawaii-based production team began rewriting David and Jeri's scripts at the behest of a cast member. The actor knew that if a network is forced to choose between backing a high-profile star or the producers, they almost always line up with the star. So they seized creative control of the show and dared Jeri and David to do something about it.

In response David and Jeri gave the network an ultimatum: *either we run the show as we see fit, as we were* hired *to do, or we quit.* Maybe they honestly believed the network might come to its senses and back their play. And maybe they knew exactly how this would go down. Either way, they had to make a stand.

The network sided with the actor.

The next day Jeri and David convened a meeting to inform the staff that they were resigning, but encouraged everyone else to remain with the show to avoid jeopardizing their relationships with the network. Despite being upset by the news, they agreed to stay on. I said nothing until the meeting was over, then closed the door to speak with them privately.

"If you're leaving, I'm leaving," I told them.

David put a hand on my shoulder and nodded absently. He assumed I was saying what I thought they wanted to hear and seeking their permission to stay. "That's okay, Joe," he said, "we made this stand on our own, it was our fight, not yours. You don't have to quit just because we are." And they started to turn away.

"I know I don't have to go," I said, "but I'm going anyway."

They turned back to me in surprise. Was I serious?

"Absolutely," I said. "Look, you guys brought me in here, not CBS. *You're* the ones who went to bat for me with the network, *you're* the ones who hired me, so as far as I'm concerned, I work for *you*, not the network. This isn't a negotiation, this isn't grandstanding, I mean it: if you go, I go."*

Toward the end of the movie *Tombstone*, Doc Holliday, half

---

* The irony was not lost on me that my last script for *Jake and the Fatman* was entitled "Goodbye."

dead from tuberculosis and barely able to walk, is riding in a posse alongside Wyatt Earp. When one of the deputies asks why he's doing this instead of staying home, Doc says, "Wyatt Earp is my friend."

The man shakes his head. "Shit, I got lots of friends."

And Doc says, simply, "I don't."

David and Jeri were more than just my friends. They had fought for me, shown me kindness, and taught me how to improve my writing. So there wasn't any other way it could go. Given how flexible loyalty is in the television industry, I don't think either of them quite believed me until I faxed my letter of resignation to CBS.

"Are you out of your mind?" my agent said when I told her my decision. "This is your first network staff job! CBS loves you! With David and Jeri leaving they may even bump you to producer next year to fill the gap. If you piss off CBS, you'll never work for them again. Look, I *understand* you're mad about this, that you're loyal to Jeri and David, but you can't keep walking off shows every time somebody pisses you off. Let's sit down over lunch to discuss this before you fire off the letter."

"I'm afraid it's too late. I already sent it. I'm off the show effective immediately."

Rather than try to describe her response, I'll just note that to this day I'm still a little hard of hearing in that ear and leave it at that.

The next day I packed up my tiny office and left the Universal lot. By now I'd heard the threat *you'll never work in this town again* enough times that it didn't scare me anymore. I was sure it wouldn't take long before I found work somewhere else.

Months passed.

As usual I'd picked the worst time to change jobs. The other network shows were winding down their seasons, and the syndicated television market had begun to implode. Every writer in town was fighting it out for the few freelance slots still available.

Meetings with my agent were cordial, but I could see in her eyes the unspoken message *I told you so. This time you went too far. This time you're screwed.*

I found it hard to argue the point. As four months without TV work slid into five I returned to prose, selling a short story, "Say Hello, Mr. Quigley," to *Pulphouse* magazine, and a second script to DC Comics, "Worldsinger," published in their *Star Trek* comic. I even flipped back to *Twilight Zone* one last time, adapting my original *TZ* spec script, "Blind Alley," for NOW Comics. It wasn't a lot of money, but it helped keep us going.

I was writing as fast as I could for anyone who might buy my stuff, but by month six I'd run out of tricks. I hated that the circumstances surrounding *Jake* had compelled me to leave, but even if I could go back in time I'd make the same decision. It was the right thing to do.

Then in spring 1991, with our bank accounts on life support, David Moessinger called. "I just got a new show," he said, "and since you were the only one to stand with Jeri and me, I wanted my first phone call to be to you. I'd like you to come on as co-producer, which is the title you walked away from when you left. So what do you say? You want to come and play?"

"Love to," I said, relieved to have a job but mostly excited at the idea of working with David again.

"What's the show?" I asked. I assumed it wouldn't be for CBS or Universal since my agent said that I'd never work for either of them again, that they would hold a grudge against me until the sun grew cold and went out. Networks were resolute like that, she said.

"It's *Murder, She Wrote*," David said, and I could feel him grinning over the phone. "We'll be back on the Universal lot again, working for CBS."

Son of a bitch.

CHAPTER 26

Paging Jessica Fletcher

*M*urder, *She Wrote* starred Angela Lansbury as Jessica Fletcher, a mystery novelist who solved murders in her spare time. For six years *Murder* had been a top-ten-rated series, but by year seven the show had become formulaic and lost its appeal. CBS and Universal were desperate to freshen up the storytelling and return the show to the top ten.

David wanted me on the show because I had a background in journalism and prose fiction that we could use to make Jessica Fletcher feel more like a working novelist. Most *Murder* stories used her background as a writer only insofar as it was one of her published books that got her invited to a gala where a murder took place, after which the story had little to do with her work. I wanted to show her actually *writing*: struggling to find the right words, meeting deadlines, battling with editors, and living the writer's life as authentically as possible. In my episodes she didn't fall asleep exhausted from a fancy dinner, she fell asleep at the keyboard.

When David came up with the idea of moving her from sleepy Cabot Cove to New York, I suggested we give her a part-time job at a college as a distinguished guest lecturer (à la Norman Corwin) teaching criminology. This would let her interact with characters who could bring a youthful energy to the show. I also moved her from a manual typewriter to a computer to make her feel more contemporary and send a positive message to older viewers concerned about adapting to new technologies.

David would write and direct the first episode bringing her to New York, and I would write the second episode, "Night Fears," establishing her new teaching job. To maintain continuity with previous seasons David also hired producer/writer Robert Swanson (or *Swanny*, as David called him), who had written many earlier episodes.

At my first meeting with Angela Lansbury and her husband, Peter Shaw, I was impressed by her sincerity, gentility, and strength of character. She could be impish when the moment called for it and strong when necessary, but this was a *lady*, no mistake. Everyone treated her deferentially, not because she asked for it but because it was simply unimaginable to regard her in any other way.

David gave me tremendous latitude to come up with offbeat stories that would challenge me as a writer. One afternoon as we were driving through the Universal lot I spotted the house that had been used in Alfred Hitchcock's *Psycho*, which is still standing.

"Wouldn't it be cool if Jessica was flown to Universal to consult about an adaptation of one of her books," I said, "and there was a murder in the *Psycho* house? We could enhance the main story with a larger meta-narrative in a way that hasn't been done on the show before."

David thought it was a weird idea but approved it anyway. A few weeks later we were shooting "Incident in Lot #7" inside the *Psycho* house, where I had the privilege of standing on the same staircase that Hitchcock used when Martin Balsam climbed to his death.

On another day, David, Bob Swanson, and I were walking across the lot through bitter wind and rain to a meeting at Universal's infamous Black Tower, which was where most of the studio executives resided.* A low, mournful wail rose and fell through the storm.

"What the hell is *that*?" David asked.

Bob nodded to the building ahead of us. "The wind around the tower."

"I think I can write an episode with that as a title," I said.

"Bet you twenty bucks you can't," Bob said, rising to the challenge.

A month later we were shooting "The Wind Around the Tower," a ghost story set in an Irish castle.

While *Jake* had been shot several thousand miles away in Hawaii, *Murder* was filmed right there on the Universal lot, which put me inside the Hollywood machine for the first time. I could take a break from writing, wander over to stage 18, and watch one of my scripts being brought to life. It was pretty heady stuff.

Jeri Taylor didn't follow David to *Murder, She Wrote* because she'd landed a gig as executive producer on *Star Trek: The Next Generation* where she became one of the show's most respected writer/producers. Since Kathryn knew Jeri through me, she had the confidence to apply for, and win, an internship on the series. Every day as I took off for Universal, Kathryn left for the Paramount studios in Hollywood. The internship position didn't pay much, but working with Jeri was a priceless opportunity for Kathryn to further develop her writing skills.

When the eighth season of *Murder, She Wrote* debuted on September 15, 1991, it returned the series to top-ten status. The reviews were positive, advertising revenues were up, Universal was happy, CBS was happy, Angela was happy. As Christmas approached we

---

* The Black Tower at Universal then was kind of like the Black Monolith in *2001*, except that it lowered your IQ when you touched it.

heard that CBS was going to give us an early pickup on season nine. Everyone was in a festive mood. So when David was summoned to a meeting at the Black Tower with Angela and the executives overseeing the show, he naturally assumed this would be a congratulatory meeting. He thought he might even get a raise.

He walked straight into a coup.

Having worked on *Murder, She Wrote* for eight years, Angela felt she deserved creative control. The executives agreed and gave her the title of executive producer. Bruce Lansbury, Angela's brother, would be supervising producer, and her son David Shaw would be executive in charge of production (later elevated to co–executive producer). Anthony Shaw, Angela's other son, was already a director on the series at her behest. She told David that he was welcome to stay with the show, but all important decisions would now have to go through her. I believe she was sincere in making the offer, but I also knew that David could never accept those terms, not after what happened on *Jake*. He'd been brought on to be the showrunner, not a hired gun.

David returned to the office pale and devastated. He had delivered on his promise to bring the show back to the top ten only to find himself caught once again between the network and a star who wanted control. Ironically, had the ratings stayed in the midtwenties, Angela might not have had the clout to push through her agenda. By bringing the show back to the top ten, he'd handed Angela the gun she used to shoot him.

After the initial shock wore off, David was surprisingly quiet and not nearly as angry as I thought he might be. He had only gentle things to say about Angela, including her courage in telling him in person rather than letting it come through others. He felt she would do a good job and told us all to get back to work.

I was already packing up my stuff when David stuck his head in my office door. "Don't you *dare* leave on my account," he said.

"I felt bad enough when you walked off *Jake*; my conscience can't handle it if you do this again. Besides, if you quit a CBS show twice, you can be damned sure they won't hire you again, and this time they'll *mean* it, trust me."

I argued that my loyalty was still to him, not the network or Universal. He wouldn't hear it.

"Put your stuff back," he said. "I *want* you to stay and I'm *asking* you to stay. So for once in your life listen to someone else and stay put, goddamnit."

I didn't like it, but respected him too much to argue further, and agreed to stay.

David left quietly and with great dignity. But the show was never the same afterward. Since Angela liked the way I portrayed her as a working writer, I was generally left to my own devices, but in every other respect the series reverted back to its formulaic storytelling.

For nearly five years, Doug Netter, John Copeland, and I had been pitching *Babylon 5* to every network, studio, and production company in town, only to be told there was no room for a space-based science fiction series other than *Star Trek*. We even pitched the show to Paramount, which was still producing *Star Trek: The Next Generation*, giving them the pilot script, series bible, and concept art. This led to a flurry of phone calls intimating that a deal was possible. Then the studio abruptly went radio silent and the door closed.

Not long afterward we booked a meeting with Evan Thompson, head of Chris-Craft Television, a consortium of independent TV stations. Rather than creating their own programs, syndicated stations traditionally only bought reruns of established series, but we'd heard that they might be interested in developing some original series, so we decided to take the shot. If he didn't buy the show, we'd have to give up because there was literally nowhere left to go. By now I'd gotten used to pitching the show to execs who didn't get it, and as we trudged down to the Chris-Craft offices in Beverly Hills I assumed this would be no different.

But Evan—tall, lean, and soft-spoken, with bright, inquisitive eyes—Got It immediately. His excitement grew as I explained the concept of a five-mile-long space station in neutral territory between several civilizations, a home to a quarter million humans and aliens attempting to find peaceful solutions to their problems. When pitching the show to other executives, I framed it as *Casablanca in Space*, but Evan didn't need any sort of high-concept shorthand.

"I really like this," he said. "We've got something in the works, I can't tell you what it is right now, but it may represent a way for us to do this show. Let me continue with that process, see where it goes, then we'll touch base when I know if it's actually going to happen."

A few weeks later news broke that Warner Bros. had partnered with several station groups—of which Chris-Craft was the largest—to create the Prime Time Entertainment Network (PTEN). Evan Thompson was co-chair of the network alongside Dick Robertson, the highly regarded head of WB Domestic Television Distribution, whose sole mandate previously had been to license syndicated reruns of series produced by Warners. PTEN would debut with two original series airing one night per week, then gradually expand into more programs over more nights. *Babylon 5* was being considered for one of those first two slots, but there were other shows also in contention. The final selections would be made during a weeklong series of meetings at Warner Bros., during which the station managers would hear pitches from various creators. I would have less than an hour to explain to these executives, most of whom had never bought an original series before, why they should pick up *Babylon 5.*

It would have to be the performance of a lifetime given what we were trying to achieve, and what we weren't telling them.

At this time in television, everything to do with space—starships, bases, planets—was done with miniatures and motion-control photography, which were limited in use and expensive to produce. *Star Trek: The Next Generation* was the costliest dramatic series of its time at an average of $1.3 million per episode. PTEN's shows, on the other hand, were budgeted at between $600,000 and $800,000. There was no conceivable way we could hit that number using conventional models and motion control.

So we decided that *Babylon 5* would use computer-generated imagery on a scale never previously attempted in television. The risks were substantial since CGI was still in its infancy, used mainly to create video transitions and primitive 3-D shapes; pulling this tech into actual production would mean rolling the dice on a new and unproven technology. So Warners was justifiably skeptical of our claim that we could make a science fiction show with a large cast, heavy prosthetics, big stunts, and tons of special effects for a PTEN budget. It didn't help that no American space-based science fiction series other than *Trek* had lasted more than three seasons in *twenty-five years.* They were even more dubious when I said that our goal was to tell one big story across five years.

And there were my own shortcomings to consider. Traditionally, TV writers spend years moving up the ladder from story editor to co-producer, producer, supervising producer, and then executive producer before being allowed to create their own series. This gives the networks a degree of confidence that you know what you're doing. Since I'd never been more than a co-producer, some of the executives at Warner Bros. felt that I was too inexperienced for the job, especially given that the PTEN shows would be straight-to-series orders. Instead of shooting a pilot and losing only $2–3 million if I screwed up, commissioning a full season meant risking $12–15 million on an untested showrunner.

To reassure the execs about using CGI for our effects, we commissioned a thirty-second demo from budding special-effects wizard Ron Thornton that featured a wide shot of a starship approaching the station from a distance of several thousand miles that turned into a close-up of the station as the ship docked, all in one continuous shot. Dramatic angles like that could never be done with models and miniatures on a television budget.

We lobbied successfully to make our presentation on the first day, when the station executives would be fresh and excited. As we waited outside the conference room for our turn to pitch, I paced back and forth, grinding my teeth nervously. Suddenly I felt a sharp *snap!* as a molar cracked lengthwise. The pain was excruciating.

"We have to get you to a dentist," Doug said. "You can't go out there like this."

I refused. If we left, they'd have to squeeze us in during the last day. By then the station owners would have heard a dozen different pitches; they'd be numb, dazed, and jaded. We had to hit them right out of the gate with something they'd remember the rest of the week. It was now or never. So I grabbed a tumbler of ice water and poured it into my mouth. The pain when it hit the exposed nerve was indescribable. I saw colors I hadn't seen since somebody dropped a tab of acid into my coffee. Just as the tooth went numb, we were summoned into the conference room. As Dick Robertson began his introduction I was secretly biting down on another shard of ice, hoping to sustain the numbness.

Then it was my turn to speak. The moment I'd been working toward for five years.

"Hello," I said, "my name is Joe Straczynski, and this is my series, *Babylon 5.*"

At least that's what I *intended* to say. What I *actually* said—not having counted on the ice giving me a massive case of rubber tongue—was closer to "He'o, muh nham ith Doe Thuzinski, ah zis ith mah theries, Ba'alon Fie."

Wanna buh suhchoklutburrs?

Had there been a gun nearby I would've shot myself in the head, but since no one had thought to bring one I was forced to continue. To this day I don't remember what I said. I'd gone in to pitch *Casablanca in Space*, but for all I can recall I might have pitched *Gunsmoke at the Bottom of the Sea*. As we were ushered out of the conference room, Doug, John, and Ron said soothing things, but I knew I hadn't done the job I wanted to do. This was our last chance to sell *Babylon 5*, and the thought that I might have screwed it up was more than I could bear.

After several weeks of waiting, the PTEN execs gave production orders to *Time Trax*, a weekly series about time travel; *The Wild West*, a limited-run documentary series from Doug Netter; and a revival of the *Kung Fu* series. We were told that the station owners liked *Babylon 5* but didn't believe we could do it for the available money.

We were dead in the water.

Then, at the eleventh hour, Evan and Dick prevailed upon the station owners to give us a chance to prove ourselves, and greenlit production of a two-hour *Babylon 5* pilot movie.

"You won't have to wait for focus groups or ratings or any of that bullshit," we were told by our Warners liaison, "just show us that a series this big can be done for the money, and we'll pull the trigger on the series order."

It wasn't what we'd hoped for, but it was a start, and in November 1991 *Babylon 5* was announced as one of four projects for the Prime Time Entertainment Network.

And we immediately almost lost it all.

I'll let Kathryn tell this part of it.

"I was in the last couple weeks of my term as a paid writer's intern with *Star Trek: The Next Generation*, and looking forward to being picked up for a second, longer internship (which usually led to writing scripts for the show), when we were all called in to a meeting with Executive Producer Michael Piller to finally learn *something* about the new, super secret *TNG* spin-off show.

"That I was called into this meeting says two things: one, that it was expected that I would still be working there when the spin-off show started; and two, that no one in that room had any idea that the premise of the spin-off would be a problem for me. But in the first minute of the meeting, when Michael said that this new show—to be called *Deep Space Nine*—would be about a space station, I shot out of my seat before I could hear anything else, and said, 'I can't be a part of this meeting any longer because my husband is also developing a space station show.'

"There was general surprise, but everybody agreed that this was the right thing for me to do, and I left the meeting. I then immediately called you and told you what had happened. It was clear from that moment that my short career at *TNG* was over. I finished out my final couple of weeks, but studiously avoided any meetings or conversations about *Deep Space Nine*.

"When I took the job at *TNG*, I had made a point of saying up front that my husband was developing a science fiction show, but I never discussed the premise and certainly never said 'space station,' only that it was a very different kind of show than *TNG*. I am 100 percent confident that before I stood up in that meeting and excused myself from the room, Jeri Taylor and the writing staff had no idea that the show you were developing and the spin-off show were both about space stations. And from the fact that Michael even had me in the meeting, not to mention the look on his face when I stood up, I am confident that neither did he. As for other Paramount executives? I couldn't possibly say."

Since the *Star Trek* and *Babylon 5* universes were nothing alike, I clung to the hope that any resemblance between the two shows would be strictly superficial. This lasted right up until I received a call from Walter Koenig, a friend who had played Chekov on the original *Star Trek*.

"I have bad news," he said. "I just had lunch with [*Trek* fan liaison] Richard Arnold, and he gave me some details about the new show. I think this could be trouble for you."

How could it be trouble? For thirty years, the various *Star Trek* series had been set aboard starships. That's the textbook definition of a trek, a journey from *here* to *there*. By contrast, the *Babylon 5* pilot was about an Earth-sponsored space station, identified by a name and a number, located in neutral territory, that served as a meeting place for alien races and diplomats, with a bar, a casino, a female second-in-charge, and a shape-changer (in the pilot).

Walter took a long breath, let it out. "Joe, it's about an Earth-sponsored space station, identified by a name and a number, located in neutral territory that serves as a meeting place for alien races, with a bar, a casino, a female second-in-charge, and a shape-changer."

And that's when it clicked.

During the five years spent pitching *Babylon 5* we'd given Paramount all of our development material. This led to several discussions with the executives that seemed to be going in a positive direction when suddenly they went radio silent. It never occurred to us that someone inside Paramount might have looked at that material and thought, *Hmmm . . . a companion series to* Next Gen *about a space station, that's a great idea.*

But why do we need these guys?

More similarities emerged in the coming weeks. Like *Babylon 5, Star Trek: Deep Space Nine* was a diplomatic and commercial outpost, a circular space station, with representatives from various races, a male war hero commander . . . *all* the elements from our show had been mysteriously beamed into this one, which was announced right after our show was picked up.

The timing felt far from coincidental. Paramount was putting together a syndicated network of their own that was competing with PTEN for the relatively small number of independent TV stations, so they had every reason to co-opt *Babylon 5* or sink it by doing something nearly identical under the *Star Trek* brand. To drive the knife deeper, Paramount would spend $12 million on their first two-hour TV movie, as opposed to our $3.5 million.

The reaction from Warner Bros. was both immediate and predictable.

"One of the reasons we hesitated to approve *Babylon 5* to series is that we weren't sure the syndication market could sustain two space-based science fiction shows, this and *Next Generation*," we were told. "But now it's worse. Can the market sustain two science fiction shows set on space stations that are nearly identical in every way, one of which has the *Star Trek* brand, while the other is an unknown? We don't know."

Over the next several weeks the pilot came within inches of being canceled. I implored Warners to take legal action, but they declined, explaining that studios rarely sue each other, and that prolonged litigation might kill both shows. With some effort Dick and Evan convinced Warners to let us keep moving ahead with the pilot, but being outspent and outgunned by *Star Trek* made the prospect of going to series highly doubtful.

For the next few months I divided my attention between working on *Murder, She Wrote* and prepping *Babylon 5* for production. When it became apparent that I couldn't do both as well as they needed to be done, I asked Angela if I could be let out of my contract. She didn't want to lose me but knew what this opportunity could mean for my career, and we parted with her best wishes for the future.[*]

As we got deeper into prep I realized just how little I knew about producing. On previous shows I never heard about decisions on cast or crew until after the fact, and had never viewed the cut of an episode until it was finished. Now I had to hire the heads of the wardrobe, art, makeup, and camera departments; sift through lists of available actors; review set designs, prosthetics, and CGI; develop budgets and shooting schedules. I'd never even *seen* a budget before. Everyone looked to me for answers as though I actually knew what I was doing. Rather than seek advice I concealed my ignorance, which was foolish and counterproductive. Asking certain questions would have exposed my inexperience, but the answers would have let me make good decisions. Instead I too often deferred to the opinions of others. *They must know what they're doing,* I thought when I found myself in over my head, *so I should respect their knowledge and let them do it their way.*

Nice in theory, but in practice it led to some very bad stumbles that would only reveal themselves much later.

I had no idea what to look for during auditions, knowing only how the characters looked and sounded in my head, so I ignored their résumés and waited until the character walked in the door with the actor, regardless of prior credits. The result was one of the best ensemble casts I've ever worked with, including Andreas Katsulas, Peter Jurasik, Mira Furlan, Jerry Doyle, Tamlyn Tomita, and Patricia Tallman, with Michael O'Hare as our lead, Commander Jeffrey Sinclair.

After the cast, the most important decision when shooting a pilot is the choice of director. It doesn't matter how good the script

---

[*] Once again, and totally by coincidence, my last script for *Murder, She Wrote* was entitled "Final Curtain." The lesson I've taken from this is that I must never write a script entitled "Joe Gets Hit by a Bus."

is if the director doesn't understand it; how solid the performances are if the director can't capture them on film; or how stellar the wardrobe, props, or set design are if the director doesn't know how to light them. Just as every writer has a unique voice on the page, a director has his own voice on the stage, so it's important to find a director whose approach lines up with your own.

And I made a terrible mistake in my choice of director.

Richard Compton came to us from one of my favorite shows, *The Equalizer*. I wanted *B5* to have a gritty, realistic look, but there's a difference between a dark and moody detective show, where directors often use haze and dim-lit alleys to conceal budgetary shortcomings, and a science fiction series, where you *want* the audience to see the new world you've created. Richard could never wrap his brain around the latter, and I didn't have enough experience to realize he was the wrong man for the job.

To prevent anyone from messing with his vision, Richard would tell you what he thought you wanted to hear rather than what he actually had in mind. He was a good *technical* director, but not a good *actors'* director. In a pilot the actors need guidance to help understand their roles, but Richard was more about the smoke, the lenses, and the lighting than the characters, and many in the cast were left to find their way alone.

Had I dug deeper into his credits I would have discovered that while Richard had directed over a dozen episodes on *The Equalizer*, he rarely directed more than one or two episodes on other shows and was not asked back on subsequent seasons. That's usually a sign of trouble, but because of my inexperience I missed the warning signs and walked blindly into the trap that was set before me.

When filming on the two-hour pilot began on August 10, 1992, Richard kept modifying the alien prosthetics at the last minute to make some of them look more cartoony, then pushed them forward to upstage the scientifically accurate aliens that I wanted to feature. Each time I complained he said it was an accident, or that the makeup didn't look good on camera, and promised to fix it for the rest of the scene. But Richard knew that once he put the extras where he wanted them in the master shot we couldn't change them later because the shots wouldn't match during editing.

John Iacovelli, production designer and head of the art department, had brought a number of amazing sets to life in a very short time, thanks to carpenters, painters, and other crew who believed in the project. They would work all night, taking naps beside their brushes before going back to work, only to find their efforts obscured by the haze and shadows Richard insisted on using in every shot. Worse still, rather than use conventional stage lights that warm the actors' faces and bring out their eyes, emphasizing their humanity, Richard opted for high-intensity xenon lights set directly above the stage. The harsh, unflattering downward light made the actors look as if they were being interrogated, and threw the rest of the set into a darkness so complete that you could barely see where you were.

"Don't worry, we can lighten it up in post," Richard said, and I believed him. I didn't understand that lightening the frame enough to dig out the background details would cause the actors' faces to bloom so much that they would practically glow.

Filming wrapped September 4, 1992, and as Richard went off to edit the pilot I couldn't shake the uneasy feeling that I'd lost control of the creative vision for the show. Two weeks later, Doug, John, and I reconvened to view the director's cut. I'd never been inside an editing suite before and was rather intimidated by my surroundings. Richard described his approach to the cut, then nodded to the editor, and we watched the pilot.

I hated it.

The pacing was slow, the scenes more about camera angles and lighting than the people inhabiting them. Whole sequences had been cut to make room for long, slow panning shots that added nothing to the story and rendered what remained incomprehensible. The cast, so lively in rehearsals, had been reduced to a dull sameness. The action scenes were clumsy, the character moments were stiff . . . the whole thing felt depressing. A three-minute scene set in hazy darkness broken by islands of harsh, unflattering lighting isn't too bad on its own, but extend that over two hours and any show will begin to feel heavy and unlikable.

When I voiced my concerns, Richard shrugged and said the edit couldn't be changed because he hadn't shot alternate coverage. What we had was what we were stuck with. "But hey, if you can do better, go for it," he said, then moved to a nearby chair and began reading a newspaper.

I sat beside the editor, my first time in the hot seat. The editor looked at me. *Well?*

I didn't know what to do or what my options were. I lacked even the language to know what to *ask* for. I felt stupid, flushed and furious at my own ignorance.

"Roll it back to the beginning," I said, and we started over.

Each change I attempted only made the situation worse. Had I been more confident in my position, or more knowledgeable, I would have said *Run off a copy, I'll take it home, make my notes, and come back tomorrow.* But I didn't know to do even that much. I figured the way we were doing it was the way you were *supposed* to do these things, right there and on the spot.

By the end I'd made only a handful of changes, none of them substantial or especially helpful. Richard looked up from his newspaper. "We done?"

"I guess so," I said.

A few days later we delivered the cut to Warner Bros., minus the CGI and other effects that would be cut in later. Their response was tepid at best.

I was sure that I'd killed our chance to get *Babylon 5* on the air as a series, and was furious with myself for not having listened to the concerns I'd had during the shoot. To make matters worse, Warner Bros. began moving the goalposts farther away. When they commissioned the pilot, they said we only had to deliver *Babylon 5* on schedule and on budget to get the series order; we wouldn't have to wait for focus groups or ratings. We'd kept our part of the bargain, but now that Warners had a pilot to test, by god they were going to test it. We complained about the unequal treatment, since the other PTEN series had been greenlit without even *producing* a pilot. Warners refused to budge, but assured us that if the show passed muster with a focus group, we would get our series order.

Despite its flaws, which were apparently more visible to me than to anyone else, the pilot earned high marks with the focus group. *We passed the test!* we told Warners. *The focus group loved us! So give us the series order!*

"We've decided we want to air the pilot first," they said, "so we can see what the ratings are like. *Then* we can decide if we want to pull the trigger."

This was absolutely contrary to how the television business works. You shoot a pilot, the network looks at it, and if they like what they see, they commission the series, for which the pilot is now episode one. We would have to wait months for an available slot *just* to air the pilot, with nothing cued up behind it. So even if we hit the desired ratings and began writing season one immediately, there would be at least a *year* between the airing of the pilot and the series debut, and it was doubtful viewers would wait around that long. Most galling of all, *Deep Space Nine* would be on the air with weekly episodes for nearly all that time, so when we finally *did* come out, everyone would think *we* were copying *them* instead of the other way around.

When *Babylon 5: The Gathering* aired on February 22, 1993, six months after we'd started filming, I could barely watch it, tortured by all the flaws I'd seen in the director's cut that still remained. But the pilot received a 10.3 national rating, which was better than the debut of all the other PTEN shows, so we were confident we would finally get our series order.

But Warners *still* held off on the pickup, saying that we might get a firm decision by the spring. *Maybe.* The delay made no sense; there had to be *something* going on in the shadows that we knew nothing about. Meanwhile, our studio liaison said that sales execs from Paramount were telling station owners that our show would look cheap, that it was a disaster in the offing, and if they bought *B5*, Paramount would yank the *Star Trek* series.

It wasn't until May 28, 1993, three months after the pilot had aired, that we finally got the series order, and only after considerable pressure from Dick Robertson and Evan Thompson. I was elated, but the news was tempered by the knowledge that much of what would have made *B5* the first of its kind had already been co-opted by *DS9.*

Still, we were finally in business on a weekly series. The kid from New Jersey who had dreamed of one day creating a science fiction series of his own had actually done it.

Recent information demands a postscript to this chapter.

In the years since *Babylon 5* went on the air, science fiction fans have debated whether or not Paramount ripped off our show to create *Deep Space Nine.* My belief at the time was that the studio co-opted the material we gave them only *after* they knew we were going into production in order to kneecap PTEN in favor of their own new network. I also accept Kathryn's sense that the *Star Trek* producers were blameless. But studio executives higher up the food chain can easily shape the direction of a show without explicitly telling the producers the source of their suggestions. *Hey, listen, guys, we really like your idea for a new* Trek *series, but instead of doing another starship show or something on a colony, let's think outside the box . . . how about a space station, you know, a port of call, with a casino, cargo ships, lots of different alien races coming through . . . a* Casablanca in Space *kind of thing. Give it some thought, roll it around for a while, and let's discuss it next week.*

That explanation was the only one that made any sense given what I knew at the time. Then in 2013 an unsolicited revelation appeared via an online statement by Steven Hopstaken, a marketing specialist who had worked as a copywriter and editor for Dick Robertson's Warner Bros. International Television Distribution from 1993 to 1994, the years that marked the births of *B5* and *DS9*. His job was to design marketing communications material for Warner TV series and films, as well as creating trade show collateral and corporate newsletters.

His statement, which first appeared on io9.com,* is reprinted below in its entirety:

I was working at Warner Bros. in the publicity department when Warner Bros. and Paramount were preparing to launch a joint network. Warner Bros. had already decided to buy *Babylon 5* for their ad hoc PTEN network (a group of independent stations that agreed to show Warner Bros. shows in prime time).

Paramount and Warner Bros. both agreed that *Deep Space 9* would be the show that would launch the new network, and there wouldn't be room for two "space" shows on the network. I was told they purposely took what they liked from the *B5* script and put it into the *DS9* script. In fact, there was talk of leaving the *B5* script intact and just

---

* http://io9.gizmodo.com/5985727/the-strange-secret-evolution-of-babylon-5

setting it in the *Star Trek* universe. I had to keep rewriting press release drafts while they were trying to make the final decision.

But then, suddenly, Paramount decided to launch a new network on their own and screwed Warner Bros. over. That sent Warner Bros. scrambling to create their own network; grabbing up any station not already committed to Paramount and getting WGN to show the WB network on cable.

So Paramount definitely knew about the *Babylon 5* script, I don't know about the *DS9* showrunners, but I find it hard to believe they didn't know.

If this is true—and an email exchange with Hopstaken in preparation for this book confirms that he stands by his story—then it's possible that Warners' reluctance to put *Babylon 5* into production was fueled by more than bureaucratic annoyance and intransigence. Perhaps they were worried that the similarities between the shows would reveal what had been going on behind the scenes by *both* studios. This might also explain their reluctance to take legal action against Paramount. That seems to make sense, but in the end only the top studio brass on either side of the contretemps really know the truth of what happened, and they ain't talking.

CHAPTER 27

Boarding Babylon

The *Babylon 5* series set up shop in what was once a spa-tub factory in Sun Valley that we converted into a working stage. It was located on a cul-de-sac that included a junkyard and a gravel pit from which a fine cloud of dust constantly blew over the lot, covering everything. To meet studio notes, Tamlyn Tomita was replaced by Claudia Christian as *B5*'s second-in-command, and Andrea Thompson came on as a telepath to replace Patricia Tallman after contractual differences arose between Warners and her agent. After adding Richard Biggs as Dr. Stephen Franklin, we began shooting in July 1993. The series debut was scheduled for January 26, 1994, over a year after the broadcast of the pilot.

Most TV series have large writing staffs: executive producers, writer-producers, and staff writers. But our meager budget didn't allow for such luxuries; with Doug and John aboard as non-writing producers, there was just enough money for me as showrunner and one story editor. In keeping with tradition, I hired Larry DiTillio to ensure continuity of vision, work with the freelancers, and build a catalog of data about the worlds and characters in our series. I also brought on Harlan Ellison as conceptual consultant as a gesture of appreciation and to give me access to his twelve-story brain. As a kid, I used to shoplift his books; now he was working for me.

Astonishing.

Showrunning a weekly TV series is infinitely more complicated than shooting a pilot. On any given day I would be writing episode A, prepping episode B, shooting episode C, editing episode D, and doing postproduction on episode E . . . all at the same time. To put that in practical terms: at 10:00 A.M. you're meeting with wardrobe to review designs for the episode you're prepping; at 11:00 you're on-set for the episode you're shooting right now; at noon you're chairing a production meeting for the episode due to start shooting in a few days; at 1:00 you eat at your desk so you can keep writing; at 2:30 you zoom across town to the edit bay to finish the producer's cut of the show you shot last week, cross town again later that day to supervise the final audio mix of the episode you're about to deliver for broadcast, then grab a bite on the way home to write through the night.

Network television has never really taken science fiction seriously, so most series had to be sanitized and scrubbed clean of content that was considered too adult in deference to kid-friendly characters free from addiction and prejudice. This was particularly true of the *Trek* universe, where poverty had been eliminated, nobody had drug or alcohol issues, humans were nearly perfect, and religion had been pish-poshed into irrelevancy. By contrast, I wanted *Babylon 5* to delve into controversy, dealing with political, social, and religious issues that would give our universe a hard-edged, gritty texture.

And then there was the issue of our five-year arc. While network soap operas often had season-long character arcs and a general sense of where they were going, neither they nor any other American TV series had attempted a single overarching story with a clearly defined beginning, middle, and end. Creators of TV series didn't *want* the shows to end, as evidenced by *General Hospital*, which went on the air in 1963 and as of this writing is *still* being produced. Nor was significant character growth allowed; at the end of each season, and the end of the series, the characters could not be substantially different from who they were at the beginning. This was especially true in science fiction TV, where the bad guy, the hero, the tough guy, the comic relief, and other key roles were set in stone at the beginning and strictly adhered to thereafter.

In our series, I wanted the characters to evolve in ways that would change the world around them, demonstrating that regardless of our circumstances or how late in the day we can still change that which seems most inevitable about us. As much as *B5* was about exploration, wars, and the rise and fall of empires, at its center were issues of personal choice, the consequences that result from those choices, and our willingness to accept responsibility for those consequences. Would our characters behave ethically when confronted by difficulty, or lean into what was more convenient? How do their seemingly small decisions result in massive events that ripple through the rest of our story?

To pull this off I would have to subvert the audience's expectations about how a science fiction show was constructed. I wanted them to take one look at the roles our characters seemed to fill at the start of the show (the bad guy, the comic relief, the hero) and assume they would remain that way, just like every other SF series. I could then start bending the story until the characters ended up 180 degrees from where they started, sending a message to the viewers that anything could happen at any time to anyone. One character would start as a terrorist, full of wrath and bloodlust, and become a religious leader who grew beyond his rage, forgiving the grievances of the past to create a better future. Another would begin as a buffoon with no power but all the choices in the world, and end up as emperor, with all the power he wanted but no choices at all. The commander of *B5* would be loyal to his government until forced by circumstance to lead an insurrection against it.

These character arcs would have to be crafted in secret and rolled out carefully because while I'd told Warners that we were doing a five-year arc (which they still didn't believe was feasible), they assumed that the characters would end the show roughly where they began. Had they known what I had in mind they would never have approved it. This left a very narrow runway for the storytelling: if the audience figured out too early where this was going, the element of surprise would be gone. If Warner Bros. figured it out too soon, *I* would be gone.

As work continued on season one of *Babylon 5*, a shadow began to loom over the show. It began with small, almost insignificant whispers that something was amiss with our lead actor, Michael O'Hare: reports of inappropriate comments made to members of the cast or staff, glitches in his performance, erratic conversations that went nowhere. The increasingly bizarre reports didn't line up with the Michael I knew, a respectful and dedicated actor who felt a responsibility to be a cheerleader for the cast and the show.

I called him into my office to find out what was going on. Tired from a long day of shooting and agitated by my inquiry, he began talking. The longer he talked, the more alarmed I became, not so much by *what* he was saying as *how* he was saying it. His sentences got tangled up in themselves, not syntactically but conceptually. He would start with A, diverge to B, switch to a completely unrelated C, then zip back to A as if the digressions somehow proved his point but which actually made no sense. I knew what stoned looked like, but this wasn't it.

Then he said he was scouring the newspapers for secret messages meant just for him, and that if he could only figure out what the messages meant, everything would be fine, just fine.

I'd heard the phrase *my blood froze* a million times, but it wasn't until this moment that I understood what that actually felt like.

He said he was getting other messages encoded in TV newscasts; that the FBI was watching him; and that sometimes he heard voices telling him things about people. I let him continue a while longer to make sure I was hearing him right, that he wasn't pulling my leg, then stood and thanked him for coming by. When he left, I shut the door and sat heavily, my head nearly between my knees. A phrase I learned while getting my psychology degree floated up from whatever deep recesses it had been hiding in all these years: *paranoid delusional behavior.*

I'd gone into the conversation assuming that there might have been issues with drugs or alcohol. But the problem wasn't the *presence* of mind-altering chemicals, it was the *absence* of them. The star of the show I'd struggled for five years to get on the air was on the verge of a psychotic break. He didn't need chiding, he needed diagnosis and treatment. He needed *help.*

At the end of the day I went to see Michael in his trailer and tried, gently but firmly, to explain that he needed to see a doctor. He refused to listen, insisting there was nothing wrong. His biggest concern was that the mysterious *they* had gotten to me and were poisoning me against him.

The walk back to my office was the longest I can remember. *Now what the hell do I do?*

We lacked the legal authority to force Michael to receive treatment if he refused to do so on his own; I wasn't a family member, and no judge or doctor would put him under involuntary observation because he hadn't demonstrated that he was a danger to himself or anyone else. The awful part was that somewhere deep inside, Michael knew he had a problem. Over the next few days I found that he could even discuss it for brief periods before sliding back into delusional behavior. He'd talk about how he was getting messages from the FBI and the CIA, I'd say he knew that wasn't true, then he'd nod and say yes, that's right, he's not getting messages, then he'd start talking about the last one he received. He was fracturing but hadn't yet broken. He was also very good at hiding his condition and could appear quite normal when he needed to put on a good face for the studio or his family. His actor's ability to shape-shift helped him in front of the cameras but would make it even more difficult to intervene.

Writing Michael out of the show for a few episodes wouldn't help because that wasn't enough time for him to start the long process of finding the right cocktail of meds to treat his condition. Nor could I make the nominal star of our show just disappear for the rest of the season. The only other option was to shut down the show. We might be able to recast and go back into production fast enough to save the rest of the season, but that would mean asking Warners to carry the cost of holding on to the crew while we were down, a dubious prospect at best. It'd be cheaper to let us stay shut down and put out a truncated season, which would almost certainly result in cancellation. But I couldn't see any other solution, so after bringing fellow executive producer Doug Netter into the loop, I waited until Michael had a light workday, when he was at his best and most self-aware, and told him what I thought needed to be done.

"No," he said, "absolutely not. Don't do it. If you pull the plug even for a little while, Warners will kill the show. Don't let me be the reason all these people are put out of work."

We went back and forth for nearly an hour, with me giving every reason why we should shut down and Michael arguing why we shouldn't. At one point, he laughed and said, "We both know I'm the crazy one here, so why am I the only one making sense?"

We fell quiet as Michael looked out the window, pale and tired but as determined as I'd ever seen him. It was already dark. In another hour the crew would wrap for the day and pour into the parking lot for Friday beers with the staff and cast, a *Babylon 5* tradition.

"Let me *do* this," he said at last. "Let me try to get through the rest of the season. If I fall down, then yeah, maybe you'll have to shut down the show, fire me, kill the character, whatever. But you don't have to do it *right now*. There are only a few episodes left, I know I can get through this, swear to God. Let me at least *try*. You can always pull the trigger later. Just give me a chance so all these people don't get fired."

Let me try. Whenever those words are spoken by someone I care about, I always do what I can to back their play. Certainly if he could finish the season on his own terms, it would be easier to convince him to seek treatment. So I agreed on the condition that if we got even the slightest indication that he was going into the red, we'd do whatever was necessary to get him the treatment he needed. He thought that sounded fair.

Since his symptoms were exacerbated by stress, I adjusted the remaining scripts to move other characters into the foreground, shaving off some of Michael's hours and reducing the weight he had to carry as the lead. This had an immediate benefit, and Michael began to exhibit fewer symptoms. His situation would have been almost manageable had there not been a personality conflict with fellow actor Jerry Doyle, who'd figured out that there was something wrong with Michael. Despite not knowing the full extent of the problem, Jerry took every opportunity to wind him up like a cheap watch just to watch him spin out.

Despite Jerry's antics, for the first time in a long while Michael actually seemed to be enjoying himself, and took great pride in proving that he could make it to the end of the season.

A few days before we finished shooting our last episode, I invited him into my office to chat. *Maybe it's not as bad as it looked,*

I thought. *Maybe he's better, and we can squeak by with him on a second season.* But fatigued at the end of a long day, he again began manifesting the same delusional behavior. After he left, I walked down the hall into Doug's office and shut the door, agonized by what had to be done.

"We can't bring him back," I said. "He's not going to get better without treatment, and that's going to take a long time. He can't do that *and* be the star of a weekly show with all the pressure that involves. We got blindsided by this and dealt with it the best we could, but we can't bring him back in good conscience until and unless he's better."

To avoid needlessly upsetting Michael, we decided to hold off on that conversation until we received definitive word about a second season; if we didn't get renewed, we'd *all* be out of a job and Michael wouldn't feel singled out.

The pickup came a few days before Michael was scheduled to appear at I-CON, a science fiction convention in Long Island where he would be feted and applauded for his work. Doug and I kept the information to ourselves as Kathryn and I flew off to I-CON to support Michael and keep an eye on things. He loved the attention of the fans, and I was happy that we'd held back the conversation so he could enjoy this moment.

At the close of the convention, Michael, Kathryn, fan liaison Rowan Kaiser, and I climbed into a van for the long freeway drive back to the airport. Twenty minutes into the trip I heard what sounded like a motorcycle roaring up alongside us. I looked out the passenger side. No motorcycle. Looked left and behind. No motorcycle. But the roar was coming from *somewhere*, and it was getting louder, fast.

Then I glanced through the front windshield just in time to see two airplane wheels starting to descend in front of us.

The driver jammed on the brakes as a small private plane made an emergency landing, missing the van by inches. The plane swung wildly from side to side, bounced hard onto the freeway, then screeched to a stop as we swerved around it.

Michael looked at me, eyes wide. "That was real, right?"

"Very," I said.

Once we returned to Los Angeles I broke the news to Michael that we'd been picked up but couldn't bring him back. A part of him knew that continuing into season two wasn't possible, but that didn't make the situation any easier. To give Michael a goal to work toward during his treatment I told him that if his condition improved, I would bring him back, even if only briefly, to tie up his character's story. I had already written a scene I wanted him to shoot for that purpose, setting up a more elaborate appearance later.

Michael expressed his appreciation, but also his concern. If news of his condition got out, it would kill his career. Nobody would ever hire him again.

"As far as I'm concerned this is just between you and me, it's nobody else's business," I said. "You're my friend and we'll deal with this privately."

Kathryn and I offered to assist with his rent and living expenses after he returned to New York, where he would have the support of his family and friends, including Sandy Bruckner, head of the *B5* fan club and Michael's de facto convention liaison. As he went through various medical regimens designed to deal with his disorder, we stayed in touch as much as possible to keep an eye on his progress, hoping that everything would work out in the end.

Meanwhile, I had to get season two on the rails. The hardest part of being a showrunner is that you're always the first one on deck, writing scripts while everyone else is on hiatus, and the last off the boat, finishing postproduction long after shooting has wrapped. To all intents and purposes you get zero time off. So while the cast and crew lounged on beaches or climbed mountains, I fired up the computer and got to work.

CHAPTER 28

The Christmas Ambush

For the role of *Babylon 5*'s new commanding officer, Captain John Sheridan,* we chose Bruce Boxleitner, best known for his work on *Tron* and *Scarecrow and Mrs. King* as well as several westerns. Bruce was the prototypical square-jawed, hard-nosed hero, an honest and honorable man who leaned into the straight-shooter image as much behind the camera as in front of it.

In addition, the actress hired to replace Patricia Tallman left to pursue other opportunities, which freed me to bring her back and get several crucial parts of the story back on track.

There was just one last hole that needed to be filled. In the season one finale, one of our characters, the second-in-command of station security, was revealed to be a traitor and shipped off the station. Since it was a fairly small role I wasn't looking for a star, just a good actor, so I was surprised when Jeff Conaway—one of the stars of *Grease* as well as the hit series *Taxi*—auditioned for the part.

---

* Yes, the same initials as Commander Jeffrey Sinclair and Joe Straczynski; I sometimes sign my work.

"He needs the job, he needs *something* to restart his career," Casting Director Fern Champion explained while Jeff waited in the hall for his audition. After being fired off *Taxi* for drug abuse he'd floated in and out of the business, doing occasional one-off roles but never landing anything permanent. "He finally went public about his addiction and entered treatment. He says he's clean now and willing to do whatever's necessary to restart his career, but I gotta be honest, you're taking a chance if you hire him and those issues come back in the middle of shooting."

I think we're all entitled to one Really Big Screw-Up in our lives; I've certainly committed more than my share. But during the audition Jeff was clear-eyed, sincere in confronting his past mistakes, and uncomplaining about having to start over. So I pushed the other producers to hire him, and a few weeks later, Jeff came on for what would become a four-year stint on *Babylon 5*.

With the series receiving solid ratings and plaudits from fans and reviewers alike, Warner Bros. reluctantly concluded we knew what we were doing and largely stopped giving us notes. This allowed me to delve into some of the issues I wanted to address: making Ivanova the first lead character of the Jewish faith as a regular in a science fiction TV series; presenting gay marriage as something so commonplace by 2259 that it's no longer even worthy of comment; and examining the death penalty and religious issues in ways that were tough but respectful.

This approach led to *Babylon 5* receiving two Emmy Awards, the Saturn Award, the E Pluribus Unum Award from the American Cinema Foundation, the Universe Award, the Space Frontier Foundation Award, and dozens of others.

The oddest recognition the show received came the afternoon Bruce Boxleitner attended a White House labor conference with his wife, actor Melissa Gilbert, who was then president of the Screen Actors Guild. "We were waiting for the meeting to start," Bruce said, "when the door opens and [political adviser to President George W. Bush] Karl Rove comes in. He blows right past Melissa, grabs my hand and says 'I just want you to know that *Babylon 5* is the best science fiction show ever.'

"Then he added, 'And the president thinks so, too.'"

I still don't know how I feel about that.

Out of all the awards the show received, the most important for me was the Hugo Award. As a kid in Newark who had to decide which science fiction books to "borrow" from liquor stores, I always looked for the words *Hugo Award Winner* on the cover. It was an indicator of excellence recognized around the world. I used to dream of one day winning a Hugo, and I was humbled and honored when my scripts for *Babylon 5* received two of them in a row.

Having grown up on Harlan Ellison's words and his work, admiring him from afar, I never imagined that we would one day become close friends. The four of us (including Kathryn and Harlan's wife Susan) traveled as a group, went to movies, and appeared together at conventions . . . though I did think it odd that whenever we convened for dinner there was almost always a third party present: a friend of Harlan's, another writer, or a celebrity who was a fan of his work (including a founding member of the '60s rock band The Turtles). One afternoon, after the fifth and sixth wheels had left and it was just the four of us gathered around the table in Harlan's Art Deco Pavilion, I asked him about it.

Harlan hesitated. Despite his reputation for crankiness, Harlan was one of the most gracious souls I have ever known; he didn't want to hurt me but he was also incapable of being less than forthright when queried. "Do you know what the definition of a bore is?" he asked at last. "It's someone who brings to a conversation nothing but his presence."

I felt my cheeks flush with embarrassment. He was right. I'd learned long ago how to ask prepared questions during interviews, relay instructions to crew members, and give practiced talks at conventions, but I'd never learned how to hold a normal conversation by initiating topics, asking spontaneous questions, or giving more than the briefest, most perfunctory responses. If I knew that a particular subject was going to come up with someone I was seeing the next day, I'd spend the night before preparing a canned first reply and a second response to what I thought they would say in return; once that ammunition was gone I would fall back on yes or no answers to even the most leading questions. Conversation was a performance I watched rather than an activity I participated in. Harlan's comment made me think back to all the parties and dinners where the conversation had stalled out when it came my turn to pick up the slack. *That* was why there was always a third party at dinner; Harlan wanted to make sure there was at least one person present with whom he could have an actual conversation.

I couldn't even bring myself to be offended. He could have easily come up with a dozen different replies to my question that were soothing and diversionary and utterly untrue. Instead he came back with something that was as hard for him to say as it was for me to hear. The question now was what to do about it. When you spend your formative years avoiding contact with people, sitting at family dinners that are marked by silence or violence and where nobody wants to hear your opinion, it's hard to pick up the skills of a raconteur.

But that was no excuse, so I returned to the mimicry I'd adopted as a child and began a careful study of Harlan and anyone else who could keep a group amused and engaged, noting what they said, how they said it, and what they were doing when they said it, compiling a catalog of behaviors that I could call up when needed, like props grabbed from a closet that I use to this day. Those who don't know me well see my behavior as natural banter, ascribing wit and stage presence to me without realizing that they're just see-ing echoes of folks far more sociable than myself, that the "me" they're seeing doesn't actually exist.

Well then, if the version of you they see isn't real, if the persona *isn't the* person, *then who are you when there's no one else around?*

The answer, even after all this time, is: I don't know. That part of my heart is sealed off from the rest of me. I'm not sad about it, I don't brood about it, and except for what's expressed for the first time in this book, I don't generally talk about it. It is what it is. The only thing I can objectively point to and say *that is a part of me* hangs in my closet as I write these words: a custom-made red-and-blue uniform with matching boots built to the exact specifications of the one George Reeves wore in *Adventures of Superman*. I've never worn it, I just like knowing it's *there*, at the edge of the rack where I can see it.

After the departure of story editor Larry DiTillio at the end of year two, my intention was to set aside a chunk of the third season's scripts for freelance writers. But Warners failed to give us an ad-vance script order, and the pickup came later than usual, putting us behind schedule before even a single word was written. The only way to hit our airdates would be if the first batch of scripts was writ-ten fast and landed on the stage ready to shoot, without the need for revisions. I couldn't trust that to outside writers so I wrote the first five scripts as a stopgap measure to get us up and running. Once filming started, however, I didn't have time to teach freelancers how to write for our show, and there were no other creative producers on staff to whom I could hand off that responsibility, so I kept going.

It wasn't my intention to write every episode of year three, but when I finally looked up from my keyboard I'd done exactly that. I didn't realize at the time that no American writer/producer had single-handedly written an entire twenty-two episode season of an hour-long dramatic series. Some had written *collaboratively* on twenty-two, but doing so alone was considered impossible or at least damned improbable. Warners was happy with the results and asked if I could do it again. I said yes. Since no one had told me it was impossible, I just went ahead and did it.

Writing that much that fast began taking a heavy toll, especially since I was still overseeing every aspect of physical production, responsibilities that on other shows are divided up between as many as a dozen people. Working eighteen to twenty hours a day, every day, led to carpal tunnel syndrome and I could only work by icing down my wrists twenty minutes for every hour spent writing. My brain was so full of story and production dilemmas that most nights I only slept an hour or two, sometimes not at all. I didn't want to take sleeping pills because I was afraid they might mess with the writing, so night after night I found myself staring at the ceiling as dawn filtered through the curtains. My immune system was so stressed out that I was constantly sick with one bug or another. Pat Tallman and Jeff Conaway began leaving jars of vitamins on my desk, and John Copeland had me undergo a physical exam normally reserved for actors so the show could be insured in case I collapsed from exhaustion or fell over dead. My hair, brown when we started *B5*, turned almost entirely white by season four.

Rather than admit that I was drowning, I pushed my feelings down and tried to pretend that everything was fine. The kid in me who was incapable of asking for help was still very much in charge. I couldn't admit, even to myself, that I was in pain. The marathon was so costly and so unusual that *Newsweek* published an article describing my situation as "Master and Slave of *Babylon 5*."

Those conditions would have tested even the strongest marriage, and ours had never been terribly deep. Tapped out, strapped to the wheel of my own creation, I lacked the bandwidth to do what needed to be done for the show *and* sustain a healthy relationship. I had to choose between them, and unfortunately the only coping mechanism I understood was isolation.

Kathryn wasn't surprised when I told her I wanted a separation. In many ways we'd been living separate lives for some time. I'd come home from work having grabbed a bite at the stage or on my way in, say hello, then go into my office to write, coming out again long after she was asleep. So she was very calm about the entire thing, in part because it wasn't *I'm leaving and want a divorce*, it was *I need to get out so I can finish this show or I'm going to lose my mind*.

Ever since I broke off contact with my family, my father had continued trying to shoehorn himself back into my life. Too cowardly to confront me directly, he hoped to provoke me into responding through a series of angry letters that he forced my mother to copy in her own handwriting, as though they were from her. The pretense was obvious because the letters reflected the word choices and grammar of someone who still thought in Russian. Even more telling, she would change pens or take a break, then begin writing again *in the middle of a word*, which no one does unless they're simply copying what's in front of them.

He only came at me directly once, when I began to speak publicly about my life in the hope that my story might help people from difficult families or limited means understand that success wasn't contingent upon having access to the best schools or a family with influence. I talked about coming from a blue-collar family that often lived in squalid conditions, constantly moving to stay ahead of creditors, and that my father had "a unique economic philosophy: blow into town, run up a lot of bills, and split."

At some point these comments ended up in a press release from Warners, which Charles saw online. Still obsessed with projecting an image of himself as the perfect father, he went batshit when I committed the unthinkable crime of breaking the Straczynski code of silence. In the past, whenever anyone in our family offered a less-than-flattering opinion of my father, he would threaten a lawsuit to shut them up, drawing upon a library of boilerplate legal forms he kept for just such occasions. These bullying tactics usually proved successful because none of his targets could afford to fight it out; the threat alone was enough to intimidate them into silence without him ever having to walk into a courtroom.

So naturally he sent an email threatening to sue me for my comments.

His email is reproduced below, edited for length as the demands go on for several pages.[*] I include this because it marks the only direct communication from my father since 1986, and represents the sole opportunity in this book to let him speak in his own voice without being characterized subjectively by me. Though the "offense" took place months earlier, he waited to send the email until December 23, giving me forty-eight hours to respond when he knew no attorneys would be working.

Item 4328103 12/23/96 20:52
From: PLASTIC@PRODIGY.NET@INET02#
To: STRACZYNSKI J. Michael Straczynski
Subject: Defamation of character
From: Charles Straczynski

On Sat April 6 1996 you and others including Babylon 5 have slandered the Straczynski family in public, to the whole world on the internet.

I am going to ask you to remove from the internet these out and out lies that were in the news release on the April, 6 date.

---

[*] I also cleaned up his spelling.

I want you to issue an apology for these lies. Apparently you are not intelligent enough to realize that you are jeopardizing Warner Bros. Productions, Babylon 5, as well as your partner Douglas Netter and yourself.

If you do not remove these lies with a retraction and an apology directly on the internet and by regular mail. I will file suit against all the above Parties.

I witnessed such underhanded and heartless actions when I was stuck in Russia during the war where children turned in their parents to the KGB who were then imprisoned and some shot due to this type of action. It seems that you developed into that type of character. I am glad that I am living in this country. You also said that you have available all these bills that you refer to.

Unless you remove this with an apology on the internet from you and Babylon 5 by Friday the 27th December 1996, this letter will appear on the internet under the following "GREAT MAKER ALSO GREAT LIAR."[*] Don't forget that Warner Bros. Babylon 5, and others might be liable. If I do decide to sue.

I want you to answer the following questions:

When was I a blue collar worker and for how long?

When was I as you remember, no longer a blue collar worker?

Can you recollect that I was in business of my own for over 21 years?

Can you remember where and what was the first and last business?

When, and name the states and towns where I used the unique economic philosophy, of running up a lot of bills and splitting? (send me copies of these bills).

Did you, in your entire life, go to bed hungry or abused?

---

[*] Great Maker was a term created by *Babylon 5* fans for me, à la Roddenberry being the "great bird of the galaxy."

Name the states and towns where we moved to every six months to a year as you claim.

Name the different schools you attended every year of your life.

Explain truthfully how bad was your existence?

How many college diplomas do you have and what for?

Name all the various colleges you attended, that you worked your way thru, and name every job you held to do this, as well as the amount of money you earned for that purpose.

Is all of your chronology of accomplished events in the news release on the internet from Babylon 5 the honest truth, or is it seeded with lies?

Who wrote that news release?

What did your mother do to you, that you heartlessly refused to speak to her for years?

I will wait until the 27th Dec. for you to do right. You know yourself that all that was a pack of lies and you are being misled by your aunt. If she has all these bills tell her to give them to you.

If you can't say anything good about a person then don't say anything at all. In the meantime go over these questions in your own mind, and see if you did the right thing.

Don't think for one minute that I won't sue the whole bunch of you, just two years ago I sued a Company in Portland Oregon called Modcom and it cost me $20,000 to do that. Just keep in mind that I will protect my family and my reputation.

> Do the right thing.
> *Charles Straczynski*

Since this tactic had proved successful in the past, he assumed his email would have its intended effect. But this time he'd picked the wrong target.

I fired back a note stating that my talks had only skimmed the surface of his past actions, and that I would happily elucidate more of them online, putting our family's whole sordid history out there with plenty of references for verification.

His reply, sent Christmas Day:

Item 6954720 12/25/96 17:40
From: PLASTIC6@JUNO.COM@INET01#
To: STRACZYNSKI
Subject: Threat to put more lies on the internet, a web letter on 12/25/96

Please go ahead with your threat to put your letter full of lies and imaginations on the web. I am anxious to see it there, we will also see how the lawyers for Warner Bros. as well as Doug Netter and others have this vetted.

That news release full of lies, was posted by Babylon five which is a part of Warner Bros and you have now twenty four hours to remove it after that a suit will be filed without any further warnings.

You now will be able to bring your evidence to court and prove all these accusations.

From now on I will deal directly with Warner Bros. I personally think that you have a screw loose and you don't realize what you are doing.

You think you know everything but let me disappoint you, you don't, so therefore it is worthless to try to convince you of anything different

I think you are a sick person.

See all of you in court

ps; I would like to see the receipts of the $20,000.00 you paid in student loans or did you skip out on them.

I'd had enough. The day he slugged me in Bourbonnais and I threatened him to his face I learned that the only way to deal with him was to come at him fists swinging.

Herewith my reply:

You want to go ahead and try and sue me, that's your choice.

But be prepared for a massive counter-suit from me for harassment, and defamation of my own character if you proceed. I can match you dollar for dollar, and I'm prepared to spend every dollar I have if it means proving my case. And I will. I will background every charge I've made, and then some; I will find, contact, subpoena and depose everyone you have known, everyone you have worked with, find every criminal charge and I will present them all in court to prove my point should you decide to sue. My character is not the issue here; you have chosen to make yours the point of your defense. If you want to walk into a courtroom and defend that, that's your decision.

Meanwhile, this is the last I want to hear from you. You do not frighten me. You can intimidate Mom and Theresa all you want, but you do not scare me. Next time you want to contact me, go through a lawyer, and I will do the same. But don't even think of threatening me any further in email, or I will have to take measures to stop you.

Twelve hours later, came the coward's reply.

Item 0755646 12/27/96 15:33
From: PLASTIC6@JUNO.COM@INET# Internet Gateway
To: STRACZYNSKI
Sub: . . . no subject . . .

Joe

Do you think I would sue you. I would never do anything to embarrass you.

I got upset when I saw that on the news release.

I got on the internet to keep up with your accomplishments and the first thing that popped up was that part where the news release is. In fact mom was going to join your fan club. This is the only way we could keep up with you since you have not ever called your mother for such a long time. Her heart was broken when Mary and Eddie Skibicki were here in Calif 2 weeks ago and told her that Theresa had an autographed picture from you.

Listen to me. She is a vindictive person. She misled me at a cost of $8000 for the trip that I took to Siberia. I tried to find my cousins address because she told me she would get it for me. When she did it was false. He and his other brother and father mama's brother were taken to Siberia during the war. The father was hung and his brother died of TB. He is the only one to survive and could not return all the way to Poland due to lack of money.

So when she had enough guts to call me and ask if I found him I called her a fool and a liar, and I know that she was feeding you a bunch of crap. She wanted for me to buy her a rascal scooter.* Why? When my mother died she grabbed all the money and didn't bother to offer me a penny. I would not take it if she offered anyway but it proves that she has greed.

What *any* of that had to do with the matter at hand, I have no idea. The email exchange ends there. Confronted by someone willing to fight back, he retired from the battlefield, backing and filling the whole time. I almost deleted the email, but one sentence caught my attention: *She misled me at a cost of $8000 for the trip that I took to Siberia.*

Siberia? Si-fucking-*beria*? What was *that* all about?

For six years my aunt Theresa was the only member of my family with whom I'd remained in contact, so during her next call I

---

* I had already bought this for her, unbeknownst to him.

asked about the Siberia thing. She explained that he'd gone to visit relatives, stopping along the way to visit some of the places they'd lived in during the war, including the train station at Bogdanova.

"Did he go anyplace else?" I asked, losing interest but looking for the end of the story. I'm a writer, it's what I do.

There was a long pause, as if she were deciding whether or not to answer, then said, "Vishnevo."

According to the bio my father had forced me to ghostwrite for him, Vishnevo was where he had seen a Jewish massacre take place, the victims herded into a cemetery before being machine-gunned to death. It seemed an odd choice for a vacation.

"Where in Vishnevo did he go?"

"The Jewish cemetery," she said. I could feel a strain in her voice. I didn't know what was causing it, but somewhere a finger was pushing down on an exposed nerve, and she dived off the phone before I could press for more information.

Vishnevo. For as long as I could remember that name had lingered at the edge of my family's history. I couldn't understand why it kept coming back into the picture. And why would my father, an avowed anti-Semite, go to a Jewish cemetery?

I might've come near an answer if I'd connected that conversation with my father's disinclination to get anywhere near a courtroom where his personal history could be dredged up. I assumed he'd backed off because he knew I could outspend him in a court of law. And that may have been the *main* reason.

But as matters turned out, it wasn't the *only* reason.

When Michael O'Hare felt stable enough to work again, I wrote a two-part episode to give his character closure and provide a chance for him to shine as an actor. He came through the experience exhausted but exhilarated. There was no way he could handle the stress of working full-time on a TV series, but this would allow him to end his role honorably and remind the town that he was available for guest roles, a prospect that helped lift his spirits. He also appreciated that his situation had been treated with discretion. "Don't worry," I told him, "I'll take this secret to my grave."

He considered this for a moment, then said, "I have a better idea: take it to *my* grave. If anything happens to me, I *want* you to talk about it publicly. If people know this can happen to a lead actor in a TV show, the commander of a space station, they'll know it can happen to anybody. Maybe that knowledge can help somebody else down the road."

And with that we parted.

As *Babylon 5* approached the end of its fourth season, the question of whether or not we would be picked up for our fifth and final season became more complicated when PTEN, bleeding money and resources, was shut down. We were the only show still standing, trying to finish our story. The cable network TNT was interested in picking us up, but at a much lower price point. The only way to make the budget work would be to eliminate one day of filming, going from a seven-day shoot to six days. Many on our crew thought this was impossible on a show as technically ambitious as *B5*.

So I made a deal with our director of photography, John Flinn, who was the heart and soul of the shooting company. We had already decided to shoot our series finale during season four, so it would be available whichever way our run concluded. We hadn't yet chosen a director, so I volunteered to do it and said if I, as a neophyte director, could get it done within the required six days, then *anybody* could do it; if I failed then we would make other adjustments to the budget, including letting go of some cast members and cutting back on extras, stunts, and CGI. I had no desire to be a director, but I needed to make a point if I was going to save my show.

Everyone on the crew knew this would be our final episode, regardless of airdate, so emotions ran high during the filming of "Sleeping in Light," which was already an emotional episode. From my position behind the monitors I could frequently hear the crew sobbing. It was six days of tears. As the director I didn't have that luxury; I had to keep everyone together and moving forward.

To Flinn's credit he didn't sandbag me during shooting, which he could have easily done to a first-time director. I suspect he was genuinely curious to see if I could pull this off or if I'd fall on my face unassisted. Everyone was an emotional wreck by the time we were done, but we still managed to wrap ahead of our six-day schedule and under budget. We'd proven the point, both to the crew and TNT.

Three weeks later, I stood on a stage in Blackpool, England, in front of thousands of fans at the biggest *Babylon 5* convention to date and announced that we would be producing our fifth season *and* four original *B5* TV movies for TNT. The crowd erupted in a roar loud enough to shake the platform beneath my feet, and the sound took me back to the moment when I stood before the assembled students of Chula Vista High School decades earlier. The seventeen-year-old version of me would never have believed where that first effort would eventually take us.

We'd made it to year five and beaten the *Star Trek* curse. There were shadows to be sure; we lost Claudia Christian at the last minute when she left the show over a contract dispute, and there were indications that Jeff Conaway was returning to his addictions, but the rest of the cast was thrilled that we would be able to finish our story. Best of all, now that I'd proven that a five-year arc could be done successfully for television, *Lost, Battlestar Galactica*, and other shows picked up the ball and ran with it, until by 2019 multi-season arcs were the rule rather than the exception.

But we did it first with *Babylon 5*.

As we began working on our fifth season,* our search for a replacement for Claudia took us to veteran actress Tracy Scoggins, who slid into the role effortlessly and very much at the last minute. Though we were now back on track, the knowledge that this was our last year made every day a bittersweet experience, and I lingered on-set as much as possible to savor those moments. When the last episode went before the cameras, the crew presented me with a Typist of the Millennium Award in recognition for writing 92 out of 110 hour-long episodes and five TV movies, a record still unmatched by any other member of the Writers Guild of America.

By this time I had been separated from Kathryn for almost three years, though we still met frequently for dinners and social events. While we were shooting *B5* I'd been boxed in, but now that I was on the other side of that crunch, I thought we should give things another chance, and Kathryn agreed. She knew that the separation had been necessary for both my sanity and the survival of *B5*, and we were together again at the end of the show.

Babylon 5 had done well enough for Warner Bros. to sense a possible franchise and they asked me to come up with a sequel. Most science fiction series put humans at the top of the pecking order, with traveling to other worlds as mundane as going to the corner store, so I decided to create a show set in a universe where humans were at the *bottom* of the totem pole. Our characters would explore ancient, dangerous worlds populated or abandoned by races

---

* For which I wrote twenty-one of the twenty-two episodes, with Neil Gaiman providing the only freelance script in three years.

billions of years ahead of us, a show that felt *alien* in the truest sense of that word.

Crusade would tell the story of the crew of the starship *Excalibur* as they searched for a cure to an alien disease that would wipe out humanity within five years. It starred Gary Cole as Captain Matthew Gideon; Daniel Dae Kim as second-in-command John Matheson; Peter Woodward as Galen, a technomage who uses advanced alien technology to simulate the effects of magic; David Allen Brooks as archaeologist Max Eilerson; Marjean Holden as Dr. Sarah Chambers; and Carrie Dobro as Dureena Nafeel, the last surviving member of her race.

During *Babylon 5* our production team had honed their craft to a fine art, so as we began filming on *Crusade* I didn't foresee any problems. Then suddenly, right in the middle of shooting episode three, TNT told us to stop production so they could reevaluate the look of the show. It seemed strange that they waited this long, but we accepted it at face value.

What none of us knew was that TNT had just received the results of a study commissioned to determine how *Babylon 5* was doing on their network. It showed that the typical TNT viewer didn't like science fiction, and that *B5* fans didn't like what TNT offered the rest of the time (mainly wrestling and westerns). When our show came on, the TNT audience tuned out, and the *B5* audience came in; at the end of the show, the *B5* audience left and the TNT audience returned. TNT had hoped we would lure new viewers who would stay for their other programs, but the strategy was going the other way, annoying viewers on both sides.

So the network executives apparently decided to use the production delay to buy time while they figured out how to get out of the deal for *Crusade*. The only way to extricate themselves without being liable for production costs on twenty-two episodes was to demonstrate that the show they were *getting* wasn't the show they'd

ordered, that we were a rogue production flouting their instructions. So after we were cleared to restart filming, they began giving
us notes that were unbelievably toxic. Based on years of receiving
network and studio notes, it seemed to me that their suggestions
weren't being made in an attempt to improve the show, *they were
notes so awful that no producer in his right mind would agree to
implement them.* Every time we said no provided another piece of
evidence they could use to demonstrate that we were refusing to
deliver the show they'd ordered.

They told us to make Dureena "a sexual explorer" who would
have intercourse with each new alien species she met in order to
better understand them. They demanded fistfights on the bridge at
every opportunity, regardless of whether or not they made sense for
the story, and insisted on big action scenes we couldn't afford within
the budget they provided. If we didn't stage those sequences, we
were chastised for going against their notes; if we did as instructed,
they complained that we were going over budget; if we were somehow able to do those big scenes *and* stay on budget, the network
insisted the scenes be removed during editing, allegedly to focus
on character, but then they did the same thing with the character
scenes, demanding pages of additional dialogue to explain things
that didn't need explaining, then yelling at us because the extra
dialogue *they had asked for* made the show "talky." We were being
whipsawed back and forth on a daily, sometimes hourly basis.

One of their more egregious notes concerned an episode entitled
"The Well of Forever." They demanded that Gideon arrange for one
of his crew members to be raped by the antagonist so they could
"catch him with his pants around his ankles" and blackmail him
into compliance.

Repeated for emphasis: the network wanted *the captain of our
ship and the star of our show* to deliberately arrange for an unwill-
ing crew member to be raped to solve a plot point.

I refused. "If I go along with this, I'll go to hell," I said to anyone within earshot. "Granted, I'm going anyway, but why accelerate the journey?"

This led to a showdown at the TNT offices. On one side of a long conference table were the network executives and lawyers; on the other were myself, Doug, John, and a Warner Bros. executive who wanted to be anywhere else that day and spent most of his time avoiding direct eye contact by watching a moth that wasn't actually there. Between us lay twenty pages of demands, most of which were on par with the rape note, while others were even more offensive. As we waited for the meeting to begin, those on our side of the table encouraged me to find middle ground, giving to get. But there *was* no middle ground. Though I didn't know the reason for their posture, it was obvious that TNT would keep grinding us down *regardless* of whether or not I agreed to implement their notes. As the meeting began I decided that if I was going to go down, I may as well do so taking a stand against demands that I considered reprehensible.

The TNT executive in charge opened the document. "Let's start with page one."

"No," I said. Very quietly, very softly, very firmly.

"No to what?"

"No to page one, no to page twenty, and to all the parts in between. I'm not doing them. I'm not doing *any* of them." Out of the corner of my eye I saw Doug wince and look away. The Warners rep paled visibly.

"So what do you want to talk about?"

I shrugged. "The weather?"

The meeting was over. And so was the show. TNT pulled the plug on *Crusade*, citing creative and contractual differences. They got what they wanted. They got *out*.

The death of *Crusade* was slow, agonizing, and unceremonious.

The thirteen episodes produced before the cancellation would still be aired, so postproduction continued even as we tore down the sets and let go of personnel. These were bitter, angry days for the crew, my partners, and Warner Bros., all of whom blamed me for letting the show go down. I accepted that blame because without access to TNT's master plan I thought I *was* to blame.

I didn't know the real story until two years later, when a TNT executive asked me to lunch after leaving the network and told me why they had worked so hard to make our lives miserable. "Once the ratings survey came in, they wanted the show gone so they could use the rest of that season's budget to buy reruns of shows more in line with what TNT viewers wanted. They were determined to get out of the deal and there was nothing you could have done to change it."

I'd spent my childhood fascinated by science fiction TV series, by *Lost in Space* and *Star Trek*, and dreamed of one day having my own show, my own *universe* to play with. I never imagined I would one day get not just one but *two* such series on the air. And while I would later return to the *Babylon 5* universe for two small projects—a pilot that didn't make it to series and a two-hour DVD movie that I would write, produce, and direct—for all intents and purposes, my time in that world was over.

It was as if the universe said, *You were staying in your comfort zone too long, so we had to blow up your life again. Nothing personal.*

It's not pain, it just feels like pain.

CHAPTER 29

Swingin' with Spider-Man

For a TV writer/producer there is no higher title than showrunner. The series budget, studios, and networks may vary in size, but as far as the actual functioning of a series is concerned, that's as far as one can go. Since only a small percentage of WGA members become showrunners, and the skills involved are considered fairly valuable, I assumed I wouldn't be out of work for long. But once you've run your own series, everybody assumes you won't work under someone else, and the only openings at the time were as seconds-in-command, so my phone remained silent.

It didn't help that the TNT fracas reinforced the perception that I was *difficult*. The truth is that I've always been willing to compromise if someone can show me, logically and objectively, a better way or where I'm simply wrong. The audience doesn't know who contributed what, so if the final script contains something infinitely smarter than what I'd originally written, I can bask in the reflected glory of that idea as though it were my own. I enjoy the back-and-forth of the notes process *when it's smart and incisive*. What I won't do is lie down to bullies or lobotomize the part of my brain that requires story logic.

But for some executives, that's a distinction without a difference.

Despite the anguish over *Crusade*, I felt quite positive about the prospect of a break in my TV career. Though it may seem counter-intuitive, I believe that being out of work can often be a good thing because it forces you to reassess your priorities. Doing the same job for years on end doesn't leave much time to ask, "Is this *really* what I want to do with my life, and if not, what is?" Quitting journalism led me to animation and firebombing my career in animation led to live-action. I'd worked in television for fifteen years because until *Crusade* augered into the ground it had been *fun*. As a kid, every new move was an opportunity to reinvent myself to fit into my new surroundings. If endings were beginnings, then a break in my TV work was another chance to decide what I wanted to do.

Working in syndicated television paid only a fraction of what was standard for network series, and the onerous contract I'd signed for *Babylon 5* ensured that I'd never see even a penny in profit from the series (and never have), but it still allowed me to sock away enough money to carry us for a few months while I figured out what to do next.

I started by taking a shot at writing the Christine Collins story as a script, only to toss it in the trash, salvaging the one piece I liked as an insert to a new edition of my writing book, painfully aware that I still lacked the skills to tell it properly. I had no desire to return to journalism, and there was no way I could go back to animation, so what was left? Having been given the amazing opportunity of unemployment, what would I *enjoy*?

The answer was obvious and immediate: comic books.

The day my father tore up all of my comics, he said, "You're never going to make a living with this crap."

Fine, I thought. *Let's prove him wrong. Again.*

My comics writing to this point was limited to just a few stand-alone issues that were breathtakingly amateurish because I was new to the form and still figuring out the rules. In a TV script you can write "He comes down the hall, kicks in the door, and enters the room." But in comics the panels don't move, so you can show the character coming down the hall, *or* kicking in the door, *or* entering the room, but not all three (unless you're going for a super-fast blur à la the Flash). I also lacked a real grasp of the techniques that would let me incorporate the artwork with the story more efficiently to create something that was visually arresting.

All right, then let's dig in and figure it out, I thought. The sensible approach would be to write more single issues for Marvel or DC, maybe some two-parters, and ease my way up the ladder until I was in a position to launch my own books and characters. The idea of going from television to writing comics full-time and creating my own books, with almost zero experience, was like an ice skater walking into the Bolshoi convinced she can be a ballerina starting *right now*. But I've never been terribly sensible; as with writing nearly all of *Babylon 5* I was so excited by the idea that I didn't stop to consider that it might be impossible.

Most of the bestselling independent comics at the time were single-character books that starred a costumed superhero marred by tragic flaws, such as *Spawn*, *Wolverine*, *Fathom*, *Witchblade*, and *The Darkness*. There were plenty of successful ensemble books, but nearly all of them were based on long-established franchises such as *The X-Men*, *Justice League*, and *The Avengers*. Creating a single-character book was the safe, commercial choice, so naturally I went the other way. I decided to create an ensemble book about super-powered characters no one had ever heard of, most of whom looked like average folks rather than being the massively muscular heroes that were pro forma in comics. Established ensemble books generally averaged half a dozen major characters, so mine would be about 113 characters, of which 20 to 25 would be center stage. To further violate the usual tropes, there would be no super-powered characters outside this group, no supervillains, and in particular, no secret identities.

I decided to go against the usual norms because in the late '90s mainstream comics had entered a creative slump. Sales at Marvel and DC had fallen to record-low numbers and most of the independent comics were artist—rather than writer—driven. From a commercial standpoint the market wasn't suited to the kind of story I wanted to tell, and my relative inexperence meant that the possibility for failure was immense.

Which of course was the biggest part of the attraction.

I decided to draw upon my experiences as an outsider in tight-knit Matawan and write about what would happen if a bunch of kids from a small town were born with unusual abilities after a mysterious cosmic event. Segregated into a camp for their own safety and the protection of others, they grow up as a dysfunctional extended family with all the attendant rivalries and jealousies. The story would focus on how the world changes them and how they change the world without the protection of secret identities because the event that birthed them was witnessed around the globe. Everyone knows who these characters *are*, but nobody knows what they *feel*, so exploring that dynamic would be the thrust of the storytelling.

In comics, whenever someone gets superpowers they invariably put on a costume and become a Hero or a Bad Guy. For this story, most of our characters would never put on a uniform or seek out careers as superheroes or villains, attempting instead to create normal lives for themselves. Characters in most comics never grow old—Peter Parker is always in his twenties, Superman somewhere in his thirties—so we would follow these characters over the course of sixty-plus years, from birth to death, as they live through shifts in friendships and rivalries, and slowly come to grips with their abilities and responsibilities.

I made every counterintuitive decision possible in the belief that if I kept going wrong, I'd eventually circle back around and end up right.

I'd survived my childhood (and much of my adulthood) by isolating myself so I couldn't be hurt no matter how hard I got pounded; the price was a veil between me and my emotions. So the first character I created was Peter Dawson, whose body is surrounded by an energy field that protects him from harm, but also prevents him from physically experiencing the world around him, unable to feel the touch of a woman's hand or the wind on his face. I'd dreamed of growing up to be a superhero, so Randy Fisk would be a comics fan with the same ambition, one of the few to don a costume and create an alter ego, which was pointless since everyone in the world knows who these characters are, but for Randy it's all about the style. I was a shy, withdrawn writer, so John Simon, a poet—and secretly the strongest of the bunch—would be similarly inclined. I grew up in different cities, adapting to my surroundings without letting anyone see who I really was, so Elizabeth Chandra would look different to everyone who saw her.

The characters were damaged, idealistic, cynical, lost, angry, hopeful, and doomed: the *Rising Stars* of the book's title, a twenty-four-issue series with a clearly defined conclusion rather than an open-ended, ongoing monthly series. Once I finished roughing out the story, I began cold-calling comics publishers to find someone interested in the book.

The first company to call back was Top Cow Comics, a division of Image Comics known for *Witchblade*, and we arranged to meet at their offices in Century City.

I knew what I wanted—a title of my own, rather than writing any of their in-house books—and was prepared to bluff as hard as necessary by piggybacking on the success of *Babylon 5*. The average top-selling comic might move 60,000 to 100,000 copies, but *B5* had millions of fans around the world; if even a fraction of them showed up, *Rising Stars* would do very well. I wanted creative freedom, no editorial interference, control of the film rights, a proprietary credit on the cover as *J. Michael Straczynski's Rising Stars*, and for the book to be published under my own imprint, Joe's Comics, with the logo right next to the Top Cow logo. I chose that name because the night my father tore up my comics he left an empty box on which I'd stenciled the words *JOE'S COMICS*. Now I would begin to refill that box with my own comics.

To my astonishment Top Cow agreed to everything.

Now I just had to figure out how to write the damned thing.

The first issue began with a mystery to hook the readers: someone has murdered Peter Dawson, the story's invulnerable man. How do you kill someone who can't be hurt? The investigation becomes a delivery mechanism to introduce the other characters as suspects and delve into their lives. It was a soap opera at a time when the emphasis was on big action books. I had no idea if it would succeed or fail, so I was just as surprised as anyone else when it became a top-selling title.

Top Cow wanted to capitalize on the success of *Rising Stars* with another series, so I reached back to an image that struck me while sitting on a bench in downtown San Diego after one of my post-mugging midnight marathons, the idea that there were two street corners, two San Diegos, two *realities* existing side by side: the daytime world of secretaries, workers, and office politics, and the midnight world of hookers, drug dealers, and violence. Both occupied the same geographic location, separated only by the tick of the clock: a daylight nation and a midnight nation. It had taken me twenty years to process that moment well enough to finally write about it.

Midnight Nation's lead character, LAPD Lieutenant Detective David Grey, is investigating what appear to be a series of gang murders when he's attacked by supernatural forces that literally steal his soul. Deprived of his anchor to this world, David passes into a shadow version of our reality populated by thrown-aways and runaways, the homeless and the lost. He learns that his soul is being held in New York by the Other Guy (the Devil, though we never specifically identify him as such) and that if he doesn't get it back he will turn into the same sort of creature that attacked him. But nothing in this world works as it should, including vehicles, so he has to *walk* there from LA, which will take a year. Along the way, he has to defeat the forces trying to stop him while fighting a more personal battle against the darkness that is slowly transforming him. And since the book would be coming out in twelve monthly installments, I could tell his story in real time.

Accompanying him on this journey is Laurel, an ancient, angelic entity who has made this journey many times before, but each attempt failed when her companions surrendered to their darker impulses. Embittered by her experiences, Laurel doesn't want to get emotionally involved with David, but gradually comes to believe that maybe this time things will work out. As they battle their way across the country, their relationship shifts from antagonism to a love story with a bittersweet but hopeful ending. An existential murder mystery where the victim is also the detective, *Midnight Nation* is a horror story, a love story, a social polemic about hope and self-sacrifice, and one of the most personal books I've ever written. The story allowed me to exorcise the demons from the night I was nearly beaten to death, and the spiritual issues I was still dealing with in terms of the God Thing.

Aided by the phenomenal artwork of Gary Frank, *Midnight Nation* proved even more successful than *Rising Stars*. After being beaten down by the bitter pill that was *Crusade*, writing comics was fun, restoring my soul and reminding me why I started writing in the first place.

In 2000, comic artist and editor Joe Quesada became editor in chief of Marvel Comics, which was suffering through one of the worst periods in its long history, marked by plummeting sales and a bankruptcy that nearly destroyed the company. Tasked with restoring Marvel to its former glory, Quesada and Marvel publisher Bill Jemas traveled to the Wizard World Chicago Comic Convention in hopes of hiring writers and artists who could help Marvel regain its position in the market.

I was there that weekend as guest of honor, and was enjoying a stroll through the dealer's room one afternoon when I heard someone yell "Stop him!" I turned to see a man in his twenties racing my way, clutching a stack of original artwork worth several thousand dollars that he had just stolen from one of the tables. As the dealer gave chase, everyone parted like the Red Sea, eager to avoid being hurt or caught in the conflict. What happened next was documented by Peter David, who was also attending the convention, in a column entitled "The Adventures of Joltin' Joe Straczynski."

> A young guy attempted to shoplift in the dealer's room. He was spotted and tried to bolt, but didn't get far. As reported by a witness, who was on the scene in the Chicago Con dealer's room:
>
> "I heard a noise, people running and yelling. And I turned and Joe and another man were converging on a young man from either side. Joe grabbed him from the right, wrapping his arm around the guy's shoulder and immobilizing him.
>
> "Another man whom I imagine to be the victimized dealer caught up with the guy, telling him not to struggle, that they weren't going to hurt him but he was definitely busted. I also heard him say, 'Do you know who this is?' pointing to Joe. The guy didn't seem to care; he just seemed angry and scared.
>
> And people wonder where Joe gets his ideas.

The thief was younger and stronger than me, but at six three I'm pretty solid. He was so surprised that anyone jumped into his path that he didn't have time to react before I put him on the floor, hard. The dealer and I then held the thief until the police showed up.

Afterward, one of the convention organizers asked me, "Why the hell did you do that? You could've gotten hurt."

I took him to where I'd been standing when the guy made a break for it, in front of a ten-foot-tall cutout of Superman. "How could I stand in front of that, in front of *him*, and do nothing?"

Later that day, still pumped on adrenaline, I was back in the dealer's room when Quesada and Jemas introduced themselves and told me how much they liked my work. "Would you be interested in doing something for us at Marvel?" Joe asked.

"Sure," I said. I assumed they wanted me to write a miniseries or something small, since both *Rising Stars* and *Midnight Nation* were limited-run books. "What did you have in mind?"

"How would you like to take over *The Amazing Spider-Man*?"

Spider-Man is Marvel's flagship character, second in worldwide recognition only to Superman. There have been a number of ancillary Spider-Man titles over the years, but *The Amazing Spider-Man* was the core title for the entire publishing division. While Superman had always been my icon, as a kid I collected every issue of *The Amazing Spider-Man* I could find, including his debut in *Amazing Fantasy* #15 (all later destroyed by my father). I was drawn to Spider-Man because like me, Peter Parker was skinny, geeky, and often bullied by other kids. For him to get amazing powers was every kid's wish come true. His impact on American culture was huge, so it made sense that they would want to start rebuilding the company with Spider-Man. As the saying goes in the comics business, "As goes Spider-Man, so goes Marvel."

And they wanted to give him to me? Spider-Man? Seriously?

"Are you sure you've got the right guy?" I asked.

They laughed and insisted they knew exactly what they were

doing. The only catch was that if I took the job I'd have to be exclusive to Marvel. So did I want it or not?

I hesitated. Having never done an open-ended, monthly comic for a major, iconic character, I wasn't sure I could pull it off. Besides, being exclusive would mean shutting down Joe's Comics. I'd just started the imprint and we had a lot of momentum going forward. Did I really want to walk away from all that? Besides, there were rumors that Marvel was going to be sold off within the year. If that happened, I would have given up Joe's Comics for nothing.

On the other hand: it was *Spider-Man*, so I said yes.

Shortly after I returned to Los Angeles, MGM called to ask if I'd like to take a shot at writing the pilot script for *Jeremiah*, a TV series that had been in development at the Showtime cable network for over a year. Based on a Belgian comic book, the story was about young characters fighting to survive a harsh, post-apocalyptic future caused by a race war years earlier. The project had stalled out in development, and MGM felt that the only way to revive the project was by walking in with a bulletproof script that would wow the network.

I was excited by the challenge of bringing a project back from the dead, so we made the deal and I began writing the two-hour pilot movie. The biggest problem was figuring out how to populate a post-apocalyptic world with young people to the near-complete exclusion of adults. My solution was a bioengineered virus triggered by the presence of certain hormones. If you were an adult, your hormones were functioning and you got the disease and died; if you were a kid, your hormones had not yet fully kicked in and you survived. It was a clean, mean solution to the problem. (In researching this, I asked several virologists if such a designer virus might one day happen. They said that it's not only possible, it is inevitable. You're welcome.)

When I didn't hear back for several weeks after turning in the script, I figured the project had dead-ended. Then I was called to a meeting with executives from MGM and Jerry Offsay, president of programming for Showtime. Jerry began by saying that he considered my script one of the best pilots he'd ever read. I didn't take his kind words too seriously, as such things were usually a prelude to a tsunami of detailed notes, leading to more drafts and more changes before ending with *good work but it's not something we want to pursue, thanks for playing and don't let the door hit you in the ass on the way out.*

"I love this so much," Jerry said, "that rather than just producing the pilot I've decided to commission the first full season based just on the script."

It took me a moment to process what he'd said. He didn't want to just shoot the pilot? Didn't want a focus group? Didn't want a dozen more revisions? He was going to *series* based on the *script*? Holy crap.

After the fall of *Crusade* I figured I'd have a lot of time on my hands before things started to break. Instead I was writing *The Amazing Spider-Man,* finishing up *Midnight Nation*, and *Jeremiah* was going straight to series.

I was sure that 2001 was going to be the best year *ever.*

To this day I remain staggered by the magnitude of that misapprehension.

CHAPTER 30

Lost in the Tall Grass with Jeremiah

n June 2001, I began writing and prepping *Jeremiah* for production in Vancouver, Canada, where I would live for the next two years. At around that same time, my first issue of *The Amazing Spider-Man* hit the stands, illustrated by the massively talented John Romita Jr., whose father was one of the original Silver Age Spider-Man artists. To freshen up the character of Spider-Man, I decided to take something we *think* we know about him and turn it upside down to see what it looks like. It's a given that Peter Parker got his powers from the bite of a radioactive spider, but nobody had ever asked *why.* Was it really just random chance, or was there some larger force involved? Did the radiation give the spider the power that it passed to Peter, or was it trying to give Peter the power it already had before the radiation killed it? The answer to those questions would provide over a year's worth of stories.

I used those early issues to repair Peter's broken relationship with Mary Jane, and to do something that I'd wanted to see for decades. Peter's aunt May had always been portrayed as a fragile, frail old woman who would fall over dead if she learned his secret. But I never bought that sexist perspective for a second. This was a woman who buried Peter's parents and her own husband, then raised a young boy alone. That takes courage, stamina, and a spine made of solid titanium. Peter may have gotten his *powers* from the spider but he got his *strength* from Aunt May, so during my run she finally discovers his secret. Not only does she not die, she embraces this side of his life and becomes his greatest ally. I wanted to show that those who love us can carry the burden of our secrets and accept the truth of who we truly are.

The relaunched *Amazing Spider-Man* performed beyond Marvel's expectations and helped set the stage for their recovery as a company. I would stay on to write seventy-four consecutive issues, one of the longest runs in the character's history.

Filming on *Jeremiah* began on September 7, 2001, at the Bridge Studios in Vancouver, also home to the *Stargate* series. Four days later I was awakened by a frantic phone call from Kathryn in Los Angeles. "Terrorists are attacking the country!" she said. "They're attacking the World Trade Center!"

Like the rest of the world I spent the next several days riveted by the tragedy, aching for the loss of those who died and the suffering of those who survived. The images of that attack will remain forever fixed in memory.

Speaking of that time much later, my editor on *The Amazing Spider-Man*, Axel Alonso said, "The Marvel office was closed on 9/12 so most of us returned to the office on 9/13. The wounds were very fresh. I was sitting at my desk, looking at a drawing of Spider-Man, when a realization suddenly hit me. I emailed Joe and said, 'I know you're working on the next script for a story-in-progress, but a thought occurred to me: Spider-Man is the quintessential New York City superhero. Wouldn't it be kind of odd for us to act like nothing happened?'

"Shortly after I got a terse reply: 'Right. Let me think on it.' And that was that."

I went radio silent because I couldn't figure out how to give Axel what he wanted. The need to drop this into the next issue meant that I would have only about three to four days to get it written, and I didn't think I had the skill set to pull it off. I was still trying to force the event to make sense for myself, let alone anybody else.

This prompted a call from Joe Quesada. "We really need to deal with this," he said. "Just because we're a comics company, that doesn't mean we should ignore it. We *can't* ignore it. Yeah, most of our readership are adults, but there are a lot of kids who read these books that don't stay up to watch *Nightline* or the evening news. They need to understand this. *We* need to understand this. Many of us lost friends in the Towers. We need to say something about this situation from within the context of the Marvel Universe.

"Yours is the best book to do that. Peter Parker is a New Yorker. Of all the characters in our universe he's the one best suited to put this in some kind of perspective. He needs to speak for himself, for the book, for *all* of us. And we think you're the guy to do it."

"I just don't think I *can*," I said. "I'm sure the words needed to address this are in the dictionary somewhere, but which ones and what order to put them in . . . I have no idea."

"Just do me a favor and think about it, see if anything comes up. It's a hot potato, no mistake. There are lots of folks who might think it's inappropriate for this to be discussed in a comic book. If you get it wrong, you'll be crucified. But if you can make it work, we'd appreciate it."

He was right about the risks. Already, the brutal murder of over three thousand innocents was being politicized to curtail civil rights, whip up prejudices, and broaden the war to those who had nothing to do with the attack but were more politically convenient. But none of that changed the fact that an act of unspeakable horror had been perpetrated and those responsible needed to be called out by every voice in the nation. I had no idea how to thread that needle. The only thing I knew for certain was that the events of 9/11 couldn't be integrated into a traditional story or fictionalized in any way because doing so would trivialize them.

But if it wasn't a story, then what *was* it?

The next day we were shooting an episode of *Jeremiah* in the Greater Vancouver Resource Development, a huge swath of ancient, old-growth forest where moss hangs off the tall trees like shawls, waving in the wind. The perfect place for reflection. While the crew set up for the next shot I retreated into the producer's trailer to make one last attempt at writing the script. My laptop was back at the office, so I opened a bound notebook and stared at the blank page. *Just write the first thing that comes to mind.*

I wrote, *There are no words.*

I stared at the page. *No words.*

Follow the thought, I decided.

Some things are beyond words. Beyond comprehension. Beyond forgiveness.

How do you say we didn't know? We couldn't know. We couldn't imagine.

The sane world will always be vulnerable to madmen, because we cannot go where they go to conceive of such things.

I struggled to keep up as the words tumbled out of my head. My pen raced across the page. Automatic writing.

What do we tell the children? Do we tell them that evil is a foreign face?

No. The evil is the thought behind the face. And it can look just like yours.

Do we tell that evil is tangible, with defined borders and names and geometries and destinies?

No. They will have nightmares enough.

Perhaps we tell them that we are sorry. Sorry that we were not able to deliver unto them the world we wished them to have.

That our eagerness to shout is not the equal of our willingness to listen.

That the burdens of distant people are the responsibility of all men and women of conscience, or their burdens will one day become our tragedy.

Or perhaps we simply tell them that we love them, and that we will protect them. That we would give our lives for theirs, and do it gladly, so great is the burden of our love.

Faster now. Writing of the retribution to come:

Whatever our history, whatever the root of our surnames, we remain a good and decent people, and we do not bow down and we do not give up. The fire of the human spirit cannot be quenched by bomb blasts or body counts. Cannot be intimidated forever into silence or drowned by tears. We have endured worse before. We will bear this burden and all that come hereafter because that's what ordinary men and women do. No matter what. This has not made us weaker. It has only made us stronger.

In recent years, we as a people have been tribalized and factionalized by a thousand casual unkindnesses. But in this we are one. Flags sprout in uncommon places, the ground made fertile by tears and shared resolve. We have become one in our grief.

We are one now in our determination. One as we recover. One as we rebuild.

You wanted to send a message, and in so doing you awakened us from our self-involvement. Message received.

Look for your reply in the thunder.

A walkie-talkie hissed at me from somewhere inside the trailer. I was overdue on set. Where the hell was I? No time. I had to get it all down because I didn't know where it was coming from or if I could ever get on this frequency again.

They knocked down two tall towers. In their memory, draft a covenant with your conscience that we will create a world in which such things need not occur. A world which will not require apologies to children. But also a world whose roads are not paved with the husks of our inalienable rights.

They knocked down two tall towers. Graft now their echo onto your spine. Become girders and glass, stone and steel. So that when the world sees you, it sees them. And stand tall.

Stand tall.

Stand tall.

I blinked hard, pulling myself back into the room. Less than an hour had passed since I'd written *There are no words*. I tore out the pages, shoved them in my pocket, and headed out to the set. That night I typed up the script and emailed it to Axel.

"I opened my mailbox," he said later, "and there was the script. So I closed my office door, put up a Do Not Disturb sign—something I never did—put my feet up on the windowsill, and read it. When I was done, I knew I was looking at an historic story. Through Spider-Man, Joe had written a love letter to New York City on behalf of Marvel Comics."

Later that day, he called to say, "Everyone here is in tears. Where the hell did this come from?"

"I don't know," I said, and I didn't. I've never written anything like it before or since.

Issue 36 of *The Amazing Spider-Man* was published in December 2001, with art by John Romita Jr. accompanying what was, essentially, a tone poem meditation about 9/11. It remains some of John's best work. When Marvel asked what they should do about the cover, I suggested a black cover. That would say all that needed saying.

Despite my concerns, the issue was taken to heart by fans and the press, including the *New York Times*. Months later it received the highest recognition that can be given to any comic book, the coveted Eisner Award presented at San Diego Comic-Con. But for me, the most important part was hearing that portions of the book were being quoted in churches, schools, and synagogues. Teachers used it to help kids understand the events of 9/11. Libraries stocked extra copies to meet the demand when the book sold out. Axel called it "one of the top three comics I'm most proud of to this day."

I wish I could take credit for all that, but I honestly can't. I still don't know where it came from. But I'd give a kidney to get back there one of these days.

As bad as things had been on *Crusade*, writing and producing *Jeremiah* was worse by several orders of magnitude. It was the most horrific, heinous, soul-killing experience of my career, and any attempt I might make to try and describe that nightmare in detail would result in a firestorm of lawsuits. I could only safely tell that story if I had all the participants assassinated, and frankly I can't afford that many ninjas.

One of the few things upon which I *can* safely comment was the disconnect between MGM and Showtime over the show's direction. Showtime wanted to brand *Jeremiah* as the kind of program that was only available on their premium cable network: an edgy, profanity-laden, and very, very *dark* post-apocalyptic series. MGM, which would syndicate the show afterward, wanted something that could exist on the broadcast end of the spectrum: a cute, fuzzy, *warmhearted* post-apocalyptic series. My attempts to walk the line between those agendas were further complicated by an executive assigned to the project who began doing everything possible to undercut my position, leading to a prolonged battle for control of the show that made every day a living hell.

Despite the behind-the-scenes drama, *Jeremiah* debuted on Showtime on March 3, 2002, to solid ratings and surprisingly positive reviews. I was desperate not to go back for year two, but my agent emphasized the importance of staying on because I was still trying to kick the "he's difficult" reputation, so I reluctantly agreed.

There was another infinitely more personal and difficult decision facing me. When Kathryn and I got married, I made a promise: *till death do us part.* I'd spent my entire life trying to prove that I wasn't my father, and that meant keeping my promises. But living alone in Vancouver for over a year reinforced the fact that I *liked* being on my own. Yes, I cared for Kathryn, and no, I wasn't seeing anyone else, I just wanted to be alone. I *liked* being alone. Just the idea of living with someone had become a source of increasingly irrational anxiety.

While there are many benefits to modeling oneself after Superman, there's one big drawback: it assumes invulnerability and precludes the possibility of weakness. But as my anxiety about living with another person continued to worsen, I had to acknowledge that something was wrong, and began seeing a therapist. He started by asking about my previous relationships and my family history. For the first time I talked about how I always felt apart from other people; the limited access to my emotions and my difficulty in reading people; my social awkwardness and the impenetrable membrane between me and the rest of the world.

"How was your relationship with your mother and father?" he asked.

"Well, I was shuttled between relatives for most of my early years rather than being with either of my parents, my mom was institutionalized for a large chunk of my childhood, and she tried on at least one occasion to murder me. My father was a violent drunk who was rarely home and kept trying to force-feed me vodka at the age of five, and—"

Gradually, the terms *Asperger's syndrome*, *reactive attachment disorder*, and *PTSD* entered the conversation. They explained my social awkwardness and all-absorbing interest in subjects like writing, comics, and, yes, Superman; also my compulsive self-reliance, lack of emotional resonance, inability to form lasting relationships, and a preference for being alone.

"Being around other people is stressful for you," he said, "so you avoid stress by avoiding people. The same goes for relationships. As you get older this tendency toward solitude will only become more pronounced. It's not so much that you're against marriage as you are against having anyone in your space. Having so little access to your emotions on an interpersonal basis may also explain why you're addicted to writing. On the one hand, writing all the time provides the perfect pretext for declining to go out and socialize. On the other, you can feel and express emotions via your characters that are otherwise off-limits, which makes you want to stay in that place as much as possible.

"In a funny way, you're able to avoid many of the downsides of solitude because you have all these voices, all these people in your head from the stories you write, so you never really feel as though you're alone. You're constantly surrounded by people, it's just that none of them actually *exist*."

Understanding the problems that had stunted my emotional growth was a revelation as profound as the day I put on a pair of eyeglasses and realized my vision was impaired. Suddenly everything in my past made sense. The therapist also helped me understand that by staying in the marriage I wasn't doing Kathryn any favors. Quite the opposite: I was hurting her. I was desperately unhappy, and it wasn't fair to keep her tied to me under those conditions.

A few days later I steeled myself and told Kathryn that I wanted out. I was afraid it would come as a terrible shock, forgetting that she's ridiculously smart and saw it coming long before I did. Her main concern was to ensure a measure of stability for herself and her parents. I assured her that no matter what happened she and they would never lack for anything. Rather than putting her on a set allowance with an end date, I would take care of all her expenses, without limit, in perpetuity.

A long time ago I gave her my word that she would never have to work in a windowless office, or anywhere else for that matter, if she didn't want to do so.

And I had no intention of letting *that* promise fall by the wayside.

As I write these words in 2019, Kathryn's future remains secure, and we are better friends than we were during most of our marriage. The pressure is off and we can be the friends we were in the beginning. We speak frequently on the phone, have dinner from time to time, I watch her cat when she goes out of town . . . we're good. We're solid.

Funny what a difference the truth can make.

I returned for year two of *Jeremiah* determined to make the best show possible under circumstances even more horrific than year one as the same executive did everything imaginable to escalate the situation through a litany of prevarications, arguments, back-channeling, and direct sabotage. At the end of the season, I told my agent that regardless of how well it performed (and it did quite well), I would not return for a third season. I'd had enough.

I finished work on *Jeremiah* in late June 2003 and moved into a house I'd purchased in the San Fernando Valley, confident that there would be no problem continuing my career. By now I'd written almost three hundred produced television episodes and had kept a show on the air for two years despite innumerable obstacles.

But the *Jeremiah* executive had spent those two years working his dark magic to blackball me with every network and studio in town. By the time I returned to Los Angeles, my career in television was effectively over. Of course I didn't know that at the time; no one ever *tells* you these things, they leave you to slowly figure it out as months pass and the phone doesn't ring.

A few weeks later, on July 3, I was awakened at nine A.M. by a caterwauling in the backyard courtesy of the outdoor cats that had moved in before I could do so. Bleary-eyed and half asleep, I staggered out to find a coven of cats surrounding one of the landscaping pipes that carried water from the sprinklers underground to the street; the cap, designed to keep leaves from falling inside, had come off. I looked down the pipe to see a six-week-old kitten staring back at me. I tried to grab him but couldn't reach that far, and he skittered away into the maze of pipes.

I called every plumber in the book but none of them wanted to come over, having already started their July 4 holiday. When I finally got someone in from animal control to scope out the situation, she noted that the mewing had stopped. "All these pipes lead to the street," she said. "I'm sure he's out by now." And with that she left.

I mewed into the pipe to see if I could provoke a response. Nothing came back. Believing that she was right and he was safely away, I went off to run errands, returning at about six P.M. It was still light when I went into the yard and mewed into the pipe. Silence.

Good, he's safely away, I thought and started back toward the house.

Then, from behind me: *Mew!*

He was still in there.

In that instant I flashed back on every cat I'd lost because of my father's twisted pathology. I remembered wrapping Midnight in one of my T-shirts and putting her in the ground, and vowed on the spot that I would not lose one more cat to the cold ground. Not this time. Maybe I couldn't save my career, but by god I was going to save that cat.

I called more plumbers. Same result. Nada.

I called the fire department. They argued against coming out because it would be dark soon, followed by pre-Fourth fireworks and the possibility of fires.

"There's a *cat* in a *pipe*," I said, "you gotta come."

Fifteen minutes later, a fire truck rumbled down the street, the firemen climbed off, and I showed them where the problem was. They dug a massive trench, pulled out a cypress tree, cut into one of the pipes, and used a mirror to look around. There was no sign of the kitten, who had moved as far as possible from the commotion.

They then departed, leaving me with a hole in the ground, a cut pipe, and a dead cypress tree. And there was still mewing going on.

I know what to do, I thought, *I'll put a can of tuna beside the hole.* But if I just left it and went back inside I wouldn't know if he or one of the other cats had eaten it. So I brought over a lawn chair and sat by the tuna fish, the cut pipe, the trench, and the dead cypress tree until one A.M. The mewing was still audible but growing weaker. Desperate not to lose him, I went back to dialing every emergency twenty-four-hour plumber I could find.

One finally arrived at three A.M. He fished a snake with a camera at one end down one of the pipes, and now we could finally see the kitten: barely conscious, wedged in tight, half covered in water, he literally had to raise his mouth out of the water to mew.

"We've got to get him out," I said, noting that he had been stuck down there for at least eighteen hours. "Use the snake to bonk him in the nose, see if we can back him up to the hole the fire department dug." As hoped, each bonk nudged him a few more inches in the right direction. When he got close, I dived into the trench, oblivious to the spiders and centipedes and god only knew what else, and put my hand in the pipe.

Then: I felt his fur brush my palm. I only had one shot at this so I waited until he pushed hard, then pulled. He *shunked* as he came out. "You're okay, buddy," I said, "you're gonna be all right." As I wrapped him in a towel I realized I was fighting tears.

I had put too many cats in the ground. Now, at last, I had taken one back out again.

Had the other cats not drawn my attention, he would have died down there, alone in the cold and the dark. Instead, Buddy lived on for fifteen years and four months as my best pal, my constant companion, and one of the most beautiful souls I have ever known.

Fall 2003 turned into spring 2004 without offers to work on existing shows or network meetings where I could pitch ideas for new series. I wrote spec pilot scripts that never left the agency. Rather than push for a job as executive producer, I said I was willing to go back to story editor or writing freelance episodic scripts for scale, starting all over again from the bottom, just let me write *something* for *some*goddamnbody.

Then: tragedy.

On May 22, 2004, Richard Biggs, who had played Dr. Franklin on *Babylon 5*, passed away from an aortic dissection, an undiagnosed genetic condition that tore his heart apart. His death was a terrible blow to everyone who had known him. On every show some cast members are liked more than others, but everyone loved Richard. Buff, seemingly healthy, and gregarious, he would hang out with fans at conventions, conduct acting workshops, and hold court at the bar, dancing late into the night. We assumed he would outlive us all. The funeral brought us together in stunned grief. His wife and family occupied the front row of the church, their souls shattered, but so proud of the man, the father, and the actor that he had been.

Richard was the first main cast member from *Babylon 5* to pass away before his time. But to the heartbreak and profound sorrow of everyone involved with the show, he would not be the last.

As 2004 turned into 2005 without any steady television work I continued writing comics, and though I loved the process, they didn't cover a fraction of what it costs to live in Los Angeles, especially since I was covering two households, two mortgages, and all the related expenses. It didn't help that I was having vision problems that cut my comics output from four books per month to one or two at most. *Babylon 5* and *Crusade* were off the air, which meant no residuals, and *Jeremiah* had bought out those residuals as part of my salary, so there was no money coming in from any of those projects. I'd been digging into my savings for nearly a year in what I hoped would be a temporary situation, but the money was going out faster than anything else was coming in.

One evening I was in a taxi crossing Los Angeles when I got a voice mail from Walter Koenig, who I had brought onto *Babylon 5* to play the role of a telepathic cop. The message was ominous in its brevity: *Call me the second you get this. It's urgent.*

"Have you heard the news about Andreas?" he asked when I called back.

Andreas Katsulas, who had worked on *Babylon 5*, was one of the best actors I'd ever known, and his portrayal of Citizen G'Kar was a fan favorite. "No, why? What's the news?"

"He's dying."

I couldn't process his words. They didn't make sense. "What do you mean he's dying?"

"I heard it from Bill." Bill Mumy, another cast member on the show, was tight with the other actors and generally knew what was going on with them.

"Bill must've misheard something," I said. "Let me call Andreas and find out what the hell's going on."

I hung up and speed-dialed Andreas. He picked up the line. "Andreas, it's Joe," I said. "Listen, I just heard—"

He started laughing before I could even finish the sentence. *I knew it, Bill got it wrong.*

But he hadn't.

"Yeah, I'm dying," Andreas said, still laughing. "Isn't that ridiculous? I'm on this great diet, I've lost weight, I'm healthier than I've ever been, and I'm dying."

He explained that during a recent checkup the doctors discovered an advanced case of lung cancer they'd missed earlier; it had been hiding behind his sternum until it was large enough to be seen on either side. "When they took the new X-ray," he said, "it winked at them."

I tried to find something comforting to say, but he brushed it aside. "Look," he said, "I've had an amazing life. I've done some really good work. Yeah, I've done some shit along the way, but I'm really proud of most of it. I've had a great run, and *Babylon*'s been a big part of that. They're going to do some chemo to try and beat this thing back, but the odds aren't great. So if this is it, well, you know, so be it. I'm good."

The cast and crew reached out to him over the coming months, but he wouldn't allow a second's grief on his behalf. Andreas was bigger than life, a Greek at full throttle, and rather than mourn what was coming, he celebrated his life and his friendships. He approached his death the same way he approached his work: he was fucking fearless.

That winter, word came that Andreas wanted to have dinner with me, *B5* producer Doug Netter, and actor Peter Jurasik, one of our most gifted cast members, with whom Andreas had often worked. Their characters were mirror opposites of each other, and the two actors had become very close.

Before dinner Andreas took enough meds to ensure that he was relatively free of pain, and we spent the night eating, laughing, and telling stories. The conversation was sufficiently profane that in a more polite century it would've gotten us burned at the stake.

Toward the end of the evening Andreas sat back from the table and smiled. "Do me a favor," he said, "tell me all the stuff I never knew about the show, all the dirt, the secrets, *all* of it. I mean, who am *I* gonna tell?"

And we did.

As Andreas began to tire we decided to take our leave. He escorted us to the door, then paused to look at each of us one at a time. When it was my turn, he held my gaze and I saw in his eyes that he was burning the moment into his memory, and mine.

Without speaking the words, he was saying good-bye.

Then he gave each of us a hug, and we stepped out into the night.

It was the last time I saw him alive.

Andreas Katsulas passed away on February 13, 2006, and to this day I remain profoundly moved by his equanimity, courage, and humor. Faced with a similar diagnosis I would have collapsed into a fetal position and never gotten up again. If I can approach my end with even a fraction of his grace, I will account myself a brave man.

By 2006 I had been out of full-time television for three years, and my savings were nearly exhausted. Friends urged me to sell the house, move somewhere else, and give up this whole Hollywood thing, maybe go teach instead. Quitting made sense; when you're shooting craps at a casino and the dice turn against you, the smart move is to cash out and run, because if you stay at the table when you're vulnerable, you could lose all of it.

I chose to stay, even though that meant taking out a second mortgage on my house and borrowing heavily from my pension plan. Alarmed by the precariousness of our situation, my accountant put pressure on me to make *something* happen fast or face dire consequences. He was especially grave the day he, I, and Kathryn met to authorize the last possible loan I could take against my retirement fund.

"I hate saying this," he said, "but you had a great run as a reporter, another solid run in television, then comics . . . very few people in this town ever get a *third* act, let alone a fourth." Then, though obviously well-meaning, he made the mistake of joining the *You're Done* chorus and said, "Maybe it's time to get out of the writing business, do something else."

I blew my stack. It would've been one thing if I'd failed as a writer, if I wasn't telling good stories anymore, but I was writing as well as I'd ever written, maybe better. The problem was that *none of my work was getting out* because a handful of people had decided I was done as a writer and were doing everything possible to ensure their prediction became reality.

"I'll get through this," I said, louder than intended.

"How?" he asked.

"*Goddamnit, I don't know!* I don't know *how* or *where* or *when* but sooner or later I *will* write my way out of this! I just need you to believe that!"

He didn't.

I signed the papers. The loan would have to be repaid quickly, and I had absolutely no idea where that money would come from.

Afterward, Kathryn and I adjourned to Mel's Diner in Sherman Oaks. I was furious at my accountant, at myself, and at the people who had decided that my career was over. As my temper cooled I glanced across the table at Kathryn, whose financial fate was inextricably linked to my own. If I stayed in the game and failed, I'd take her down with me; we'd *both* go bankrupt. She was entitled to a voice in that decision.

"Is he right?" I asked at last. "Should I just admit defeat and get out of the business?"

She sat back and crossed her arms, head tilted in the signature way that told you she was clicking through responses with laser-like speed. "You said back there that you can write your way out of this," she said. "Do you honestly believe that?"

"Yes, I do."

"Then keep fighting," she said. Like it was the most obvious thing in the world.

From Kathryn, much later: "I must have looked at you like you had the proverbial two heads because of course I didn't think you should quit! Never have, never will. It's not only what you do, it's who you are. And that's a good thing, in my opinion. It's what makes you so good at both writing and producing. It's what lifts you out of the ordinary."

Just in case anyone was wondering why we're still friends.

By now I had arrived at the kind of cold, clinical understanding that comes with any terminal diagnosis that if I didn't do something soon to jump-start my career, I would no longer *have* one. When a writer, actor, or director is unemployed for three years, he passes from *he's in a transitional period* to *he's hard-core unemployable, he's been off the market too long.* Not only was I at the far edge of that timeline, I was fifty-two. By that age the studios figure they've seen everything you have to offer, so they wander off after the next shiny object, secure in the belief that you have no more surprises left, no new colors left to show. You are what they *think* you are, and if they think it's over for you . . . it's over.

Nearly all the TV writers you knew during the '80s have fallen by the wayside, a part of my brain whispered. *They're either out of the business completely or their careers are on life support. Why should you be the exception? Why put that kind of pressure on yourself? They're right, the odds of you getting a fourth act are pretty slim. Maybe you* should *just let it go.*

Suddenly I was right back in that ambulance in Chula Vista, racing toward a hospital after six guys tried to kill me. I'd gotten angry that night, angrier than I'd ever been before, because I still had stories to tell. Now that rage returned tenfold. I hadn't come so far, worked so hard, and sacrificed so much of my life to the work only to see it end in this humiliating fashion.

Never let them stop you from telling the story you want to tell.

Fucking A.

I didn't leave the house for days, then weeks. I didn't want to see anyone. I needed to be alone. Voice mails accumulated: *Are you okay? Nobody's heard anything from you in ages.* I didn't return them. I needed to let the anger build into a fire big enough to show me a way out.

When I hit critical mass, ready to claw my own skin off, I went to Santa Monica and walked to an empty bench at the end of the pier. I sat there for hours, looking out at the water, running options through my head like a rat in a box, desperately trying to chew its way through to a solution. Nothing came. The afternoon turned to shadows. I stayed put. The shadows turned to cold night. Wearing just a light shirt, I shivered in the dark.

Tough shit, we're not leaving. We're going to figure this out if we have to sit here all week.

Then another voice came drifting up out of my subconscious, something Harlan Ellison had written years earlier, which I quoted in the frontispiece of my scriptwriting book.

Don't be afraid. That simple. Don't let them scare you. There's nothing they can do to you . . . a writer always writes. That's what he's for. And if they won't let you write one kind of thing, if they chop you off at the pockets in the market place, then go to another market place. And if they close off all the bazaars then by god go and work with your hands till you *can* write, because the talent is always there. But the first time you say, "Oh, Christ, they'll kill me," then you're done. Because the chief commodity a writer has to sell is his courage, and if he has none he is more than a coward. He is a sellout and a fink and a heretic, because writing is a holy chore.

Writing is a holy chore.

I stared up at the moon. Back in San Diego I'd spent every penny to buy writing supplies instead of food, determined to keep going despite starvation, failure, and all the people who refused to believe in me, ready to do whatever was necessary to make it as a writer or die trying.

If you're still there, I thought at my younger self, *then we need to work together to get out of this. There are stories I still need to tell, and I refuse to give up on them. If that means selling the house and everything I own to buy time to make this work, then that's what I'll do. I choose to stay and fight, to write my way out of this, but I need your help to figure out how.*

With that thought, a flare went up somewhere deep inside my brain. For the last ten years, a box had been sitting in my office containing hundreds of pages of letters, transcripts, and newspaper articles detailing the case of Christine Collins. I'd failed repeatedly to crack that story because I lacked the skills needed to properly honor what she endured while fighting for her missing son.

Can I pull this off now? I wondered. I've always envisioned whatever talent I have as existing outside me, whispering into my ear from just behind my right shoulder, the connection between us thinner than a spider's thread. I fired a question down the web. *Do I finally have enough tools in my toolbox to write this?*

The reply came back, *I think so.*

You think so or you know so?

There's only one way to find out. But it has to be a movie, not a television script.

It made sense. Writing a feature script would let me go around my TV agent at the Creative Artists Agency (CAA)* to Martin Spencer, an agent in the film division. I'd never had much contact with Martin, so I had no way to predict how he would react to the material, but at least he wouldn't be biased against me. I had no illusions about selling the screenplay, let alone seeing it produced, but if it passed muster with Martin, it would go to movie executives who wouldn't know or care about my history or that I was "difficult" because once a studio buys a screenplay they're done with the writer; they wouldn't have to live with me. The best I thought I could hope for was that the script might give me a chance to pitch on other projects.

It was nearly dawn when I finally stood, sore and shivering, and made my way off the Santa Monica Pier. I'd come there alone, but now there were two of us walking back. In the past, whenever the bullies, the muggers, and my father came at us we fought back until we couldn't get up off the ground and we *still* wouldn't back down. This was no different. The people who had put us in this position wore suits and ties and worked in expensive offices, but they were just another kind of bully. They were sure that if they kept pounding us long enough and hard enough sooner or later we'd shut up and they could say they'd won. But we'd never given them that satisfaction before, and we weren't about to do so now.

As I headed home, the title for the screenplay floated up at me: a term out of mythology for one child substituted for another. It seemed apt given what Christine endured when the LAPD brought

---

* Q: What do you get when you cross an agent from CAA with a ham sandwich? A: A ham sandwich that never returns your calls.

back a child they insisted was her missing son but was in fact some-one else. But it also applied to this attempt to reinvent myself one last time, to win a fourth act and replace one career, one life, with another.

I would call it *Changeling*.

CHAPTER 31

What Was I Thinking?

O ver the years, I'd managed to accumulate several hundred pages of documentation about Christine Collins, but to tell the story properly I would need every bit of available information. So I returned to sifting through dark basements and microfiche reels at the Los Angeles Police Department and City Hall archives, the LA County Hospital historical files, the *Los Angeles Times* morgue, and the LA Public Library, gathering over two thousand pages of reference material. The crown jewel, the record that had eluded me for years, was the transcript of the murder trial. These documents finally allowed me to triangulate the three sides of the puzzle behind one of the most heinous crimes in Los Angeles history.

On one side of the triangle was Christine Collins, a single mother who never aspired to politics or sought the limelight. But after her son was kidnapped and the LAPD tried to force her to accept a boy they mistakenly identified as her own, she went to war with the police, a battle that exposed a serial killer and brought down the chief of police and the mayor of Los Angeles.

On another side was Gordon Stewart Northcott, a psychopath who kidnapped young, defenseless children and brought them to a ranch in Riverside where they were assaulted and killed, their bodies dismembered, burned, and buried.

The final side of this story was occupied by the LAPD, which in 1928 was infamous for its brutality and lack of accountability for violent acts committed against the citizens of Los Angeles. The police owned Los Angeles and were willing to do whatever was necessary to maintain control. This led to protests and a demand for reform by newspapers and private citizens. The LAPD was desperate for some positive press, and returning a lost child to his tearful mother would give them exactly the boost they needed. So rather than admit their mistake when they brought back the wrong child, they threw Christine into an asylum to pressure her into accepting this interloper as her own. The LAPD's refusal to acknowledge the truth allowed a serial killer to continue his work unimpeded.

Once all the research was in place I set out to write the script as fast as I could to avoid second-guessing myself. Drawing on my experience as a reporter, I hewed closely to the facts, quoting dialogue verbatim from articles, letters, and public records because the events were so bizarre that if I got even one thing wrong it would call the whole story into question. I threw every bit of myself into that script: my background in psychology informed the scenes of her incarceration; the memory of my mother's institutionalization propped up Christine's time in the asylum; and for one of the most disturbing scenes, in which Northcott tries to entice a young boy into his car, I hearkened back to my experience of being chased by unknown parties through the streets of Paterson.

For two weeks I barely ate or slept, writing in white heat to the exclusion of everything else until I typed *Fade Out*. Since the story was so unbelievable, I took the unusual step of seeding the screenplay with photos and newspaper clippings designed to prove that yes, this actually happened.

At three in the morning on the last day of that writing jag, I printed the final version of the script, bound it with brass brads, and just *looked* at it for a long time, too scared to send it off. In the past I'd whined that my work could've been so much better if not for the interference of networks and studios. Now the universe had called my bluff: this time there had been no compromises. More than anything in years *Changeling* represented who I was as a writer. If it was good enough to draw positive attention, then I'd been right to stick it out. But if the script wasn't good enough, if it hit the wall and bounced, then maybe I *didn't* have what it takes and should find another career.

Physicist Erwin Schrödinger postulated that if you place a cat in a box containing a vial of poison gas with a 50/50 chance of being released, the cat is not alive *or* dead but simultaneously alive *and* dead, existing as two quantum possibilities. It's only when you look inside the box that the two quantum possibilities fold into one reality: a live cat or a dead one. As long as I didn't attach the script to an email and hit send, my career was simultaneously alive and dead. But the moment it went off, one of those quantum possibilities would emerge as my new reality, and I was terrified it would be the wrong one.

Get it over with, I thought, and emailed it to Martin Spencer's office with a note to his assistant asking her to print it and leave it on his desk so he'd find it first thing when he came in. I hadn't told him what I was working on, fearing that I might not be able to pull it off, so when he called later that day he was surprised and intrigued.

"What's this?" he asked brightly as he scanned the title. "*Changeling* . . . science fiction? Horror?" It was a reasonable assumption. Both genres were popular in the marketplace, the title sounded SFish, and I was known almost exclusively for working in those arenas.

"It's a mainstream drama," I said.

"Okay," he said. It obviously wasn't the answer he'd hoped for, but he remained chipper. "Contemporary though, right?"

"Actually, it's a *period* mainstream drama."

"Ah." The enthusiasm left his voice. Those three words are considered the kiss of death since they usually result in the script never being bought at all, or at most a small sale to an independent producer who might never make the damned thing.

"So what's it about?" he asked, rising to the challenge.

"A serial killer."

"Lots of serial killer specs making the rounds these days. Really needs to be something special to compete with that. Who does he kill?"

"Children."

If it's possible to hear someone wince over the phone, I heard Martin wince.

"It's the story of the mother of one of the boys who gets kidnapped," I added quickly. "She goes on a crusade to try and save her son."

His voice brightened. "So she finds him?"

"Umm . . . no, actually, she doesn't."

In the voice of someone who doesn't want you to know he feels a headache coming on, Martin thanked me for sending the script then promised to read it that evening and get back to me.

Idiot, I thought. I'd just blown my chance to enlist someone who might believe in me and my work. Why *hadn't* I written a big SF movie? Or a horror film? Or *anything* other than a depressing period drama about a woman who gets thrown into an asylum after her son goes missing and is presumed sliced into little pieces? What the hell was I *thinking*?

In my head I turned to the twelve-year-old version of myself for support.

What're you looking at me *for?* he said. *I don't even understand* girls *yet.*

I barely slept that night, worried that he might not respond positively to the material. And even if he *did* like it, the odds of one script having a significant effect on my career were somewhere between slim and none.

He called the next day, very excited, to say that the script was one of the best he'd ever read. "I think this is a Ron Howard film," he said. "Is it okay if I give it to him?"

Ron Howard? *Apollo 13, Da Vinci Code, A Beautiful Mind*? *That* Ron Howard?

"Sure," I said, "why not?" I assumed it would lead to a polite *not for us thanks* rejection, but just knowing that Martin thought it was worth Ron's time meant that I'd pulled off the writing. I finally had an agent at CAA who believed in my work enough to let it actually leave the building.

None of this helped resolve my money problems, however, which were growing more substantial by the day. Having exhausted the last loan possible against my retirement fund, I was now officially out of options. I'd put so much time into working on *Changeling* that there was no time to write anything else that could be sold quickly to pay mortgages and bills. After a week without news, I reconciled myself to the reality that I would have to sell my house. I'd just started contacting realtors when Martin called.

"I thought you might like to know that Ron read the script," he said.

I nodded absently, mentally filling in the rest of what I expected him to say. *He liked it, but he had a few problems with the story, and it's not really his sort of film, so he passed. I have some ideas on other people we can approach with this, but it might be a long, slow haul . . .*

"He liked it," Martin said.

"Great," I said, awaiting the hammer.

"He wants to buy it."

I froze. "He *what*?"

"He wants to buy it, *and* he wants to direct it."

I leaned against the desk for balance. I couldn't breathe. My heart was trying to tear its way out of my chest. I gradually realized that Martin was still talking.

"We should get a call in a few days from Universal business affairs to start negotiations. Since this is your first original screenplay deal, and because Universal is playing hardball on spec acquisitions, we won't get top dollar, but when someone like Ron steps up to the plate they have to factor that in, so we might be able to get around six hundred thousand, maybe six-fifty."

Six hundred thousand? *Dollars?*

American?

There was some more talk after that: Ron would want to meet after the deal closed, there might be revisions, and there were no guarantees that it would actually get made because Ron had a lot on his plate. I tried to play it cool.

Martin hung up. I hung up.

And I screamed as loudly as I've ever screamed in my entire life.

I wouldn't have to sell the house! I could pay off all my bills and then some!

But the very *best* part was that Ron bought the script based solely on the words on the page. He hadn't agreed to buy it because I was a nice guy, or someone he owed a favor . . . and he hadn't *declined* to buy it because I was *difficult*. A director as well respected as Ron Howard liked the script enough to buy it on its own terms.

I should call somebody, I thought, *starting with Kathryn.*

But I didn't reach for the phone. No one else in the world knew that my life had just been profoundly changed, and I wanted to savor that secret knowledge for just a little longer. I wouldn't *really* understand what it meant for some time, but I was cognizant enough to realize that once word of the sale got out, there wouldn't be time to sit and live in the moment. And I *wanted* that moment. During my time in Community I'd come across a word in the Book of Psalms, *Selah*, that was a signal for the audience to be silent for a moment and appreciate what was just said. It means *Pause, and consider.*

I allowed myself half an hour before I started making calls.

Selah.

On June 27, 2006, after weeks of negotiation between Martin, my attorney Kevin Kelly, and Universal Studios business affairs, the front page of the film industry trade magazine *Daily Variety* broke the news that "Universal Pictures and Imagine Entertainment have purchased J. Michael Straczynski's thriller *Changeling*, which is being eyed by Ron Howard to direct."

And the world exploded.

I assumed the sale would open some doors, but having never worked in the film business, I didn't understand that when an A-list director buys a script that he plans to direct, the curious alchemy of filmmaking also transmutes the writer into an A-lister. Prior to hitting send on *Changeling*, I was just another out-of-work television writer *and* I was fifty-two years old, a damned unlikely age to begin a career in the movie business.* But once news broke about the sale, every studio executive in town wanted to meet me. Most of them had no idea that I'd previously worked in television. Some even thought *Changeling* was my first script.

Offers to write and rewrite movies began showing up on Martin's desk. My life had gone from *Get lost, bub* to *We'd love it if your client would consider this* and *Do you think Joe would have*

---

* In June 2008 *Daily Variety* named me one of their Top Ten Screenwriters to Watch, a list of up-and-coming writers who were otherwise all in their twenties or early thirties. In photos taken at a party given to mark the occasion, I look like somebody's father sent to drive them home after the festivities.

time in his schedule to write this for us? These weren't just requests for meetings, there were offers attached. Real offers. For real
money. *Serious* money. Every day felt as though I had awakened in
someone else's life, and I kept worrying that at any moment he was
going to call and ask for it back.

Producing *Changeling* would require finding a lead actress with
a name big enough to convince Universal to pull the trigger, but
there weren't many of those and most had long-term commitments
that took them out of the running. The odds went down another
notch when Ron reviewed his list of commitments and realized he
wouldn't have an available slot to direct *Changeling* for at least
another year, maybe two. Movies get made when there's heat and
urgency; when they grow old and cold, they fade away. Ron said
he'd look for another director, and my agent began to do the same,
but I didn't hold out much hope.

Ron then sent the script to Clint Eastwood, who promised to
read it on the plane coming back from Europe. I was pleased to
think that Clint was going to read something I'd written, but I didn't
think for a minute that it would lead anywhere.

Martin called back a few days later, wonder in his voice. "Clint
read the script. He loves it and wants to direct it. He has a window
to shoot it this October *if* we can find a star by then, but nobody's
holding their breath. It has to be someone who's available for that
specific window *and* has the star power to move the needle at
Universal."

To start filming in October, Clint would have to start prep in
August, which meant having a deal with an actress by May. By now
we were well into April, so once again the odds of success weren't
great.

Then: another call from Martin.

"Angelina Jolie read the script," he said. "She wants to do
it, she's available in October, and she's one of the few actresses

who could get this made, so Universal is going to greenlight the movie."

When *Daily Variety* announced that *Changeling* was going into production, with Ron Howard and Brian Grazer producing through Imagine Entertainment, Clint Eastwood directing, and starring Angelina Jolie, the world exploded *again*. Deals and contracts stacked up like planes waiting to land at LAX. There was a waiting list for producers to hire me.

A *waiting* list!

One of these assignments was to adapt Max Brooks's *World War Z*, a series of faux reports written after a fictional zombie outbreak wipes out most of the world's population. Brad Pitt's company had spent a buttload of money to option the property, but since it lacked a main character or narrative through-line, they couldn't figure out how to adapt it into a movie. So I created the character who would have written those reports and gave him a family, filling out the roster of characters with his boss and others from the United Nations and then putting him in the middle of incidents carefully chosen from the book.

Some of the films I worked on would go into production, others would not, but that's par for the course. After enduring decades of frustration and scorched-earth network politics I was having the time of my life working with some of the most creative people in the industry, including Steven Spielberg, Paul Greengrass, and James Cameron. Finally, *finally* I was doing the only thing I ever wanted to do in the first place: telling stories.

A few weeks before *Changeling* was scheduled to start filming, I met with Clint and producer Rob Lorenz at their offices on the Warners lot. Clint was quiet, almost shy, and rarely looked directly at me as we spoke, preferring the view of the opposite wall or the piles of reference material he'd accumulated to ensure that the look was true to the period. He wanted to know where the story came from, how I'd stumbled upon it, and any details I'd left out that could inform his approach as a director.

As our meeting drew to a close I asked Clint if he wanted any changes made to the script. After all, we were still going off my original spec screenplay and no first draft of a movie script ever goes into production unchanged.

For the first time he turned and *looked* at me with eyes I'd seen in countless movies, and suddenly it was Clint Fucking Eastwood. *Do you feel lucky, punk? Well,* do *you?*

"You know how many movies I've made?" he growled.

"A lot?" I said, sounding like a mouse addressing a very large cat that was trying to decide if I would taste better sautéed or pan-fried.

"A *lot*," he said. "But I've gotten more calls on this project from people I don't even *know* telling me not to screw this up than on anything else I've done. So the way I see it, my job isn't to change things, my job is to not screw it up."

The script would be shot exactly as written. First draft. Word for word.

Unbelievable.

That fall, I was invited to a Marvel Comics creative retreat in Manhattan where we would work out the story for their upcoming Civil War publishing event. (Much of the structure we came up with during that retreat ended up in the *Captain America: Civil War* movie, including material from my run on *The Amazing Spider-Man*.)

On the second day of the retreat, publisher Dan Buckley mentioned that they were hoping to bring Thor back into Marvel's publishing line after a two-year absence. The problem was that no one knew what to do with him. Known for spouting corny-sounding semi-Chaucerian dialogue, Thor wore a costume that was stuck in the '60s, had a confusing mythology, and a nearly invincible power set that made it difficult to put him into real jeopardy.

Having grown up on mythology, Shakespeare, and the Bible, I knew *exactly* what to do with the character. I raised my hand, volunteering for the job.

They offered it to writer Mark Millar, who ran screaming out into the night.

Standing right here, I thought. *Hello?*

Next they emailed Neil Gaiman to ask if he'd like to tackle the book. It's not Neil's style to say *no fucking way* because he's a gentleman, but if you were to run his reply through the Polite British Person to Americanese Translation System, the response would be *no fucking way*.

Finally, almost reluctantly, they said *Fine, let Straczynski take a shot at it.*

When they asked what I had in mind, I said I wanted to shift Thor's diction to something that leaned into the classic sensibility but was easier on the ears, more Christopher Fry than Shakespeare. I also wanted to work with the artist to modernize the look of his costume.

They had no problem with any of this.

Then they asked, "What about Asgard? Nobody ever knows what to do with Asgard. You want to put it back in a Norse setting? In the sky? In another dimension?"

"I want to put Asgard in Oklahoma."

A silence vast as space hung in the air for a moment. "You want to do *what?*"

"Thor standing beside Iron Man or Spider-Man isn't much of a contrast, they're all major powers. But Thor in a small town makes him more godlike, while close proximity to ordinary folks will humanize Thor, making him more relatable. In classical mythology gods often roamed freely among the people. You could be crossing a field and run into Diana or Odin or Dionysus. They were practically your neighbors. So there's plenty of precedence for it."

"Yeah, but . . . Okla*homa*?"

"The visual contrast of terrains will be great," I said. "It's flat-flat-flat-flat-ASGARD-flat-flat-flat-flat."

They thought I was nuts, but to their credit went along with it. When my first issue of *Thor* landed in September 2007 with a re-designed costume, a new approach to his dialogue, and Asgard set firmly in Oklahoma, the book sold out immediately, and every issue thereafter was in the top ten of all comics published that month.

On April 23, 2008, Universal announced that *Changeling* would premiere in official competition at the Cannes Film Festival in May, and that they were sending me, Brian Grazer, Clint, Angelina, and Brad Pitt for the event. I was excited by the news but didn't fully appreciate the enormity of the situation since as a TV guy I hadn't paid much attention to the festival. I'd never attended *any* film festival other than the Festival of Animated Cartoons at San Diego State University in 1979, a tiny affair that was more about creating a safe space for students to smoke pot and watch semi-pornographic cartoons than fostering an appreciation for the art of filmmaking. I had a pretty good idea that Cannes would be a larger and more prestigious event than the one at SDSU, but the extent of my imagination ended there.

From the moment we checked into the Hotel du Cap-Eden-Roc—a stunning French villa built in the 1870s as a writers' retreat, which is ironic considering that few writers can afford to stay there—we were besieged by photographers. They weren't there for me, of course; they were trying to get shots of Brian, Clint, Brad,

Angelina, and other camera-ready celebrities. But since I was traveling with showbiz royalty, I was frequently caught in their wake, blinded by lightning storms of flashbulbs and requests to turn this way or that. The nights were a blur of galas overlooking the French Riviera attended by overly cologned men in tuxedos and beautiful women wearing diamonds big enough to be seen from space. Private yachts the size of shopping malls filled the bay. The festival was a tsunami of cameras, booze, food, booze, nearly naked women, booze, six-inch Louboutin fuck-me heels, exotic cars, and just a goddamn lot of booze.

It was a long way from living in a Skid Row shanty, half starved and covered in lice and roaches, and it would have been easy to fall for the glamour of Cannes, to get all *look-at-me-I'm-so-important*. But I knew that I was just a very small piece lodged in the gears of a filmmaking machine that needed celebrities and press to survive, and I was more than happy to keep the madness swirling around me at arm's length. As a reporter I'd seen the dangers of getting hooked on that kind of attention. There's something very seductive about opening a newspaper and seeing your photo all over the place, or doing a web search on your name to discover five hundred new hits that day. And there's an equally massive crash when you open the newspaper or go online and *don't* see your name. To be mentioned is to be validated, to be important, to *exist*; to be forgotten is death. Which is why some celebrities go out of their way to feed the publicity machine, often to their own detriment: they leak their schedule to paparazzi or create scenes at parties or events because they *need* that day's fix of headlines to confirm they're still alive, still relevant, still *important*. It's as addictive and destructive as cocaine.

Journalist Linda Ellerbee noted that when the circus arrives, they pick someone in authority, usually the mayor, to ride the elephant in a parade from the train station to the tents across town.

The person atop the elephant thinks the people below are waving at him. They're not. They're waving at the elephant, which he just happens to be sitting on at that particular moment.

The press and the attention weren't there for me. I was just riding the elephant.

But there was one moment at Cannes that changed my life. Unfortunately I can't explain it in a way that makes sense. I can only try to describe what it felt like.

The night before the premiere of *Changeling*, the festival arranged for an outdoor screening of *Dirty Harry*, which Clint would introduce. I arrived to find rows of low-slung chairs set up on a beach facing a movie screen floating on pontoons just offshore. As the sun set, composer Angelo Badalamenti and his musicians took position in front of the screen and began to play music from *Twin Peaks*.

Sunset in the South of France is a magical experience under any circumstances, but as I sat on the beach, watching the most beautiful sunset I'd ever seen, listening to the kind of music that lends itself to introspection, on the eve of the debut of my first feature film, a profound calmness came over me.

For years I'd been going through my career like a man running for a bus: red-faced and short of breath, hurtling from one job to the next, always afraid of coming up short, trying to convince people that I had what it took to become a writer. During *Babylon 5*, Patricia Tallman once said, "Whenever I think of you, I always see you with your dukes up, fighting your way out of a corner."

And there was truth to that. I'd been backed up to the wall so many times that fighting my way out became a lifestyle. It wasn't just a matter of slugging it out with censors and studio executives; I'd spent my whole life shadowboxing with my past: my family and my father, the bullies who'd tormented me, and the doubters who wanted to see me fail and fall and not get back up again. I didn't know how *not* to fight. I was like a boxer, eyes pounded shut, swinging wild, leading with my chin, refusing to surrender an inch of ground, trying to prove something to people who had stopped thinking about me years ago.

But that evening, on the beach at Cannes, I realized that whatever I'd set out to prove, to others but most of all to myself, *I'd proven it*, or I would not have been sitting on *that* beach at *that* moment. Even if I had done nothing before *Changeling*, the involvement of Clint Eastwood, Ron Howard, and Angelina Jolie assured that this film would live on forever. Factor in the rest of my body of work and finally, for the first time, I knew that the wind would not take away my name. With that knowledge I felt light. Lighter than I had ever felt.

Light enough? I wondered, as a thought came back to me from the child I had once been.

If we want to live forever, we need to learn to fly.

But what if we try and fail? What if we fall off the roof?

We won't, a voice answered back. Firm. Resolute. The voice of someone I'd known and trusted since I was a child. *We won't fall off the roof. Not this time.*

I closed my eyes and saw myself standing up out of the beach chair. Looking off into the infinite horizon, I pulled open my shirt to reveal the symbol I had been carrying in secret for so many years: *that* symbol, *his* symbol. Then, digging my toes into the soft sand, I bent slightly at the knees, and pushed off with the barest of efforts, rising into that perfect sunset. The land spun out beneath me as I arced higher, gathering momentum, speeding out of the blue and into the black, until with one last surge I pierced the veil of the atmosphere.

And suddenly everything was quiet, and calm, and I could see the curve of the earth.

And for the first time in my life, I was weightless.

And I let go. I let go of *all* of it, as though a part of my brain said *You can take off the boxing gloves now, there's no one left to fight.* Watching the last thin ribbon of sunset fade into a night of unimaginable beauty was like watching one life end and another begin. I was at peace with my past. Finally. At peace.

I should come back down now, a part of me thought.

No, it's okay, you stay up here, on patrol. I've got it covered down there.

You sure?

Yeah. I'm sure. You've earned the right to fly, anywhere you want.

Thanks. It's awful pretty up here. Catch you later?

I'll be here.

That sense of calm has stayed with me ever since as a steadying influence on my work and my life. Rather than return from Cannes puffed up like a banjo player after a big meal, full of misplaced self-importance, I came back quieter and more centered than I'd left. No matter what the future may hold, I did what I'd set out to do, and no one can ever take that away.

I sometimes look up at the night sky in case I might catch a glimpse of a familiar blue-and-red silhouette passing by overhead, and take great joy in the thought that I'm still up there somewhere.

The night of the *Changeling* premiere, we boarded limousines and were escorted by police through the crowded streets to the Palais des Festivals et des Congrès, where a red carpet as long as an airport runway was lined by hundreds of photographers. Video screens above the theater showed the event as it was being broadcast live to a worldwide audience of twenty million viewers. There's something very sobering in the knowledge that if you do anything as stupid as adjusting your underwear or picking your nose, you'll be seen by an audience only slightly smaller than the population of Australia.

Clint and the other luminaries involved with *Changeling* lined up at one end of the red carpet, waiting for their names to be announced on loudspeakers so they could begin the long walk. It was glorious, it was exciting . . . and if I needed any further evidence of the place of the writer in the entertainment industry, this was it.

Clint Eastwood's name was announced, and he started up the red carpet.

The photographers went crazy taking pictures of him.

Angelina and Brad were announced; they clasped hands and started up the red carpet.

The paparazzi taking photos went even further out of their minds.

My name was announced; I started up the red carpet—

—as the photographers kept taking pictures of Clint, Brad, and Angelina.

I paused. Kind of waved a little. *Hi . . . writer here . . . wrote this thing . . .*

Nothing.

At another time of my life I might've been annoyed. But I was so happy just to *be* there, so calmed from the night before, that I smiled, laughed, and stopped in the middle of the runway to pull out my cell phone and take a photo of Clint, Angelina, and Brad—everyone else was doing it, so why not?—before continuing unnoticed up the red carpet into the Palais and the premiere of *Changeling*.

When we returned to Los Angeles, Universal began its Oscar campaign for *Changeling*, a ritual that involved screenings, press junkets, PR appearances, interviews, and photo sessions. The studio hoped to get me an Academy Award nomination for Best Original Screenplay, and paid for magazine ads and billboards bearing my name and *For Your Consideration*, but the odds were small given that I was a stranger to the voting members of the Academy and this was my first feature film. So when *Changeling* was nominated for three Oscars, including Best Actress for Angelina Jolie, but not Best Screenplay, I was absolutely fine with it.

So I was pleasantly surprised when I was nominated for a BAFTA Award from the British Academy of Film and Television Arts (their equivalent of the Oscar) for Best Screenplay. The night of the awards ceremony, I showed up in a Savile Row tuxedo sufficient to conceal my true identity, and mingled with Penelope Cruz, Mickey Rourke, Kate Winslet, and a hectare of filmmakers infinitely more gifted than myself, who had no idea that there was an alien among them. I didn't win, nor did I expect to; I was ridiculously happy just to be the beneficiary of an astonishing sequence of events that began on a cold night all alone on the Santa Monica Pier.

CHAPTER 32

Being Superman

After *Changeling* I was again working twelve to sixteen hours a day to meet deadlines on the movies I was being asked to write, but where that schedule had previously burned me out, now the reverse was true. I felt revived, renewed. *This is what you've been working toward for all these years: enjoy it, drive flat out, live on the bleeding edge of what you can write, and never look back.*

Between assignments I wrote another spec screenplay, this one about the friendship between Harry Houdini and Arthur Conan Doyle. When DreamWorks heard about it, they bought the script for a *million dollars*. As a rule, screenplay fees are broken into separate payments for start-up, outline, first and second drafts. Since this was a finished script, I asked DreamWorks if I could get the full amount in one lump sum because I'd never seen a check for a million dollars before. It was a silly request on every conceivable level, but somewhere deep inside me the impoverished kid who lived in the projects of Newark, who had gone dumpster-diving for Coke bottles to redeem to buy comics, and who lived in unheated houses in the dead of winter, *that* kid wanted to see *that check*, goddamnit.

DreamWorks understood the request and graciously sent along the full amount.

The day the check arrived I stared at it for what felt like forever. Five years earlier I had come within inches of losing everything, and now here was this amazing gift.

A copy of that check is framed in my office alongside the first check I ever received: fifteen dollars for the Uri Geller interview in the *San Diego Reader*, when my family thought I was wasting my time with this whole writing thing.

Sweartagod: it's a good life, if you don't weaken.

During the course of six years, I wrote five produced movies that collectively earned $1.5 billion at the box office: *Changeling*, *Ninja Assassin*, *Underworld: Awakening*, *World War Z*, and *Thor*, the last of which was based on both my run on the book and an outline I'd written for the film. When Kenneth Branagh came on to direct *Thor*, he thought it would be fun to have me do a cameo in the movie. I explained to Sir Kenneth that my face on-screen would only send audiences fleeing, but he persisted, and soon I was in wardrobe at a desert location east of Los Angeles. I thought I'd just be standing in a line with a bunch of other guys as the camera drifted past, but Sir Kenneth decided against all evidence to the contrary that I could act.

The scene takes place after Thor's hammer is thrown out of Asgard and craters into Earth. "I want you to be the one who discovers the hammer," Sir Kenneth said, pointing to a red pickup truck. "You're going to drive up, get out, and react to seeing the crater where the hammer has landed. Then you clamber down to the hammer and try to pick it up."

Swell.

As I did the scene, I hearkened back to the days spent reading

Thor comics in my aunt's house. Now here I was, years later, acting in a *Thor* movie based on my own material.

I had disappeared into my own narrative.

Could my life get any weirder?

Why, yes, it could.

In 2009 I was appearing at New York Comic Con when Dan DiDio, editor in chief of DC Comics, invited me up to their booth for a private chat. It was common knowledge that my exclusive contract with Marvel was at an end, so the invitation was not unexpected. But I could never have guessed what he had in mind.

"We want to give you Superman," he said.

It took about ten seconds for my brain to stop Robby-the-Robot-flashing before I could ask what the hell he was talking about.

"A lot of college-age comic book fans have never read a Superman title," he began. "They read Batman, they read X-Men, they read your runs on Spidey and Thor, but there's no point of entry for them on Superman. They think he's old-fashioned. They call him the Big Blue Boy Scout, and they're not wrong. He's the one character in our roster who writers have the hardest time figuring out how to write. We've published good books by good writers, and we're proud of them, but that doesn't help if new readers aren't coming around to read those stories.

"So we're going to launch a series of prestige, hardcover graphic novels that will let us redefine our core characters for a new audience. We're packaging it as a publishing event for mainstream bookstores around the world. Superman will be the first one out the door.

"We want you to reinvent Superman for the twenty-first century, make him fresh and dynamic: modern, smart, and emotionally accessible, someone who can bring in a whole new audience. If this first volume does well, we'll do two more for a three-book arc.

"So . . . you want it or not?"

Superman had always been a beacon of hope, someone I strove my entire life to emulate. Like Clark, I had always been a "strange visitor from a distant world" who had to fit in with people who felt alien to me. Taking this job would bring me full circle. I'd based my moral code, my values, and much of my personality on Superman. Now I would be creating Superman based on my values and beliefs.

Joe Straczynski had spent his entire life becoming Superman.

Now, in a way, Superman would become Joe Straczynski.*

Did I want the job?

Hell, yes.

I started work at once, filling out the rest of my time with limited runs on *Wonder Woman*, *The Brave and the Bold*, and the monthly *Superman* title. One of the most personal stories in the regular *Superman* run was about a young boy who keeps waiting for Superman to save him from his abusive father. The cover featured a boy in a Superman suit looking silently out at the reader, his face bruised, one eye blackened. There are no words to describe how I felt looking at a young version of myself looking out at the older me from the cover of a *Superman* comic book.

In writing the graphic novel, I thought back to the years I spent in Vancouver working on *Jeremiah*. Every Wednesday I went downtown to the comics store on Granville Street, an area known for a heavy presence of runaways in their teens and twenties. Many of them had come to the city in search of opportunities that never appeared, while others were simply lost. Sometimes they wandered into the comics store, desperate for something to ease the burden of life on the streets. They would pull back their rain-soaked hoodies and walk down the rows of garishly colored comics, searching for anything that spoke about the world they lived in. But when they

---

* So technically we could've entitled this book *Superman Becoming Joe*, but that would have been weird and I don't think it would have sold many copies.

reached the end of the display, and found nothing they could relate to, disappointment settled into their faces and they left the store empty-handed.

I wanted to write something for those kids: a Clark Kent who comes to Metropolis with dreams and extraordinary abilities, but without knowing how best to use them: a young man who was infinitely powerful but also infinitely lost. Rather than one more story about what he can *do*, I wanted to write about his attempts to figure out who he *is*, where he fits in, and what he wants to become.

My background as a reporter helped make the *Daily Planet* feel more authentic, and I put the words of Norman Corwin into the mouth of Perry White as he helped his reporters perfect their craft. I wrote Lois as a no-nonsense professional who doesn't simply fall into Superman's arms because she's supposed to, and made Jim Olsen the badass that most newspaper photographers have to be in order to get the right shot at the right moment. I worked harder on that book than anything I'd written since *Changeling*. It deserved no less. *He* deserved no less. A few months later, when the script was paired with the artwork of Shane Davis, bound, and prepped for shipping, I could only hope that I'd done it right.

Superman: Earth One debuted in 2010 at the number one spot on the *New York Times* bestseller list for hardcover graphic novels and stayed on the list for thirty-two weeks. The next two volumes also hit the bestseller list. But the best part since then has been the steady flow of readers coming to my signings year after year, a copy of that book in hand. "I never read a Superman book until *Earth One*," they say, "and it's like I finally have a Superman who belongs to me. He gives me somebody to aspire to, someone to be like, you know?"

Someone to aspire to. Someone to be like. Yeah, I know.

I had spent most of my life trying to become Superman even though a part of me knew that this goal was fundamentally unattainable. I would never actually fly or deflect bullets, would never be faster than a locomotive, bend steel in my bare hands, or leap tall buildings in a single bound. My ambition was always doomed to failure.

But after spending three novels in Clark Kent's head, each of us mirroring the other in a *which came first, the chicken or the egg?* kind of way, I finally realized that *becoming* Superman isn't the point; the trick is *being* Superman on a moment-by-moment, day-by-day, choice-by-choice basis.

Being kind, making hard decisions, helping those in need, standing up for what's right, pointing toward hope and truth, and embracing the power of persistence . . . those were the qualities of Superman that mattered to me far more than his ability to see through walls. Because all of us can do those other things, can *be* those things; we can be *Superman* whenever we choose.

We just have to be willing to choose.

That's all. That's it. That's the secret.

And it only took me a lifetime to figure that out.

CHAPTER 33

The Truth Unearthed

For ten years, the dark undercurrent of my family had continued to bubble in the background, punctuated by the long, rambling letters my father dictated for my mother to transcribe, making elaborate excuses for his behavior. Quoting one such letter, thirteen handwritten pages long:

"—your father (is) of Russian heritage, which is a dark, violent and mostly unhappy heritage . . . this is probably because in over 2000 years White Russia was always ruled by some other country and there was nothing but war there most of the time and that made the people there the way they were."

Later: "He can't help how he is for he is a product of his heritage for where he came from the way he behaves is perfectly normal."

Translation: don't blame him, blame two thousand years of wars that happened before he was born, in a country he didn't live in until he got stuck there as a teenager for seven years, with the rest of his life being spent in the United States.

"He does drink, yes, but that is the way of the part of the world he came from. Over there they drink with their food and drink some after dinner to deaden a little of their lives for they work from morning to sundown but get very little of any of what they make, their lives are very dead. They just got in electricity a couple of years ago, maybe two or three people of the village will have refrigerators or ice boxes or even telephones. Very few even have cars."

What did my father's drinking have to do with electricity or cars in villages thousands of miles away? The answer, obviously, was nothing and everything. Addicts and abusers always try to rationalize away their behavior.

It's not my fault, I had no choice.

Yes, you did, and yes you do, I had always wanted to shout at him, but held back to avoid collateral damage to the rest of my family. *You didn't have to become what you experienced. You could have chosen another way. To say "I have no choice" is the worst kind of cowardice because you think it gives you license to hurt other people then hide behind your past where you think nobody can touch you. If our past determines our present, then I should be the biggest asshole on the face of the planet, a monster, because I had you as a father for twenty-plus years of my life. But I chose to go a different way, so if your argument is that we're trapped in the prison of the past, that we must do unto others what was done unto us in all its cruelty and violence, forever and ever amen, then my choice just disproved your entire thesis, you racist, misogynist, drunken, wife-beating piece of shit.*

The letters stopped when my mother finally decided she'd had enough of his abuse and filed for divorce. It was one of the last decisions she made before Alzheimer's began to rip out the neural connections in her brain.

"Charles kept up his regular beating schedule all the way to the end," my sister Theresa said later. "Even in the last three or four years she was with him, they're both old, but that wouldn't stop him. In fact, the schedule seemed to have accelerated. She's hunched over from the arthritis in her back, and that made him very angry. (Of course it never occurred to him that the kicking he gave her in the back the day she got out of the hospital after back surgery might have something to do with it.) She was slowing down, and could never do the work in the shop to his satisfaction. He had slowed down too and couldn't chase her as well, so he improvised and started using chains and belts to whip her from a distance. Even when he was mostly getting around by wheelchair, he found ways, usually by waiting until she was in a room where he could block her in with his chair."

My father was relentless in fighting the divorce, determined not to relinquish his control over her. He didn't want her free to tell the world what she knew about his past, or to allow her access to the $3 million he had accumulated over the years from his plastics company. He even refused to pay for Evelyn's hospitalization when she was conveyed to a constant-care facility for long-term support. Instead he escaped to Las Vegas, bought a house for cash, then hid the rest of his money in bank accounts in the United States, Canada, and the Cayman Islands. He vowed that not a penny of "his money" would go to her, oblivious to the fact that he'd only acquired "his money" by pressing her and the rest of us into working for him without pay.

"One day I went to visit Mom while she was in the hospital," Theresa would say much later, "and she was having a more lucid day than usual so I took her outside for a walk. Suddenly she ran away from me and hid under a tree. When I caught up to her I asked what she was doing. She said that she'd seen Satan, that 'the Devil's over there!'

"I looked where she was pointing and a man was standing there. He looked like Charles."

I was working at home one afternoon when my aunt called to inform me that Charles had digitized the story he'd forced me to write about his time in Russia during the Second World War and uploaded it to several online websites dealing with the Holocaust. I told her I didn't care what he did with something I'd written forty years earlier at his behest. Later, driven by perverse curiosity, I did a Google search that led to the sites where "The Vacation I Am Trying to Forget"* had been uploaded and which, as of 2019, can still be found online. The document was every bit as wretched and overwritten as when I'd first typed it back in high school. I was about to click away when I came to the section about the massacre at Vishnevo. Some sections had been updated, but the crucial parts remained intact.

I saw around 60 or 70 people standing in formation in the yard, some were fully dressed others had only pants. German SS and the police surrounded them. I could not get into the yard because of the activity that was taking place, so I waited across the street. After a few minutes, around twenty five more Jews carrying shovels and surrounded by guards marched up from the Ghetto and stopped on Vilna St. about fifty feet past the Gmina. The SS gave the order to move out and they marched out towards the street and made a right turn, joining the others wondering what was going on. So I followed behind at a distance. They marched past the Orthodox Church then made a right turn on the road where the Jewish cemetery was located.

I cut across the field and hid in an old first world war bunker across from the cemetery and waited. When the Jews arrived a few minutes later the Gestapo and police prodded the Jews towards the hole that had been dug previously. There were shouts, I could not hear very well what

---

* The back-and-forth discussion and upload described here and further downstream can be found at http://www.eilatgordinlevitan.com/vishnevo/v_pages /vstories_forget.html.

was being said, but I assume that they were ordered to line up in front of the holes. Some moved very slowly and reluctantly. Others were shoved towards the hole. A signal was given. The guns fired loudly piercing the still air. The prisoners slowly slumped and fell into the open holes.

From the bunker where I was hiding I could plainly see that some were still alive but already they had a crew ready to cover them up with dirt to smother and die.

The document also contained his account of the day that Sophia was warned by neighbors to leave the area or risk being killed as collaborators: "The Partisans felt that my mother was a collaborator because she worked at the station cooking for the Germans." Even as a kid I never understood this part. Plenty of innocent civilians—Jews and Gentiles alike—were forced by the Germans to work at factories and farms but weren't considered collaborators because saying no usually ended in being shot. Collaborators *chose* to work with the Nazis of their own free will. Why would Charles's family be considered collaborators if they had no other choice?

Then I remembered my father's description of the young Jewish girls who worked for Sophia as little more than slave labor. Not *with* her, *for* her, implying that she was in charge. And there was the matter of the German uniform made for Charles by the soldiers he considered his friends. He'd kept that uniform in pristine condition for the rest of his life, despite telling the rest of the family that he had destroyed it, a clear indication that it held great significance for him.

What if the threat from partisans wasn't based on a misunderstanding? What if they *were* collaborators? There's nothing like parading around in your own custom-made Nazi uniform to give the locals the impression that you just *might* be on the wrong side of history. It would also explain why my grandmother became nervous whenever anyone talked about their relationship with the Germans who ran the train station, insisting that they had only casual contact with them, and no contact of *any* kind with the SS officers who regularly came through on their way to eliminate "undesirables." She always characterized their condition as one of subservience, doing hard labor under difficult circumstances, and said they were never allowed to stray far from the station. To hear her tell it they were little more than prisoners, dressed and fed poorly.

But that description contradicted the photos that had been on display in her house all the years I was growing up, pictures that showed my grandmother wearing expensive clothes and shoes, walking arm in arm with German officers as they shopped together. Had I spent so much time ignoring her photos and shrugging off my father's old stories that I hadn't paid proper attention to what was right in front of me the whole time?

The key part that remained unchanged between the two versions of my father's story was his statement that he watched the Jews being killed as he "hid in an old first world war bunker."

"From the bunker where I was hiding I could plainly see . . ."

We had always accepted his story because we didn't know any better. But now the story had been posted to websites by and for people *who had been there at the time*, and their recollections were quite different, including a description of the massacre written by a survivor named Shlomo Elishkevich, reprinted in part below.

> During that month the Germans killed people almost every day. One day they gathered thirty-eight Jews and brought them to the Jewish Cemetery. Among them there were Yaacov-Hirsh Elishkevich and his son Avraham Binyamin, Hirshe Rogovin, Ayzik Rogovin and others. The Germans forced them to dig a big trench. When they finished digging, they were shoved into the trench and were gunned down by the Germans with a machine gun. The machine

gun stood near the cemetery on a hill which was located on top of a German bunker left over from WWI. Then the victims were covered over with the ground. Gentile witnesses told that for up to three days following the slaughter the ground covering the mass grave moved, as some of the victims were still alive.

This was the line that brought a chill to my blood:

The machine gun stood near the cemetery on a hill which was located on top of a German bunker left over from WWI.

As I scrolled down I found a post my father had written arguing with that description: "The other inaccurate writing was that the Jewish people that died at the cemetery in Vishnevo were killed by a machine gun on top of a 1st world war bunker. That is not true. From where the bunker was it would be impossible to carry that out. All the action was conducted at the cemetery and I was watching all this from the bunker on that day."

Another web page contained notes from my father that he accidentally posted publicly in reply to private emails he had apparently received from other survivors.* One such reply was written to a woman named Dvora Helberg, who said that "all of the victims were Jews and were murdered by the Nazis *and their local collaborators.*" (Emphasis mine.) Though I do not have her note to my father, I can only assume that during their exchange she, too, mentioned the machine-gun nest atop the World War I memorial, because in response my father wrote:

What I do remember and it's stuck in my mind and will be there forever of people being butchered at the cemetery

---

* His reply is located at http://www.eilatgordinlevitan.com/vishnevo/v_pages /vish_gb_archive1.html.

while I watched it from the wwl German bunker across from the cemetery. There was no machine gun on top of the bunker, only wide eyed me.

My father said there was no machine gun on the World War I memorial bunker.

But multiple survivors insisted just as adamantly that there *was* a machine gun there, and that it had fired into the crowd of Jews.

My father had said that he and his family were suspected of being collaborators.

The survivors said the victims were murdered by the Nazis "and their local collaborators."

By his own words, both in the document and directly via his online responses, my father—a suspected collaborator—had placed himself squarely on that memorial bunker *as the massacre was taking place*. The same bunker that others confirmed as the source of the machine-gun fire.

Those statements seemed like a contradiction. But what if they *weren't*?

What if they were *both* correct?

What if the survivors were telling the truth when they said the machine-gun fire came from a World War I bunker, and my father was telling the truth when he said that he watched the massacre from that same bunker, carefully omitting the fact that *he had been a part of it*?

Charles was able to make that omission work when he told us the story because there was no one to contradict him. But he couldn't do the same with survivors who had personally witnessed the massacre and, much to his inconvenience, lived to tell about it.

I went back to the sites in question to see if there was any more information to be found, only to discover that my father had blipped off all of them, never to return. Perhaps he thought that deleting his account would also delete his messages, but they remained and, as of this writing, are still online.

Without hard evidence it would be pointless to confront my father about my suspicions. There was only one person who could tell me the truth about what *really* happened that day. Someone who had hinted for years that she knew something ominous about my father, information she used repeatedly to punish him into silence with one word: *Vishnevo!*

There are things I know about your father I can only tell to a dog.

I wanted to gather more information before calling my aunt, but there was little more to be found online and she was in failing health; there was danger in waiting too long. So in the fall of 2008, I called her at her home in Paterson. We talked for a few minutes about nothing in particular, then I steeled myself for what was to come. "Can I ask you a question?"

"Sure, shoot," she said, and laughed. "Why so formal all of a sudden? Don't forget I used to change your diapers when you were a baby, so there's nothing about you that I haven't seen." For reasons I'll never understand she always took great pleasure in reminding me of that.

"I want to ask you about Vishnevo."

The other end of the phone went silent. I could hear her breathing, the tension palpable. "Uh-huh," she said at last, her voice flat, volunteering nothing.

"Were you there the day of the massacre?"

"No," she said firmly. "I was with Mama at the train station. You have to remember I was still recovering from polio. Walking anywhere was hard, and the roads were terrible, so I stayed close to home."

"But my father was there that day."

"Uh-huh." Again, noncommittal. "Joey, why are you asking me about things that happened over fifty years ago? Where's all this going?"

I realized that as long as she thought she had room to maneuver, she would never give up the truth. My only choice was to bluff. I told her what I'd dug up online and said that I'd found other, definitive sources indicating that my father had been involved in the massacre.

"Before I decide what to do about this," I said, "I want to hear what you have to say." I left the *what to do about this* part deliberately vague, letting her mind flit from the possibility of private confrontation to the risk of public exposure.

The silence on the phone lingered. At any moment I expected her to hang up. *Come on*, I thought, *just this once, please, just this once.*

Then I heard her exhale, a resigned sigh exorcising decades of secrets. "You have to understand we never talked about this to anybody outside the family. I told Ted a little, but even he never knew the whole story, not him, not Frank, nobody.

"If I tell you, I want you to promise you won't use this or tell anyone what I said as long as I'm alive, okay? I don't want that son of a bitch coming after me, I have enough troubles of my own. Say you promise and I'll believe you."

"I promise. I just want to know the truth as you saw it, that's all."

She took a long breath, then slowly began talking. It should be noted that while some of what follows was described in previous chapters for purposes of continuity in the storytelling, this was the first time I was hearing most of it.

She started by describing their flight to the train station after the blitzkrieg and Sophia's affair with some of the officers, one of whom considered Charles a potential stepson. In keeping with the tradition of the Hitler Youth, he began to educate Charles in all matters Nazi.

"The SS were always hanging around the station," she said. "Some of them were posted nearby, and there were always more going and coming on the trains. Mama cooked for the soldiers who worked there, and sometimes, you know, she did *more* for them, not because she had to, but because she liked to. They'd bring her gifts, take her on trips, and buy her expensive clothes. She practically ran that place, and when the work got to be too much, she had them bring Jewish girls to work for her. She used to love pushing them around and making them work while she sat with the soldiers, drinking and laughing.

"Your father loved the uniforms, the guns, and the way the Nazis could push people around. He used to follow them around all day. They practically adopted him. They let him run errands, even made that ridiculous uniform for him. He used to wear it all the time, even when we were alone upstairs at the station, just staring at himself in the mirror with that swastika. Then he started tagging along when they went on patrol at night. He'd carry water, food; whatever they needed him to do, he did it.

"One morning he ran upstairs to where we lived above the station and told me that while he was out with the soldiers they came across a bunch of Jews on the road. The soldiers wanted to know where they were going and started beating them when they didn't answer fast enough. They used rubber pipes or hoses, something like that, and your father jumped right into it, beating them just as hard as the soldiers. It was exciting, he loved it. After that he joined up whenever a patrol went looking for Jews or anyone else they could beat up."

With those words I finally understood why my father used to go out at night with friends to beat up any "queers" they found on the street: he was reliving those experiences, just as he did the afternoon he forced me to put on his uniform.

With all that as context, she came to the day of the incident.

"A bunch of soldiers and SS came on the train, more than usual. They picked up some of the soldiers who were already there and started loading everybody into trucks, heading to Vishnevo. They said something big was going to happen. Charlie practically begged them to let him come along. They said yes, so he jumped in and they drove off.

"When they came back, he told me the SS and the soldiers had started pulling people out of their houses, making them dig their own graves, then shooting them. Then they set up a machine-gun nest on a World War I bunker and started firing into the crowd, and your father . . ."

She hesitated. I closed my eyes, silently urging her to keep going.

Her voice went low and soft. "At first he stood with the soldiers as they fired the machine gun, feeding bullets. He said it was like shooting fish in a barrel. Then one of the soldiers said, 'You want to do it?'

"And he did.

"They let him take over the machine gun for a while and he just started shooting people, killing them, one after another, like it was a game. When one of the SS officers came toward them, the soldiers took the machine gun back because they were afraid of getting in trouble.

"He said it was the most amazing thing he'd ever done, and he couldn't wait to do it again."

"And did he? Do it again?"

She paused. I could feel her weighing her answer. "Why?" she asked at last, a certain canniness in her voice. "Is there anything else, anything *specific* you wanted to ask me about?"

"No," I said. I didn't have anything else because I hadn't considered the possibility that there might *be* anything else.

"Then no, he didn't do it again," she said, in a tone of voice that suggested just the opposite. It was her way of saying *I'm tired of talking about this, so unless you've got something, unless you* know *something, I'm not going to volunteer.*[*]

---

[*] I later remembered my father's description of a second attack on Vishnevo that he

"How much did Sophia know about all this?"

"All of it," she said. "Why do you think she was so afraid of anyone looking too close at our history? Don't forget, back then there were Nazi hunters everywhere looking for collaborators."

Then she said she had to go to a dinner at the church and hung up.

I sat without moving for what felt like a very long time. It was dark when I looked up again.

A cold knot formed in my stomach. My father was a murderer. My father was a *war criminal.*

With that realization, all the pieces of my family's history that had never made sense began to line up like dominoes. Whatever the real cause of my step-grandfather's death, natural or unnatural, he'd allegedly told Sophia that he'd been a collaborator, which may have prompted her to assist with his demise. Why would Sophia be worried about people poking into Walter's past unless she was afraid that she might be compromised in the process? That same fear was almost certainly what prompted Theresa to interrogate Ted's brother Frank about his father's activities during the war, looking for anything that might harm them from that side of the family.

And there was my father's itinerant lifestyle to consider. Twenty-one moves in eighteen years. Maybe the reason behind those moves was just what it seemed, getting out of town to stay ahead of bill collectors. But what if it wasn't the *only* reason? Did my father keep moving to make things harder for anyone who might be looking for him? Then there was the matter of the aliases, using Stark for business papers, apartment rentals, and anything else that might leave a paper trail. My school records were always under Straczynski, but nobody was looking for twelve-year-old collaborators.

The whispered conversations, veiled hints of some terrible scandal, outbursts of violence, the German uniform, my grandmother's

---

"happened" to witness, and wonder to this day how much more there may have been to that story.

paranoia, my father's rabid anti-Semitism, and his penchant for beating "inferiors" . . . suddenly it all made sense.

With one exception: Why would my father upload the story to websites created for victims of the Holocaust, where his lies might be exposed?

It's possible that he had grown overconfident. Having told his version of the massacre for so long without challenge he may have believed he could keep doing so indefinitely. Maybe it never occurred to him that there were people still alive who'd been there that day and would give close scrutiny to his story. *Too* close, given how quickly he rabbited when awkward questions arose about where he'd been standing when the killing started.

But there's another explanation for my father's choice of websites that goes straight to the heart of his twisted pathology. His posts made it abundantly clear that he uploaded the story to elicit sympathy from other users of the system. *This was the terrible thing I endured* was the subtext of his messages, *feel sorry for me.*

Whenever he beat my mother or inflicted damage on the rest of us, he would try to evoke sympathy from us afterward. He wanted us to believe that it wasn't his fault, it was our mother, it was how he was raised, it was *our* fault. He would pluck at every string he could find to get us to feel sorry for him, because in his mind, receiving sympathy from those he harmed equaled forgiveness.

So it's altogether possible that he chose those sites because if he could get sympathy from the survivors of Vishnevo, *from the very people he harmed*, it would be tantamount to expiation. A part of him must have craved forgiveness as he grew older and the imminence of death loomed larger. Following that line of thought, one might assume he revisited the Jewish cemetery in his later years because he was compelled by guilt to confront his actions, and was seeking forgiveness from God before passing on to the other side. But it's far more likely that he returned to the cemetery to relive the happiest moment of his young life: the day he had been given permission to kill men, women, and children without repercussion. I think he felt nostalgia for an opportunity that had never come again.

At least I *assume* it never came again, barring whatever the hell *else* my aunt knew about him.

Theresa Straczynski-Skibicki passed away January 28, 2009, at the age of seventy-seven, taking with her whatever secrets still remained about my family. I spent months afterward trying to find more information to conclusively prove what my father had done, desperate to expose him to the world. But he was not an official part of the extermination unit, so there was nothing to be found in the public record. Then my father's health went into a sharp decline as years of drunken excess finally caught up with him. Rather than go to top-flight hospitals, he checked in and out of various bargain-basement facilities, fearing that if he withdrew any of the money he'd hidden away in various bank accounts, my mother's attorneys would seize it all.

Had he simply been willing to look after her from the beginning, he would have had access to that money and better care for himself. By going out of his way to harm her, he ended up hurting himself just as badly, if not worse.

I rather like the symmetry of that.

The degree to which my father never came to grips with his actions is borne out by his own words, as reported by my sister Lorraine. Lying in a hospital bed, dying and riddled with disease, he kept saying, over and over, "What did I ever do to deserve this?"

I was having a late-night cup of coffee and a hazelnut-and-banana crepe at a restaurant on the Third Street Promenade in Santa Monica when my phone dinged with an email notifying me that my father had died. The cause of death was ventilatory-dependent respiratory failure that led to aspiration pneumonia, septic shock, and full-blown cardiorespiratory arrest. It had apparently been a long, slow, agonizing death.

I finished reading the email and ordered a side of ice cream to celebrate.

Charles Straczynski, wife beater and alcoholic, the monster of my childhood and last alleged participant in the Vishnevo Massacre, died at the age of eighty-one at 5:00 A.M. on January 28, 2011, two years *to the day* after my aunt's death. Free at last from his threats, I can imagine her clawing at him from the other side, dragging him to a place where those he had harmed eagerly awaited his arrival.

As word got out that my father had died, friends and acquaintances reached out to comfort me. When I told them that I didn't need to be consoled, they asked how I could have any kind of closure since I'd never tried to talk to him before he died.

My father was all about control, and he was willing to say or do whatever was necessary to make sure you were never outside his power, so he could do to you whatever he wanted and your only option was to take it. The very worst thing I could ever do to him was to take away that control and punch him in the face with twenty-five years of silence.

And *that* is some serious fucking closure.

Courtesy of a military amnesty program offered years earlier, my father had turned his general discharge into an honorable discharge, which entitled him to a military burial at the Southern Nevada Veterans Memorial Cemetery in Boulder City, Nevada. It's appropriate that my father, a deadbeat who sponged off others, got the US military to spring for a hero's burial that provided the last brushstroke in his twisted self-portrait as a good and honorable man.

Though no family members attended the funeral, he didn't go into the ground alone. Four people were present, three of whom had been hired to work with my father in the days leading up to his death and knew very little about him. Among them was Jerry Samplawski, a Las Vegas resident who introduced himself to me in an email after the funeral. He'd met Charles while doing volunteer work with various hospitals and noted that right up to the end my father was talking about how he "hated all Jews," thus pretty much negating the *seeking forgiveness* idea.

In the months that followed, attorneys for my mother and sister tried to untangle Charles's finances to seize what they could to assist in my mother's care, but the Cayman Island banks refused to acknowledge their authority to access the funds. When we learned there was a will setting out what should be done with his $3 million in assets, I said I wanted no part of an inheritance. Better it should go to my sisters or to a battered women's shelter.

As it turned out, the gesture was unnecessary.

Correspondence discovered between Charles and his estate planners at the Royal Bank of Canada's Cayman Trust Planning in October 2008 laid out the details of his will and made sure that they could not be challenged by any of us. The document allocated a few personal bequests to people who had worked for my father in his last days, or who he had known years earlier, then stipulated that my sisters and I would receive a check for one hundred dollars each, a deliberate insult launched from the other side of the grave.

The remaining funds, nearly $2.5 million, were donated to the University of California, Davis, School of Veterinary Medicine, in Davis, California.

Why a veterinary hospital?

Because whenever someone my father hated would come to him

for financial assistance he would decline, saying with a sneer, "I'd rather give it to the dogs."

That's why a veterinary hospital.

He gave it to the dogs.

On October 27, 2012, my mother died at the age of seventy-seven. The lawyers handling my father's estate tried to use a provision in his will to have her buried beside Charles, who wanted his control over her to literally extend beyond life itself. My sister Theresa and I vowed to stop this. I had no affection for my mother, but if we could deny my father's last wishes, then I was totally fine with going to war. The battle lasted several weeks, during which her body was moved from one mortuary to the next. At one point we even discussed literally stealing the body.

When one of the attorneys asked if there was any scenario under which I would allow my mother to be buried beside Charles, I said, "Yes, absolutely. I will go along with this if we can carve an arrow on *her* headstone, pointing to *his* headstone, saying *I'm with stupid.*"

In the end, my sister got custody of the body, which was subsequently cremated.

A year later, after nearly three decades of separation, I met with Theresa in the lobby of the Harbor Marriott hotel in San Diego. One might think that after being apart for so long we would have volumes of things to discuss, but the hour was filled with the kind of awkward, pause-riddled small talk you make at parties with people you don't know and will likely never see again. Other than being born into the same gene pool, we had nothing in common; we were strangers who had been warehoused together. But she was well, and happy, and that was all that mattered.

Not long thereafter, I received six large boxes from the Las Vegas attorney who had been handling the disposition of my father's physical property: his computer, binders filled with documents, the Cayman Island correspondence, souvenirs, the original manuscript I'd written decades earlier, and letters he'd sent to the American and German governments in an attempt to get reparations for the trauma of being exposed to the events of World War II. Right up until the end he was running scams, trying to profit by playing the victim when he was the aggressor.

More significant was what *wasn't* in those boxes: no Christmas cards or letters to or from relatives expressing affection, and no photos of Evelyn, me, or my sisters. There were only letters threatening lawsuits against those who had crossed him, business correspondence, boilerplate legal forms, and photos of his factory in Chula Vista. There was nothing in his computer that was not angry at someone for something. The documents painted the picture of a bitter man who had nothing to live for beyond the prospect of inflicting pain on others.

I didn't want to touch any of it, but since there might be more family secrets lurking inside, or information that might conclusively link him to the incident at Vishnevo, I went carefully through each box until only one remained, the kind of thin, flat container used to transport framed paintings. With no expectations of finding anything useful, I cut one end of the box and felt around inside until I found the edge of a picture frame. It refused to budge. I asked my assistant, Stephanie Walters, to grab the other end of the box while I pulled.

With one last tug the frame popped out of the box and I fell backward onto the floor. I sat up to find myself staring at my father's shrine to all things Nazi, the one I had seen every day for most of my young life. With it was another framed selection of photos that I *hadn't* seen before, featuring German soldiers from the train station where he had lived, identified in captions as *kameraden*, friends and comrades.

As I studied the photos I realized that I'd been wrong about something. My father's possessions *had* included photos of his family. But his family wasn't me, or my sisters, or my mother. We had never *been* his family. His family were the SS and German soldiers who gave him the opportunity to exhibit cruelty without conscience and kill without consequence.

It was then that I realized there was one more task ahead of me. Yes, my father was dead, but he wasn't *quite* dead enough to suit me.

As a kid I'd watched all the Universal Pictures horror movies— *Frankenstein*, *Dracula*, *The Wolf Man*—and in the last of those I had seen my father. During the day, he seemed to others a respectable businessman and father. At night, the monster came out. In *The Wolf Man* the world only discovered what Lawrence Talbot really was after the monster's skin was penetrated by silver, exposing the truth. As a teenager seeing my father beating my mother one time too many, I'd reached for the gun and the clip to put down the monster, but the bullets were nowhere to be found. Now, decades later, I had the power to kill the creature and reveal his true face to the world, but the task would require a very particular kind of bullet. A silver bullet to kill the monster of the drunken midnights; the monster of blood and hatred and violence; the monster that had brutalized me, my sisters, my mother, and countless others, and who I believe committed acts far more terrible than anything I could have imagined.

And I realized what that silver bullet would be.

You are holding it in your hands.

CHAPTER 34

Selah

A brief pause before the end; the deep breath before the plunge.
Selah.

Lines from earlier in this book.

Funny what a difference the truth can make.

I wanted to show that those who love us can carry the burden of our secrets and accept the truth of who we truly are.

"Don't worry, I'll take this secret to my grave."

I come from a family of secrets, but we do not have a monopoly on the unspoken.

And secrets often come at considerable cost.

When Jeff Conaway joined the cast of *Babylon 5*, we knew that he'd had prior issues with drug abuse. It was only after his actions led to him being fired off *Taxi* that he came clean about his problems and addressed them. By the time he showed up at our door he was strong in every sense of that word. He was solid, he was clear-eyed, he was *Jeff.*

Around the start of season five, some of us began to notice a difference in him. He often seemed groggy and disconnected; he stumbled over lines that earlier would have posed no difficulty.

Whispers came to my office from the set: *We think he's backsliding.*

I began visiting Jeff in his trailer when he wasn't needed on-set. *Is everything okay? How are you doing? We're kind of worried about you.*[*]

Each time he brushed aside my concerns. *I'm fine, Joe, just tired . . . I'm staying up late working on my music, and there's a lot going on in my life right now, but I'm good . . . better than good, I'm great.*

Except he wasn't.

When we reached episode one hundred, a milestone for any series, the cast and crew assembled for a group photo to commemorate the occasion. But there was a face missing from the roster. While everyone else gathered on-set, Jeff was in his trailer, too drugged to come out. Production assistants sent to drag him out if necessary were rebuffed and booted out, the door slammed and locked behind them. We waited as long as we could, then took the photo.

Hours later, Jeff staggered out of his trailer, angry and upset. He said that he'd just been taking a nap and nobody had bothered to wake him up for the shoot.

"Step into my office," I said, and closed the door.

I told him he wasn't fooling anyone; he needed to face up to the fact that his bad habits had returned, and get back into treatment.

At first he refused to admit that there was a problem, but as the conversation sanded him down he reluctantly allowed that he'd slipped up. "I can't go back into treatment, if I do it'll get around and my career's dead. In this business if you fall down once, people can accept it; fall down twice and you're done."

---

[*] In these and similar conversations, I wasn't idly sticking my nose in his business. When you're the showrunner, anything that can affect production is your business. In a way, you're the dad of the production team, which on reflection means maybe I wouldn't have been a bad father after all.

I thought he was wrong, and said so. It just bounced off.

Jeff's downward slide accelerated after *Babylon 5*. He took bit parts, worked in shorts and reality TV, anything that didn't require him to remember lots of lines. By this time we had fallen out of contact—I think he didn't want to see me again after our conversation—but others in the cast urged him to admit his problems and seek help. He refused, insisting that he could, and would, get through it alone and nobody would ever need to know.

Had he sought treatment, which, yes, carried some risk of exposure, he might have been able to hold on and escape what came later. Instead, his determination to keep anyone from knowing his secret ended up with the whole world finding out about it during a full-blown meltdown during a taping of the reality series *Celebrity Fit Club*. Out of control, nearly incoherent, and barely able to walk in a straight line, he pulled off his shoes and shirt, yelled profanities, and threatened members of the cast.

And the cameras caught it all.

Over the next several years, Jeff battled multiple addictions to cocaine, alcohol, and painkillers. Unable to get scripted work, he was only able to pay bills by making more appearances on reality shows. Networks, studios, and producers profited from the spectacle of a man in free fall, slowly and agonizingly self-destructing on national television. By the time he hit *Celebrity Rehab* in 2008 Jeff was virtually unrecognizable: gaunt and hollow-eyed, wracked by self-pity, depression, and fits of screaming rage.

Those of us who had worked with Jeff watched the footage, horrified and grief-stricken, and found nowhere there the man we had known.

The spiral continued until May 26, 2011, when Jeff, his body twisted and weakened by years of addiction, passed away from complications of pneumonia and encephalopathy caused by multiple drug overdoses. *Determination to keep his condition secret and refusing to ask for help when it might've made a difference* could also have been added to the death certificate.

Jerry Doyle was better than Jeff at hiding his alcoholism, but the cost was no less substantial. He was slick, and funny, and could function on-set as if nothing was amiss. "I don't have an alcohol problem," he'd say. "As long as there's alcohol, I don't have a problem."

But I'd grown up with an alcoholic, and knew the signs very well. The few times we touched upon the topic in private he'd change subjects, reluctant to discuss it. So I began putting the words I wanted him to hear into the mouth of his character, Michael Garibaldi, who was also and not coincidentally a recovering alcoholic.

"Don't think I don't know what you're doing," Jerry said as he passed my office one afternoon, after the latest script dealing with Garibaldi's alcoholism had been distributed. I kept hoping the words would get through, but they never did. During the finale of *Babylon 5*, when everyone leaves the station for the last time, Jerry paused beside the elevator and, in an unscripted moment, picked up a shot glass off the bar and carried it away with him. It was his way of telling me *I'm not gonna change, I am what I am*.

After putting in five years as a lead on a TV series, Jerry was confident that there would be plenty of work waiting for him after *Babylon 5* came to an end. Instead he drifted from one small part to the next without ever managing to land another recurring role. After his run for Congress in 2000 ended in a humiliating defeat, and his conservative radio show *The Jerry Doyle Show* began tapering off, he entered 2015 hemorrhaging sponsors and money, and drinking heavily.

To his credit, Jerry reached out a little, to a few friends who he felt could help with his problem, but still refused to seek formal treatment, fearing it would jeopardize his career. His decision not to let anyone know he was suffering meant that there was no one to help him on July 27, 2016, eleven days after his sixtieth birthday. With his financial resources nearly tapped out, confronted by the fact that his career had flamed out, Jerry consumed so much alcohol so quickly that he essentially drank himself to death. The coroner ruled his death as *technically* accidental but also ascribed it to complications from chronic alcoholism.

Anyone who knew Jerry would tell you that he could talk non-stop for hours on any subject.

But he was incapable of seeking help at the one moment when he needed it most.

"I'll take this secret to my grave." It was the promise I made to Michael O'Hare.

"I have a better idea: take it to *my* grave. If anything happens to me, I *want* you to talk about it publicly. If people know this can happen to a lead actor in a TV show, the commander of a space station, they'll know it can happen to anybody. Maybe that knowledge can help somebody else down the road."

After his last appearance on *Babylon 5*, Michael's condition continued to improve for the next few years. But there were some around him who, perhaps embarrassed by his need to stay on constant medications, suggested that he didn't need them, that they were just getting in the way of his career. Whether he stopped taking his meds at their behest, or if he did so on his own, the fall was precipitous and frightening. For months I made calls and posted online messages asking if anyone knew where he was before finally receiving an email from a relative saying that Michael was in a halfway house, paid for by the family and the state.

Sandra Bruckner, Kathryn, and I tried to reach out, but the door was shut. I was told he didn't want to see anyone from his past, then that he might be open to it; that he was better, and that he was worse. As one of his family members noted in an email, the Michael O'Hare that I had known was pretty much gone. "He's on his meds again and the clinic is making sure of that, but the thing is, each time it's been like less Michael comes back. Even on meds his delusions are a permanent fixture now, he's just better able to seem normal to people who don't know him well. His parents talk to him regularly and they can tell, from odd things he says and doesn't say. They have offered to get him a phone but he doesn't want one, I don't think he wants anyone to be able to call him, he calls them from a pay phone."

The strain of his condition eventually led to a heart attack followed by a coma, where he remained until his passing on September 28, 2012, at the age of sixty.

Seven months later, during a celebration hosted by Phoenix Comic Con to commemorate *Babylon 5*'s twentieth anniversary, I kept my promise to Michael and spoke for the first time about what he had endured. He wanted people to know that showing vulnerability is not the same as being weak; that there is no shame in asking for or receiving help to get past the nightmares and difficulties of the present moment; that those who love us are capable of bearing our secrets, our failings, and our truest, most flawed selves.

Sometimes we keep secrets because we are afraid of what will happen to us.

And sometimes we keep them because we are afraid of what someone will *do* to us.

My mother failed to ask for help out of fear of exposure or retribution, while my sisters and I had been trained into a state of conditioned helplessness, believing that no one could help us and that Terrible Things Would Happen if we talked about what was really going on inside our family. We failed to understand that abusers carefully create a sense of terror that is far out of proportion to what they can actually *do*. Abusers use that vague, unspecified, free-floating-fear to keep their targets within range long after they've reached a point where they could simply walk away.

I call this Elephant Rope Syndrome.

In the days of traveling circuses, elephants were kept from escaping by slender ropes that were tied around their ankles and anchored to small stakes in the ground, restraints they could have easily shaken off, but didn't. Why? Because when the elephants were still young, they were kept in place with thick chains around their ankles that led to long stakes set so deep into the ground that they couldn't be pulled out. This gradually conditioned the elephants to believe that as long as there was something on their ankle, they couldn't escape.

If you talk to anybody about this, you're in trouble . . . you'll do what I tell you or else . . . if you leave I'll come after you and then you'll get what's coming to you . . . those are the chains and stakes that keep us immobilized as children, preventing us from asking for help or telling people what's going on behind closed doors.

By the time we become adults, those chains of possible consequence have given way to the limits of what can actually be done to us, becoming ropes that we can pull out at any time by telling the truth, asking for help, or simply walking away. The trick is to shake off those years of conditioning to see the situation for what it really is. Had my mother or I walked into a doctor's office and shown them the bruises and the cuts, if I had told teachers or counselors about the violence inside our home, we would have been plucked out immediately, just as when Grace convinced the police to escort Evelyn to safety during the first years of their marriage. Would the aftermath have been easy? No, of course not. Would it have been worse than the world we were living in daily? Almost certainly not.

If you are in pain, or know someone who is; if you feel there is no one who can relate to what you're going through; if you have been frightened into immobility by secrets you believe you have to maintain to protect yourself, your family, or your career, understand that you are only as alone as you choose to be. One phone call, one email, one text to the right person or agency can make the very literal difference between life and death.

You just have to decide to do it.

Selah.

EPILOGUE

I n 2014, after an eleven-year break, I decided that it was time to get back into television and teamed up with Lana Wachowski, for whom I'd rewritten the movie *Ninja Assassin*. During three days spent at the home she shares in San Francisco with her wife, Karin Winslow, we talked politics, religion, philosophy, the internet, and evolution. The overriding theme to emerge was connectivity. I've always believed that as a species we are better together than we are apart, that despite our divergent cultures we are alike in more ways, and in more *important* ways, than we are different. As a kid in Newark I was sure that if one of those cops could authentically walk around inside the mind of an African American protestor, once the shock wore off he'd find that the man he considered his enemy wasn't nearly as alien as he'd imagined.

Having always had difficulty in expressing my emotions there was a lot of wish fulfillment in this idea. It would be so much easier if someone could just peek inside my head to see what's there, and I suspect that feeling is not uncommon. Despite being factionalized, tribalized, and marginalized to within an inch of our lives, there is something in the human spirit that longs for connection, for community. On any given day, internet-friends who have never actually met in person will go online, cue up a movie or a TV show, and hit play at the same time, commenting on it in texts and chats, sharing an experience in real time despite being separated by thousands of miles.

This led me to wonder if it would be possible to tell a story about connectivity that could be produced on a planetary scale, bigger than anything previously attempted for television. Not an American story set against international backdrops, but one big saga told through eight stories taking place simultaneously around the world; not just a shared story, but a shared *experience* as each character drifts in and out of the others' minds. Rather than exploring someone's point of view *of* a story, we would be using point of view *as* story.

Linked telepathically, our characters would be able to experience one another's memories, skills, and most importantly, their secrets, because we are often defined by the things we choose not to express. The concept was too complex to pitch verbally, so we (now including the other half of the Wachowski duology) decided to write the pilot script. The process was fun, so we wrote another. Then a third.

Once these were done, we scheduled appointments to pitch the show to every major cable and streaming service in Los Angeles during a weeklong period. Prior to the meetings, we gave them the scripts to help them understand what we were trying to do. Our first appointment was at Netflix at eleven A.M. on a Tuesday. Rather than the usual "here's the plot, the action, and the bad guys" pitch, we spent most of our time talking about identity, gender, privacy, and empathy. It was more of a dialectic than a pitch, and after the meeting we went to lunch thinking we had probably been just a *tad* too obscure for our own good, demonstrating once again the dangers of a liberal arts education.

But at one o'clock the Netflix executives called to make a pre-emptive offer to buy the show, taking it off the market before we could go to the rest of our meetings. They gave us a straight-to-series commitment, and how fast could we start shooting this thing?

We decided early on that there would be no stage work; the series would be shot entirely on location. The average television episode is shot in eight or ten days, most of which are spent on a stage where you can control your environment. Shooting everything on location meant we'd be working without a safety net in nine cities on three continents. If there were issues with weather or if we lost a location at the last minute, we'd be screwed. The scope of the production, the scale of the storytelling, and the international cast made *Sense8* the biggest and most complex production any of us had ever been involved with.

In the end, we wanted *Sense8* to be about hope, about the idea that while humanity has advanced *technologically* through conflict, it's only through the social-evolutionary engines of compassion, understanding, and empathy that we will be able to attain a better and nobler future. We believed viewers were hungry for a story in which kindness trumps cruelty, and the common coin of our shared humanity is stronger than whatever would try to drive us apart.

Sense8 debuted on Netflix June 15, 2015, where it ran for two seasons, and I am desperately proud of the work we did on that series.

For years my comics output had been steadily diminishing due to eye problems that made it difficult to meet deadlines. After a series of surgeries and transplants in 2015 that were still considered fairly experimental, I emerged with 20/25 vision. Now that I was finally back up to speed, there was nothing to stop me from writing as many comics as before.

Except for the return of the familiar, intimate voice in the back of my head that had been whispering stories since I was seventeen. The same voice I heard when I knew it was time to leave San Diego for Los Angeles, when I walked away from journalism and, later, animation. For years that voice, representing some part of my psyche eager for new challenges, had forced me to walk away from what I knew I could do in order to start over with something less certain.

You've been writing comics long enough that you've become comfortable. You're done. Move on. Let's find a new challenge, where we can start all over at the bottom.

The weight of that decision felt like a fist closing around my heart.

I don't want *to move on. This isn't fair. I love comics.*

Tough. You've done this too long. It's time to step outside your comfort zone and try something else, where there's a good chance you'll fail, something that will force you to take chances.

Like what?

Go back to novels and plays. Those are the two areas where you never really established yourself. Maybe you'll succeed, and maybe you won't. But it's time to try.

So on July 22, 2016, I announced at San Diego Comic-Con that I was taking a sabbatical from the comics business. As of this writing I am still on hiatus, but if the right project, with the right degree of creative freedom came along, I might be enticed to return. If not, it's been a hell of a run: sixteen years of work resulting in the sale of thirteen million issues.

Meanwhile, the time I would normally spend writing comics for companies eager to publish them is being spent writing novels that publishers may never buy and plays that may never get produced. Once again I'm starting over from scratch, from absolute zero.

It's terrifying.

It's exhilarating.

It's life, you know?

In recent years I reached out to my uncle Ted's brother, Frank Skibicki, the only remaining member of my extended family who had been there during my family's early years in Paterson. We exchanged letters and Christmas gift baskets, and when I told him I was writing my autobiography, I asked if he'd be willing to give it a look. I emphasized that the book had to be as accurate as possible, so if there were any discrepancies between the text and his own memory I would lean into the latter. He graciously agreed.

Several months later, I traveled to Paterson for the first time in forty-five years, excited about the reunion and nervous about the coming critique. I'd spent years piecing together my family's history from scraps and the slow, steady unraveling of secrets, and was worried that somewhere along the way I might've gotten something wrong.

After a warm welcome, we moved to his kitchen for tea and conversation. Turning to the manuscript, he said he'd found only two small mistakes, both of which were corrected prior to publication. As far as he could tell, everything else concerning my family's history was accurate down to the smallest detail. *You got it right*, he said. *All of it.*

As we continued talking, audio recorder whirring, it became clear that despite my aunt's decision not to tell him about my father's involvement in the atrocity at Vishnevo, he'd always known *something* significant had happened given how often she referred to that village as a way of shutting down my father when he got out of hand.

"Theresa would allude to it whenever Charles would start talking about that time," he said.

"She would remind him, 'How about that little village?' and that sort of did it. Why did she keep mentioning this village? Because atrocities were done there. Charlie wouldn't admit his particular involvement in them, he just said, 'I happened to be in the area.' He was always squashing it a bit. He didn't want to talk about it. Certainly he never spoke to me about the war.

"He was always a bit evasive about some of his actions or things that were going on while he was at the railway station. Theresa would fill in some of the details when she chose to. She only mentioned that Charlie always tried to please those who were around him, and that she and her mother were worried that he was going to get them into some serious trouble."

I asked if he was surprised by Theresa's revelation that my father had taken part in the massacre, or if it simply confirmed his own suspicions. He looked down thoughtfully, composing his thoughts before replying.

"No, I wasn't surprised," he said at last. "He was touched by that evil Nazism and it stayed with him the rest of his life."

He was also very cognizant of my father's fear of being arrested as a collaborator. "One time he was visiting and he showed me this pouch he wore around his neck all the time. He kept a cashier's check for a quarter million dollars inside in case he ever needed to get out of the country fast."

Then he said, "Do you remember Tscherin Soobzokov?"

The name didn't ring a bell, but when I checked Wikipedia I recognized the photo as a friend of my father who we knew as Tom, an Americanized version of Tscherin. My father would often invite him to our home, saying that Tom had been a very important man during the war.

"When I was living with Ted and Theresa," Frank said, "I was going to school and working for a corporation about a block away from the house, the Seale Corporation. Charlie worked there for a while, and he got to know Soobzokov, who was accused by the Jewish Defense League of New York City of collaborating during the war. He was a Gestapo lieutenant as part of the resettlement program for Polish people. The JDL bombed his home. He and Charlie were friends. Why were they friends? Probably because they shared similar experiences during the war, especially with the Gestapo."

After returning to Los Angeles I looked more deeply into Soobzokov's story, and one of the last remaining mysteries about my father's past finally became clear.

During World War II Soobzokov, then an officer in the Waffen-SS, was assigned to an execution operation in the Circassia region. The *New York Times* identified his Wehrmacht unit as being responsible for "the deaths of a million Jews on the Russian front." Those who survived his campaign dubbed him "the Führer of the North Caucasus."

After the war, Soobzokov fled to the United States and settled in Paterson, where he tried to pass himself off as a respectable businessman, much as my father did. But his role in the war caught up with him when his abandoned first wife began telling people about his past. Other survivors who immigrated to Paterson brought similar stories, which led to attempts by Jewish authorities to extradite him for trial. When he fought those efforts to a standstill, an individual who identified himself as being with the JDL detonated a pipe bomb beneath his porch. He died from his wounds on September 6, 1985.

It was just a few weeks later that my father instructed his attorneys to draft a prenuptial agreement for my mother to sign, creating a non-disclosure clause as a prerequisite to their confidential marriage. There's little that can motivate a change in lifestyle faster than seeing your friend get bombed into tiny bits because of loose talk by a first wife.

I returned home from meetings one afternoon to find a package from Harlan Ellison waiting for me. A year earlier he had asked me to write an introduction to the new prestige edition of his anthology

Ellison Wonderland, one of the first books I ever owned outright. At last the book was here, signed and personalized by Harlan. I quote the beginning of that introduction.

> Harlan Ellison and I have almost nothing in common.
>
> Harlan is Jewish and loves to bargain, to *hondle*, to drive sales managers almost to the verge of suicide in the course of seeking the best possible deal.
>
> I am Gentile, and cannot bargain my way out of a paper sack. (For which see my forthcoming short story, "I Have No Jews, And I Must Buy Retail.")
>
> I am tall.
>
> Harlan is . . . not as tall.
>
> (At a PEN International fundraiser a few years ago, we approached Ed Asner only to have him break into laughter at the sight. He explained that side by side, we looked like the New York World's Fair Perisphere and Trylon.)
>
> Harlan comes from Cleveland. I hail from New Jersey.
>
> I have multiple degrees from San Diego State University.
>
> Harlan was booted out of Ohio State University with the lowest GPA in history, by record.
>
> At 80, Harlan still has all his hair.
>
> At 60, I . . . well, let's just say I'm always the first one in a crowd to know when it's raining. But then, I stand considerably closer to the sky.

I was moved to see that the man who had been my inadvertent mentor for over forty years, and my friend for nearly thirty, had mentioned me in the book's dedication, and signed the front page *To Joe—Ever and always my best pal & trail-pard! Yr. Friend— Harlan Ellison.*

I'd told Harlan that I was writing my autobiography, in which he featured prominently, and promised to get the manuscript to him for his review as soon as it was ready. I wanted him to understand, from deep inside the words, what he had meant to me as a friend and role model.

How's the book going? he would ask. *When can I see it?*

It's going well, I would reply, *and soon, I promise.* I wanted the draft to be letter perfect.

But I should not have awaited perfection.

After a stroke in 2014 left him bedridden and nearly paralyzed on his right side, Harlan went into a state of slow decline. The last time I saw him . . . well, this takes some explaining. As a younger man, Harlan owned a waterbed that was built into an impressively raised platform accessible by carpeted steps on either side. Given the many photos taken of models draped over that bed in provocative poses, surrounding a rather dashing Harlan, I think he considered it a sorta-kinda Mayan temple dedicated to his frolicsome sensibilities.

After his stroke, it became his prison and an impediment to visitors. Located in the corner of the bedroom, there was only about a foot of space between the last step and the wall, which made standing there difficult. The long steps on the other side put visitors several feet away and forced them to stand since sitting in a chair would put them out of his line of sight, adding more layers of isolation to his condition.

During our last visit, I began by standing in the narrow space on his left between the bed and the wall, but I could see that he was having difficulty raising his head to look up that high, so I circled around to the other side, which was even worse.

Screw it, I decided, and climbed into the bed beside him.

For two hours we talked about everything, anything, and nothing in particular. His voice was still strong but his eyes were sunken and tired, as though his soul was trying to sneak out of the room without anyone noticing. When Susan left to prepare dinner, he confessed to feeling like he was slowly disconnecting from the world; he was tired of the struggle and ready to check out.

"You're a fighter," I said. "You'll be around long after I'm gone."

He waved away the reassurance. "How's the book going?" he asked.

"Still sanding it down," I said. "So you're going to have to stick around to read it."

"Well, I definitely want to read it," he said, "though I'm not sure I want to see *you* again."

We laughed for quite a while at that one. The line was typical of his acerbic humor, but I could tell there was something more to it. Then Susan returned to let him know it was time for dinner.

As I sat up to take my leave, Harlan reached over and, to my surprise, kissed the back of my hand. When it came to other guys, Harlan was not a terribly affectionate man, and I could feel my eyes stinging with the kindness of that gesture.

Then he glanced up at me, and I could see the thought behind his gaze as clearly as if he had said the words aloud. *Good-bye, my friend, and don't come back. Don't see me like this again.*

Harlan Ellison, who was the closest thing I had to a father figure outside of a comic book, passed away in his sleep on June 28, 2018, at the age of eighty-four, and though he never had the chance to read this manuscript, *I* know that *he* knew how much I learned from him, and what that relationship meant to me.

As a kid who grew up on Harlan's work, I never imagined that I would have the chance to meet him and become his friend . . . that the trajectory of these two eccentric bullets, fired from different ends of the country, would one day strike in midair, forever altering both. What are the odds that a street kid in New Jersey with dreams of becoming a writer, who looked to the words of a complete stranger in California for succor in times of distress, would end up as his friend? What are the—

Wait a second.

What actually *are* the odds? Let's deconstruct the math for a moment, because this is important.

The chances of me ending up in LA aren't too bad. Becoming a writer? A bit less likely. Becoming a *successful* writer? More doubtful still. Getting to know Harlan? Not probable but not unthinkable. Becoming his friend? Rather difficult given how high he kept the walls. Having the opportunity to help him as he helped me? The odds aren't great, but they pale into insignificance against the chances of doing all that *and* being asked to write an introduction to a new edition of *one of the very first books I ever owned.*

Conservatively, I'd put the odds of hitting every one of those at about a million to one. The number is probably much higher if I were to sit down and really do the math, but let's say a million to one to make this easier.

Next item: What are the odds that a kid from nowhere who loved comic books like *Spider-Man* would become a successful writer in the comic book business, including a six-year run on *Spider-Man*?

The odds against that are ridiculous. But let's keep them at a million to one.

Item the Third: What are the odds that someone who grew up in love with *Lost in Space, Star Trek*, and other science fiction television shows would become one of a very small number of people to create a new science fiction universe in his own TV series?

Much higher than a million to one. But again, conservatively, let's keep it there.

Item the Fourth: Having used the Hugo Award as my standard for what books to read, what are the odds that I would win not just one but *two* Hugos, especially since only eight writers have won two or more Hugos since they started giving them out in 1967?

Million to one. Easy.

Item the Fifth: What are the odds that a kid who based his personality on Superman's values would be given the chance to re-imagine that character for a new generation, something only a few writers have had the opportunity to do? Or that this new iteration would repeatedly land on the *New York Times* bestseller list?

Ditto. Million to one. The odds of landing on the *NY Times* list *alone* are that high.

Item the Sixth: What are the odds that a kid who loved *The Twilight Zone* and admired Rod Serling would meet him in person, become one of only a handful of people to be on staff on a new version of *The Twilight Zone*, and write a script in posthumous collaboration with him?

Let's stick to a million to one. But you and I know that the odds are *much* higher.

Item the Seventh: What are the odds that a kid from the inner-city streets of Newark and Skid Row would go on to write movies for Ron Howard and Clint Eastwood and Angelina Jolie and Brad Pitt and Kenneth Branagh and be nominated for a British Academy Award?

A million to one. At least.

I could go on, but the point's been made: the odds of any *one* of those things happening are a million to one against.

But in the aggregate, the odds of any one person doing *all* of those million-to-one things are a tredecillion to 1 against.

Which is another way of saying 1 to the 42nd power.

That's a 1 followed by 42 zeroes.

Written out, the odds are 1,000,000,000,000,000,000,000,000, 000,000,000,000,000,000 to 1 against all those things happening to the same person.

But all of those things *did* happen, and they happened to *me*, so the question becomes: Why?

I'm not a social creature or a glad-hander. I'm riddled with social anxiety, not terribly good looking, not great at public speaking, and frankly I'm a pain in the ass. Some might even say I'm "difficult." By all rights I should be hard-core unemployable.

So again: Why?

As kids, we embrace that which gives us joy because we don't know any other way. We spontaneously sing, act, dance, and tell stories until someone—usually an adult—says *stop that* or *you're embarrassing yourself* or *you're not very good at that* or *wait until you're older* or *let someone else do that*. It's the tyranny of reasonable voices alluded to previously. Those voices cause us to unlearn our passions inch by inch until that which gives us joy is sanded away, leaving behind a shell that does what it is told by family, friends, teachers, and employers.

I think the reason so many unlikely things happened to me is because I never listened to those voices; because I came out of the womb snarling at anyone who told me there was something I couldn't do; because I learned that to win I only had to say *yes, I will* one more time than somebody else could say *no, you won't*. I never walked away from what gave me joy, never surrendered my dreams to those who would profit by eradicating them.

All the things I loved and believed in as a child—not just science fiction movies and TV shows and comic books, but also the importance of kindness, of doing the right thing for no other reason than that it *is* the right thing—I still love and believe in today. And one of the most important things I believe is that if we love something and have even an inch of aptitude, we can become successful at it because our love for the work will sustain us through the hard times required to get good enough at it to earn a living. It may not be the best possible living, you may not be able to afford a yacht, and from time to time you may find yourself teetering at the edge of the abyss, but wouldn't you rather make a thin living doing what you *love* than a slightly better living doing what you *hate*?

It's easy to fall asleep in our lives, lulled into somnolence by routine, by the day-to-day sameness of work and responsibility until suddenly something happens to wake us up: a divorce, a wedding, a death, a birth, or a diagnosis. In that instant we're awake in ways we previously were not, and for the first time in a very long while, we ask: *Is this it? Is this the sum total of my life? Is this the way it has to be?*

Taken in order, the answers are: no, it's not, and it doesn't have to be.

When I sold *Changeling*, not one studio executive cared about my age, if it was my first script or my fiftieth, where I went to school, what my grades were, or where I grew up. All they cared about were the words on the page.

It doesn't matter if you're seventeen or fifty-seven, if you come from a poor background or a rich one, if you went to the best schools or the worst. It. Doesn't. Matter.

What matters is listening to the small voice at the back of your head that says *This is what gives me joy.*

It's about fighting naysayers and self-doubt when you feel you can't fight for even one more second. It's about standing up when all you want to do is lie down until life stops hitting you. It's not easy. It was never *meant* to be easy. But it can be done if we *choose* to do it.

"Whenever I think of you, I see you with your dukes up, fighting your way out of a corner."

I believe that if we do what we love fearlessly, with joy and commitment, the universe bends to our intent. Quantum mechanics tells us that the observer affects the observed. We are the observers; our lives and the world around us are the observed. If time is a matter of perspective, if speed and movement are relative to perception, if Schrödinger's cat is both alive and dead until we look inside the box, then the same *must* apply to our capacity to envision the lives we want for ourselves and to make that happen.

If my life stands for anything, it's to offer proof that it's possible to choose your own path, to break the cycle of violence, abuse, and doubt; that it's possible to fight and win.

That's all. Not that winning is guaranteed, just that it's *possible*.

Here's why that matters:

The threshold theory of human development holds that people will generally fail to do something as long as they think it's impossible. The ones who succeed are those who can see past the horizon and imagine themselves doing it, and slowly, through struggle and self-programming, convince themselves that *the impossible is possible*.

For the whole of human history no one had run a sub-four-minute mile until British runner Roger Bannister in 1954. On its own, that's an interesting factoid. But what's more interesting is what happened *afterward*, when John Landy *also* broke the four-minute mile within just a few months of Bannister's achievement. In the years that followed, others did the same.

They had not become significantly faster runners than they had been before, nor did they train any differently. They were the same after Bannister's achievement as they were before it. So what made the difference? Why could they do *then* what they couldn't do before?

Because they knew it was possible.

Believing the task impossible, they had been unable to achieve it.

Knowing that it could be done, they did it.

And *that* is the point of this digression: not that success is guaranteed when we decide to pursue our dreams, just that it's *possible*.

One of the dopiest things DC Comics ever did was to declare that the *S* on Superman's chest was a Kryptonian letter symbolizing hope. That symbol is an icon around the world because it means something different to everyone who sees it. To some, sure, it may mean hope; but to others it means strength, honesty, freedom . . .

it means what you *need* it to mean, allowing us to project onto a fictional character the better and nobler aspects of ourselves. We cherish images of Superman doing amazing things because they let us imagine that we are capable of doing such things ourselves, that they are *possible.*

For me, Superman represented all those qualities plus persistence, the refusal to surrender in the face of overwhelming odds. No matter how badly he got hurt or how many stood against him, you just *knew* that he would get up and keep fighting, that he would die before giving up.

If he could do it, then I could do it.

And if *I* can do it, frankly, *anybody* can do it.

We have no control over who beats us up or knocks us down, or the obstacles that stand between us and our dreams. But we have *absolute* control over how we choose to respond.

You didn't come from the best schools.

Doesn't matter, get up, keep fighting.

Your parents were alcoholics, violent, or abusive.

Doesn't matter, get up, keep fighting.

Your friends and family don't believe in you.

Doesn't matter, get up, keep fighting.

They've got you pinned down in the schoolyard, the office, the house.

Doesn't matter, get up, keep fighting.

You come from the streets, the farm, the projects, from nowhere.

Doesn't matter, get up, keep fighting.

The bullies are bigger than you are, will *always* be bigger than you are.

Doesn't matter, get up, keep fighting.

Doesn't matter.

Get up.

Keep fighting.

By taking responsibility for our lives, our mistakes, and our dreams, we break the patterns of the past and free ourselves to fight for our future, for what gives us joy, and for the possibilities of a better future.

And with that choice ridiculously beautiful and powerful things begin to happen.

As I write these concluding words, it is November 2018, and despite everything that has happened in my past I am struck by how profoundly fortunate I am: I get to spend my days and nights making up stories about things that never happened, but which feel as if they did.

Online and at conventions I'm approached by fans who, as kids, watched *He-Man*, *She-Ra*, and *The Real Ghostbusters*, progressed as teens into *Captain Power*, were old enough for the more complex stories of *The Twilight Zone*, hit *Babylon 5* and my comics work in their twenties, then later discovered my work in movies and on *Sense8*. Some among those fans are writers themselves, who graciously insist that they learned their craft by studying my work. If that is as advertised, then I am a doubly fortunate man.

My home is my Fortress of Solitude, containing mementos of past battles, both the losses and the victories. The walls are covered in comic book art, so that everywhere I look, a friend is looking back at me, and on my desk is a statue of the Superman I birthed.

How unlikely. How *marvelous*.

Every day I go into my office, turn on the computer, and apply fingers to keyboard.

I have no idea where the words will take me next.

I know only that the journey will be *amazing*.

ABOUT THE AUTHOR

J. Michael Straczynski began his career writing for the *Los Angeles Times,* the *Los Angeles Herald Examiner,* the *San Diego Reader*, and TIME Inc. as well as publishing novels and short stories. He has written hundreds of produced television episodes for such series as *He-Man*; *She-Ra*; *The Real Ghostbusters*; *The Twilight Zone*; *Walker, Texas Ranger*; *Murder, She Wrote*; *Babylon 5*; *Crusade*; *Jeremiah*; and *Sense8*, the latter four of which he also created. His movie work includes Clint Eastwood's Oscar-nominated *Changeling*; *Ninja Assassin*; *Thor*; *Underworld: Awakening*; and *World War Z.*

Straczynski has worked for Marvel and DC Comics, writing *The Amazing Spider-Man*, *Fantastic Four*, *Thor*, *The Silver Surfer*, *Wonder Woman*, and *Superman*, selling more than thirteen million issues in total, and his *Superman: Earth One* graphic novel series appeared consistently on the *New York Times* bestseller list.

He has won the Hugo Award, the Saturn Award, the Ray Bradbury Award from the Science Fiction Writers of America, the Eisner, Icon, and Inkpot Lifetime Achievement Awards, the Space Frontier Foundation Award, and the Eagle Award; he shares in two

Emmy Awards; and was nominated for a British Academy Award for his screenplay for *Changeling*.

Straczynski has been profiled in *Time* magazine, *Newsweek* selected him as one of their Fifty for the Future, *Daily Variety* selected him as one of their top-ten screenwriters to watch, and he has had an asteroid officially named after him by the International Astronomical Union, straczynski-3469, chosen because he and the asteroid have "an eccentric orbit."

He's not entirely sure how he feels about that part.